第5辑
Volume 5

# 管理会计师协会教学案例
# IMA Educational Cases

（汉英双语版）

瑞夫·劳森（Raef Lawson） 编

杨继良 主译
胡金凤 赵 澄 校

经济科学出版社

图书在版编目（CIP）数据

管理会计师协会教学案例. 第5辑／（美）劳森（Lawson, R.）编：杨继良译. —北京：经济科学出版社，2014.1
ISBN 978-7-5141-3976-1

Ⅰ. ①管… Ⅱ. ①劳… ②杨… Ⅲ. ①管理会计-案例 Ⅳ. ①F234.3

中国版本图书馆 CIP 数据核字（2013）第 267580 号

图字：01-2014-0198

管理会计师协会教学案例（第5辑）
IMA Educational Cases-Volume 5

© 2014 Institute of Management Accountants
© 2014 中英文双语专有出版权属经济科学出版社

All rights reserved. No part of this book may be reproduced in any form without the written permission of Institute of Management Accountants and Economic Science Press.

未经管理会计师协会（IMA）和经济科学出版社的书面许可，本书的任何部分均不可以任何形式翻印。

责任编辑：周国强
责任校对：隗立娜
责任印制：邱　天

### 管理会计师协会教学案例
（第5辑）

瑞夫·劳森（Raef Lawson）　编

经济科学出版社出版、发行　新华书店经销
社址：北京市海淀区阜成路甲28号　邮编：100142
编辑部电话：88191350　发行部电话：88191540
网址：www.esp.com.cn
电子邮件：esp@esp.com.cn
天猫网店：经济科学出版社旗舰店
网址：http://jjkxcbs.tmall.com
北京密兴印刷有限公司印装
787×1092　16开　18印张　500000字
2014年2月第1版　2014年2月第1次印刷
印数：0001—3000册
ISBN 978-7-5141-3976-1　定价：49.00元
（图书出现印装问题，本社负责调换。电话：010-88191502）
（版权所有　翻印必究）

## 始于1919年的管理会计专业机构——美国管理会计师协会

美国管理会计师协会（The Institute of Management Accountants，简称IMA®）成立于1919年，是全球领先的国际管理会计师认证和服务机构，属非营利性组织，总部设在美国新泽西州，在全球120个国家、200个分会中拥有超过6.5万名会员，并通过设立在苏黎世、迪拜和北京的办事处为会员提供本土化服务。

在国际上，作为COSO委员会的创始成员和国际会计师联合会（IFAC）的主要成员，IMA在管理会计、公司内部规划与控制、风险管理等领域始终参与最前沿的实践。此外，IMA还在美国财务会计准则委员会（FASB）和美国证券交易委员会（SEC）等组织中发挥举足轻重的作用。

自2007年进入中国以来，IMA发展迅速，已经成为凝聚财务高管和企业决策制定者的高端平台。IMA会员遍布工商界、学术界、政府部门以及各类非营利机构内部，这些财务专业人士凭借其先进的财务理念、出色的战略思维、卓越的管理能力和严格的道德准则，不断推进企业和机构整体绩效的提升。

## 40 年的卓越铸就黄金证书——CMA 认证

IMA 旗下的美国注册管理会计师（Certified Management Accountant，简称 CMA®）认证是对会计和财务专业人士的权威鉴定。2012 年恰逢 CMA 认证推出 40 周年，在这 40 年的卓越历程中，CMA 一直秉承 IMA 的使命，即用最实用的知识体系培养管理会计精英，用最严格的测评标准保证认证的权威性，现已发展成为全球财务的黄金标准。

CMA 知识体系具有很强的实践性。其所侧重的预算预测、内部控制、决策分析、风险管理等内容非常符合企业对会计人才的需求。

CMA 认证提供英文和中文两种考试语言。作为唯一一个进行汉化的管理会计认证，CMA 认证专注测试知识体系和专业技能，让更多的中国财务专业人士全面、透彻地了解管理会计的精髓。2009 年 11 月，中国国家外国专家局培训中心与 IMA 签约，将 CMA 认证列为国家人才重点培养项目，在国资委和大型央企的支持下，培养高层次、国际化的管理会计人才。

CMA 认证是高薪"敲门砖"。IMA 2012 年中国区会员薪酬调研显示，持有 CMA 认证的会员平均年薪为 27.8 万元，比非持证者高 34%。

**IMA 学习资源**

- CMA 学习教材　CMA Learning System

- 《管理会计公告》Statement of Management Accounting

- 《管理会计季刊》　Management Accounting Quarterly

- 《IMA 教学案例期刊》 IMA Educational Case Journal

- 《战略财务杂志》 Strategic Finance Magazine

- 《管理会计在中国》 Management Accounting In China

- 《财务报告内部控制与风险管理》 Financial Report, Internal Control and Risk Management

# 译者的话

到2012年底，IMA的教学用案例（*IMA Educational Case Journal*，IECJ），已经有五年历史了。头三年（2008～2010）的案例，经过主编瑞夫·劳森博士（Dr. Raef Lawson）重新编排，于2012年由北京的经济科学出版社发行第1～3辑双语版。现在呈现在读者面前的，是后两年（2011～2012）的案例，仍是双语版，编排成第4～5两辑，使每一辑都包含了主要的课题内容。

双语版倍增了篇幅，对于只需要汉语的读者，携带不便。但是，英语逐渐成为我们与世界沟通的重要手段。国内的一些大学，纷纷采取双语教学，双语版有利于教学。因而第四、第五辑仍维持双语版。

我个人在最近六、七年里，把翻译管理会计方面的资料，作为退休生活的主要内容，以此为乐。但翻译这套案例，也实在是一次"再教育"。翻译之难，远远超过我过去的想象。这套案例中，不但有许多会计和相关学科中的新名词，而且涉及重工业、医疗保健、食品饮料、运动娱乐、信息技术等各行各业的情景和词汇，常常束手无策。尤有甚者，作者会不时用一些美国新潮的俚语，更令人目瞪口呆。

我的一些朋友，伸出了援手。迈麦克（Mike Meiser）是一位退休的飞行员，和我同住在美国边陲的安吉雷奇市，我们成了好朋友。我翻译的每一篇案例，都会有近二十条疑问，他都很细心地查资料、为我作答。我曾做过统计，平均每页我都会遇到一个吃不准的问题，而我的猜想中，大约20%是理解不全面、另外20%是完全错了！如果没有他的帮助，读者会看到每十页中平均有两页有重大错误，严重误导了读者。有不少"译者注"，是按照他的解释写成的，便于读者了解美国生活中的细节。

上海第十医院财务处长费峰教授，解答了医疗保健词汇中的许多难题；现在美国的慕勇教授，详细审阅（甚至重新翻译）了有关信息技术方面的章节；重庆理工大学一些电算化系的同学，也帮了不少忙，我都不知道他们的姓名，都算无名英雄吧。

我个人在2012年初，动了一次大手术。现在还在逐渐恢复，终究是八十多岁的人了。于是，在翻译2011～2012年的案例中，组织了一个团队，包括了两位已经在大学任教的硕士、一位已应永道会计事务所之聘的、另外一位在读的研究生。同时，增强了校订，每一篇在译成后都经过两道校订，事实证明这样做完全有必要。在每一篇的第一页底部，都具体地列出了译者和初校、二校者的姓名。

  从我们译、校者来讲，出双语版的目的，是便于读者找出翻译中的差错。我们诚恳地希望能收到大家的批评指正。来函请寄杨继良（jiliang_y@163.com）、赵澄（chengjxufe111@163.com）、陈秀云（bear12345@qq.com）、胡金凤（hujinfeng023@126.com）或余辉（cherishth@qq.com）。我们引颈以待。

杨继良

2013 年 11 月 1 日

# Translator's Words

By the end of 2012, *IMA Educational Case Journal* (IECJ) had been published for five years. Cases for the first three years (2008 ~ 2010) were published by the Economic Science Press, Beijing, in bilingual version in three volumes in 2012. Now we are presenting the Fourth and Fifth Volumes based on the chief editor of the IECJ, Dr. Raef Lawson's rearrangement for cases published in 2011 to 2012. Each volume includes the main topics of management accounting.

The bilingual version doubles the length of the book. This might cause some inconvenience for readers who only read Chinese. However, English gradually becomes an important tool for Chinese to communicate with the outside world. More and more Chinese business schools are adopting bilingual teaching. Therefore, Volumes IV and V are still published in bilingual version.

For the most recent seven years, translating materials on Management Accounting is the most enjoyable contents of my retired life. However, this job is very challenging, far beyond my capalbility. These cases are full of technical terms as well as business environments related to heavy industry, healthcare, food and beverage, sports and entertainment, and information technology, which I am not familiar with. Furthermore, some authors use quite a few current American slangs. My dictionary just could not help.

Some of my friends extend their hands to help. Mr. Mike Meiser, a retired pilot, also lives in Anchorage, Alaska, in our neighborhood. He becomes my best friend. I have about one question in each page. I give him my guess. He spends much time doing research with all available sources. Averagely speaking, in my ten questions, two of my guesses are not complete, Mike gives me full explanation which I use in footnotes; another two of my guesses are absolutely wrong. Without his help, every ten pages of my translation would have two serious mistakes!

Professor Fei Feng, director of the Financial Department of No. 10 Hospital in Shanghai helps me with healthcare terms. Professor Mu Yong carefully proofreads cases related to information technology, sometimes even retranslate many paragraphs. Graduate students majored in Computerized Accounting also lend their hands. I don't know their names. They are "unknown heroes".

I had a major operation in January 2012, recovering smoothly though slowly due to my age. I am 82, not able to translate these cases all by myself in these days. For translating cases comprised of Volumes IV and V, we have formed a team, including two college instructors, one PwC staff, and one student pursuing his Master's degree. Three of them were my students when I lectured at the Chongqing Polytechnic University. They translated about half of the cases in Volumes IV and V (bilingual version). All these cases are proofread for at least twice for quality purposes. The names of the specific translator and proofreaders appear at the bottom of the first page of each case.

As translators and proofreaders, the purpose for publishing these cases in bilingual version is inviting our readers to find out errors in our work. We sincerely expect your criticism and correction. Please send to Yang Jiliang (jiliang_y@yahoo.com), Zhao Cheng (chengjxufe111@163.com), Chen Xiuyun (bear12345@163.com), Hu Jinfeng (hujinfeng023@126.com), or Yu Hui (cherishth@qq.com). We are "raising our heads" ——eagerly looking forward to your criticism.

**Yang Jiliang**
November 1, 2013

# 序　言

本书是《管理会计师协会教学案例杂志》（IMA Educational Case Journal）的案例研究合辑。管理会计师协会（IMA）出版这些案例研究的翻译版本，其目的是在全球范围内提升管理会计课程的教学质量，从而促进管理会计职业的发展进程。

采用案例研究教学方法，学员需要分析和讨论现实生活中的实例，这些实例涉及有关组织所面临的决策、症结及问题等事项。案例研究教学方法与传统的教学方法完全不同，在传统课堂上，学员参与分析与讨论的机会少之又少，而案例教学方法则要求学员积极参与课堂讨论。

如果学员过去接受的是传统教学方法，现在就会认识到这种学习方法必须加以改变。一则案例研究不仅仅是一道问题。一道问题只有一个正确答案，而一则案例研究往往没有独一无二的正确答案。决策者在面临案例研究所描述的情形下，通常可以在多种备选的做法中选取一种，而这些备选做法都有理有据。

案例研究会提供详细而有趣的信息，来对企业的实际情况展开说明，这会大大增加了学员学习案例所涉及概念的兴趣。案例所述的实例都涵盖了某些管理上的理论概念，因而也能加深学员对管理理论的理解。

采用案例教学的好处还不止这些。通过学习案例的分析方法和在课堂上的演示方法，学员所掌握的技能就会得以提升，这些技能对于学员未来作为商界专业人士的生涯是极为重要的。案例研究方法能提高学员针对具体症结而提出恰当问题的能力，也能提升学员针对具体情形而识别和把握症结所在的能力（而不只是提出一些抽象的问题）。案例研究反映了现实生活中管理决策的实际情况，在现实生活中管理决策往往是建立在不充分的信息基础之上。案例研究将要告诉学员管理决策伴有模糊性和复杂性。案例研究还能使学员获得管理工作的整体视野，因而做出管理决策往往需要把各种理论和概念综合起来，而这些理论和概念又来源于营销和制造等不同的职能领域。

在本辑案例中，我加入了一则案例的教案，其目的是让使用这些案例教学的教员们了解这一教案资源。所有这些案例的教案在 IMA 的网站上对 IMA 教师会员开放。

提供教案的目的不仅仅在于简单地给出案例的"正确"答案。除了建议解决案例的方法，一则好的教案传达了作者使用案例的经验，即：建议学习案例材料的其他可供选择的方法、讨论如何根据案例所使用的课程修改案例、提供案例（如果是一则"现实生活"中的实例）中公司实际采取的行动的信息，以及可能提供其他一些参考资源。

IMA 教师会员可以从 http：//www.imanet.org/网站上获得所有案例的教案。如果您有任何关于教师会员会籍的问题，请拨打 IMA 中国办事处咨询热线：4000 - 462 - 262，或发邮件到 imachina@ imanet.org。

祝君成功！望大家喜欢这些案例。

瑞夫·劳森，PhD，CFA，CMA，CPA
IMA 常驻教授、研究副主席
IMA 教学案例期刊编辑
管理会计师协会

# Editor's Preface

This book contains a selection of case studies published in the *IMA Educational Case Journal*. Through publication of the translations of these case studies, the Institute of Management Accountants (IMA) is pursuing its goal of enhancing the teaching of management accounting world-wide, thereby furthering the development of the global management accounting profession.

The case study method entails learning by analyzing and discussing a real-life situation involving a decision, problem, or issue faced by an organization. Unlike traditional lecture-based teaching where student participation in the classroom is minimal, the case study method requires students to be actively involved and to participate in the classroom discussion.

If you have been exposed only to traditional teaching methods, you will find that you need to change your approach to learning. A case study is not a problem. A problem has a unique, correct solution. On the other hand, there typically no unique, correct answer to a case study. A decision-maker faced with a situation described in a case study can usually choose between several alternative courses of action, each of which can be supported by logical argument.

By providing detailed, interesting information about real business situations, case studies can make learning about the concepts covered in a case more interesting. Cases will also enhance your grasp of management theory by providing real-life examples of the underlying theoretical concepts.

But the use of case studies does much more than that. By learning how to analyze and present a case study, you will be developing skills that are essential to your future career as a business professional. These include the development of analytic and decision-making skills and learning how to express your views. The case study method will improve your ability to ask the right questions in a given problem situation and to identify and understand the underlying problems in a given situation rather than the superficial issues. Case studies reflect the reality of managerial decision-making in the real world, where often decisions are based on insufficient information. Cases reflect the ambiguity and complexity that accompany most management decision-making. They can also provide an integrated view of management, as managerial decision-making frequently involves integration of theories and concepts learnt in different functional areas such as marketing and manufacturing.

In this volume I have included the Teaching Note for one of the cases in order to acquaint faculty using these cases with this resource. Teaching Notes for all of these cases are available to IMA Academic members on the IMA website.

The purpose of a Teaching Note is more than simply presenting the "correct" answer to a case. Besides suggesting an approach to solving a case, a good Teaching Note conveys the author's experience in using the case, suggests alternative ways to approach the material in the case, discusses how to modify the case based on the course in which it is used, provides information on the actions actually taken by the company in the case (if a "real world" case), and may provide references to additional resources.

Teaching notes for all of these cases are available to IMA academic members on http://www.imanet.org/. For any questions regarding academic membership registration, please contact IMA China office by dialing the hotline 4000-462-262 or sending email to imachina@imanet.org。

I wish you success and hope you enjoy these cases!

*Raef Lawson, PhD, CFA, CMA, CPA*
*Professor-in-Residence and Vice President of Research*
*Editor, IMA Educational Case Journal*
*Institute of Management Accountants*

# 目 录

## 成本习性与成本管理

派克斯维尔闪电：对策略性业务扩展机遇的评估 / 3
   **教案**  派克斯维尔闪电：对策略性业务扩展机遇的评估 / 22
加勒比海啤酒公司：转移定价、道德和公司治理 / 54

## 成本计算方法

德尔格公司：为生命的技术 / 71

## 战略实施

医疗保健网络联盟：利用平衡计分卡促进变革 / 99

## 编制计划与预算

会计师有时未能预算 / 121
SEWMEX 公司：国际背景下的短期利润规划 / 136
田纳西河流域管理局：电力成本 / 158

## 业绩考核与报酬

联合利华：一家全球性公司的信息技术服务外包的财务启示 / 183

## 公司治理与职业道德

詹森制药：一出公司治理的角色扮演 / 209
Alchemy——一则内部审计案例 / 234

## 可持续发展

索莱亚的可持续战略部署 / 245

# Contents

### Cost Behavior & Cost Management

Pikesville Lightening: Evaluating Strategic Business Expansion Opportunities / 13
   TEACHING NOTE Pikesville Lightening: Evaluating Strategic Business Expansion Opportunities / 37
Caribbean Brewers: Transfer Pricing, Ethics and Governance / 61

### Costing Methodologies

Dräger Medical Systems, Inc.: Technology for Life / 83

### Strategy Implementation

Alliance Healthcare Network: Using a Balanced Scorecard to Motivate Change / 108

### Planning & Budgeting

Sometimes Accountants Fail to Budget / 128
SEWMEX: Short-Term Profit Planning in an International Setting / 146
The Tennessee Valley Authority: The Cost of Power / 169

### Performance Measurement & Compensation

Unilever: The Financial Implications of Outsourcing Information Technology Services in a Global Organization / 193

## Corporate Governance & Ethics

Jensen Pharma: A Governance Role-Play / 220
Alchemy-An Internal Auditing Case / 238

## Sustainability

Deploying Sustainability at Solea / 258

# 成本习性与成本管理
Cost Behavior & Cost Management

# 派克斯维尔闪电：对策略性业务扩展机遇的评估[1]

*Thomas G. Canace*
*Wake Forest University*

*Paul E. Juras*
*Babson College*

## 简介

派克斯维尔闪电球队的所有者葛瑞格·斯顿（Greg Storm）有一句常常被人引用的话："我并未拥有一支棒球队；我卖的是热狗！"这句话很切合于棒球小联盟最近的策略，即把这项运动转变成为"家家户户都能负担起的一种享受"，也就是它不只是一项运动，更是一项娱乐活动。不仅如此，斯顿还是一个梦想家，他重视创造性思维，并不懈地努力寻求独特的方法发展他的企业，成为市场上的主导者。斯顿需要帮助来打出"全垒打"；因为只靠"一垒打"[2]，不能为这个行业带来革命性的转变，或者使这种季节性的行业能够长期持续不断地发展。

## 背景

1882年美国组成了棒球的"西北联盟"。然而，此后不久，各地联盟的负责人与"全国联盟"和"全美联盟"[3]签订协议，从而确定了各地协会的职权，尤其是对各个球队定出"大"、"小"联盟（"major"或"minor" league）的棒球队之别。依据此项协议，西北联盟成为了第一个公认的小联盟棒球队。后来，又签订了协议，确定"大联盟球队"有选用"小联盟球

---

\* 本篇译者为杨继良，校订者为胡金凤、赵澄。

[1] 编写本案例的目的是为了给学生提供一个解说、分析、估价、归纳和交流对一个管理会计问题的解决方案的机会。——原注

棒球是美国人非常喜爱的一种球赛，从孩童时代就开始着迷。这则案例的球队和故事都是虚构的，但反映了这项球赛有很强的季节性，为了谋求全年都有持续的收入，作者假设一个球队计划把业务扩展到非比赛季节。故事中有些情节看来不完全属实，例如把球队的标记印到家庭用的加热炉上和热狗面包的包装上，就未必有实用价值。如何把球队的收入不局限于赛季，对于棒球队来讲，确实是个问题。原文题目的拼法有误，已改正。Pikesville是个实有的地名，故该球队的名称按词典译成中文。——译者

[2] home run（全垒打），棒球术语，指一击就得了一分；与此相对的"一垒打（one-base hit）"则需要数击才能取得一分。——译者

[3] National League and American League，后者在原文中作 American Association，系笔误，应改正。这是两个全国性的大联盟，各管辖十四五支球队。——译者

队"球员之权，从而形成了一种"棒球手培养系统"④。在这一系统下，偏僻、落后、缺乏人才的小镇，也能培养出参加大联盟球队的选手。

这样组织起来的棒球队最初只限于美国的西南地区；但到19世纪末、20世纪初，就迅速扩展到全国。虽然到20世纪中叶，小联盟俱乐部的数量减少颇多，但到20世纪80年代，参加小联盟的球队数激增，自从50年代以后，出席观看的人数第一次超过2000万人。这一成就促使参加大、小两级联盟的球队之间的业务合作关系大为加强，这一合作关系迄今仍然存在于职业棒球协议下的两级联盟之间。在20世纪90年代时签订的新协议下，大联盟仍然支付经营费用的大部分，但小联盟也需要把在它们棒球场的售票所得（按最低标准），分一部分给大联盟了。如今许多粉丝和观察家都没有注意到，大联盟组织享有决定本季度参加小联盟的是哪些球员的绝对权力。事实上，许多棒球分会俱乐部已提出意见，因为往往在球季开始之前一个月，他们才知道最后参加球赛的球员名单。当然，小联盟球队的所有者对棒球运营的控制权有限，他们都清楚地认识到他们仍然在地方层面经营业务、使之兴旺繁荣，然而这些组织的经营业绩都仅仅为"小"（微不足道）的。

事实上，多亏新一代球队所有者的策略性思维和企业家精神，这些球队都被经营得如一流的职业体育俱乐部，在设计独特的棒球场上打球，也为许多家庭提供了一种新的娱乐方式。这些所有者认识到，尽管在表面上他们的任务在于组织年轻的球员参加大联盟的"球赛"，但更重要地，他们的盈利能力很大程度上取决于，是否能成功地成为一个娱乐场所。许多评论家常分析到：各参加小联盟的球队与各个电影院之间为娱乐收入展开竞争；它们门票售价划一，期望通过提供的副食和娱乐服务来增加利润。因此，尽管在大联盟球赛上赢得球赛是争取吸引观众的关键，然而各小联盟球队的经营成功与否，更多地取决于提供便宜的其他非棒球娱乐项目。

## 派克斯维尔闪电

"派克斯维尔闪电"是俄亥俄州派克斯维尔市的一个小联盟球队，它隶属于东部联盟的中区。1976年的赛季以来，这个球队曾是"匹兹堡海盗队"（the Pittsburgh Pirates）的3A会员队，近年在"瀑布体育场"（Waterfall Stadium）打球。这个现代化的体育场于2006年在克利夫兰附近建成。斯顿公司是这个球队主要的所有者，全权拥有场内的商店和娱乐服务的经营权。食物和娱乐服务的收入对该组织的总体盈利能力至关重要，正如它的所有者葛瑞格·斯顿常被人引用的一句话："我并非拥有一个棒球队；我卖的是热狗！"这句话很切合于最近小联盟组织最近提出的策略，即把这项运动转变成为"家家户户都能负担得起的一种享受"，也就是它不只是一项运动，而

---

④ farm system，体育用词，通常指一个球队或体育俱乐部的任务在于向年青的球员提供经验或训练，并通过协议规定：成功的球员可以在某个时间转给高一级的球队。这一体制可采取各种不同形式，可以是正式的，也可以是非正式的。——原注

是要使它更成为一项娱乐活动。除了多种多样的食物、饮料、零食以外，斯顿还想到孩子们的需要，把棒球场设计成在球场周边提供各项娱乐服务的场地。为了使家长和孩子们回到棒球场来，斯顿坚信，除了球队在棒球内场上取得胜利外，还必须辅之以让每一场比赛都为这些家庭带来快乐。表1列示了在赛季中为球迷们提供娱乐所提出的一些创意的范例。

---

**表 1**
**派克斯维尔闪电的主要举措**

**A 部分——为全体观众在比赛的日子里提供的活动**
1. 赛后烟火和音乐会
2. 儿童的快乐时间——让儿童免费到"游乐场"玩耍
3. 大联盟的历任球员意外来访
4. 与球员见面之夜
5. 在周末时担任总经理之职
6. 免费公路之旅——与球队一起旅行观看一次客场比赛
7. 赢得一次在"闪电商店"一小时的抢购狂欢
8. 球赛的"全明星"孩子——按照每次球赛入场预报单，选择一个孩子为"全明星"
9. "梦幻家庭"——选择一个幸运家庭与球队队员同席
10. 天降祥瑞——与球队的吉祥物"闪电博尔特"同席而坐

**B 部分——特别游戏日的经历**
1. 生日派对——食物、游泳、在"游乐场"玩游戏，享受"贵宾"待遇
2. 开球仪式——包括球帽、由球员签名的棒球、并与球队合影
3. 公司郊游和派对
4. 专属包厢出租——享受球队老板专用包厢一晚

---

斯顿是一个富有远见的人，他重视创造性思维，并且不懈地努力寻求独特的方法发展它的经营，成为市场上的主导企业。虽然许多参加小联盟的球队也同样地找到一些在赛季中增加卖座和提高忠诚度的方法，斯顿对他的雇员说得很清楚：他认为这项经营不应该局限在赛季。

# 扩展盈利能力

与斯顿扩大经营的目标相呼应，他采取的第一项创举是将球场的一些体验送入粉丝们的家庭，让他们在非赛季时也能享受到，而不会遗忘球队。公司从制造商购得了经销权，独家经销"POG 烤箱"（以"派克斯维尔闪电"球队的标志 为商标，通过电话和互联网销售）。"POG"是一种在棒球场销售的热狗，它已成为各个年龄段的"派克斯维尔"迷的至爱，并被许多运动场售货公司冠以"全垒打[5]"的标签。其烤箱是特制的，它们的尺寸要比球场上常用的烤箱小一些。

眼看 2010 会计年度即将来临，斯顿这位早先曾担任首席财务官（CFO）的人，就要求分部的会计组开始对烤箱的销售额作出盈利计划。为提供编制

---

[5] out of this park，一球被击到很高远的地方，远远超球场的范围，就是"全垒打"的意思。——译者

2010年度财务预算的必要数据，会计组抽出了一些容量数据，从总分类账中抽出一些财务数据，汇编出成本构成的一些主要项目（表2）。

表2
部分财务及其他数据

A 部分——热狗烤箱业务的数量数据

| 季度 | 销售数量 | 千瓦特小时 | 季度 | 销售数量 | 千瓦特小时 |
|---|---|---|---|---|---|
| 2006 会计年度： | | | 2008 会计年度： | | |
| 第一季度 | 9 100 | 4 300 | 第一季度 | 10 000 | 4 000 |
| 第二季度 | 14 700 | 5 250 | 第二季度 | 16 000 | 5 000 |
| 第三季度 | 16 900 | 6 310 | 第三季度 | 18 000 | 6 000 |
| 第四季度 | 14 800 | 10 011 | 第四季度 | 15 000 | 10 000 |
| 2007 会计年度： | | | 2009 会计年度： | | |
| 第一季度 | 9 500 | 11 777 | 第一季度 | 11 000 | 12 000 |
| 第二季度 | 15 100 | 10 966 | 第二季度 | 17 000 | 11 000 |
| 第三季度 | 17 000 | 9 120 | 第三季度 | 20 000 | 9 000 |
| 第四季度 | 15 000 | 8 320 | 第四季度 | 13 000 | 8 000 |

B 部分——总分类账数据

| 从 Oracle 总分类账下载的原始数据 | | 从 Oracle 总分类账下载的原始数据 | |
|---|---|---|---|
| 当前数据 | | 当前数据 | |
| 获自总分类账科目 | 年度/季度/科目 | 获自总分类账科目 | 年度/季度/科目 |
| 功能性货币 | 美元 | 功能性货币 | 美元 |
| 利润中心 | 1000 派克斯维尔烤箱 | 利润中心 | 1000 派克斯维尔烤箱 |
| 分配渠道 | 10 个最终客户销售商 | 分配渠道 | 10 个最终客户销售商 |
| 产品 | PG－101 POG 烤箱 Plight 101 | 产品 | PG－101 POG 烤箱 Plight 101 |
| 打印页码 | 1/2 | 打印页码 | 1/2 |

| 项目 | 总账科目编号 | 实际 | 会计年度 | 季度 | 项目 | 总账科目编号 | 实际 | 会计年度 | 季度 |
|---|---|---|---|---|---|---|---|---|---|
| 保险 | 000100100 | 5 000 | 2006 | 1 | 运输费用 | 000100122 | 110 000 | 2008 | 1 |
| 保险 | 000100100 | 5 000 | 2006 | 2 | 运输费用 | 000100122 | 176 000 | 2008 | 2 |
| 保险 | 000100100 | 5 000 | 2006 | 3 | 运输费用 | 000100122 | 198 000 | 2008 | 3 |
| 保险 | 000100100 | 5 000 | 2006 | 4 | 运输费用 | 000100122 | 165 000 | 2008 | 4 |
| 保险 | 000100100 | 5 000 | 2007 | 1 | 运输费用 | 000100122 | 121 000 | 2009 | 1 |
| 保险 | 000100100 | 5 000 | 2007 | 2 | 运输费用 | 000100122 | 187 000 | 2009 | 2 |
| 保险 | 000100100 | 5 000 | 2007 | 3 | 运输费用 | 000100122 | 220 000 | 2009 | 3 |
| 保险 | 000100100 | 5 000 | 2007 | 4 | 运输费用 | 000100122 | 143 000 | 2009 | 4 |
| 保险 | 000100100 | 6 250 | 2008 | 1 | 折旧费用 | 000100123 | 32 655 | 2006 | 1 |
| 保险 | 000100100 | 6 250 | 2008 | 2 | 折旧费用 | 000100123 | 32 655 | 2006 | 2 |
| 保险 | 000100100 | 6 250 | 2008 | 3 | 折旧费用 | 000100123 | 32 655 | 2006 | 3 |
| 保险 | 000100100 | 6 250 | 2008 | 4 | 折旧费用 | 000100123 | 32 655 | 2006 | 4 |

表2 转一下页

**表2**
**部分财务及其他数据**
接上页

**B部分——总分类账数据**

| | | | | | | | | | |
|---|---|---|---|---|---|---|---|---|---|
| 保险 | 000100100 | 8 737 | 2009 | 1 | 折旧费用 | 000100123 | 32 655 | 2007 | 1 |
| 保险 | 000100100 | 8 737 | 2009 | 2 | 折旧费用 | 000100123 | 32 655 | 2007 | 2 |
| 保险 | 000100100 | 8 737 | 2009 | 3 | 折旧费用 | 000100123 | 32 655 | 2007 | 3 |
| 保险 | 000100100 | 8 737 | 2009 | 4 | 折旧费用 | 000100123 | 56 000 | 2007 | 4 |
| 行政人员薪酬 | 000100110 | 18 000 | 2006 | 1 | 折旧费用 | 000100123 | 56 000 | 2008 | 1 |
| 行政人员薪酬 | 000100110 | 76 099 | 2006 | 2 | 折旧费用 | 000100123 | 56 000 | 2008 | 2 |
| 行政人员薪酬 | 000100110 | 76 099 | 2006 | 3 | 折旧费用 | 000100123 | 56 000 | 2008 | 3 |
| 行政人员薪酬 | 000100110 | 78 689 | 2006 | 4 | 折旧费用 | 000100123 | 56 000 | 2008 | 4 |
| 行政人员薪酬 | 000100110 | 78 689 | 2007 | 1 | 折旧费用 | 000100123 | 70 000 | 2009 | 1 |
| 行政人员薪酬 | 000100110 | 82 455 | 2007 | 2 | 折旧费用 | 000100123 | 70 000 | 2009 | 2 |
| 行政人员薪酬 | 000100110 | 82 455 | 2007 | 3 | 折旧费用 | 000100123 | 70 000 | 2009 | 3 |
| 行政人员薪酬 | 000100110 | 86 555 | 2007 | 4 | 折旧费用 | 000100123 | 70 000 | 2009 | 4 |
| 行政人员薪酬 | 000100110 | 138 016 | 2008 | 1 | 公用事业费用 | 000100184 | 17 850 | 2006 | 1 |
| 行政人员薪酬 | 000100110 | 138 016 | 2008 | 2 | 公用事业费用 | 000100184 | 20 099 | 2006 | 2 |
| 行政人员薪酬 | 000100110 | 138 016 | 2008 | 3 | 公用事业费用 | 000100184 | 23 100 | 2006 | 3 |
| 行政人员薪酬 | 000100110 | 138 016 | 2008 | 4 | 公用事业费用 | 000100184 | 33 024 | 2006 | 4 |
| 行政人员薪酬 | 000100110 | 140 777 | 2009 | 1 | 公用事业费用 | 000100184 | 32 550 | 2007 | 1 |
| 行政人员薪酬 | 000100110 | 140 777 | 2009 | 2 | 公用事业费用 | 000100184 | 31 000 | 2007 | 2 |
| 行政人员薪酬 | 000100110 | 140 777 | 2009 | 3 | 公用事业费用 | 000100184 | 28 999 | 2007 | 3 |
| 行政人员薪酬 | 000100110 | 140 777 | 2009 | 4 | 公用事业费用 | 000100184 | 25 997 | 2007 | 4 |
| 广告费用 | 000100121 | 192 506 | 2006 | 1 | 公用事业费用 | 000100184 | 18 000 | 2008 | 1 |
| 广告费用 | 000100121 | 192 506 | 2006 | 2 | 公用事业费用 | 000100184 | 21 000 | 2008 | 2 |
| 广告费用 | 000100121 | 192 506 | 2006 | 3 | 公用事业费用 | 000100184 | 24 000 | 2008 | 3 |
| 广告费用 | 000100121 | 192 506 | 2006 | 4 | 公用事业费用 | 000100184 | 33 000 | 2008 | 4 |
| 广告费用 | 000100121 | 197 896 | 2007 | 1 | 公用事业费用 | 000100184 | 35 000 | 2009 | 1 |
| 广告费用 | 000100121 | 197 896 | 2007 | 2 | 公用事业费用 | 000100184 | 33 000 | 2009 | 2 |
| 广告费用 | 000100121 | 197 896 | 2007 | 3 | 公用事业费用 | 000100184 | 30 000 | 2009 | 3 |
| 广告费用 | 000100121 | 197 896 | 2007 | 4 | 公用事业费用 | 000100184 | 27 000 | 2009 | 4 |
| 广告费用 | 000100121 | 203 883 | 2008 | 1 | 维修费用 | 000100191 | 6 980 | 2006 | 1 |
| 广告费用 | 000100121 | 203 883 | 2008 | 2 | 维修费用 | 000100191 | 7 800 | 2006 | 2 |
| 广告费用 | 000100121 | 203 883 | 2008 | 3 | 维修费用 | 000100191 | 9 040 | 2006 | 3 |
| 广告费用 | 000100121 | 203 883 | 2008 | 4 | 维修费用 | 000100191 | 11 650 | 2006 | 4 |
| 广告费用 | 000100121 | 210 000 | 2009 | 1 | 维修费用 | 000100191 | 7 869 | 2007 | 1 |
| 广告费用 | 000100121 | 210 000 | 2009 | 2 | 维修费用 | 000100191 | 11 250 | 2007 | 2 |
| 广告费用 | 000100121 | 210 000 | 2009 | 3 | 维修费用 | 000100191 | 9 980 | 2007 | 3 |
| 广告费用 | 000100121 | 210 000 | 2009 | 4 | 维修费用 | 000100191 | 9 200 | 2007 | 4 |
| 运输费用 | 000100122 | 100 100 | 2006 | 1 | 维修费用 | 000100191 | 6 500 | 2008 | 1 |
| 运输费用 | 000100122 | 161 700 | 2006 | 2 | 维修费用 | 000100191 | 7 500 | 2008 | 2 |
| 运输费用 | 000100122 | 185 900 | 2006 | 3 | 维修费用 | 000100191 | 8 600 | 2008 | 3 |
| 运输费用 | 000100122 | 162 800 | 2006 | 4 | 维修费用 | 000100191 | 11 700 | 2008 | 4 |
| 运输费用 | 000100122 | 104 500 | 2007 | 1 | 维修费用 | 000100191 | 12 000 | 2009 | 1 |
| 运输费用 | 000100122 | 166 100 | 2007 | 2 | 维修费用 | 000100191 | 11 800 | 2009 | 2 |
| 运输费用 | 000100122 | 187 000 | 2007 | 3 | 维修费用 | 000100191 | 10 000 | 2009 | 3 |
| 运输费用 | 000100122 | 165 000 | 2007 | 4 | 维修费用 | 000100191 | 9 600 | 2009 | 4 |

表2转一下页

### 表 2
### 部分财务及其他数据
接上页

#### C 部分——其他综合数据

按历史数据，每台烤箱的销货成本为 35 美元，销售佣金等于销售额的 6%。预计在 2010 会计年度中，这些数据不会发生变化。斯顿还告诉会计组：广告费用必须与上一年保持不变，行政人员工薪和保险费均根据通货膨胀率提高 3%。如本表的 B 部分所示，这些项目在 2010 会计年度之前 16 个季度的成本数据，均可自总分类账得到。运输、电力、维修和折旧费用，也可以从总分类账得到过去 16 个季度的数据。如本表的 A 部分所示，公司的销售组和业务组也提供了过去 16 个会计季度的有关数据。

公司的管理层也已打算在 2010 会计年度第一季度的资产负债表上，披露新置的价值为 500 000 美元的卡车，以帮助运输产品；并向 POG 烤箱投资 100 万美元（该分部的固定资产政策为，对当年购入的固定资产计提一整年的折旧费用，而不考虑购入的时间）。这些卡车预期使用寿命为十年。在编制计划时，分部不考虑财务措施对税金的影响，因为税金是在公司层面上计算、按总体经营情况向各分部分配的。工程师们预期在 2010 会计年度的第一季度将耗费电力 13 000 千瓦小时。

在编制 2010 会计年度第一季度的计划时，斯顿关心三种情景下的财务预算数据：(1) 基础方案：假定出售 12 000 台烤箱，每台按 100 美元出售；(2) 市场渗透策略：假定以 5% 的折扣销售，有望提高销售量 10%；(3) 市场溢价策略：假定把价格提高 15%，销售额预期减少 15%，同时把烤箱上的商标做得更大一些，这会使每台烤箱的销售费用增加 5 美元。

为便于编制计划，斯顿向公司的会计人员描绘了一种独特的利润表的格式，可以用于编制将由他审阅的收益情况。他把这一格式称为"混合式损益表[⑥]"，因为这种利润表既包括了以公认会计原则（GAAP）为基础制定的内容，又包括了以贡献毛利为基础的内容。为避免词不达意的误解，他在纸上描绘了自己的想法，见表 3。

### 表 3
### 混合式的利润表图示

| 混合式损益表 | |
|---|---|
| | 销售 |
| 减： | 销货成本 |
| 等于： | 毛利 |
| 减： | 营业费用：**变动费用** |
| 等于： | 贡献毛益 |
| 减： | 营业费用：**固定费用** |
| 等于： | 营业利润 |

---

[⑥] "损益表（Profit and Loss Statement）"，现在改称为利润表（Income Statement）。——译者

## 未来的愿景

### 为未来的扩张提出的倡议

正当斯顿认为他这第一个倡议是"迈向正确的方向"（step in the right direction）时，他已经提前开始考虑下一项重大突破。他和其他球队的所有者不同的是，他认为赛季过去之后的时刻，有许多待开发的发财机会在等待着他，所以并不想在这段时间休假。他把公司的会计组视同为咨询师，渴望他们提出有关球队营销和娱乐活动的战略方向的意见。再者，他希望将这有关赛季后的倡议看作扩展经营季节的方法。而这一倡议必然比 POG 烤箱更为重大。他希望将这些设施投资资本化，使粉丝们全年都参与到球队的活动中。他认为这会充分地引起当地媒体的注意，甚至于能够在全国的电视屏幕上看到这一项有创意的突破。

从营业角度来看，赛季结束后，球队多数的基本设施都呈闲置状态，而有些业务费用是固定费用，他相信从非赛季时获得的新收入中的相当一部分会增加球队的利润，扩展其整体的盈利能力。他对于这样的前景感到兴奋，特别是因为他知道其他球队的所有者中，没有一个人是这样想的，这给了他先人一步的优势。人们常听到斯顿这样讲，"我们仅仅局限于自己的创造性"。此时他要用这句话来检验他公司的会计组了，期望在棒球小联盟球队的娱乐活动中取得历史性的突破。

### 提高球队的战略财务管理

斯顿除了为公司创造一个战略性的重大突破，他还希望建立一个框架来治理公司日常的财务管理策略。他认为，如果没有这样一个框架，公司的会计部门将永远被看作是个写写算算的机构，不能充分施展其能力、作出战略性的贡献。由于他的财会工作的背景，他完全相信：公司的成长和繁荣，取决于采用一个比较好的营业合伙模式。这一模式能鞭策会计人员的聪明才智，使他们的工作不限于传统的业务处理，而能成为公司策略的咨询人员，坚持不懈地解决各种经营中的问题。

最近，他还回忆到在他职业生涯的初期，他曾接触过商业战略伙伴（strategic business partner, SBP）[⑦] 角色的 C – 框架（见表 4），而他至今还没有在他这个企业中实施过该框架。他决定把这一框架展示给他的会计组。他希望将这个框架付诸实践的任务交给他们，使这个框架"合身"于他们的情况和组织。当他开始向他们介绍这一框架时，他强调这一治理模式可通

---

⑦ 在以下的表 4 中，可以看到要尽到商业战略伙伴（Strategic Business Partner, SBP）的责任，企业的 CFO 应该从四方面对企业三方面产生影响，因英文中都以字母 C 开头，所以称为"C 框架"。下面"他们会把自己 C 作企业的合作伙伴"，就是从这里来的。作者在这里一语双关，因为 C 与"see"同音，表明会计部门将自己看作企业的合作伙伴，也表明在该框架的作用下，会计部门可作为企业的合作伙伴。——译者

过合作伙伴的方式提供一种具体有形的方式来促进自觉的思考战略财务管理的重要性，并超越过去只是算出基本数据的局限性。

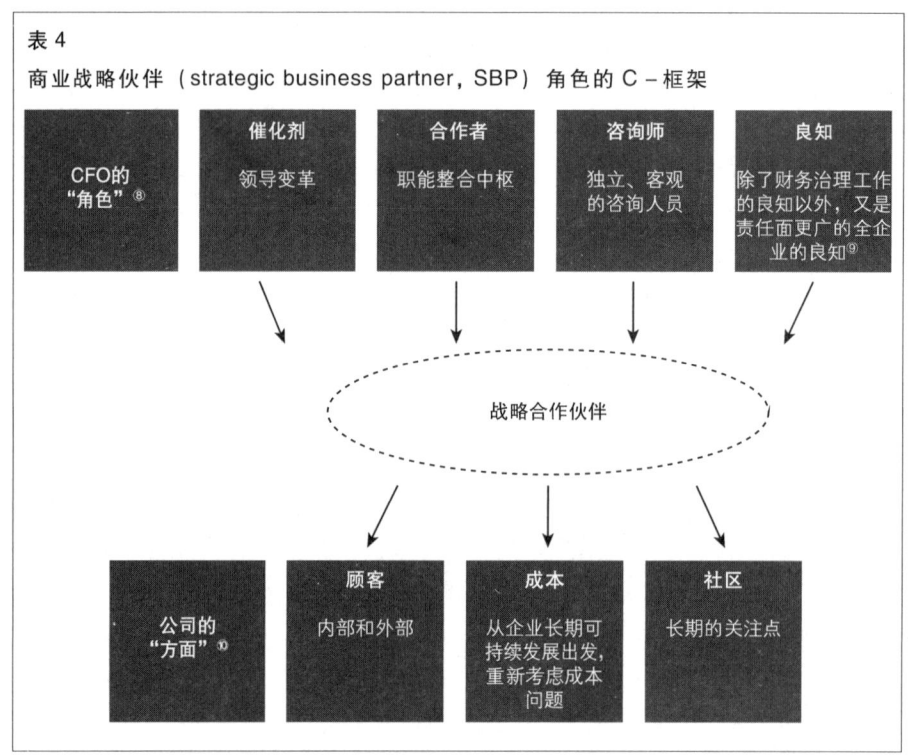

他的解释是，在框架的顶端有若干个方面，相关人员可从这几方面协助公司的CFO，使他更好地成为整个公司经营的合伙人（CFO的角色）。这些方面起着信息输入的作用。首先，会计部门可以成为帮助引进和实施新策略、引导企业实现变革的催化剂。其次，他们作为合作者，可成为整合企业的各项职能（诸如采购、销售、人事和信息技术）的中枢。第三，会计人员将对企业领导提供独立、客观的咨询意见，扮演咨询师的角色。最后，从近来流传的几则丑闻来看，会计部门显然必须成为企业的良知，这不但指报告的财务报表，还包括它有责任向领导提供意见使其策略产生更广泛的影响。

会计部门在企业中充当企业的催化剂、合作者、咨询师和良知，并成为企业领导的合作伙伴，每一方面最终必将一起影响到整个公司的产出（公司对三方面）。首先，在CFO层次上所采取的每一个行动都应该对客户产生正面的影响——所谓客户，包括依赖于会计部门提供的建议和信息的企业内部合伙者（内部客户），以及外部为企业创造收入的粉丝们（外部客户）。其次，CFO的每一项角色都应该帮助企业的成本结构达到足以使企业长期

---

⑧ CFO "lever"，指CFO应该作为以下四种角色（作为催化剂、合作者、咨询师、良知），对企业施加影响。——译者

⑨ 即必须遵循职业道德。——译者

⑩ company "lever"，指企业应对三个方面（顾客、成本、社区）起到影响。——译者

可持续发展的水平。没有一家企业能够安于现状，而不考虑对未来的影响。最后，第一层次的影响者应该致力于当地以及范围更为广阔的社区的提高和收益。

斯顿宣称，一旦提出上述框架并使之适应于派克斯维尔球队，这个框架会存在于会计部门日常工作中，而整个企业也会因为将财务职能与企业的决策策略联结起来而获益。在每一项为企业所执行的任务中，他们会把自己"C"作企业的合作伙伴。为了激励他们奔向这一目标，他提醒到：他们当前为实施非赛季时期的各项倡议所做的工作，正是他们已经跳出了"写写算算"的圈子、开始担当帮助经营企业的任务的一项最好的例证。

# 挑战

对会计组来说，斯顿显然对他们的工作和企业的未来都有很高的期望。他要求他们打出一个思想上的"全垒打"，因为单是"一垒打"不足以变革这个行业，也不能对这项季节性的营业提供长期、持久的发展。

他将会计人员看作咨询顾问，不仅具备提供财务和分析信息的专业技能，而且也具有战略思维，可对他和公司领导提出有价值的意见，帮助企业提高盈利能力和企业的扩展潜力。他深信，如果他们按他所要求的那样去做，他们也会将自己看作是战略财务经理——企业的合作伙伴——支持并协助企业做出决策。

斯顿要求会计组编制一份报告供他审阅。他要求报告书针对现存和未来的各项问题，以推动企业走向长期发展：

- 请提供一份概述企业现状的综合报告，列示财务分析中的主要指标情况，以及你对企业的战略建议。
- 财务分析——运用统计和财务方法，对POG烤箱分部的计划执行情况作一分析评价。内容包括：
  - 一份概述成本结构中各要素成本性态的表格；
  - 为2010会计年度的第一季度，编制一份混合式的利润预算表（包含支持论点的分析）；
  - 对斯顿所提出的混合式利润表的优点和用途，作一概述。
- 策略分析——未来的扩展
  - 请选择一项很可能提高盈利性的非赛季的扩张策略提出你的意见，向斯顿作一概述。在你的意见中，应就执行策略中需耗用的各项资源（如营业费用、资本支出、筹资费用、人事和外聘咨询人员的费用）作出估计。
- 策略分析——采用C-框架
  - 应用C-框架，向斯顿概述应如何改进战略财务管理的意见。概述中包括把CFO各种角色的投入，与公司的三方面产出联系起来，作一全面的探讨。

# Pikesville Lightening: Evaluating Strategic Business Expansion Opportunities[1]

*Thomas G. Canace*
*Wake Forest University*

*Paul E. Juras*
*Babson College*

## INTRODUCTION

Greg Storm, team owner, has often been quoted as saying, "I don't own a baseball team; I sell hot dogs!" This line ties in well with the recent strategy of minor league organizations to transform games into an "affordable family experience" offering much more entertainment than just the game. Still, Storm is a visionary who values outside-the-box thinking and who continually strives to be a market leader in finding unique ways to grow his business. Storm needs help "hitting a home run," because base hits alone would not revolutionize the industry or provide long-term, sustainable growth for the seasonal business.

## BACKGROUND

In 1882, the Northwestern League of baseball was organized. Soon after its inception, however, league officials signed an agreement with the National League and the American Association that established territorial rights and essentially assigned "major" or "minor" league status to teams. From this agreement, the Northwestern League became the first recognized minor league in baseball. Further agreements established the rights of major league teams to draft minor league players, resulting in the "farm system" where players trained for the major leagues in obscure one-horse towns with little pizzazz.

Such organized baseball was confined to the northeastern United States at first, but quickly expanded throughout the country by the turn of the century.

---

[1] This case was prepared to provide an opportunity for students to interpret, analyze, evaluate, synthesize, and communicate a solution to a management accounting problem.

Although the number of minor league clubs had decreased considerably by the mid-twentieth century, by the 1980s minor league baseball had exploded, with attendance exceeding 20 million for the first time since 1950. This success prompted the business relationship between the two leagues that exists today under the Professional Baseball Agreement. Under the new agreement set forth in the 1990s, the majors continued to pay a large share of the operational expenses, but minors were now required to share ticket revenues and establish minimum standards at their ballparks. To this day, many fans and observers are unaware that the major league organization has full authority to decide who plays for the minor league team for the season. In fact, many farm clubs have commented that it is not unusual for them to learn their final rosters about one month before the start of the season. Of course, while the minor league owners have limited control over the baseball operations, all clearly recognize that they are still running a business that must thrive at the local level, and the operating performance of these organizations has been anything but "minor."

In fact, thanks to the strategic thinking and entrepreneurial spirit of a new breed of team owners, these teams are run like top-flight professional clubs, playing in uniquely designed ballparks while also offering a new entertainment alternative for families. These owners have recognized that, while on the surface, their mission is to "play ball" by preparing young players for the big leagues, more importantly their profitability depends largely upon their successful establishment as an entertainment venue. Many observers have often made the analogy that minor league teams compete with movie theaters for entertainment revenue, charging a flat-rate admissions fee but hoping to expand the bottom line by providing ancillary food and entertainment services. Hence, while winning games is key to filling the ballpark at the major league level, operating success for minor league teams is driven more by affordability and alternative non-baseball entertainment.

# THE PIKESVILLE LIGHTNING

The Pikesville Lightning organization is a minor league baseball team based in Pikesville, Ohio, and plays in the Central Division of the Eastern League. Since the 1976 season, the team has been the AAA affiliate of the Pittsburgh Pirates, and currently plays in Waterfall Stadium, a state-of-the-art facility built in 2006 near Cleveland. Storm Enterprises is the primary owner of the organization, and maintains full ownership of park vending and entertainment operations. Food and entertainment revenue is so vital to the overall profitability of the organization that owner Greg Storm has often been quoted as saying, "I don't own a baseball team; I sell hot dogs!" This line ties in well with the recent strategy of minor league organizations to transform games into an affordable family experience with much more entertainment offered than just the game. In addition to the wide array of foods, drinks, and snacks, Storm designed the ballpark with kids in mind by providing various forms of entertainment around the perimeter of the park. To keep parents and children coming back to the park, Storm firmly believes that team success on the diamond must be complemented by family fun at every game. Table 1 provides a sample of some strategic initiatives he has put in place during the season to entertain fans (Table 1).

Storm is a visionary who values outside-the-box thinking and who continually strives to be a market leader in finding unique ways to grow his business. While many minor league organizations have also found ways to improve attendance and loyalty during the season, Storm has made it very clear to his employees that he does not want to be limited by the seasonality of the business.

Table 1

Top Initiatives of Pikesville Lightning

Panel A-Game Day Events for All

1. Post-game fireworks and concert
2. Kids Happy Hour-free hour in FunZone for kids only
3. Surprise Major League visitor from the past
4. Meet-the-players night
5. Become a general manager for the weekend
6. Road trip give-away-travel with the team to a road game
7. Win a 1-hour shopping spree in the Lightning Shop
8. All-star kid of the game-one child selected before each game based upon pre-entry
9. The Magical Family-one family selected to sit with team
10. Mascot encounter-sit with the "Lightning Bolt" team mascot

Panel B-Special Request Game Day Experiences

1. Birthday party-food, swimming, FunZone games and special VIP treatment
2. Ceremonial first pitch-includes cap, autographed baseball, and team picture with you
3. Corporate outings and parties
4. Buy-a-box: Rent the owners' box for a night for your event

# EXPANDING PROFITABILITY

In recognition of his stretch goal for the business, Storm developed a first-step initiative to bring some of this ballpark experience into the homes of fans even during the off season to keep fans thinking about the team. The company obtained an exclusive franchise from its manufacturer to purchase "POG" ovens (branded with the Pikesville Lighting team ⚡ logo for distribution via phone and Internet orders.) A "POG" is a special type of hot dog sold at the ballpark that has become a hit with Pikesville fans of all ages, and has even been labeled "out of this park" by many sports vending companies. These ovens were special because they were smaller replicas of the ovens used at the park.

With fiscal 2010 on the horizon, Storm, a chief financial officer (CFO) earlier in his career, has asked the divisional accounting team to begin planning profitability from oven sales. To provide the necessary data to prepare the budgeted financials for fiscal 2010, the accounting team pulled together some volume data, accessed the general ledger to pull financial data, and summarized some key elements of the cost structure (Table 2).

Table 2
Selected Financial and Other Data

Panel A-Volume Data for Hot Dog Oven Business

| Quarter | Units Sold | Kilowatt Hours | Quarter | Units Sold | Kilowatt Hours |
|---|---|---|---|---|---|
| FY2006: | | | FY2008: | | |
| Q1 | 9 100 | 4 300 | Q1 | 10 000 | 4 000 |
| Q2 | 14 700 | 5 250 | Q2 | 16 000 | 5 000 |
| Q3 | 16 900 | 6 310 | Q3 | 18 000 | 6 000 |
| Q4 | 14 800 | 10 011 | Q4 | 15 000 | 10 000 |
| FY2007: | | | FY2009: | | |
| Q1 | 9 500 | 11 777 | Q1 | 11 000 | 12 000 |
| Q2 | 15 100 | 10 966 | Q2 | 17 000 | 11 000 |
| Q3 | 17 000 | 9 120 | Q3 | 20 000 | 9 000 |
| Q4 | 15 000 | 8 320 | Q4 | 13 000 | 8 000 |

Table 2 continues on next page

---

② The division's fixed asset policy is to take a full year's worth of depreciation on assets purchased during the year, regardless of the date of acquisition.

## Table 2
### Selected Financial and Other Data (Continued)
#### Panel B-General Ledger Data

| Raw Download from Oracle General Ledger | | | | | Raw Download from Oracle General Ledger | | | | |
|---|---|---|---|---|---|---|---|---|---|
| Current data | | | | | Current data | | | | |
| GL Account Retrieval | year/quarter/account | | | | GL Account Retrieval | year/quarter/account | | | |
| Func. Currency | usd | | | | Func. Currency | usd | | | |
| Profit Center | 1000 Pikesville-Oven | | | | Profit Center | 1000 Pikesville-Oven | | | |
| Distr. Channel | 10 Final customer sales | | | | Distr. Channel | 10 Final customer sales | | | |
| Product | PG – 101 POG Warmer Oven PLIGHT 101 | | | | Product | PG – 101 POG Warmer Oven PLIGHT 101 | | | |
| Page feed | 1 of 2 | | | | Page feed | 2 of 2 | | | |
| Lead column | GL number | Actual | Fiscal year | Quarter | Lead column | GL number | Actual | Fiscal year | Quarter |
| insurance | 000100100 | 5 000 | 2006 | 1 | shipping | 000100122 | 110 000 | 2008 | 1 |
| insurance | 000100100 | 5 000 | 2006 | 2 | shipping | 000100122 | 176 000 | 2008 | 2 |
| insurance | 000100100 | 5 000 | 2006 | 3 | shipping | 000100122 | 198 000 | 2008 | 3 |
| insurance | 000100100 | 5 000 | 2006 | 4 | shipping | 000100122 | 165 000 | 2008 | 4 |
| insurance | 000100100 | 5 000 | 2007 | 1 | shipping | 000100122 | 121 000 | 2009 | 1 |
| insurance | 000100100 | 5 000 | 2007 | 2 | shipping | 000100122 | 187 000 | 2009 | 2 |
| insurance | 000100100 | 5 000 | 2007 | 3 | shipping | 000100122 | 220 000 | 2009 | 3 |
| insurance | 000100100 | 5 000 | 2007 | 4 | shipping | 000100122 | 143 000 | 2009 | 4 |
| insurance | 000100100 | 6 250 | 2008 | 1 | depreciation | 000100123 | 32 655 | 2006 | 1 |
| insurance | 000100100 | 6 250 | 2008 | 2 | depreciation | 000100123 | 32 655 | 2006 | 2 |
| insurance | 000100100 | 6 250 | 2008 | 3 | depreciation | 000100123 | 32 655 | 2006 | 3 |
| insurance | 000100100 | 6 250 | 2008 | 4 | depreciation | 000100123 | 32 655 | 2006 | 4 |
| insurance | 000100100 | 8 737 | 2009 | 1 | depreciation | 000100123 | 32 655 | 2007 | 1 |
| insurance | 000100100 | 8 737 | 2009 | 2 | depreciation | 000100123 | 32 655 | 2007 | 2 |
| insurance | 000100100 | 8 737 | 2009 | 3 | depreciation | 000100123 | 32 655 | 2007 | 3 |
| insurance | 000100100 | 8 737 | 2009 | 4 | depreciation | 000100123 | 56 000 | 2007 | 4 |
| admin. salaries | 000100110 | 18 000 | 2006 | 1 | depreciation | 000100123 | 56 000 | 2008 | 1 |
| admin. salaries | 000100110 | 76 099 | 2006 | 2 | depreciation | 000100123 | 56 000 | 2008 | 2 |
| admin. salaries | 000100110 | 76 099 | 2006 | 3 | depreciation | 000100123 | 56 000 | 2008 | 3 |
| admin. salaries | 000100110 | 78 689 | 2006 | 4 | depreciation | 000100123 | 56 000 | 2008 | 4 |
| admin. salaries | 000100110 | 78 689 | 2007 | 1 | depreciation | 000100123 | 70 000 | 2009 | 1 |
| admin. salaries | 000100110 | 82 455 | 2007 | 2 | depreciation | 000100123 | 70 000 | 2009 | 2 |
| admin. salaries | 000100110 | 82 455 | 2007 | 3 | depreciation | 000100123 | 70 000 | 2009 | 3 |
| admin. salaries | 000100110 | 86 555 | 2007 | 4 | depreciation | 000100123 | 70 000 | 2009 | 4 |
| admin. salaries | 000100110 | 138 016 | 2008 | 1 | utilities | 000100184 | 17 850 | 2006 | 1 |
| admin. salaries | 000100110 | 138 016 | 2008 | 2 | utilities | 000100184 | 20 099 | 2006 | 2 |
| admin. salaries | 000100110 | 138 016 | 2008 | 3 | utilities | 000100184 | 23 100 | 2006 | 3 |
| admin. salaries | 000100110 | 138 016 | 2008 | 4 | utilities | 000100184 | 33 024 | 2006 | 4 |
| admin. salaries | 000100110 | 140 777 | 2009 | 1 | utilities | 000100184 | 32 550 | 2007 | 1 |

Table 2 continues on next page

## Table 2
### Selected Financial and Other Data (Continued)
#### Panel B-General Ledger Data

| | | | | | | | | | |
|---|---|---|---|---|---|---|---|---|---|
| admin. salaries | 000100110 | 140 777 | 2009 | 2 | utilities | 000100184 | 31 000 | 2007 | 2 |
| admin. salaries | 000100110 | 140 777 | 2009 | 3 | utilities | 000100184 | 28 999 | 2007 | 3 |
| admin. salaries | 000100110 | 140 777 | 2009 | 4 | utilities | 000100184 | 25 997 | 2007 | 4 |
| advertising | 000100121 | 192 506 | 2006 | 1 | utilities | 000100184 | 18 000 | 2008 | 1 |
| advertising | 000100121 | 192 506 | 2006 | 2 | utilities | 000100184 | 21 000 | 2008 | 2 |
| advertising | 000100121 | 192 506 | 2006 | 3 | utilities | 000100184 | 24 000 | 2008 | 3 |
| advertising | 000100121 | 192 506 | 2006 | 4 | utilities | 000100184 | 33 000 | 2008 | 4 |
| advertising | 000100121 | 197 896 | 2007 | 1 | utilities | 000100184 | 35 000 | 2009 | 1 |
| advertising | 000100121 | 197 896 | 2007 | 2 | utilities | 000100184 | 33 000 | 2009 | 2 |
| advertising | 000100121 | 197 896 | 2007 | 3 | utilities | 000100184 | 30 000 | 2009 | 3 |
| advertising | 000100121 | 197 896 | 2007 | 4 | utilities | 000100184 | 27 000 | 2009 | 4 |
| advertising | 000100121 | 203 883 | 2008 | 1 | maintenance | 000100191 | 6 980 | 2006 | 1 |
| advertising | 000100121 | 203 883 | 2008 | 2 | maintenance | 000100191 | 7 800 | 2006 | 2 |
| advertising | 000100121 | 203 883 | 2008 | 3 | maintenance | 000100191 | 9 040 | 2006 | 3 |
| advertising | 000100121 | 203 883 | 2008 | 4 | maintenance | 000100191 | 11 650 | 2006 | 4 |
| advertising | 000100121 | 210 000 | 2009 | 1 | maintenance | 000100191 | 7 869 | 2007 | 1 |
| advertising | 000100121 | 210 000 | 2009 | 2 | maintenance | 000100191 | 11 250 | 2007 | 2 |
| advertising | 000100121 | 210 000 | 2009 | 3 | maintenance | 000100191 | 9 980 | 2007 | 3 |
| advertising | 000100121 | 210 000 | 2009 | 4 | maintenance | 000100191 | 9 200 | 2007 | 4 |
| shipping | 000100122 | 100 100 | 2006 | 1 | maintenance | 000100191 | 6 500 | 2008 | 1 |
| shipping | 000100122 | 161 700 | 2006 | 2 | maintenance | 000100191 | 7 500 | 2008 | 2 |
| shipping | 000100122 | 185 900 | 2006 | 3 | maintenance | 000100191 | 8 600 | 2008 | 3 |
| shipping | 000100122 | 162 800 | 2006 | 4 | maintenance | 000100191 | 11 700 | 2008 | 4 |
| shipping | 000100122 | 104 500 | 2007 | 1 | maintenance | 000100191 | 12 000 | 2009 | 1 |
| shipping | 000100122 | 166 100 | 2007 | 2 | maintenance | 000100191 | 11 800 | 2009 | 2 |
| shipping | 000100122 | 187 000 | 2007 | 3 | maintenance | 000100191 | 10 000 | 2009 | 3 |
| shipping | 000100122 | 165 000 | 2007 | 4 | maintenance | 000100191 | 9 600 | 2009 | 4 |

#### Panel C-Other Summary Data

Cost of Goods Sold has historically amounted to $35 per oven sold, while sales commissions represent 6% of sales. These figures aren't expected to change for fiscal 2010. Storm has also advised the team that advertising expenses must remain flat relative to the prior year, while administrative salaries and insurance expenses are each subject to inflationary increases of 3%. Cost data for the prior 16 quarters is available for these items in the general ledger, as shown in Panel B. Cost data for shipping, electricity, maintenance, and depre-ciation are available for the prior 16 quarters in the general ledger as well. The sales and operations teams have also provided relevant volume data over the last 16 fiscal quarters, as shown in Panel A.

Management has also planned to build up the balance sheet during the first quarter of fiscal 2010 with capital expenditures of $500, 000 for additional trucks to assist in the ground distribution of the product and with a $1 million investment in POG ovens. (The division's fixed-asset policy is to take a full year's worth of depreciation on assets purchased during the year, regardless of the date of acquisition.) The trucks are expected to have a useful life of 10 years. For planning purposes, the division doesn't tax-effect its financials because taxes are calculated at a corporate level and allocated to the divisions based upon overall performance. Engineers expect to use 13, 000 kilowatt hours during the first quarter of fiscal 2010.

In planning for the first quarter of fiscal 2010, Storm was interested in three scenarios for the budgeted financials: (1) Base Case: Assume 12, 000 ovens sold at a price of $100 per oven; (2) Market Penetration Strategy: Assume the company can sell 10% more ovens by offering a 5% price discount; (3) Market Premium Strategy: Assume the company loses 15% of its planned customers if it attempts to sell the ovens at a 15% premium and spending $5 more per unit to make the logo bigger.

As an aid in planning, Storm described a unique income statement format he wanted the accountants to use when preparing the budgeted information for his review. He referred to it as a "Hybrid P & L" because it was comprised of the GAAP-based and contribution margin based income statement. To ensure there was no miscommunication, he illustrated the concept for them on a piece of paper as shown in Table 3:

Table 3
Illustration of Hybrid Income Statement

Hybrid P-and-L

|  |  |
| --- | --- |
|  | Sales |
| Less: | Cost of Goods Sold |
| Equals: | Gross Profit |
| Less: | Operating expenses: **Variable** |
| Equals: | Contribution Margin |
| Less: | Operating expenses: **Fixed** |
| Equals: | Operating income |

# A VISION FOR THE FUTURE

### Future Expansion Initiatives

While Storm considered his first initiative a "step in the right direction," he was already starting to think ahead to the next breakthrough. Unlike his peers in the world of team ownership, he really did not want to take time off during the off season while there could be a wealth of unexplored opportunities awaiting him. He valued his accounting team as consultants and was eager to receive their input about the strategic direction of team marketing and entertainment events. Once again, he wanted to consider off-season initiatives as a way to expand the seasonality of the business. But this had to be bigger than the POG oven initiative. He wanted to capitalize on his facilities' investments and really get the fans involved to provide a year-long experience. He knew this would get a great deal of attention from the local media, and could even hit the national radar screen as an innovative breakthrough.

From a business standpoint, since much of the capital infrastructure became idle during the off season and some of the operating expenses were fixed, he believed that a high proportion of new revenue from off-season ventures could drop to the bottom line and expand his overall profitability. He was excited about these prospects especially because he knew that no other team owners were considering such a strategy, so this would give him a first-mover advantage. Storm was routinely heard saying, "We are limited only by our own creativity," and now he would put this phrase to test with his accounting team in the hopes of making history in the world of minor league baseball entertainment.

## Enhancing Organizational Strategic Financial Management

In addition to creating a new strategic breakthrough for his organization, Storm was interested in developing a framework for governing the ongoing strategic financial management of his business. Without such a framework, he believed his accounting organization would not be empowered to unleash its strategic contribution to the business, but would forever be seen only as the "numbercrunchers." Given his roots in accounting and finance, he wholeheartedly believed that the growth and prosperity of his business depended upon adopting a better business partnering model. Such a model would rein in the intelligence of his accountants to add value beyond the traditional transaction processing and would enable them to become strategic advisors continuously working toward business solutions.

Recently, he recalled that, early in his career, he was exposed to a framework that he had never implemented for his business: the C-framework for the strategic business partner (SBP) role (Table 4). He decided to present this framework to his accounting organization. He wanted to place the onus on them to bring this framework to life by "fitting" it to their situation and organization, however. As he began introducing the framework to them, he emphasized that such a governing model would provide a tangible way to consciously think about the importance of strategic financial management through business partnering, and to avoid "slipping" back into a role that fails to see past the mere production of the fundamentals.

He explained that, at the top of the framework, there were several dimensions along which individuals could assist the CFO in becoming a better partner to the overall business (CFO levers). These dimensions serve as inputs. First, the accounting organization could act as catalysts in leading change for the business by helping to introduce and implement new strategies. Second, they could take on the role of collaborator by serving as a hub to integrate the functional aspects of the business such as purchasing, sales, human resources, and information technology. Third, the accountants would assume the role of consultant by acting as an independent, objective advisor to the business leaders. Finally, recent scandals have made it clear that the accounting organization must provide a conscience to the business-not only with respect to the reported financials but also by advising how strategy could have broader ramifications.

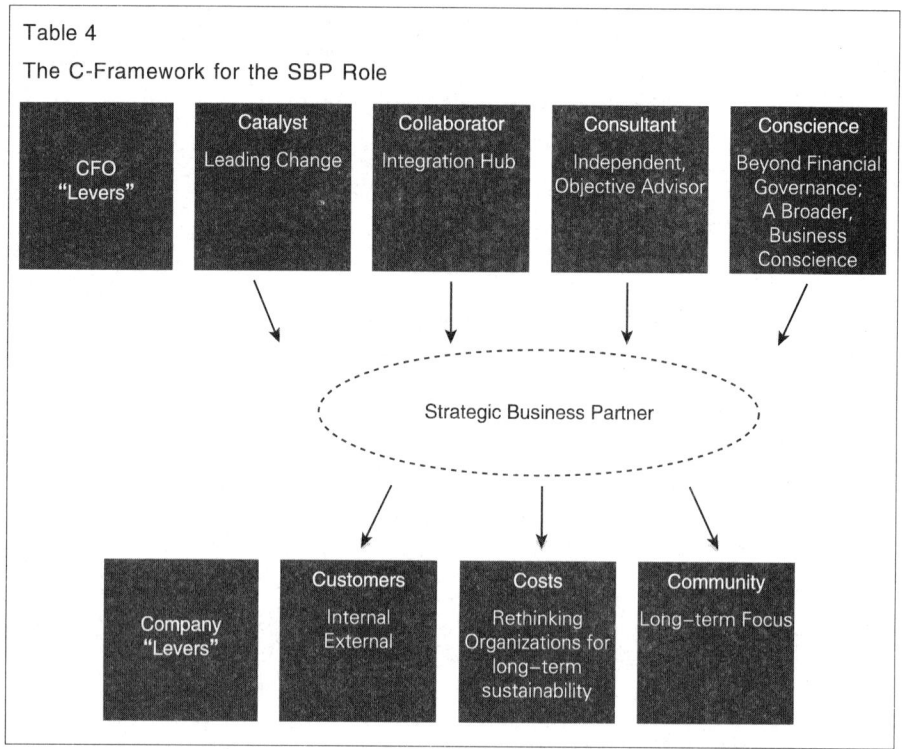

Table 4
The C-Framework for the SBP Role

By acting as a catalyst, collaborator, consultant, and conscience for the business to partner with the business leaders, each of the dimensions should ultimately impact the company along several dimensions (company levers) that serve as outputs. First, each action at the CFO level should positively impact the customers of the organization-both internal partners who rely on information and advice from the accountants and the external revenue-generating fans. Second, each CFO lever should assist the business in achieving a cost structure that allows for long-term sustainability. No business can live for the present without considering ramifications for the future. Finally, the first-tier levers should work toward the advancement and benefit of the local and larger community.

Storm declared that, once developed and tailored to the Pikesville organization, the framework would be lived by the accounting team every day and the entire business would reap the rewards of linking the financial function into the strategic aspects of the decision making. They would "C" themselves as business partners in every task they perform for the business. To motivate them toward this goal, he reminded them that their current task of developing the off-season initiative was a prime example of how they already go beyond just "counting beans" and have begun to step into a role of helping to run the business.

# THE CHALLENGE

It was clear to the accounting team that Storm had high expectations for their work and for the future of his organization. Storm challenged them to "hit home runs" with their thinking, for base hits alone would not revolutionize the industry or provide long-term, sustainable growth for the seasonal business.

He viewed his accountants as consultants who not only had the technical skills to provide financial and analytical information, but who also had the strategic thinking to provide valuable input to him and the business leaders to help improve the profitability and expansion potential of the business. He was confident that, by performing the work he was asking them to do, they, too, would begin to view themselves as strategic financial managers-business partners-who would support and assist with the decision making of the business.

Storm asked the team to prepare a report for his review. He wanted the report to address the following current issues and future prospects that could propel the business toward long-term growth:

- Provide an executive summary that outlines the current situation, key metrics from your financial analysis, and your strategic recommendations for the business.
- Financial Analysis – Using statistical and financial methods, provide an analytical assessment of the planned performance for the POG oven segment including
  - A table that outlines the cost behavior of each element of the cost structure;
  - A hybrid-format budgeted income statement for Q1FY2010 [provide supporting analysis];
  - Outline the benefits and usefulness of Storm's hybrid income statement approach.
- Strategic Analysis-Future Expansion
  - Outline your advice to Storm about one specific high-impact potential off-season expansion strategy to be employed for achieving greater profitability. Include in your discussion an assessment of the resources (e.g., operating, capital, financing, personnel, and external consultants) necessary to execute the strategy.
- Strategic Analysis-Employing the C-framework
  - Use the C-framework to outline your advice to Storm about how to improve its strategic financial management function. Include a thorough discussion of the framework by linking each CFO-lever input to each of the three company-lever outputs.

教案

# 派克斯维尔闪电：对策略性业务扩展机遇的评估

*Thomas G. Canace*
*Wake Forest University*

*Paul E. Juras*
*Babson College*

葛瑞格·斯顿（Greg Storm）是一位棒球队所有者，他力求找到独特的发展经营方法，让他的企业成为行业的领军球队。他将会计人员看作是咨询顾问，不仅具备专业技能，而且还具有策略性思维，可对他和公司各领导提出有价值的意见，帮助企业提高盈利能力和企业的扩展潜力。本案例要求学生扮演球队会计组的一位成员，对企业的经营结果进行财务和策略分析。案例也要求学生将会计人员看作战略合作伙伴的角色，提出具体的策略性建议，以改进和提高企业的经营成果。

关键词：成本性态、利润预算表、策略性分析

## 概述

该案例向学生们呈现了：为一个虚构的小联盟棒球队"派克斯维尔闪电"编制一套财务和策略的任务。本案例的主题是通过识别和分析新的商业机遇，扩展企业的盈利能力。要完美地实现这一目标，企业的管理会计师应成为企业的合作伙伴，把自己看成是企业的战略咨询人员来协助决策的制定。我们假定学生在派克斯维尔闪电公司担任这项职务。他们在该公司的主要所有者葛瑞格·斯顿领导下，帮助公司经营在球场内销售和各项娱乐活动。

斯顿曾是一位财务总监（CFO），他深信创造性思维方法。由于斯顿曾在赛季实施了一些重要的倡议来改善企业提供的娱乐活动，因此来球场的家庭不管老少都可度过愉快的一天。案例的表1列示了这些倡议。棒球赛会将粉丝们吸引到球场来观看比赛，斯顿意识到这个活动的季节性特点，因而他还采取措施，通过其他项目来扩展企业的盈利能力。最近，他实施了倡议中的一项，让粉丝们在一年的任何时间都能在家里品尝到球场上出售的食物。他从球队的烤箱制造商购得了经销权，通过电话和互联网向公众出售独家经销的以球队标志为商标的小型热狗烤箱。这些烤箱仿效烹饪一种在球场销售

---

\* 本篇译者为杨继良，校订者为胡金凤、赵澄。

的特制红肠面包（称为"POGs"），POGs已成为各年龄段粉丝们的至爱。他认为把他的这个品牌带到每个粉丝的家庭和厨房，是让粉丝们全年都关注球队的至关重要的第一步。

这一最先提出来的倡议，有助于实现斯顿使球队成为小联盟组织中最佳球队的宏伟目标，他还要求对该倡议作一些财务分析。他还和他的会计组成员讨论两项具体的策略方面的问题。他解释了，利用球场设施的投资来向粉丝们提供全年服务的需要。他要求会计组就非赛季的"策略性突破"提出建议，以扩展季节性的经营。他还向会计组展示了一种框架，对公司的战略财务管理进行持续治理。他把这称为战略合作伙伴模式的C-框架（见案例的表4的图解）。这一框架的中心主题在于，会计人员不能仅仅把自己看作为"写写算算"的人。相反，他们必须成为战略咨询人员，不断地寻求独特的经营方式和扩张的机会。他相信，把全体员工的智慧开发出来，是彻底改革这一行业的关键性的一步。他要求会计组把C-框架加以调整使之适应于派克斯维尔球队，用它来治理其战略性合作伙伴模式。

## 适用的课程

本案例旨在用于高年级本科生或初级水平研究生的管理会计课程。如果用于本科生的入门管理会计课程，则宜对课外作业部分的内容加以修订。在本案例的教案中，将列示作业的修订意见。

## 案例的重点和目的

案例提出的问题，要求学生对基本的成本结构作一分析，进而用所得的信息计算"POG"倡议中两种定价方案下的边际贡献和无差别点[①]。与以决策目的的混合式利润表的价值评估相关联的其他课题，包括：在了解企业当前情况的基础上提出战略方案，以及改进战略管理会计职能。

为了帮助派克斯维尔闪电棒球小联盟队和它的主要所有者葛瑞格·斯顿，案例首先要求学生在财务和策略两方面尽到职责帮助企业。要求学生对三个相互关联的问题提交答案。第一项任务是对小型"POG"烤箱这一近期小规模扩张企业业务的倡议，进行财务分析。为这项任务，学生将直接应用财务分析方法来支持关于如何影响组织未来的盈利能力的决策制定。更重要的是，这一财务分析任务也让学生对内部财务报表产生一种新的认识——混合式的利润表法。学生必须思考这一方法的好处和用途，并用它来分析经营扩展倡

---

① point of indifference，指在某种情况下两种选择的结果（例如采用不同的生产方式生产同一个产品所花费的成本）相同的那个点。例如，假定有方程式"A方式下的固定成本合计（3 081）+在A方式下每单位的变动成本（2.03）×产量（X）=在B方式下的固定成本合计（5 991）+在B方式下的每单位的变动成本（1.33）×产量（X）"，解这个方程式，找出"X"值为4 157。这个4 157就代表如果产量在这一点上，两种生产方式生产同一种产品的总成本没有差别。当产量小于4 157时，A方式下总成本小于B方式下的总成本；大于4 157时，则相反。等于4 157时，两种情况的总成本相同。这一点（4 157）即"无差别点"。——译者

议。这一思考便把学生引向与前述内容相关联的第二项任务。

第二项任务要求学生对突破性的扩张倡议进行战略考虑，学生需要对扩展业务季节性的非赛季项目提供详细的建议。在这项任务中，学生只需要把财务信息间接地应用到决策过程之中，并需要直接应用战略眼光来支持决策，确定决策如何影响组织未来的盈利能力。在这里，学生将结合经营计划的若干要素提出一种创新性的解决方案。作为建议的一部分，学生必须详细说明混合式利润表作为前景分析的潜在工具，应如何应用于当前的任务。这是关键性的一步，因为它能证实学生是否能够把这一工具的好处应用于欠佳的情况和环境中。

第三项任务也属于策略性质，它要求学生"裁剪"出合作伙伴框架使其合身于派克斯维尔公司。一旦这个框架得到应用，它就能成为一个活生生的实例，说明公司将如何通过财务职能与策略方面的决策制定联结起来而受益。重要的是，这第三项任务把先前的财务和策略任务结成一体，着力于本案例的核心内容——今天的管理会计师必须成为战略合作伙伴，结合企业的财务和战略两部分来支持决策制定。会计人员只有将自己"C"（看）作企业管理的伙伴，才能发挥他们的能动性。在派克斯维尔闪电公司这则案例中，就是要把 C - 框架的应用融入企业的扩展机会。

## 案例的使用指南

作者曾对本科生讲授本案例。我们采用调查的方法，向学生取得反馈，并对调查的结果作了总结，见附录 A。从调查所得的自由评语，说明学生比较喜欢对不很传统类型的企业作出分析，另外是从一堆看似"混乱的"数据中找出对成本性态的估计数，能够长进见识。这也说明这则案例对学生的全部要求，可能对本科的管理会计基础入门课程，太难了些。尽管如此，涉及成本结构、边际贡献和敏感性分析的第一组作业要求，肯定适用于本科生的入门课程。

## 案例的参考问题及其目的

### 财务分析

1. 运用统计和财务方法，对 POG 烤箱分部的计划执行情况作一分析评价。

a. 写出成本结构的每一要素的成本公式。简要阐述你根据这些成本各自的性态得出的结论。简要阐述（用一两句话）为什么你对你的成本公式感到有把握。列示/提供支持你论点的计算式和表格，证明你算出的数字正确。将你算得的每一项结果列示在表格中，如下所示。

| 成本项目 | 成本公式 | 成本性态 | 说明/假设 |
|---|---|---|---|
|  |  |  |  |
|  |  |  |  |

b. 按表 2 的 C 部分结尾处所示的基本方案和拟实施的市场渗透和溢价策略，为 2010 会计年度第一季度编制一份贡献毛利格式的预计利润表（在另外一页纸上，整齐、清楚地列示出来）。利润表将以三种可能的前景列示为三列。阐述所有相关的假设。

c. 对前面所提到的基础方案、市场渗透策略和溢价策略，为回答问题 1，编制一份 2010 会计年度第一季度的以美国公认会计准则为基础的利润预算表（在另外一页纸上，整齐、清楚地列示出来）。在利润表的独立空栏中，并列报告三种策略的每种情况。阐述所有相关的假设。

d. 结合以上问题 b 和问题 c 的结果，编制一份 2010 会计制度第一季度的混合式的利润预算表（包含相应的分析）。

e. 对斯顿所提出的混合式利润表的优点和用途，作一概述。在答案中，请详细提及混合式方法与以公认会计原则为基础方法的对比。

2. 请编制不确定性分析——敏感性分析：

a. 销量为多少时，市场溢价策略下的息税前利润（EBIT）会等于基础方案下的息税前利润（无差别点）？根据此计算，管理层认为的顾客流失百分率（与基础方案相比）会为多少（安全边际）？

b. 售价为多少时，市场渗透策略下的息税前利润（EBIT）等于基础方案下的息税前利润（无差别点）？根据计算，表明渗透策略的定价应如何？

c. 假定该分部打算更积极地渗透市场。假定该分部能够通过每台降价 $0.5，而增加销售 250 台，请编制前五次降价策略各自的息税前利润的一览表（降价依次增加 0.5 美元，而降价每增加 0.5 美元，销量增加 250 台）。假定溢价策略能够实现，则在哪一点上（销售量和单价）能使市场渗透策略与市场溢价策略下的利润一致？

## 策略分析

3. 未来的扩张

a. 请提供一份概述企业现状的综合报告，列示财务分析中的主要指标情况，以及你对企业的策略建议。

b. 请选择一项很可能提高盈利性的非赛季的扩张策略提出你的意见，向斯顿作一概述。

c. 请就你会如何实施该项计划提出具体的做法。在你的意见中，应就执行策略中需耗用的各项资源（如营业费用、资本支出、筹资费用、人事和外聘咨询人员的费用）作出估计，以及评估企业是否需要增添这些资源。请考虑混合式利润表的优势，简述这一分析工具如何有助于计划和控制你所提出的突破性项目。在你的整个建议之中，可考虑如下各项问题：

  i. 这一计划实施的时间安排是怎样的？
  ii. 可能会出现哪些问题，你对不可预见的情况有什么计划吗？
  iii. 在实施这一计划之前，你还会需要哪些信息？
  iv. 请述明你计划如何使这一竞争优势保持下去？

4. 采用 C - 框架

a. 应用 C - 框架来概述你对斯顿提出的关于如何改进战略财务管理职能的建议。建议中应包括如何把该框架与 CFO 各角色的投入与公司的三方面产出联系起来的讨论。

b. 请述明这对企业达成斯顿所设定的目标将有何帮助。

## 参考答案和评分的指导意见

### 财务分析——扩展盈利能力

各组学生必须解决的首要任务之一就是：整理从 ERP 系统[②]总分类账模块取得的"杂乱的"原始数据。他们将利用这一数据编制下一年度第一季度的预计利润表。如下所述，这一利润表将采用美国公认会计原则财务报表的格式，同时又将各成本按其固定与变动的特性加以分列。这就要求在电子数据表格的模式中，首先按照成本性态将成本结构分别确认为固定、变动和混合成本。学生将根据固定和变动成本的定义对这些成本加以分类，但同时还将采用比较复杂的统计分析方法（例如回归分析），使用一个计算公式确定混合成本。完整的分析不仅需要"机械地"执行统计分析，而且必须考虑其他的判断因素，诸如（i）确定最适用的成本动因，和（ii）检查各成本项目的季度数字，确定整体的成本模式是否适用于该项成本，以及是否需要把这一项移作异常值处理。以下的表 TN - 1 为各成本项目和公式的汇总表。

学生要利用成本结构数据，根据案例表 3 所讨论和描述的"混合式利润表"的方法编制季度的利润预算表。热狗烤箱分部第一季度的利润预算表列示于表 TN - 4；它是将表 TN - 2 所示的供内部使用的利润（贡献毛利）表，与表 TN - 3 所示的供外部使用（按公认会计原则编制）的利润表合并。

---

② ERP 系统（enterprise resource planning system），即企业资源规划系统。ERP 系统是指建立在信息技术基础上，以系统化的管理思想为企业决策层及员工提供决策运行手段的管理平台。——译者

### 表 TN-1
### 成本结构汇总

| 成本项目 | 成本公式 | 成本种类 | 分析说明 |
| --- | --- | --- | --- |
| 销货成本 | 单位售价 $35 | 变动 | 已于案例中提供 |
| 销售佣金 | 销售收入的 6% | 变动 | 已于案例中提供 |
| 运输费用 | 售出的单位运输费用 $11 | 变动 | 根据变动成本的定义 |
| 保险费用 | 每个季度 $9 000 | 固定 | 根据固定成本的定义（包含 3% 的通货膨胀） |
| 行政人员薪酬 | 每个季度 $145 000 | 固定 | 根据固定成本的定义（包含 3% 的通货膨胀） |
| 广告费用 | 每个季度 $210 000 | 固定 | 根据固定成本的定义 |
| 折旧费用 | 每个季度 $82 500 * | 固定 | 根据固定成本的定义 |
| 公用事业费 | $10 055.67 + $2.08 (x) | 混合 | 统计分析法，此处成本动因 (x) 为千瓦小时 |
| 维修费用 | $4 146.46 + $.06825 (x) | 混合 | 统计分析法，此处成本动因 (x) 为千瓦小时 |
| 维修成本说明： | | | |
| 如果离群值包括在回归分析之中 | $5 018.73 + $0.5431 (x) | 混合 | 统计分析法，此处成本动因 (x) 为千瓦小时 |
| 如果以销售量作为成本动因 | $6 514.77 + $0.2035 (x) | 混合 | 统计分析法，此处成本动因 (x) 为销售量 |

\* 如果现有不动产、工厂和设备（根据总分类账）未来每个季度的折旧费计作 70 000 美元，加上当期的资本支出 12 500 美元（成本 $500 000/使用寿命 10 年/每年 4 个季节）。请注意：投入存货的资金，不需要加以分析。

表 TN-4 列示了根据案例提供的信息和表 TN-1 所概述的成本结构而得出一种的参考解答，此外还有两点值得注意。首先，编制前瞻性报表是关键的第一步，这项练习的主要好处是让学生能够审视其内容，思考这一独特格式作为分析工具的有效性。这个问题，将在表 3 中做进一步的讨论。第二，由于报表中的一些项目能够直接计算出来，而另一些项目则需要进一步作判断，因而答案不唯一。因此，学生的答案虽然可能与表 TN-4 中的参考答案不同，但可作为一个出发点审视其各成本项目和总利润与表 TN-4 之间大小方向上的差异。为帮助教师评估学生的前瞻性报表的质量，下面表 TN-4a 提供了简略指南。

### 表 TN-2
**边际贡献**

派克斯维尔闪电热狗烤箱分部

2010 会计年度第一季度三种情况下的利润预算表

|  | 基础方案 | 市场渗透策略 | 市场溢价策略 |
|---|---|---|---|
| 销售收入 | 1 200 000 | 1 254 000 | 1 173 000 |
| 变动成本： |  |  |  |
| 销货成本 | 420 000 | 462 000 | 408 000 |
| 销售佣金 | 72 000 | 75 240 | 70 380 |
| 运输费用 | 132 000 | 145 200 | 112 200 |
| 公用事业费 | 27 053 | 27 053 | 27 053 |
| 维修费用 | 8 872 | 8 872 | 8 872 |
| 变动成本合计 | 659 926 | 718 366 | 626 506 |
| 边际贡献 | 540 074 | 535 634 | 546 494 |
| 固定成本 |  |  |  |
| 行政人员薪酬 | 145 000 | 145 000 | 145 000 |
| 广告费用 | 210 000 | 210 000 | 210 000 |
| 保险费用 | 9 000 | 9 000 | 9 000 |
| 折旧费用 | 82 500 | 82 500 | 82 500 |
| 公用事业费 | 10 056 | 10 056 | 10 056 |
| 维修费用 | 4 146 | 4 146 | 4 146 |
| 固定成本合计 | 460 702 | 460 702 | 460 702 |
| 分部的息税前利润 | 79 372 | 74 932 | 85 792 |

### 表 TN-3
**公认会计原则为基础**

派克斯维尔闪电热狗烤箱分部

以公认会计原则为基础，三种情况下的 2010 会计年度第一季度利润预算表

|  | 基础方案 | 市场渗透策略 | 市场溢价策略 |
|---|---|---|---|
| 销售收入 | 1 200 000 | 1 254 000 | 1 173 000 |
| 销货成本 | 420 000 | 462 000 | 408 000 |
| 毛利 | 780 000 | 792 000 | 765 000 |
| 营业费用 |  |  |  |
| 广告费用 | 210 000 | 210 000 | 210 000 |
| 销售佣金 | 72 000 | 75 240 | 70 380 |
| 运输费用 | 132 000 | 145 200 | 112 200 |
| 公用事业费 | 37 109 | 37 109 | 37 109 |
| 维修费用 | 13 019 | 13 019 | 13 019 |
| 行政人员薪酬 | 145 000 | 145 000 | 145 000 |
| 保险费用 | 9 000 | 9 000 | 9 000 |
| 折旧费用 | 82 500 | 82 500 | 82 500 |
| 营业费用合计 | 700 628 | 717 068 | 679 208 |
| 分部的息税前利润 | 79 372 | 74 932 | 85 792 |

### 表 TN-4
**混合式利润预算表**

派克斯维尔闪电热狗烤箱分部

2010 会计年度第一季度的利润预算表—仅供内部管理用

|  | 金额 | 占销售收入% |
|---|---|---|
| 烤箱销售收入（12 000 台，每台 100 美元） | $1 200 000 | 100% |
| 销货成本 | 420 000 | 35 |
| 毛利 | 780 000 | 65 |
|  |  |  |
| 营业费用：变动 |  |  |
| 销售佣金 | 72 000 |  |
| 运输费用 | 132 000 |  |
| 公用事业费 | 27 053 |  |
| 维修费用 | 8 873 |  |
| 变动营业费用合计 | 239 926 | 20 |
| 边际贡献 | 540 074 | 45 |
|  |  |  |
| 营业费用：固定 |  |  |
| 行政人员工薪 | 145 000 |  |
| 广告费用 | 210 000 |  |
| 保险费用 | 9 000 |  |
| 折旧费用 | 82 500 |  |
| 公用事业费 | 10 056 |  |
| 维修费用 | 4 146 |  |
|  |  |  |
| 固定营业费用合计 | 460 702 | 38 |
| 分部的营业收益 | $79 372 | 7% |

### 表 TN-4a
**评价混合式利润预算表指南**

1. 行政人员薪酬和保险费用：这两项成本是根据总分类账最近一季度的数字，加上3%的通货膨胀率的调整后的数据。调整之前的金额分别为 140 777 美元和 8 737 美元。

2. 运输费用：这是一项完全的变动成本，每销售一台的费用 11 美元，此数以总分类账上的历史数据为基础算得。如果学生不能理解这一点，他们或许会试着将其分为固定成本和变动成本两部分。如此一来，他们会将这项成本同时计入营业费用的变动和固定两部分。

3. 公用事业费和维修费用：学生根据他们所作的统计分析，获得的数字可能各不相同。例如，他们所用的成本动因可能不一致、可能未能排除离群值，或者可能对一项或对两项成本都采用了多元回归分析法。这些都可能引起不同的计算结果。这些计算差异中有些已列示于本教案的表 1 中。此外，学生所采用的成本公式可能是正确的，但对固定和变动成本的分配并不正确，可能错误的将成本全部列为固定成本或变动成本，也可能错误的列为了混合成本。这是一项比较严重的错误，说明学生对如何用成本公式算出财务报表上的数字理解不够。

下一步财务考虑，要求学生对混合式利润表的优点和用处作一概述。学生识别混合式利润表是很重要的。学生识别利润表的主要特点固然重要，但了解这种内部财务报表的新思维方法比完成具体的任务更为重要。表 TN-5 提示了几类优点和用处。这份清单并未详尽，对学生的评估还可以按其回答与其他学生的比较情况进行考虑。总之，混合式利润表可以提供更详尽的情况，考虑了成本结构进行了进一步盈利能力分析，同时又维持对外报送的财务报表的完整性。在案例中，混合式财务报表特别适用于这种信息比较明确的财务方面，但学生还必须在随后的案例部分中重温这一概念，而这一部分的情况则没有这么明确。

---

**表 TN-5**
**混合式利润表的优点和用处**

效率：
- 维持按照美国公认会计原则编制的财务报表的整体格式要求。
- 比较容易利用对外报送的报表编制出来。
- 不需要总分类账明细。
- 虽然企业的管理当局所确定的成本性态分类不够精确，但由于它包含了公认会计原则所要求的全部信息，他们可能比较倾向于在内部管理上使用这些数据。

详尽：
- 这种利润表能披露三种利润数字，比单纯按公认会计原则要求的格式、或按边际贡献的格式提供的信息更为详尽。
- 保留了毛利的计算——确保管理当局不至于忽略毛利。这对于参考其他单位的数据作标杆分析极为重要。

分析：
- 促使在估测短期或长期可控成本时，考虑固定和变动成本的因素。
- 它是一种简易的分析工具，可以用来对固定和变动成本作基于一个特别的基础的分析，或者技术性较复杂的分析。
- 报表上既列出毛利，又列出边际贡献，因而能够对制造/营业部门，以及辅助部门（销售、设施等）如何更好地管理盈利性提供更深入的见解。
- 兼有两种利润表的优点。

---

# 敏感性分析

下面这一组要求与敏感性分析有关。第一个要求是计算市场溢价策略下，销售量达到多少时，其息税前利润可以与基础方案下息税前利润相同，即达到无差别点。第二个要求是计算在扩展市场策略下，售价为多少时，其息税前利润可以达到与基础方案下息税前利润相同。在表 TN-6 中所披露的成本公式和解答所需要的信息都可从表 TN-1 获得。请注意：成本公式过于复杂，会使学生感到困难。Excel 中的求解功能是解决这一问题的最简单的方法。在第一种情况下，需设定目标函数等于当前的息税前利润，求解规划则会推算出相应的销售量。在第二种情况下，需设定目标函数等于当前的息税前利润，求解规划则会推算出相应的销售价格。

| 表 TN-6 无差别点 | |
|---|---|
| **成本项目** | **成本公式** |
| 销货成本 | 每销售一台为$35（按照市场溢价策略，需要增价$5.00） |
| 销售佣金 | 销售价格（SP）的6% |
| 运输费用 | 每销售一台为$11 |
| 公用事业费 | 每千瓦（KW）$2.08 |
| 维修费用 | 每千瓦（KW）$.06825 |
| 据工程师预计，本季度耗用13 000千瓦 | |
| 保险费用 | $9 000 |
| 行政人员薪酬 | $145 000 |
| 广告费用 | $210 000 |
| 折旧费用 | $82 500 |
| 公用事业费 | $10 055.67 |
| 维修费用 | $4 146.46 |
| **溢价策略下的成本公式** | |
| (40.00+11.00)×销售数量+(2.08+.06825)×KW+0.06×SP+固定成本 | |
| 我们需要解决销售数量（QTY）问题 | |
| (2.6735×13 000+460 702+目标利润)/边际贡献（CM） | =QTY |
| 此处边际贡献（CM）=SP-51-6.90=57.10 | |
| (35 926+460 702+79 372)/57.10 | =10 088 |
| **市场渗透策略下的成本公式** | |
| (35.00+11.00)×QTY+(2.08+.06825)×KW+0.06×SP+固定成本 | |
| 我们需要解决销售价格（SP）问题 | |
| (2.6735×13 000+460 702+目标利润)/边际贡献（CM） | =QTY |
| 因为销售价格（SP）是未知数，因此边际贡献（CM）也是个未知数 所以，上式中的分母为SP-0.06×SP-46=0.94SP-46 | |
| (35 926+460 702+79 372)/(0.94SP-46) | =13 200 |
| (35 926+460 702+79 372)/13 200 | =0.94SP-46 |
| 43.636363 | =0.94SP-46 |
| 89.64 | =0.94SP，因而SP=$95.36 |

学生只是计算出结果是不够的，还需对这些结果进行解释。在溢价策略下，预计的销售水平比维持现状多112台（10 200-10 088）。此时，安全系数只有1%（112/10 200）；这意味着管理层进行估计时允许出错的余地很小。在第二种情况下，每台定价95美元，预计的销售量不足以达到当前

的利润水平。这就只能提高售价,从而会增加将预计销售量调低于 13 200 台之数的威胁。管理层在选择走哪条路之前,应考虑作进一步的敏感性分析。

最后一种情况,要求学生着眼于一种比较激进的渗透策略,即假设该分部能够通过降低单价 0.50 美元,而增加销售 250 台。目的是为使利润达到溢价策略下的水平,即 85 792 美元。学生需要编制一份详列前五次降价(每次 0.50 美元)和销售量依次增加 250 台情况下的息税前利润的一览表。计算的结果见表 TN-7。从该表可见,降价 1.00 美元并不能完全达到目标利润水平,而降价 1.50 美元则能使利润超过目标数。看来,降价 1.50 美元能使安全系数有所提高,因为销量会低于 13 950 台,同时也达到目标利润水平。

表 TN-7
方案概况

|  | 当前数值 | 每台减价 $0.50 | 每台减价 $1.00 | 每台减价 $1.50 | 每台减价 $2.00 | 每台减价 $2.50 |
| --- | --- | --- | --- | --- | --- | --- |
| 销售数量 | 13 200 | 13 450 | 13 700 | 13 950 | 14 200 | 14 450 |
| 销售价格 | $95.00 | $94.50 | $94.00 | $93.50 | $93.00 | $92.50 |
| 息税前利润 | 74 932 | 79 436 | 83 704 | 87 738 | 91 536 | 95 100 |

# 策略分析

学生需要对派克斯维尔闪电的两种策略作一评估。基于他们答案的创新性和可行性不同,以及他们的策略和思维过程的完整性不同,这一要求为学生们提供了一个使其答案与众不同的机会。此外,应就学生们所提出的建议是否使人信服,以及制定的决策的是否经过深思熟虑,对他们作出评估。

### 未来扩张的倡议

第一项策略,是考虑采用未来扩张的倡议,以提高企业的盈利能力。斯顿意欲使企业的经营不受球赛季节的限制,并且已经开始有了"POG"烤箱的倡议。学生此前对烤箱的倡议进行过了财务分析后,现在他们还必须提出一项"突破性的倡议",即对非赛季的扩张策略的建议,使粉丝们一年四季都关注这个球队。除了说明这项策略以外,斯顿还要求对执行该策略所需要的财务和非财务资源进行详细的估测。

该答案不唯一,而以实例说明。但下面列举了最近一堂管理会计课程中出的一些建议。

1. 冬季瀑布
- 室外人造溜冰场，附有出售食品衣物的货摊[③]、现场演出、圣诞村，并能举行私人的或慈善性的活动。
2. 冬季乐园
- 游乐区的游戏将以冬季为主题重新装修，购置一台造雪车来模拟下雪天、增加气氛。
- 出售冬季装备，诸如印有球队标志的长袖衬衫、汗衫、长裤和帽子等。
- 室外大屏幕的电影之夜。
- 儿童活动夜。
- 节日期间的音乐会、日间溜冰、果酒、奶酪和其他零食。
3. 把场地改装为临时的曲棍球场，通过中学组织青少年参加球赛和免费溜冰。研究表明，美国的中西部地区（尤其是俄亥俄州）的人们在曲棍球上花费了相当多的时间。
4. 室外休闲场所——包括乘坐雪圈[④]、溜冰、篝火和暖和的食物。这与建造一个可以举行多种活动的水上公园相似，只不过是在冬季举行，所以是一个雪季的娱乐场所，设有供冰上和/或雪上用的滑雪板、雪圈等物。

案例的这一部分内容依各人的主观想法而异，因而在下面的表 TN-8 中列示了一般和具体注意事项，作为评估学生建议的指导意见。在下面所列示的各项内容中，至关重要的一点是，学生应该考虑如何利用混合式利润表来分析倡议未来的盈利能力，并将混合式利润表体现在他们的思维过程中来支持他们的想法。这样就可验证，学生是否能够把这个方法用于情况和环境不够充分的条件之下。

# 运用 C-框架

第二项策略性任务是，要求学生对这一管理会计部门作为公司商业战略伙伴角色的模式展开讨论。此处，学生将讨论案例表 4（以战略合作伙伴为任务者的 C-框架）中所列示的 CFO 的四个角色的投入，如何与公司其他部门合作，对公司的三项产出即顾客（customer）、成本控制（cost control）和社区（community）产生影响。通过讨论，学生将对框架原则进行"裁剪"，使其合身于派克斯维尔组织。

这里再重复提一次：案例的该部分属于主观想象。在下面的表 TN-9 中，列示了一般的和具体的事项，可以作为学生就该框架的原则如何适用于派克斯维尔组织所提出的论点进行评估的指导意见。

---

[③] 这种货摊通常由个人或慈善机构经营，向场主（在本例为这个棒球队）支付小额费用。——译者
[④] snow tubing，人乘坐在橡胶圈内，在雪地里从高处向下滑行的一种游戏。——译者

## 表 TN-8
**评估各项扩张倡议中宜考虑的问题**

- 该建议是否考虑到案例中提到的全部问题？
- 建议的策略是否独特/具有创造性？
- 策略是否清晰并表述清楚？策略是否易于理解？
- 所提出的建议如何与斯顿所描述的公司使命和愿景的战略适应？
- 策略是否证实可行、经得起质疑、获得充分的支持？各项观点是否能够经得起反对意见、有充分的事实根据？
- 策略是否考虑到各方面的受众——包括斯顿和顾客？
- 策略与需要的资源之间，是否具有内在一致性？
- 策略是否可以实施？
- 策略的各项建议，是否与采用现实假设作出的财务分析结果相一致？
- 从内容和陈述两方面来看，建议是否专业化？
- 整体建议是否对问题提出了具有远见的、透彻的分析？
- 所提出的建议是否体现了把混合式利润表用于企业的未来分析的好处？该建议是否能在实际情况和环境条件不充分的情况下，也能实现它应得的好处？
- 提出的建议是否体现了合理的决策制定方法？
- 提出的建议是否有完整的研究为支撑，该研究是否突出了所有的预期风险？研究是否相关、可靠和足以支撑该项策略？
- 所提出的建议是否考虑了其优势、劣势、机遇和威胁（SWOT分析）？
- 对各项资源的讨论是否具体和可行？提出的建议中确定的所需资源是否完整？
- 建议的时间安排是否切实可行、合乎逻辑和完整无缺？
- 倡议的持续性是否具有明确的支撑？

## 表 TN-9
**应用 C-框架的建议事项**

- 这一框架是否适用于本行业？是否适用于本单位？
- 讨论中是否把斯顿作为主要的听众？
- CFO 的各项角色是否与公司的各个方面都联系了起来？CFO 的各项角色是否与公司的三方面相连接？
- 学生是否对每一项连接都有深刻理解？
- 框架中的各项内容是否都被采用和讨论了？
- 每一项内容的讨论是否有针对会计部门如何才能成为一个更好的合作伙伴、并在战略性决策的制定中尽职？
- 讨论中是否涉及该观点，即会计人员所必须提供的不仅仅是机械性的财务数字？
- 学生是否提供了具体的、实实在在的例子，以支撑自己的论点？
- 学生的讨论是否考虑到，这项框架会对突破性的倡议产生什么样的影响？
- 讨论中是否表明，学生对下述事项有清晰的理解：(1) 谁是外部顾客和内部顾客？(2) 为实现企业长期地可持续发展，需要考虑的关键性的成本有哪些？(3) 企业为什么必须将它所处的社区作为长期关注点？
- 在讨论中，是否明确的识别/考虑了其他受商业战略伙伴角色影响的职能部门？这一点是否和企业的整体策略连接起来了？
- 在讨论中，是否包含任何可实施的独特的/有创意的建议？
- 在讨论中，是否考虑到企业内部可能对合作伙伴关系实施产生的阻力？
- 讨论中，是否考虑到采用这一模式会带来的长期利益？
- 讨论中，是否有请外部研究人员参与，证实或支持论点所根据的各项假设？

## 附录 A
### "派克斯维尔闪电"案例学生反馈意见调查表

近年来，这则案例曾用于管理会计入门课程的三个班级。其中一个班级在使用了财务方面的要求之外，还使用了策略性方面的要求；其余两个班级则只使用了财务方面的要求。以下是为取得反馈意见而采用的调查内容。请在下有中圈出你认为适当的数字。

1. 案例向我们提供了企业的现实情况。

   10　　　　20　　　　30　　　　40　　　　50　　　　60　　　　70　　　　80　　　　90　　　　100
   强烈不同意　　　　　不同意　　　　　　　　中立　　　　　　　　同意　　　　　　强烈同意

2. 学习这则案例令人愉快。

   10　　　　20　　　　30　　　　40　　　　50　　　　60　　　　70　　　　80　　　　90　　　　100
   强烈不同意　　　　　不同意　　　　　　　　中立　　　　　　　　同意　　　　　　强烈同意

3. 这则案例在团队合作方面，给我们上了很好的一课。

   10　　　　20　　　　30　　　　40　　　　50　　　　60　　　　70　　　　80　　　　90　　　　100
   强烈不同意　　　　　不同意　　　　　　　　中立　　　　　　　　同意　　　　　　强烈同意

4. 案例帮助我更好地理解如何处理从会计体系（例如，总分类账数据）中获得的原始资料。

   10　　　　20　　　　30　　　　40　　　　50　　　　60　　　　70　　　　80　　　　90　　　　100
   强烈不同意　　　　　不同意　　　　　　　　中立　　　　　　　　同意　　　　　　强烈同意

5. 案例帮助我更好地理解如何应用统计方法分析数据以作出决策。

   10　　　　20　　　　30　　　　40　　　　50　　　　60　　　　70　　　　80　　　　90　　　　100
   强烈不同意　　　　　不同意　　　　　　　　中立　　　　　　　　同意　　　　　　强烈同意

6. 案例帮助我更好地理解成本结构的信息是如何对财务报表产生影响的。

   10　　　　20　　　　30　　　　40　　　　50　　　　60　　　　70　　　　80　　　　90　　　　100
   强烈不同意　　　　　不同意　　　　　　　　中立　　　　　　　　同意　　　　　　强烈同意

7. 案例使我学到，在作出决策时，如何把策略和财务因素整合起来。

   10　　　　20　　　　30　　　　40　　　　50　　　　60　　　　70　　　　80　　　　90　　　　100
   强烈不同意　　　　　不同意　　　　　　　　中立　　　　　　　　同意　　　　　　强烈同意

8. 案例教我如何应用先进的电子数据表软件来建立数据表模型。

   10　　　　20　　　　30　　　　40　　　　50　　　　60　　　　70　　　　80　　　　90　　　　100
   强烈不同意　　　　　不同意　　　　　　　　中立　　　　　　　　同意　　　　　　强烈同意

9. 学习完这则案例，你还有什么其他评语吗？

   _____

   _____

   _____

下表概括了上列调查的结果：

| 同时使用了财务和策略要求的一个班级 | | | | | | | | |
|---|---|---|---|---|---|---|---|---|
| | 现实情况 | 娱乐性 | 团队合作 | 原始资料 | 统计方法 | 财务报表的影响 | 整合性 | 电子数据表 |
| 调查表份数 =20 | 1 | 2 | 3 | 4 | 5 | 6 | 7 | 8 |
| 平均数 | 85.5 | 76.0 | 80.5 | 89.0 | 84.0 | 85.5 | 84.5 | 87.0 |
| 中位数 | 90.0 | 80.0 | 80.0 | 90.0 | 90.0 | 90.0 | 80.0 | 90.0 |
| 众数 | 90.0 | 70.0 | 80.0 | 100.0 | 100.0 | 90.0 | 80.0 | 100.0 |
| 仅使用了财务要求的两个班级 | | | | | | | | |
| | 现实情况 | 娱乐性 | 团队合作 | 原始资料 | 统计方法 | 财务报表的影响 | 整合性 | 电子数据表 |
| 调查表份数 =42 | 1 | 2 | 3 | 4 | 5 | 6 | 7 | 8 |
| 平均数 | 82.7 | 64.1 | 68.2 | 79.1 | 74.1 | 77.7 | 74.1 | 77.3 |
| 中位数 | 80.0 | 65.0 | 75.0 | 80.0 | 80.0 | 80.0 | 80.0 | 85.0 |
| 众数 | 80.0 | 80.0 | 70.0 | 80.0 | 80.0 | 80.0 | 80.0 | 100.0 |

尽管布置学生完成财务和战略要求表明，学生对此体验给予了较好的评价。而完成整套要求对学生而言，可能显得过于困难，并要求教师花更多时间提供教学指导。

TEACHING NOTE

# Pikesville Lightening: Evaluating Strategic Business Expansion Opportunities

*Thomas G. Canace*
*Wake Forest University*

*Paul E. Juras*
*Babson College*

GREG STORM, OWNER, IS STRIVING TO make his organization a market leader by finding unique ways to grow the business. He views his accountants as consultants who not only have the technical skills to provide financial and analytical information, but who also have the strategic thinking to provide valuable input to him and the business leaders to help improve the profitability and expansion potential of the business. This case asks the student to play the role of a member of the accounting team and perform some financial and strategic analysis of operating results. The student is also asked to view the role of accountant as that of a strategic business partner by making a specific strategic recommendation to improve the operating results of the organization.

Keywords: cost behavior, budgeted income statement, strategic analysis.

## SYNOPSIS

Students are presented with a set of financial and strategic tasks for a fictional minor league baseball team, the Pikesville Lightning. The central theme of the case is expanding business profitability by identifying and analyzing new business opportunities, which is best achieved when managerial accountants become business partners who see themselves as strategic advisors to assist with decision making. Students assume such a role in the accounting organization of the Pikesville organization. They work under the leadership of primary owner, Greg

Storm, supporting the park vending and entertainment operations of the business.

Storm is a former CFO who has strong beliefs in outside-the-box thinking. A day at the ballpark has become a day of family fun for people of all ages because Storm has implemented key initiatives during the season to improve the entertainment venue of his business. These initiatives are shown in Table 1 of the case. In recognition of the seasonal nature of bringing fans to the ballpark to enjoy baseball games, however, he has also taken steps to expand business profitability through other programs. Recently, he implemented one such initiative to give fans the opportunity to experience some of the ballpark food at home all year long. He obtained an exclusive franchise from the team's oven manufacturer to purchase mini-replica hot dog ovens branded with the team logo for resale to the public via phone and Internet orders. These ovens simulate the cooking experience of special hot dogs (called "POGs") that are sold at the ballpark and have become a hit with fans of all ages. He believes that bringing his brand to the homes and kitchens of fans is a critical first step toward achieving year-long interest in his team.

This first initiative supports Storm's more grandiose goal for his organization of becoming a best-in-class minor league organization, and asks for some financial analysis of the initiatives. He also discusses two specific strategic challenges with the members of his accounting organization. He explains the need to provide a year-long experience to fans to capitalize on his facilities' investments. He asks the team to develop a recommendation for an off-season "strategic breakthrough" initiative as a way to expand the seasonality of the business. He also presents the team with a framework for governing the ongoing strategic financial management of his business. He refers to this as the C-framework of strategic business partnering (illustrated in Table 4 of the case). The central theme of this framework is that his accountants cannot merely view themselves as "number-crunchers." Rather, they must become strategic advisors who continuously work toward unique business solutions and expansion opportunities. He believes that tapping into the intelligence of all employees is a critical step toward revolutionizing the industry. His mandate to the team is to tailor the C-framework to the Pikesville organization to be used as model to govern its strategic business partnering.

# INTENDED COURSES

This case is intended for use in upper-level undergraduate or introductory-level graduate management accounting courses. The assignments could be modified for use in an introductory undergraduate managerial accounting course, and suggested modifications for such use are presented within this teaching note.

## CASE FOCUS AND OBJECTIVES

The suggested questions require an analysis of basic cost structure and the subsequent use of that information to compute contribution margin and point of indifference with respect to two pricing alternatives for the "POG" initiative. Other topics relate to the assessment of the value of a hybrid income statement for decision-making purposes, development of strategic alternatives based on understanding of the organization's current situation, and improvement of the strategic managerial accounting function.

In supporting the Pikesville Lightning minor league baseball organization and its primary owner, Greg Storm, the first task asks students to assist in both financial and strategic roles. The submission requires responses to three interrelated tasks. The first part requires financial analysis to support the organization's recent small-scale business expansion initiative involving the mini-replica "POG" ovens. In this task, students will directly apply financial analysis techniques to support decision making about how to impact the future profitability of the organization. More importantly, the financial task also exposes students to a new way of thinking about internal financial statements-the hybrid income statement approach. The students must reflect upon the benefits and usefulness of such an approach as a tool to analyze the operations of the expansion initiative. This reflection provides a segue into the second task.

The second task involves strategic consideration of a "breakthrough" expansion initiative where students must provide detailed recommendations for an off-season project to expand the seasonality of the business. In this task, students will only indirectly apply financial information to the decision-making process, but will now be required to directly provide strategic vision to support decision-making about how to impact the future profitability of the organization. Here, students will provide a creative solution that incorporates some of the ingredients of a business plan. As part of their recommendation, students must articulate how to apply the hybrid income statement to the current task as a possible tool for future analysis. This is a critical step because it validates whether the students can translate the benefits of such a tool to a less-developed set of facts and circumstances.

The third task is also strategic, as it requires the students to tailor the business partner framework to the Pikesville organization. Once applied, the framework will become a living model for how the organization will benefit from linking the financial function into the strategic aspects of the decision making. Importantly, this final task synthesizes the prior financial and strategic tasks to focus on the central theme of the case-that today's managerial accountants must become strategic business partners by unifying both the financial and strategic components of the business to support decision making. The accountants will have achieved this dynamic role once they develop the ability to "C" themselves as business partners. In the case of the Pikesville Lightning organization this translates into "C-ing" the business expansion opportunities.

## IMPLEMENTATION GUIDANCE

The authors have experience with using the case in an undergraduate setting. An example of a survey instrument used to obtain student feedback, along with a summary of the survey's results, appears in Appendix A. The open-ended comments indicated that the students appreciated a less traditional type of organization used for an analysis and there was insight gained from having to deal with "messy" data to develop estimates of cost behavior. This experience also revealed that the full set of case requirements could possibly be overwhelming for an introductory undergraduate managerial accounting course. Still, the first set of requirements involving cost structure, contribution margin, and sensitivity analysis are certainly appropriate for an introductory undergraduate course.

## SUGGESTED QUESTIONS AND RELATED OBJECTIVES

### FINANCIAL ANALYSIS

1. Using statistical and financial methods, provide an analytical assessment of the planned performance for the "POG" oven segment.

a. Provide cost formulas for the each individual item of the cost structure. Briefly explain what conclusions you can make about the behavior of each of these costs. Briefly explain (one or two sentences) why you feel confident about your cost formulas. Show/provide supporting calculations and schedules to support your amounts. Present your answer for each item in a table, as shown below.

| Cost Item | Cost Formula | Cost Behavior | Notes/Assumptions |
| --- | --- | --- | --- |
|  |  |  |  |
|  |  |  |  |

b. For the base case and for penetration and the premium strategies mentioned at the end of Panel C of Table 2, provide a contribution margin format budgeted income statement for Q1 FY2010 (on a separate page and in good form). Report each of the three scenarios side-by-side in separate columns of the income statement. Identify all relevant assumptions.

c. For the base case and for the penetration and the premium strategies mentioned above, prepare a U. S. GAAP-based budgeted income statement for Q1 FY2010 (on a separate page and in good form). Report each of the three scenarios side-by-side in separate columns of the income statement. Identify all relevant assumptions.

d. Combine your results from b) and c) above to prepare a hybrid format budgeted income statement for Q1FY2010 [provide supporting analysis].

e. Outline the benefits and usefulness of Storm's hybrid income statement approach. As part of your response, make specific reference to the hybrid method versus the GAAP-based approach.

2. Planning for uncertainty-sensitivity analysis:

a. At what level of sales is the market premium strategy profit before interest and taxes (EBIT) equal to the base case (the point of indifference)? What does this say about the percentage of customers that management thinks would be lost relative to the base case (margin of safety)?

b. At what sales price is the market penetration strategy's EBIT equal to the base case (point of indifference)? What does this say about pricing for the planned penetration strategy?

c. Assume the division wants to penetrate the market more aggressively. Assuming the division can increase sales units by an additional 250 units for every $0.50 in further price reduction, provide a schedule showing the EBIT for the strategy for the first five reductions (in increments of $0.50 price cuts and 250 unit increases). Assuming the premium strategy targets would be met, at what point (sales units and price) would the penetration strategy yield the same earnings as the market premium strategy?

## STRATEGIC ANALYSIS

3. Future Expansion

a. Provide an executive summary that outlines the current situation, key metrics from your financial analysis, and your strategic recommendations for the business.

b. Outline your advice to Storm about one specific high-impact potential off-season expansion strategy to be employed for achieving greater profitability.

c. Provide specific information about how you would implement this plan. Include in your discussion an assessment of the resources (e. g., operating, capital, financing, personnel, and external consultants) necessary to execute the strategy and whether these resources would be incremental to the business. Considering the benefits of the hybrid income statement, briefly articulate how this tool for analysis could assist in the planning and control of your breakthrough project. As part of your overall recommendation, some other potential considerations are provided below:

i. What is the proposed timeline for "going live" with the plan?

ii. What could go wrong and what contingencies have you planned for?

iii. What other information would you need before implementation?

iv. Articulate how you plan to make this competitive advantage sustainable over time.

4. Employing the C-Framework

a. Use the C-framework to outline your advice to Storm about how to improve the strategic financial management function. Include a thorough discussion of the framework by linking each CFO-lever input to each of the three company-lever outputs.

b. Articulate how this will assist the organization in achieving the goals laid out by Storm.

# SUGGESTED SOLUTIONS AND GUIDANCE FOR EVALUATION

## FINANCIAL ANALYSIS-EXPANDING PROFITABILITY

One of the first tasks student teams must tackle is to work through some "messy" data exported from the general ledger module of the enterprise resource planning system. They will use this data to construct a forward-looking income statement for the first quarter of the next fiscal year. As discussed below, the income statement will take on the complexion of a U. S. GAAP financial statement, but will also include separation of costs into their fixed and variable components. This requires spreadsheet modeling first to organize the cost structure by behavior into fixed, variable, and mixed costs. Students will categorize these costs by applying the definitions of fixed and variable costs, but will also apply more sophisticated statistical analysis (e. g., regression analysis) to determine a cost formula for mixed costs. A thorough analysis will require not only "mechanically" performing statistical analysis, but also necessitates considering other judgmental factors such as ( i ) determining the most appropriate cost driver and ( ii ) examining the quarterly data for each cost item to determine whether any costs are not representative of the overall pattern of costs and should be considered for removal as outliers. A summary table outlining the cost items and formulas is provided below in Table TN – 1.

### Table TN – 1
### Summary of Cost Structure

| Cost Item | Cost Formula | Cost Type | Notes for Analysis |
|---|---|---|---|
| Cost of Goods Sold | $35 per unit sold | Variable | Provided in case |
| Sales Commissions | 6% of sales revenue | Variable | Provided in case |
| Shipping Costs | $11 per unit sold | Variable | Apply definition of variable cost |
| Insurance | $9 000 per quarter | Fixed | Apply definition of fixed cost; include 3% inflation |
| Administrative Salaries | $145 000 per quarter | Fixed | Apply definition of fixed cost; include 3% inflation |
| Advertising Expense | $210 000 per quarter | Fixed | Apply definition of fixed cost |
| Depreciation Expense | $82 500* per quarter | Fixed | Apply definition of fixed cost |
| Utilities Expense | $10 055.67 + $2.08 (x) | Mixed | Statistical analysis, where cost driver (x) is kilowatt hours |
| Maintenance Expense | $4 146.46 + $.06825 (x) | Mixed | Statistical analysis, where cost driver (x) is kilowatt hours |
| Note for Maintenance costs: | | | |
| If Outlier included in regression | $5,018.73 + $0.5431 (x) | Mixed | Statistical analysis, where cost driver (x) is kilowatt hours |
| If Cost Driver used was units sold | $6,514.77 + $0.2035 (x) | Mixed | Statistical analysis, where cost driver (x) is units sold |

*Forward-looking depreciation expense per quarter is calculated as $70 000 for existing property, plant, and equipment (from general ledger) plus $12 500 for current capital expenditures calculated as $500 000 cost ÷ 10 – year life ÷ 4 quarters per year. Note that the investment in inventory is not needed for the analysis.

Using the cost structure data, students will prepare the budgeted quarterly income statement using the "Hybrid P&L" approach discussed and illustrated in Table 3 of the case. The budgeted first quarter income statement for the hot dog oven division is provided in Table TN – 4 and reflects a merging of the internal (contribution margin) income statement Table TN – 2, and the external (GAAP) income statement Table TN – 3.

## Table TN-2
### Contribution Margin

Pikesville Lightning Hot Dog Oven Division

Contribution Margin Income Statement Budget under Three Scenarios for the first quarter of Fiscal Year 2010

|  | Base Case | Market Penetration | Market Premium |
|---|---|---|---|
| Sales | 1 200 000 | 1 254 000 | 1 173 000 |
| Variable Costs: |  |  |  |
| Cost of Goods Sold | 420 000 | 462 000 | 408 000 |
| Sales Commissions | 72 000 | 75 240 | 70 380 |
| Shipping Expense | 132 000 | 145 200 | 112 200 |
| Utilities Expense | 27 053 | 27 053 | 27 053 |
| Maintenance Expense | 8 872 | 8 872 | 8 872 |
| Total Variable Costs | 659 926 | 718 366 | 626 506 |
| Contribution Margin | 540 074 | 535 634 | 546 494 |
| Fixed Costs |  |  |  |
| Administrative Salaries | 145 000 | 145 000 | 145 000 |
| Advertising Expense | 210 000 | 210 000 | 210 000 |
| Insurance Expense | 9 000 | 9 000 | 9 000 |
| Depreciation Expense | 82 500 | 82 500 | 82 500 |
| Utilities Expense | 10 056 | 10 056 | 10 056 |
| Maintenance Expense | 4 146 | 4 146 | 4 146 |
| Total Fixed Costs | 460 702 | 460 702 | 460 702 |
| Divisional EBIT | 79 372 | 74 932 | 85 792 |

## Table TN-3
### GAAP Based

Pikesville Lightning Hot Dog Oven Division

US GAAP Income Statement Budget under Three Scenarios for the first quarter of Fiscal Year 2010

|  | Base Case | Market Penetration | Market Premium |
|---|---|---|---|
| Sales | 1 200 000 | 1 254 000 | 1 173 000 |
| Cost of Goods Sold | 420 000 | 462 000 | 408 000 |
| Gross Profit | 780 000 | 792 000 | 765 000 |
| Operating Expenses |  |  |  |
| Advertising Expense | 210 000 | 210 000 | 210 000 |
| Sales Commissions | 72 000 | 75 240 | 70 380 |
| Shipping Expense | 132 000 | 145 200 | 112 200 |
| Utilities Expense | 37 109 | 37 109 | 37 109 |
| Maintenance Expense | 13 019 | 13 019 | 13 019 |
| Administrative Salaries | 145 000 | 145 000 | 145 000 |
| Insurance Expense | 9 000 | 9 000 | 9 000 |
| Depreciation Expense | 82 500 | 82 500 | 82 500 |
| Total Operating Expenses | 700 628 | 717 068 | 679 208 |
| Divisional EBIT | 79 372 | 74 932 | 85 792 |

Table TN – 4

**Budgeted Hybrid Income Statement**

Pikesville Lightning Hot Dog Oven Division

Budgeted Hybrid Income Statement For the first fiscal quarter 2010

—for internal management use only—

|  | $ Amount | % of Sales |
|---|---|---|
| Sales of ovens (12 000 ovens at $100 per unit) | $1 200 000 | 100% |
| Cost of goods sold | 420 000 | 35 |
| Gross Profit | 780 000 | 65 |
|  |  |  |
| Operating Expenses: Variable |  |  |
|    Sales commissions | 72 000 |  |
|    Shipping expense | 132 000 |  |
|    Utilities expense | 27 053 |  |
|    Maintenance expense | 8 873 |  |
| Total Variable Operating Expenses | 239 926 | 20 |
| Contribution Margin | 540 074 | 45 |
|  |  |  |
| Operating Expenses: Fixed |  |  |
|    Administrative salaries | 145 000 |  |
|    Advertising expense | 210 000 |  |
|    Insurance expense | 9 000 |  |
|    Depreciation expense | 82 500 |  |
|    Utilities expense | 10 056 |  |
|    Maintenance expense | 4 146 |  |
|  |  |  |
| Total Fixed Operating Expenses | 460 702 | 38 |
| Division Operating Income | $79 372 | 7% |

While Table TN – 4 provides one suggested solution based upon the information provided in the case and the cost structure outlined in Table TN – 1, two other points are worth noting. First, while preparation of the forward-looking statement is a critical first step, a major benefit of the exercise is for students to examine the contents to reflect on the usefulness of such a unique format as an analytical tool. This will be discussed further below in conjunction with Table 3. Second, while some components of the statement are straightforward to calculate, others require more judgment and are, therefore, subject to more variability in response. Hence, while student responses may differ from the suggested solution provided in Table TN – 4, the solution provides for a starting point in examining the magnitude and direction of any differences for a specific line item and for the overall profit calculation. To assist in assessing the quality of students' forward-looking statements, a brief guide is provided in Table TN – 4a below.

> **Table TN – 4a**
> 
> **Guide for Evaluating Budgeted Hybrid Income Statement**
> 
> 1. Administrative salaries and insurance expense: These costs reflect a 3% inflationary adjustment relative to the most recent quarterly data in the general ledger. In the absence of the adjustment, the amounts would be $140,777 and $8,737, respectively.
> 
> 2. Shipping expense: This is a pure variable cost at $11 per unit sold, based upon application of the historical general ledger data. Failing to understand this, students may attempt to ascribe a fixed and variable component, in which case they would report the cost under both sections of operating expenses.
> 
> 3. Utilities and maintenance expense: Students may obtain different numbers based upon their statistical analysis. For instance, they may use a different cost driver, fail to spot the outlier, or may use a multivariate regression ap-proach for one or both of these costs. All of these may contribute to calcula-tion differences. Several of these calculation differences have been identified in Table 1 of the teaching note. Further, students may correctly calculate the cost formula but may allocate the costs incorrectly between fixed and variable or may distribute all costs as either fixed or variable. This is a more serious error, as it indicates a lack of understanding of how the cost formulas are translated into financial statement amounts.

The next financial consideration requires students to outline the benefits and usefulness of the hybrid income statement approach. While it is important for students to identify key attributes of the income statement, their exposure to new ways of thinking about financial statements internally transcends the specific tasks of the competition. Table TN – 5 provides suggested key considerations under several categories. This is not an all-inclusive list, and students can also be assessed by the salience of other responses. In summary, the hybrid format is an efficiently constructed income statement that provides more detail to assist management with further profitability analysis by considering the cost structure while also maintaining the integrity of the externally reported financial statements. While the hybrid financial statement is specifically addressed in this more-defined financial aspect of the case, students must revisit this concept later in the strategic component of the case when the situation is less defined.

# SENSITIVITY ANALYSIS

The next set of requirements relates to sensitivity analysis. The first of these calculations requires a calculation of the level of sales under the market premium strategy to reach the same profit before interest and taxes (EBIT) as the base case, which is known as a point of indifference. The second calculation requires the determination of the sales price under the market penetration strategy to reach an EBIT equal to the base case. Drawing from the information in TN – 1, the cost formulas and solutions to the two requirements are presented in TN – 6. Note that the complexity of the cost formula could cause difficulty for the students. The Solver function in Excel is the easiest way to approach the problem. In the first case, it would entail setting the objective function equal to the current state EBIT level and letting Solver change the number of units sold. In the second case it would entail setting the objective function equal to the current state EBIT level and letting Solver change selling price.

---

**Table TN – 5**
**Benefits & Usefulness of Hybrid Income Statement**

Efficiency:

- Maintains the overall formatting of GAAP-based financial statements.
- Provides easier transition from external reporting.
- Does not require separate general ledger.
- Since it includes all GAAP information, management may be more inclined to implement internally even if they have less precision to determine fixed and variable components.

Detail:

- Provides more detail than GAAP or contribution margin formats alone, includ – ing three profit measures.
- Maintains the gross profit measure -ensures management does not lose focus of gross profit, which is vital for external benchmarking purposes.

Analysis:

- Motivates consideration of fixed and variable costs to assess controllable costs in both the short and long run.
- Simple analytical tool that can be constructed on an ad – hoc basis or using sophisticated techniques for analyzing fixed and variable costs.
- Reporting both gross profit and contribution margin provides more insight to both the manufacturing/ operating units and supporting units ( sales, facilities, etc. ) about how to better manage profitability.
- Merges the benefits of both income statements.

---

Simply performing the computations is not enough. The students are asked to interpret the results. For the premium strategy, the projected sales level is 112 units ( 10 200-10 088 ) above the amount needed to remain as well off as the current state. That is a margin of safety of only 1% ( 112/10 200 ), meaning there is little room for error in management's estimates. In the second scenario the projected volume is insufficient to reach the current state profit level at the $ 95. 00 price. The price would have to be increased, which raises the threat of moving the sales below the projected level of 13 200 units. Management should consider doing some additional sensitivity analysis before choosing a path.

The final scenario asks the students to look at a more aggressive penetration strategy by assuming the division can increase sales units by an additional 250 units for every $ 0. 50 in further price reduction. The goal is to reach a profit level equal to that of the premium pricing strategy, which is $ 85 792. The students are asked to provide a schedule showing the EBIT for the strategy for the first five reductions in increments of $ 0. 50 price cuts and 250-unit increases. The results are presented in TN – 7 and show that a cut of $ 1. 00 will not quite reach the target profit level while a price cut of $1.50 will put them over the target profit. It seems the $1.50 price cut offers a bit of a safety margin in that sales could be below 13 950 and the target profit level could be reached.

### Table TN-6
### Point of Indifference

| Cost Item | Cost Formula |
|---|---|
| Cost of Goods Sold | $35 per unit sold (the premium strategy calls for a $5.00 increase) |
| Sales Commissions | 6% of selling price (SP) |
| Shipping Costs | $11 per unit sold |
| Utilities Expense | $2.08 per kilowatt (KW) |
| Maintenance Expense | $.06825 per kilowatt (KW) |
| The engineers expect to use 13 000 kilowatts this quarter | |
| Insurance | $9 000 |
| Administrative Salaries | $145 000 |
| Advertising Expense | $210 000 |
| Depreciation Expense | $82 500 |
| Utilities Expense | $10 055.67 |
| Maintenance Expense | $4 146.46 |

**Cost formula for premium**

(40.00 + 11.00) x QTY + (2.08 + .06825) x KW + .06xSP + Fixed costs

We need to solve for the quantity to be sold (QTY)

| $\dfrac{2.6735 \times 13\,000 + 460\,702 + \text{profit target}}{CM}$ | = QTY |
|---|---|

Where CM = SP − 51 − 6.90 = 57.10

| $\dfrac{35\,926 + 460\,702 + 79\,372}{57.10}$ | = 10 088 |
|---|---|

**Cost formula for penetration**

(35.00 + 11.00) x QTY + (2.08 + .06825) x KW + .06xSP + Fixed costs

We need to solve for the selling price (SP)

| $\dfrac{2.6735 \times 13\,000 + 460\,702 + \text{profit target}}{CM}$ | = QTY |
|---|---|

CM in unknown because the SP is unknown.
Therefore the denominator becomes SP − .06 x SP − 46 = .94SP − 46

| $\dfrac{35\,926 + 460\,702 + 79\,372}{.94SP - 46}$ | = 13 200 |
|---|---|
| $\dfrac{35\,926 + 460\,702 + 79\,372}{13\,200}$ | = .94SP − 46 |
| 43.636363 | = .94SP − 46 |
| 89.64 | = .94 SP so SP = $95.36 |

Table TN-7
Scenario Summary

|  | Current Values | Cut $0.50 | Cut $1.00 | Cut $1.50 | Cut $2.00 | Cut $2.50 |
|---|---|---|---|---|---|---|
| Units Sold | 13 200 | 13 450 | 13 700 | 13 950 | 14 200 | 14 450 |
| Sales Price | $95.00 | $94.50 | $94.00 | $93.50 | $93.00 | $92.50 |
| EBIT | 74 932 | 79 436 | 83 704 | 87 738 | 91 536 | 95 100 |

# STRATEGIC ANALYSIS

Students are required to evaluate two strategic aspects of the Pikesville organization. This requirement of the case offers teams the opportunity to differentiate their responses based upon the creativity and feasibility of their responses as well as the completeness of their strategy and thought process. Further, students should be evaluated based upon whether their recommendations are cogent and embody characteristics of well contemplated approaches to decision making.

# FUTURE EXPANSION INITIATIVES

The first strategic task is a consideration of future expansion initiatives to grow the profitability of the business. Storm intends to grow the business beyond the limitations of the baseball season, and has already begun to do so with the "POG" oven initiative. While students have performed financial analysis for the oven initiative, they must now articulate a "breakthrough initiative" with a recommendation for an off-season expansion strategy that keeps the fan base engaged throughout the year. In addition to articulation of the strategy, Storm has asked for a detailed assessment of the financial and nonfinancial resources necessary to execute the strategy.

There is no single answer, but by way of illustration, here are several examples of student suggestions from a recent undergraduate course.

1. Winter Waterfall
   - Outdoor synthetic skating rink with concessions, live entertainment, a Christmas village, and the ability to host private or charity functions.
2. Winter Wonderland
   - Fun Zone games will be redecorated and themed for winter, and a snow machine will be purchased to imitate snow and add to the experience.
   - Winter gear such as long-sleeved shirts, sweatshirts, pants, and hats with the team logo will be available.

- Movie night on big screens in the outdoors.
- Activity night for children
- Festival with concerts, daily ice-skating, wine, cheese, and other snacks.

3. Conversion of field to temporary hockey rink to host youth through high school games and free skate. Research shows that the Midwest (especially Ohio) spends considerable time playing hockey.

4. Recreation park for outdoors-including snow tubing, ice skating, fire pits, and warm food. This would be similar to creating a flexible water park, but instead, it would be for wintertime, and, therefore, it would be a snow season park with slides and tubes, etc., for use on snow and/or ice.

As this component of the case is subjective, an outline of suggested general and specific considerations is provided in Table TN – 8 below as a guideline for assessing the quality of students' recommendations. Among the other facets listed below, it is critical that students incorporate the hybrid income statement approach into their thought process to support how it can be used as tool to analyze future profitability of the initiative. This provides the opportunity to validate whether the students can translate the benefits of such a tool to a less-developed set of facts and circumstances.

# EMPLOYING THE C-FRAMEWORK

The second strategic task requires a discussion of the model that will govern the strategic business partnering role of the accounting organization. Here, students will tailor the tenets of the C-framework to the Pikesville organization by discussing how each of four CFO levers serves as an input for the accounting organization to partner with the rest of the business to impact each of three company levers, which serve as the outputs of the framework.

Once again, this component of the case is subjective. In Table TN – 9 below, an outline of suggested general and specific considerations is provided as a guideline for assessing the quality of students' discussion of the framework as it fits into the Pikesville organization.

### Table TN-8

**Suggested Considerations for Assessing Expansion Initiatives**

- Does the recommendation consider all of the questions asked in the case?
- How unique/creative is the proposed strategy?
- Is the strategy clear and well articulated? Is the strategy easy to comprehend?
- What is the strategic fit of the recommendation with the overall mission of the organization and the vision as articulated by Storm?
- Is the strategy well justified, defended, and supported? Are views supported with critical arguments and evidence?
- Does the strategy consider the audience-both Storm and the customer base?
- Is there internal consistency between the strategy and the resources required?
- Is the strategy feasible to implement?
- Does the strategic recommendation incorporate financial analysis using realistic supporting assumptions?
- Is the recommendation professional in both content and presentation?
- Does the overall recommendation provide an insightful and thorough analysis of the issue?
- How well does the recommendation incorporate the benefits of the hybrid income statement as a tool for future analysis of the business initiative? Does the recommendation adequately translate the benefits to a less developed set of facts and circumstances?
- Does the recommendation exemplify a sound decision-making approach?
- Does the recommendation use thorough research to support the position and does the research highlight any expected risks? Is the research relevant, reliable, and applied to support the strategy?
- Does the recommendation consider strengths, weaknesses, opportunities, and threats?
- Is the discussion of resources specific and actionable? Does the recommendation exemplify completeness with respect to the identified required resources?
- Is the proposed timeline realistic, logical, and complete?
- Is the sustainability of the initiative clearly supported?

### Table TN-9

**Suggested Considerations for Employing the C-Framework**

- Is the framework tailored to this industry? Organization?
- Does the discussion consider Storm as the main audience?
- Are the levers linked across the CFO and company dimensions? Is each CFO lever linked to each company lever?
- Do students have a firm grasp of the meaning of each link?
- Are all levers in the framework employed and discussed?
- Does the discussion of each lever specifically address how the accounting organization can become a better business partner to serve in a strategic decision-making role?
- Does the discussion embrace the notion that the accountants must provide more than mechanical financial outputs?
- Do students provide specific, tangible examples to support their discussion?
- Does the discussion consider how the framework could impact the breakthrough initiative?
- Does the discussion demonstrate a clear understanding of the following considerations: (1) Who are the external and internal customers? (2) What are the critical costs to consider in achieving long-term sustainability? (3) Why must the business consider the community in its long-term focus?
- Does the discussion specifically identify/consider other internal functions that will be impacted by the strategic business partner role? Is this tied into the overall strategy of the business?
- Does the discussion include any unique/creative suggestions for implementation?
- Does the discussion consider any resistance to business partnering that might exist in the business in response to implementation?
- Does the discussion consider the long-term benefits of using such a model?
- Does the discussion use external research to validate or support the assumptions?

## Appendix A

**Pikesville Lightning Case Study Student Feedback Questionnaire**

The case was recently used in three sections of an introductory managerial accounting course. One section used the strategic requirements in addition to the financial requirements, while the other sections used only the financial requirements. The following is the survey instrument used to obtain feedback.

Circle the appropriate number using the scale below.

1. The case provides a realistic business situation.

| 10 | 20 | 30 | 40 | 50 | 60 | 70 | 80 | 90 | 100 |
| Strongly Disagree | | Disagree | | | Neutral | | Agree | | Strongly Agree |

2. I enjoyed working on the case.

| 10 | 20 | 30 | 40 | 50 | 60 | 70 | 80 | 90 | 100 |
| Strongly Disagree | | Disagree | | | Neutral | | Agree | | Strongly Agree |

3. The case was a good lesson in teamwork skills.

| 10 | 20 | 30 | 40 | 50 | 60 | 70 | 80 | 90 | 100 |
| Strongly Disagree | | Disagree | | | Neutral | | Agree | | Strongly Agree |

4. The case helped me to better understand how to work with raw data from an accounting system (i.e., general ledger data).

| 10 | 20 | 30 | 40 | 50 | 60 | 70 | 80 | 90 | 100 |
| Strongly Disagree | | Disagree | | | Neutral | | Agree | | Strongly Agree |

5. The case helped me to better understand how to apply statistical methods to analyze data for decision making.

| 10 | 20 | 30 | 40 | 50 | 60 | 70 | 80 | 90 | 100 |
| Strongly Disagree | | Disagree | | | Neutral | | Agree | | Strongly Agree |

6. The case helped me to better understand how cost structure information affects financial statements.

| 10 | 20 | 30 | 40 | 50 | 60 | 70 | 80 | 90 | 100 |
| Strongly Disagree | | Disagree | | | Neutral | | Agree | | Strongly Agree |

7. The case taught me how to integrate strategic and financial factors for decision making.

| 10 | 20 | 30 | 40 | 50 | 60 | 70 | 80 | 90 | 100 |
| Strongly Disagree | | Disagree | | | Neutral | | Agree | | Strongly Agree |

8. The case taught me how to model spreadsheets using advanced spreadsheet functionality.

| 10 | 20 | 30 | 40 | 50 | 60 | 70 | 80 | 90 | 100 |
| Strongly Disagree | | Disagree | | | Neutral | | Agree | | Strongly Agree |

9. Do you have any other comments regarding the case study?

_____

_____

_____

The tables below summarize the results

Single section using both financial and strategic requirements.

|  | Realistic | Enjoyment | Teamwork | Raw Data | Stat. Methods | FS Effects | Integration | Spreadsheets |
|---|---|---|---|---|---|---|---|---|
| N = 20 | 1 | 2 | 3 | 4 | 5 | 6 | 7 | 8 |
| MEAN | 85.5 | 76.0 | 80.5 | 89.0 | 84.0 | 85.5 | 84.5 | 87.0 |
| MEDIAN | 90.0 | 80.0 | 80.0 | 90.0 | 90.0 | 90.0 | 80.0 | 90.0 |
| MODE | 90.0 | 70.0 | 80.0 | 100.0 | 100.0 | 90.0 | 80.0 | 100.0 |

Two sections using just financial requirements.

|  | Realistic | Enjoyment | Teamwork | Raw Data | Stat. Methods | FS Effects | Integration | Spreadsheets |
|---|---|---|---|---|---|---|---|---|
| N = 42 | 1 | 2 | 3 | 4 | 5 | 6 | 7 | 8 |
| MEAN | 82.7 | 64.1 | 68.2 | 79.1 | 74.1 | 77.7 | 74.1 | 77.3 |
| MEDIAN | 80.0 | 65.0 | 75.0 | 80.0 | 80.0 | 80.0 | 80.0 | 85.0 |
| MODE | 80.0 | 80.0 | 70.0 | 80.0 | 80.0 | 80.0 | 80.0 | 100.0 |

While the students asked to perform the financial and strategic requirements indicated more favorable evaluation of the experience, the complete set of requirements could prove to be a bit overwhelming for the students and require more time on the part of the instructor to provide instructional guidance.

# 加勒比海啤酒公司：转移定价、道德和公司治理

Douglas Kalesnikoff
University of Saskatchewan

Suresh Kalagnanam
University of Saskatchewan

## 简介

2011年4月，你用刚获得的商学学位在加勒比海啤酒股份有限公司（位于加勒比海安提瓜岛）获得了一份管理工作——财务总监（CFO）的顾问。加勒比海啤酒股份有限公司是格拉国际（一个从事啤酒酿造和配送的企业集团）旗下控股75%的一家子公司。你工作还不满一个星期，就需要你处理一些重大项目了。

## 格拉国际

在过去的半个多世纪，格拉啤酒已经是信誉卓著的国际啤酒品牌，通常位居世界啤酒畅销品牌的前三名。一直到2005年，总部设在德国慕尼黑的格拉国际，开始在一家位于牙买加的啤酒厂为加勒比海地区酿造格拉啤酒。随着运输成本的持续增长，从位于加勒比海西部的牙买加到加勒比海东部诸岛的物流出现问题。在21世纪初，格拉国际就已经着手在加勒比海东部寻找一个合适的厂址。在严格评估了多个地点后，格拉国际决定在安提瓜岛新建酒厂。

安提瓜岛有68 000人口，是加勒比海东部的背风群岛中说英语的最大岛屿。1784年霍雷肖·纳尔逊海军上将（Admiral Horatio Nelson）航行至此，安提瓜岛便成为了英国最重要的加勒比海基地。地处东加勒比海群岛的中间，安提瓜岛经常在向风群岛（圣·卢西亚、格林纳达、多米尼加和圣·文森特）与背风群岛（圣·凯特斯、圣·马丁、蒙特色拉特岛和安圭拉岛）之间起到商业和交通枢纽的作用。在北边它天然邻近波多黎各和多米尼加共和国，在南边它天然邻近巴巴多斯和特立尼达拉岛，这些岛屿都是人口比较稠密的地区。

---

\* 本篇译者为赵澄，校订者为胡金凤、余辉。

安提瓜岛上已经有一家经营非常成功的啤酒厂,这家啤酒厂生产提瓜啤酒,是安提瓜岛和整个东加勒比海地区很受欢迎的一个品牌。在 2000 年,安提瓜岛的酿酒厂与安提瓜政府就提瓜啤酒的销售收入达成了协议,15 年内对提瓜啤酒销售收入免征所得税。综合考虑到安提瓜岛位于东加勒比海的中心位置,提瓜啤酒生产线的成功,及提瓜啤酒的税收优惠,使得安提瓜岛成为格拉国际的一个较优的选择。2005 年,它购买了安提瓜岛啤酒厂 75%的股权,改名加勒比海啤酒股份有限公司。加勒比海啤酒股份有限公司剩余的 25%的普通股仍然由高管层和其他员工持有。加勒比海啤酒股份有限公司是格拉国际控制下的不同规模的众多子公司之一。

2008 年,加勒比海啤酒股份有限公司扩充了生产设备,因此,其产能有效地翻了一倍。这次规模扩张的资金来源于,以 10%固定利率向格拉国际借入的 10 年内分期偿还的借款。工厂扩大规模后,销往加勒比海东部地区的格拉啤酒的生产全部被转移到了加勒比海啤酒股份有限公司。在图表 1 中提供了加勒比啤酒股份有限公司相应的生产数据。

图表 1
销售额(每箱 24 瓶)

|  | 格拉啤酒 |  | 提瓜啤酒 |  |
| --- | --- | --- | --- | --- |
|  | 国内 | 出口 | 国内 | 出口 |
| 2007 | 380 000 | 55 000 | 875 000 | 45 000 |
| 2008 | 389 000 | 59 000 | 868 000 | 48 000 |
| 2009 | 401 000 | 825 000 | 897 000 | 51 000 |
| 2010 | 411 000 | 1 190 000 | 911 000 | 53 000 |

# 最近的问题

当你就任新的职务时,你会发现加勒比海啤酒公司的一切并不是那么乐观。在你上班的第二天,生产经理乔森·乔瑟弗(Jason Joseph),大家都亲切地叫他 JJ,就来到你的办公室并且把门关上了。JJ 已经做了几十年的生产经理,并且被誉为酿酒大师,曾在 20 世纪 90 年代晚期和 21 世纪早期,凭借提瓜啤酒获得过多项殊荣。在会面中,JJ 很明显不高兴并且很压抑。他解释到,在格拉国际介入啤酒厂之前,一切都很好;JJ 之前拥有加勒比海啤酒股份有限公司 25%的所有权,而现在减少到 8%。作为生产经理,他之前总能拿到 100 000 美元的薪酬,同时还有奖金和每年股利分红的收益。自从格拉国际成为大股东,从来都没有进行过股利分红。此外,JJ 的奖金建立在控制平均总生产成本和质量控制两者结合的基础上,从工厂规模扩张以来就全部都没有了。至于生产成本,只要总的生成成本不超过销售额的 43%,JJ 和其他生产人员就有资格获得奖金。图表 2 包含了一份报告的形式，可以用来评估生产效率并计算奖金。

JJ解释到，酿造啤酒的生产工艺在过去的几十年里基本上是相同的，如附录1所示。前两个步骤，即碾碎和搅拌酒料，占总生产成本的50%。提瓜啤酒需要更长和更时间密集型的生产过程，以达到麦芽汁生产出来的阶段；因此与格拉啤酒相比，提瓜啤酒在该阶段会多消耗一倍的制造资源。在麦芽汁生产完工后，不同品牌啤酒的生产工艺和成本就相同了。

啤酒的直接成本并不总是占那么大的比重；啤酒的98%的成分是水，并且24瓶每箱的原材料成本仅约3美元。瓶盖和标签的成本和材料成本差不多，每箱大约3美元。24瓶每箱的瓶子的押金成本是8美元；然而，这不能算作一项正式成本，因为24瓶每箱的8美元押金可以从市场收回，包括所有的国内市场和提瓜啤酒的出口市场。而与正常商业惯例不同的是：对于格拉啤酒而言，出口市场的此项支出是不能收回；因此，与出口的格拉啤酒瓶子相关的成本要费用化。

由于生产效率的下降，如图表2所示，JJ的奖金就遭殃了。JJ坚信生产设备即使没有更加有效，但也能像扩张以前一样有效的运转，他还担心图表2中的生产成本的分配方法正在侵蚀他的奖金。"规模扩张之前，我重点关注每箱啤酒的生产成本。格拉国际现在让我们负责生产成本占销售额的百分比——这将夺走生产人员的控制权。我也不理解为何出口的格拉啤酒的瓶子成本也计入我们工厂的费用，"JJ极度郁闷地说。他还解释到，格拉国际还

**图表 2**
**生产成本占销售额的比例**

|  | 2007 |  | 2008 |  | 2009 |  | 2010 |  |
|---|---|---|---|---|---|---|---|---|
| 销售额 | $66 375 000 |  | $66 725 000 |  | $88 075 000 |  | $98 500 000 |  |
| 生产成本 |  |  |  |  |  |  |  |  |
| 变动成本： |  |  |  |  |  |  |  |  |
| 　原材料 | $4 037 900 | 6.1% | $4 078 360 | 6.1% | $6 587 220 | 7.5% | $7 874 550 | 8.0% |
| 　瓶子 | 440 000 | 0.7% | 472 000 | 0.7% | 6 600 000 | 7.5% | 9 520 000 | 9.7% |
| 　瓶盖和标签 | 4 092 100 | 6.2% | 4 146 560 | 6.2% | 6 630 700 | 7.5% | 7 823 250 | 7.9% |
| 变动成本合计： | $8 570 000 | 12.9% | $8 696 920 | 13.0% | $19 817 920 | 22.5% | $25 217 800 | 25.6% |
| 制造费用： |  |  |  |  |  |  |  |  |
| 　公共事业设施费 | $4 539 250 | 6.8% | $4 433 000 | 6.6% | $6 739 400 | 7.7% | $7 695 000 | 7.8% |
| 　工厂维持成本 | 1 084 000 | 1.6% | 1 050 280 | 1.6% | 1 521 800 | 1.7% | 1 539 000 | 1.6% |
| 　人员工资 | 7 452 500 | 11.2% | 7 229 200 | 10.8% | 10 435 200 | 11.8% | 11 286 000 | 11.5% |
| 　折旧费 | 5 420 000 | 8.2% | 5 456 000 | 8.2% | 8 696 000 | 9.9% | 10 260 000 | 10.4% |
| 制造费用合计： | $18 495 750 | 27.9% | $18 168 480 | 27.2% | $27 392 400 | 31.1% | $30 780 000 | 31.2% |
| 生产成本合计： | $27 065 750 | 40.8% | $26 865 400 | 40.3% | $47 210 320 | 53.6% | $55 997 800 | 56.9% |

**注释**：为了简化，假定销售量就等于生产量。

时不时抱怨出口到加勒比海其他国家的格拉啤酒的质量，继而拒绝向加勒比海啤酒股份有限公司支付运输费用。JJ坚信啤酒的质量一如既往的好，并且迫切想要证明质量差的说法是毫无根据的。他还认为格拉国际为了少支付一些运输费用，而制造出啤酒质量有问题的谣言。"我不明白为何总部会说我们的质量差；我从来没有听到过当地顾客对格拉啤酒的任何抱怨。我做这一行已经很久了，能分辨出啤酒的质量优劣；我能够并且通常能在事情失控前对生产过程采取纠正措施。"

在离开你的办公室前，JJ说道，他非常的郁闷，并且正在慎重考虑离开这家公司去特立尼达拉岛的一家酿酒厂担任总酿酒师和生产经理，这家酿酒厂是加勒比海啤酒股份有限公司的一个主要竞争对手。这将会是公司的一项重大损失。

这一天晚些时候，总会计师将来自于安提瓜岛税务局（IRD）（相当于美国的国税局）的一封信交给你，信中提到税务审计人员会在下个月来公司审查截至2008年、2009年、2010年年末的纳税申报。你调查发现为了享受提瓜啤酒的税收豁免，在准备年度纳税申报时，加勒比海啤酒股份有限公司根据应税和非应税产品类别编制了利润表。图表3提供了两种产品类别的分配。

加勒比海啤酒股份有限公司是安提瓜岛的纳税居民，因此，要按利润的30%缴纳所得税。当你开始为应对税务审计做准备时，你发现如下问题：

- 格拉啤酒出口销售额全部归属于格拉加勒比海公司，一家格拉国际的全资子公司，它位于免税管辖区的百慕大群岛（见图表4所示的交易图）。
- 由于成本和物流原因，所有出口的啤酒都直接运送到加勒比海东部的各个岛屿，并在这些岛屿销售，只有发票被送到百慕大（见图表4）。
- 从国内来看，24瓶每箱的格拉啤酒售价为50美元，但是，给格拉加勒比海公司开具的发票上注明的用于出口的格拉啤酒却是每箱25美元。
- 除了每箱售价50美元外，加勒比海啤酒股份有限公司能收回可回收的提瓜啤酒瓶的押金每箱8美元，包括国内销售的和出口的。与这项正常商业惯例不同的是，对于出口格拉啤酒这项业务，在给格拉加勒比海公司开具的发票上没有这项押金。
- 然而，格拉加勒比海公司向加勒比海东部区域的其他岛屿开具的发票售价为50美元/箱，还外加了每箱的瓶子押金8美元。

你需要尽快研究安提瓜岛的所得税法（ITA），并浏览一下一般税的反避税章节（见图表5）。

**图表 3**
**纳税和非纳税收入分配**

| 2008 | 合计 | 非纳税的提瓜啤酒 | 纳税的格拉啤酒 |
|---|---|---|---|
| 销售量（每箱24瓶） | 1 364 000 | 916 000 | 448 000 |
| 销售额 | $66 725 000 | $45 800 000 | $20 925 000 |
| 生产成本 | $26 865 400 | $18 041 574 | $8 823 826 |
| 销售费用 | 4 670 750 | 3 206 000 | 1 464 750 |
| 管理费用 | 4 003 500 | 2 748 000 | 1 255 500 |
| 利息费用 | 543 000 | 372 715 | 170 285 |
| 净利润 | $30 642 350 | $21 431 712 | $9 210 638 |
| 2009 | 合计 | 非纳税的提瓜啤酒 | 纳税的格拉啤酒 |
| 销售量（每箱24瓶） | 2 174 000 | 948 000 | 1 226 000 |
| 销售额 | $88 075 000 | $47 400 000 | $40 675 000 |
| 生产成本 | $47 210 320 | $20 586 653 | $26 623 667 |
| 销售费用 | 5 284 500 | 2 844 000 | 2 440 500 |
| 管理费用 | 4 844 125 | 2 607 000 | 2 237 125 |
| 利息费用 | 3 257 000 | 1 752 845 | 1 504 155 |
| 净利润 | $27 479 055 | $19 609 502 | $7 869 553 |
| 2010 | 合计 | 非纳税的提瓜啤酒 | 纳税的格拉啤酒 |
| 销售量（每箱24瓶） | 2 565 000 | 964 000 | 1 601 000 |
| 销售额 | $98 500 000 | $48 200 000 | $50 300 000 |
| 生产成本 | $55 997 800 | $21 045 567 | $34 952 233 |
| 销售费用 | 5 614 500 | 2 747 400 | 2 867 100 |
| 管理费用 | 5 220 500 | 2 554 600 | 2 665 900 |
| 利息费用 | 2 932 000 | 1 434 745 | 1 497 255 |
| 净利润 | $28 735 200 | $20 417 688 | $8 317 512 |

注释：出口的格拉啤酒售价是25美元，其他是50美元。
　　　总的生产成本以销售量（销售箱数）为基础进行分配。
　　　销售费用、管理费用和利息费用以销售额为基础进行分配。

### 图表 4
### 集团交易流程图

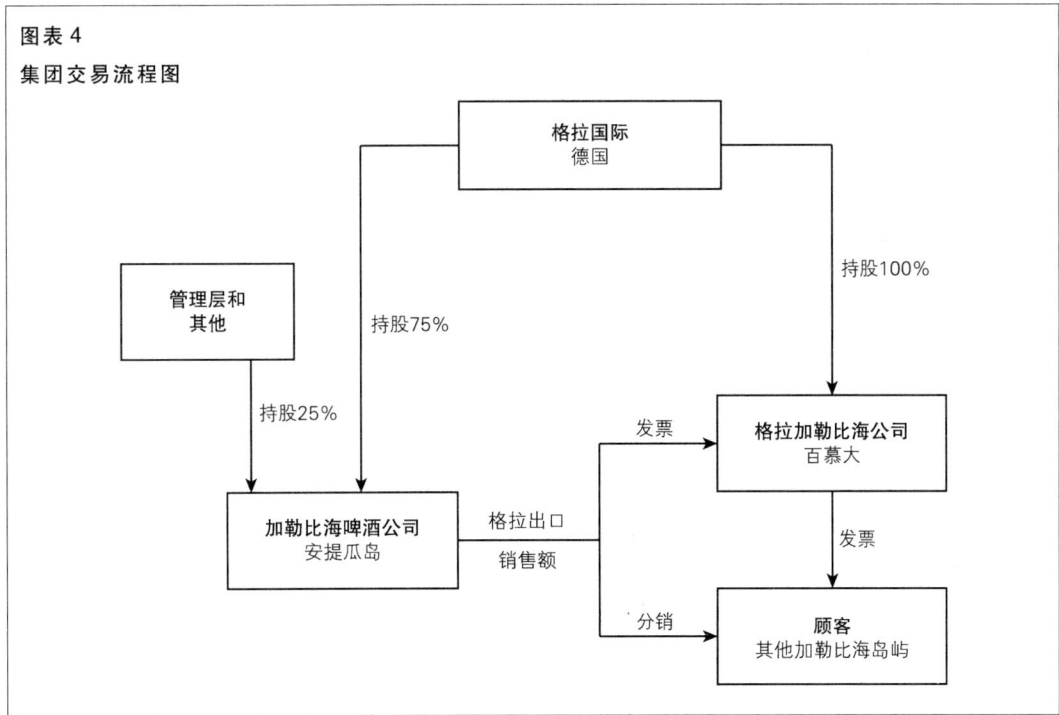

### 图表 5
### 安提瓜岛所得税法案 第 23 条
### 关联方交易的纳税义务

一家本国公司在与一家外国公司进行业务往来时，由于公司之间的关联方关系，他们之间的交易过程被操纵了，而致使本国公司在交易过程中获得的利润少于与不存在这种关系的公司进行交易预期可产生的利润。国家税务局可以一个合理的方式来确定本国公司是否需要将额外的利润确认为本国公司的应纳税所得。

### 附录 1
### 啤酒酿造流程的九个步骤

1. 碾磨——啤酒酿造是以干净的大麦谷类（又称麦芽）开始的，通过碾磨机挤压将干燥的麦粒剥离，并将其碾碎为粗糙的粉末。
2. 搅拌大酒桶——碾磨后的谷粒被倒进装有特定温度的温水（取决于酿造的配方）的搅拌大酒桶中；谷粒粉和水混合在一起成了浆——浓稠、甜味的液体，即麦芽汁。
3. 过滤——麦芽汁被倾倒入一个称之为过滤大酒桶的容器内（德语称为"净化缸"），在这个容器内，利用一个巨大的过滤网或过滤器床过滤出"废弃"的谷粒和谷壳。
4. 煮沸——将麦芽汁放入大罐或麦芽铜器中煮沸，再配上啤酒花香料继续煮90分钟。
5. 发酵——冷却后，麦芽汁被转移到发酵缸中，在这里，糖分产生新陈代谢变化成为酒和碳氧化物，得到的混合物就被称为嫩啤酒。
6. 回湿——啤酒被冷却到冰点左右，这促进了酵母活动，进而使得蛋白质变稠；啤酒变得更加爽口和干净。
7. 过滤——这个阶段的过滤是去掉多余的酵母、蛋白质和其他不溶解物质，同时稳定口味，这样一来啤酒变得更加透明和清澈。
8. 巴氏杀菌——用巴氏杀菌法消除啤酒内的任何剩余的酵母和其他的微生物。
9. 包装——完工后的啤酒接下来进行机械化装瓶或装桶。

## 将要面临的挑战（或者说前面的路）

你仔细考虑了从 JJ 那里听到的每一件事。你也反思了一下你的新职责，特别是关于你将要带头拟订的详尽的新计划和预算程序。你被告知这些程序非常重要，这将使得格拉加勒比海公司与其他分部在资源分配、绩效考核、估价和报酬上统一使用标准的程序。你应该思考"一个集团公司应该走标准化的道路，还是让每个子公司都走灵活性的道路？"

下周将召开一次董事会会议。弗瑞德瑞克·沃斯坦（Frederik Verstam），格拉国际的长期高级管理人员，被空降到加勒比海啤酒股份有限公司担任 CEO 和董事会主席。加勒比海啤酒股份有限公司的其他董事会成员包括：来自总部的格兰德威尔·高德勒（Grandview Goerdler）和德罗瑞斯·贾斯德（Delores Garstad），他们从慕尼黑飞过来参加季度会议；爱德华·伍慈（Edward Woods），当地的政府官员；以及拜荣恩·杰克逊（Byron Jackson），安提瓜岛当地的一个拥有加勒比海啤酒股份有限公司 2% 股权的商人。

你收到了董事会的会议议程，并告诉你需要准备如下报告：
1. 解决不断提高的生产成本问题的报告，如图表 2 所示。
2. 关于成本和质量控制的生产人员的绩效考核体系的报告。
3. 与即将到来的所得税审计相关的薄弱点或风险的报告。

除了上述要求的报告，你还需要关注格拉啤酒出口相关的转移定价政策。这会对小股东，如 JJ，产生怎样的影响？董事会将如何应对不利于少数股东权益的陈述？最能代表大股东权益的是什么？

根据提供的信息，你需要思考，怎样处理 JJ 的担心和准备董事会会议。作为一个新人、有责任感的专业人士，你还要考虑在董事会会议中应该提出的与公司治理有关的管理层控制方面和其他方面的问题。

# Caribbean Brewers: Transfer Pricing, Ethics and Governance

*Douglas Kalesnikoff*
*University of Saskatchewan*

*Suresh Kalagnanam*
*University of Saskatchewan*

## INTRODUCTION

It is April 2011 and you have used your newly acquired business degree to secure a management job as advisor to the chief financial officer with Caribbean Brewers Inc., located in Antigua in the Caribbean Sea. Caribbean Brewers Inc. is a 75%-owned subsidiary of Gera International, a conglomerate in the business of brewing and distributing beer. It is barely a week since you started your job and you already have major projects to deal with.

## GERA INTERNATIONAL

Gera beer has been a well-established international brand of beer for over half a century, usually ranked among the top three selling brands of beer in the world. Up until 2005, Gera International, head-quartered in Munich, Germany, brewed Gera beer for the Caribbean region at a brewery located in Jamaica. As transportation costs continued to increase, the logistics of shipping from Jamaica, which is located in the western Caribbean, to islands in the eastern Caribbean became problematic. In the early 2000s, Gera International set out to find a suitable location for a plant in the eastern Caribbean. After due diligence investigations on a number of locations, Gera International decided on Antigua.

Antigua, with the population of 68 000, is the largest of the English-speaking Leeward Islands of the eastern Caribbean. Antigua became Great Britain's most important Caribbean base when Admiral Horatio Nelson sailed there in 1784. Situated in the middle of the eastern Caribbean chain of Islands, Antigua often serves as a business and transportation hub between the Windward Islands of St. Lucia, Grenada, Dominica, and St. Vincent and the Leeward

Islands of St. Kitts, St. Martin, Montserrat, and Anguilla. It is also in reasonable physical proximity to the more populated islands of Puerto Rico and Dominican Republic to the north and Barbados and Trinidad to the south.

Antigua already had a successful brewery that produced Tigua beer, a popular brand in Antigua and throughout the eastern Caribbean. In 2000, the Antiguan brewery had negotiated a 15-year income tax holiday with the government of Antigua on income earned from sales of Tigua beer. The combination of the central location of Antigua in the eastern Caribbean, the success of the Tigua beer line, and the tax concession on Tigua beer made Antigua a good choice for Gera International; it purchased 75% of the Antiguan brewery, Caribbean Brewers Inc., in 2005. The remaining 25% of the common shares of Caribbean Brewers remained held by senior management and other employees. Caribbean Brewers is one of the many subsidiaries of varying sizes under Gera International's control.

The production facilities of Caribbean Brewers were expanded in 2008, thereby effectively doubling the productive capacity. This expansion was funded through a 10-year amortized loan from Gera International at a fixed interest rate of 10%. All of the production of Gera beer for the eastern Caribbean region was transferred to Caribbean Brewers after the plant expansion. The resulting production figures for Caribbean Brewers are provided in Figure 1.

Figure 1
Sales Volume (cases of 24)

|  | Gera | | Tigua | |
| --- | --- | --- | --- | --- |
|  | Domestic | Export | Domestic | Export |
| 2007 | 380 000 | 55 000 | 875 000 | 45 000 |
| 2008 | 389 000 | 59 000 | 868 000 | 48 000 |
| 2009 | 401 000 | 825 000 | 897 000 | 51 000 |
| 2010 | 411 000 | 1 190 000 | 911 000 | 53 000 |

# RECENT ISSUES

Upon arrival in your new position, you discover that all is not rosy at Caribbean Brewers. On only your second day in the office, the production manager, Jason Joseph, affectionately known as JJ, comes into your office and shuts the door. JJ has been production manager for decades and has been heralded as a master brewer, having won multiple awards for Tigua beer in the late 1990s and early 2000s. It is clear during the meeting that JJ is unhappy and distressed. He explains that prior to Gera International's involvement in the brewery, things were better; JJ previously had a 25% ownership in Caribbean Brewers, which is now reduced to 8%. He had always received a salary of about $ 100 000 as the production manager, but had also benefited by a bonus and an annual dividend. Since Gera International became the majority shareholder, there have been no dividends. In addition, JJ's bonus, which is based on a combination of controlling average total production costs and quality control, has all but been eliminated since the plant expansion. With respect to production costs, JJ and other production personnel are eligible for a bonus provided that total production costs do not exceed 43% of sales. Figure 2 contains the format of the report that is used to assess production efficiency and bonus calculations.

### Figure 2
### Production Costs as a Percentage of Sales

|  | 2007 |  | 2008 |  | 2009 |  | 2010 |  |
|---|---|---|---|---|---|---|---|---|
| Sales | $66 375 000 |  | $66 725 000 |  | $88 075 000 |  | $98 500 000 |  |
| Production Costs: |  |  |  |  |  |  |  |  |
| Variable Cost: |  |  |  |  |  |  |  |  |
| raw materials | $4 037 900 | 6.1% | $4 078 360 | 6.1% | $6 587 220 | 7.5% | $7 874 550 | 8.0% |
| bottles | 440 000 | 0.7% | 472 000 | 0.7% | 6 600 000 | 7.5% | 9 520 000 | 9.7% |
| caps and labels | 4 092 100 | 6.2% | 4 146 560 | 6.2% | 6 630 700 | 7.5% | 7 823 250 | 7.9% |
| Total Variable Costs: | $8 570 000 | 12.9% | $8 696 920 | 13.0% | $19 817 920 | 22.5% | $25 217 800 | 25.6% |
| Overhead: |  |  |  |  |  |  |  |  |
| utilities | $4 539 250 | 6.8% | $4 433 000 | 6.6% | $6 739 400 | 7.7% | $7 695 000 | 7.8% |
| plant maintenance | 1 084 000 | 1.6% | 1 050 280 | 1.6% | 1 521 800 | 1.7% | 1 539 000 | 1.6% |
| personnel | 7 452 500 | 11.2% | 7 229 200 | 10.8% | 10 435 200 | 11.8% | 11 286 000 | 11.5% |
| depreciation | 5 420 000 | 8.2% | 5 456 000 | 8.2% | 8 696 000 | 9.9% | 10 260 000 | 10.4% |
| Total Overhead: | $18 495 750 | 27.9% | $18 168 480 | 27.2% | $27 392 400 | 31.1% | $30 780 000 | 31.2% |
| Total Production Costs | $27 065 750 | 40.8% | $26 865 400 | 40.3% | $47 210 320 | 53.6% | $55 997 800 | 56.9% |

Note: For simplicity it is assumed that sales units are equal to production units.

JJ explains that the production process for brewing beer has been fundamentally the same for decades, as outlined in Appendix 1. The first two steps, i.e., milling and mash tun, account for 50% of the total production overhead costs. Tigua beer has a longer and more time-intensive production process up to the stage where the wort is created; this results in the Tigua beer consuming 100% more overhead resources up to this stage compared to Gera beer. After the creation of the wort, the process and cost are the same regardless of the brand.

The direct costs of the beer are not all that significant; 98% of the beer is water and the cost of the raw materials is only about \$3 per case of 24. The costs of the bottle cap and label are as much as raw materials, about \$3 per case. The cost of the bottles is \$8 per case of 24; however, this is not normally treated as a cost because a deposit of \$8 per case of 24 is collected for all returnable markets, which include all domestic markets and export of Tigua. Contrary to this normal business practice, no deposit is collected on the export market for Gera beer; as a result, the cost of the bottles pertaining to Gera beer exports are expensed.

As a result of the decline in production efficiencies, as measured in Figure 2, JJ's bonus has suffered. JJ is adamant that the production facility is operating as efficiently as, if not more efficiently than, before the expansion, and is concerned that the cost allocations used in Figure 2 for production costs are penalizing his bonus. "Prior to the expansion, I focused on production cost per case. Gera International now holds us accountable for production cost as a percentage of sales-this has taken away control from the production people. I also don't understand why the exported Gera beer bottle costs are charged to our plant," JJ exclaimed in sheer frustration. He also explained that Gera International has on occasion complained about the quality of Gera beer exported to other Caribbean countries, thereby refusing to pay Caribbean Brewers for some shipments. JJ is adamant that the quality of the beer is consistent and desperately wants to be able to prove the allegations of poor quality as groundless. He is concerned that Gera International is making false allegations about the quality to justify not paying for some of the shipments. "I do not understand how head office can say that our quality is poor; I have not heard any complaints from our local customers of Gera beer. I have been in the business long enough to know when quality is bad; I am able to and usually do take corrective actions during the process itself before things go out of hand."

Before leaving your office, JJ explains that he is very frustrated and is seriously considering leaving the company to be the master brewer and production manager of a brewery in Trinidad, a major competitor of Caribbean Brewers. This would be a major loss to the company.

Later the same day, the head accountant provides you with a letter from the Inland Revenue Department (IRD) of Antigua (equivalent to IRS in the United States of America) explaining that tax auditors will be coming out next month to review the tax filings for the years ending December 31, 2008, 2009, and 2010. You investigate and find that in order to benefit from the tax exemption of Tigua beer, Caribbean Brewers prepares profitability statements along taxable and nontaxable product lines when filing the annual tax return. This allocation between the two product lines is provided in Figure 3.

### Figure 3
### Allocation of Taxable and Non-taxable Streams

| 2008 | Total | Non-taxable Tigua | Taxable-Gera |
|---|---|---|---|
| Volume in cases of 24 | 1 364 000 | 916 000 | 448 000 |
| Sales | $66 725 000 | $45 800 000 | $20 925 000 |
| Production Costs | $26 865 400 | $18 041 574 | $8 823 826 |
| Sales Costs | 4 670 750 | 3 206 000 | 1 464 750 |
| Administrative Costs | 4 003 500 | 2 748 000 | 1 255 500 |
| Interest Costs | 543 000 | 372 715 | 170 285 |
| Net profit | $30 642 350 | $21 431 712 | $9 210 638 |
| **2009** | **Total** | **Non-taxable Tigua** | **Taxable-Gera** |
| Volume in cases of 24 | 2 174 000 | 948 000 | 1 226 000 |
| Sales | $88 075 000 | $47 400 000 | $40 675 000 |
| Production Costs | $47 210 320 | $20 586 653 | $26 623 667 |
| Sales Costs | 5 284 500 | 2 844 000 | 2 440 500 |
| Administrative Costs | 4 844 125 | 2 607 000 | 2 237 125 |
| Interest | 3 257 000 | 1 752 845 | 1 504 155 |
| Net profit | $27 479 055 | $19 609 502 | $7 869 553 |
| **2010** | **Total** | **Non-taxable Tigua** | **Taxable-Gera** |
| Volume in cases of 24 | 2 565 000 | 964 000 | 1 601 000 |
| Sales | $98 500 000 | $48 200 000 | $50 300 000 |
| Production Costs | $55 997 800 | $21 045 567 | $34 952 233 |
| Sales Costs | 5 614 500 | 2 747 400 | 2 867 100 |
| Administrative Costs | 5 220 500 | 2 554 600 | 2 665 900 |
| Interest | 2 932 000 | 1 434 745 | 1 497 255 |
| Net profit | $28 735 200 | $20 417 688 | $8 317 512 |

Notes: Sales price of Gera Exported beer is $25 while all others are $50.
Total production costs allocated on the basis of volume (# of cases).
Sales and Administrative and Interest expense allocated on the basis of sales dollars.

Caribbean Brewers is a tax resident of Antigua and thus subject to taxes of 30% of profits. As you begin preparing for the tax audit you find out the following:

- All export sales of Gera beer are made to Gera Caribbean, a wholly-owned subsidiary of Gera International, which is located in Bermuda, a tax-free jurisdiction. (See Figure 4 for a chart of the transactions.)

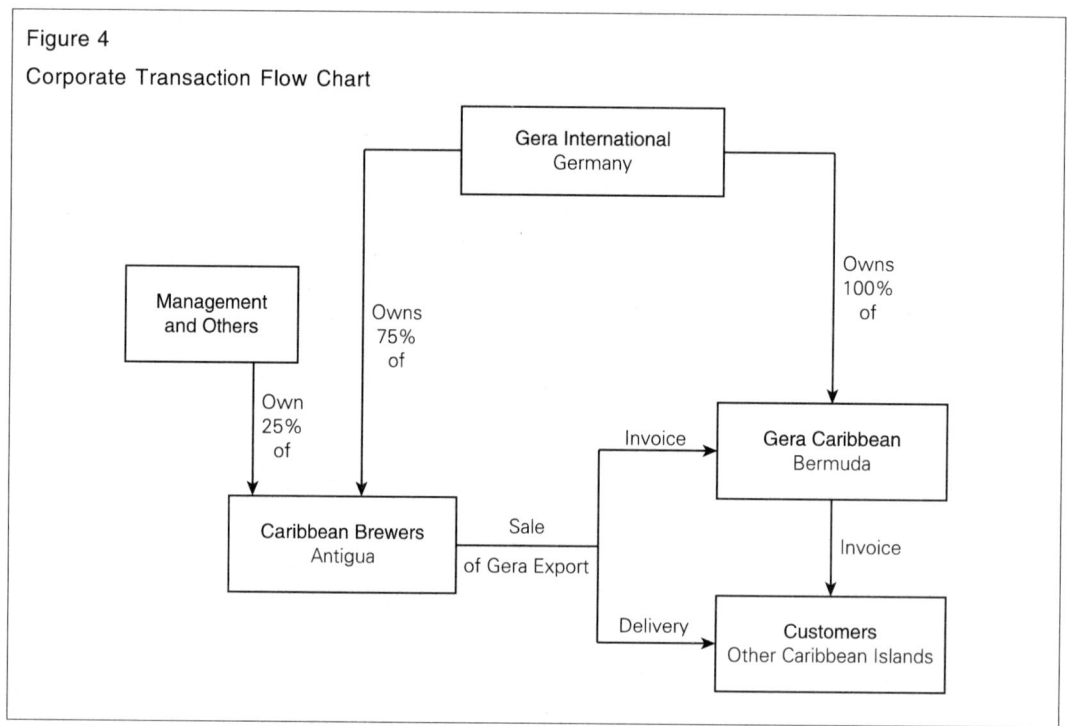

Figure 4
Corporate Transaction Flow Chart

- For cost and logistical reasons, the exports are shipped directly to the Island where the beer will be sold in the eastern Caribbean while only the invoice is sent to Bermuda (see Figure 4).
- Domestically, a case of 24 Gera beer sells for $50, but the exported Gera beer is invoiced to Gera Caribbean for $25 per case.
- In addition to the $50/case, Caribbean Brewers collects a returnable bottle deposit of $8 per case on domestic sales and exported Tigua beer. Contrary to this normal business practice, no deposit is invoiced to Gera Caribbean for exported Gera beer.
- Gera Caribbean in turn invoices the other Islands in the eastern Caribbean for $50/case plus an $8/case deposit for the bottles.

You quickly research the Antigua Income Tax Act (ITA) and come across a general tax anti-avoidance section (see Figure 5).

Figure 5
Antigua ITA Section 23
Related Party Transactions Involving Liability to Tax
Where a resident corporation carries on business with a non-resident corporation and by reason of the relationship between such corporations the course of business between them has been so arranged that the business done by the resident produces less profits than those which could be expected to arise from that business if such relationship had not existed, Inland Revenue may determine in a reasonable fashion whether any additional profits should be deemed to be assessable income of the resident corporation.

## Appendix 1

### The Nine-Step Process of Beer Making

1. **Milling**-Beer brewing begins with polished barley grains called malt, which are passed through a milling machine to crack the dried kernels and grind them into a coarse powder.

2. **Mash tun**-The milled grain is dropped into the mash tun with warm water of a certain temperature, depending on the brew recipe; the grain and water are mixed together to create a mash-a thick, sweet liquid called wort.

3. **Lautering**-The wort is then drained off in a vessel called a lauter tun (German for "purification tank") where the husks are used like a giant sieve or filter bed for filtering out the "spent" grain.

4. **Boiling**-The wort is boiled and spiced with hops for up to 90 minutes in a large kettle, or wort copper.

5. **Fermenting**-After it is cooled, the wort is then transferred to a fermentation tank where the sugars are metabolized into alcohol and carbon dioxide, and the resulting mixture is then called young beer.

6. **Conditioning**-The beer is cooled to around freezing point, which encourages settling of the yeast and causes proteins to thicken; the beer becomes crisp and clean.

7. **Filtering**-In this stage the filtering removes excess yeast, protein, and other insolubles, as well as stabilizes the flavor so that the beer becomes bright and clear.

8. **Pasteurizing**-The beer is pasteurized to kill off any of the remaining yeast and any other microorganisms.

9. **Packaging**-The finished beer is then mechanically filled into bottles or kegs.

# THE CHALLENGES AHEAD (OR THE ROAD AHEAD)

You ponder everything that you have heard from JJ. You also reflect upon your new responsibilities, particularly with respect to new elaborate planning and budgeting processes that you will be spearheading. You have been told that these processes are extremely critical and will bring Gera Caribbean in line with the other segments in terms of using standard procedures for resource allocation, performance measurement, evaluation, and reward. "Is a corporate group standard approach the right way to go, or should each subsidiary have some flexibility?" you wonder.

There is a board of directors meeting scheduled for next week. Frederik Verstam, a long-time executive of Gera International, has been parachuted in as the CEO and chairman of the board of Caribbean Brewers. The other members of the board of directors of Caribbean Brewers are Grandview Goerdler and Delores Garstad from the head office, who fly in for the quarterly meetings from Munich; Edward Woods, a local politician; and Byron Jackson, a local businessman in Antigua with a 2% ownership interest in Caribbean Brewers.

You receive an agenda for the board meeting and note that you are required to prepare the following reports:

1. Report addressing the rising costs of production, as illustrated in Figure 2.

2. Report on the performance measurement system for production personnel with respect to both cost and quality control.

3. Report on any vulnerability or risks associated with the upcoming income tax audit.

In addition to the requested reports, you have some concerns over the transfer pricing policy in relation to exports of Gera Beer. How is this affecting the minority shareholders such as JJ? How will any presentation of adverse consequences to minority shareholders be received by the board, which is most heavily represented by the majority shareholder?

Based on the information provided, you ponder as to what you can do to address the concerns of JJ and prepare for the board meeting. As a new, responsible professional, you also wonder what management control and other issues you should bring up at the board meeting that relate to matters of governance.

# 成本计算方法
## Costing Methodologies

# 德尔格公司:为生命的技术

*Paul Mulligan*
*Babson College*

*Alfred J. Nanni, Jr.*
*Babson College*

## 简介

德尔格医疗公司(Dräger Medical Systems, Inc.)[①] 的战略经营经理比尔·尼克森(Bill Nicholson)面临着一项艰巨的任务……也或许是一项很好的机遇?德尔格公司的管理层最近宣布了一项计划,即打算关闭在马萨诸塞州丹佛斯的生产部门;如果达到预期条件的话,再把原设在该地的病人监护仪的生产经营,迁移到该公司设在马萨诸塞州安多弗的监护仪和信息技术产品总部。在宣布这一决定时,管理层注意到如果把研发业务和生产营运设在同一个地点会有许多好处。比尔也知道,公司的管理层期望,在支付合并所花费的成本之后,这一合并措施能带来显著的成本节约。成本的节约、两种业务设在同一地点的好处,这都是好消息……然而挑战何在呢?

首先,丹佛斯生产设施的场地面积为 33 000 平方英尺,而安多弗的可用面积约为 18 000 平方英尺。虽然面积有所减少,管理层仍然明确要求,迁入新厂后,必须维持在丹佛斯的生产场地的产量。事实上,管理层还期望,如果市场需求增加,新的设施可有更高的产量。比尔不禁自言自语地道出了他内心的疑虑:"现在我们已经在很高的利用率水平上运行了。整个系统并没有任何闲置。而我们在丹佛斯没有多余的面积。我们怎么能够把整个生产系统迁移到一个面积少 45% 的新址,而又维持甚至增加我们的生产能力呢?当然,如果我们能够做到,我们可能成为德尔格公司内其他附属机构业务流程再造的典范。"

---

\* 本篇译者为杨继良,校订者为胡金凤、赵澄。
本文作者对德尔格公司战略经营经理比尔·尼克森和德尔格公司生产工程经理马赫什·罗文达为本案例编写所给予的合作和支持,深表谢意。

[①] 德尔格公司在中国设有分公司,例如上海的上海德尔格医疗器械有限公司。本案例用的公司译名据此。——译者

## 公司简况

德尔格公司的总部在德国的吕贝克[2]，在医疗和防护技术方面处于国际领先地位。德尔格公司成立于1889年，到现在已是家族的第五代在经营企业了。据该公司网站[3]所述，公司取得长期的成功归功于它一贯信守自己的承诺——"价值导向的公司文化具备四大核心力量：与顾客的密切合作、员工的专长、不断的创新和卓越的质量。为生命开发技术是我们的指导原则和使命。凡公司所开发的（包括临床设施、工业和采矿或急救服务等）产品都旨在保护、支持和救护生命。"

德尔格公司两个主要的经营单位[4]，分别经营安全产品和医疗产品。安全产品分部向客户提供整套的事故管理设施，专注于人身安全和预防的生产设施。当前产品中包括固定的和移动性的气体检测系统、呼吸保护、消防设备、专业潜水设备、酒精和各种毒品检测仪器。

医疗产品分部的产品系列包括麻醉工作站、供医院重病特别护理和家用的通风设备、可移动的紧急通风设备、婴儿保暖治疗设备、病人监护设备以及临床应用的信息技术和软件。德尔格公司越来越多的客户选择购买整套的综合设施，而非单独购置各项设备。因此，德尔格公司应把当前生产的监护仪，看作为一组产品中的一个组成部分，而非看作为一项单独的设备。这一把重点放在综合设施上的做法，提高了德尔格公司的临床信息技术和软件产品的重要性。过去，各项监护仪通常只反映护理的病人的某一项信息。而今天的许多监护仪能同时追踪病人多种情况、综合显示病人各方面的信息。

## 社会责任和环境保护

德尔格公司管理层强调，所有的员工都必须担负起保护生命的责任，指出"当人们选用我们的产品，那就是信任我们，并把他们价值最高的财产——即生命交付给我们。这就是为什么我们所涉及的问题，远远超过我们公司的场地范围，影响涉及我们的客户、员工、投资者和整个社会。"

德尔格公司的战略是鼓励在设计的过程中谨记可持续发展，并以节约使用各项资源为目标。1998年以来，在吕贝克市的公司的所有经营活动都已获得了 DIN EN ISO 14001[5] 的认证，这项认证是团体认证的一部分。这一

---

[2] 德国北部港口城市。——译者

[3] www.draeger.com——原注

[4] business unit，经营单位；指一个组织机构的任何部分，或未分成各个部分的整个企业实体。有时视为一个利润中心（引自美国管理会计师协会所编《CMA考试所用词汇的专业词典》）。——译者

[5] ISO 14000所规定的标准可对不满足于单纯按法规办事的经理人员提供一定的帮助——这一标准可以视为经营企业的一项成本。该标准适宜于有远见的经理人员，他们理解实施这一项战略方针可为环保措施方面的投资带来回报（资料来源：ISO网址）。——原注

认证未来将适用于德尔格公司全部分公司。该公司把相当一部分注意力集中于防止浪费和回收利用、减少水的消耗、重塑生产线等方面，以满足较高的环境标准。此外，公司时常开展旨在降低二氧化碳排放的项目。这些项目包括：

- 建造一座热电站：德尔格公司在吕贝克建造了一座以煤气为动力的热电站。这座工厂于 2008 年投产，采用最新式的把发热和发电结合起来的技术，生产电力的同时产生热能，这可减少能源损耗和二氧化碳的排放。
- 实施可以重复利用的包装系统：德尔格公司已经采用"通勤者"⑥包装系统多年。这种环保的、可以再次利用的包装方法，在供应商、生产、物流以及客户之间往返流通使用，能够帮助德尔格公司避免大量木材和硬纸板的浪费。这也使员工减少暴露在灰尘之中，通过人体工程学设计保护他们的健康，并且其生命周期长因而降低了包装和装卸成本。
- 活性炭生产：在涉及化学制品时，德尔格公司的活性炭生产设施在帮助减少废气排放、确保有效的防爆以及达到高安全标准方面起到重要的作用。通过有效地清除充满尘埃的烟道气体、最先进的烟道气体洗涤器、气体测量和控制的综合技术以及各种高性能的过滤器，确保生产设施能适应环境和自动防止故障地运转。

图表 1 归纳了德尔格公司在实施可持续发展方面所做努力的成果。

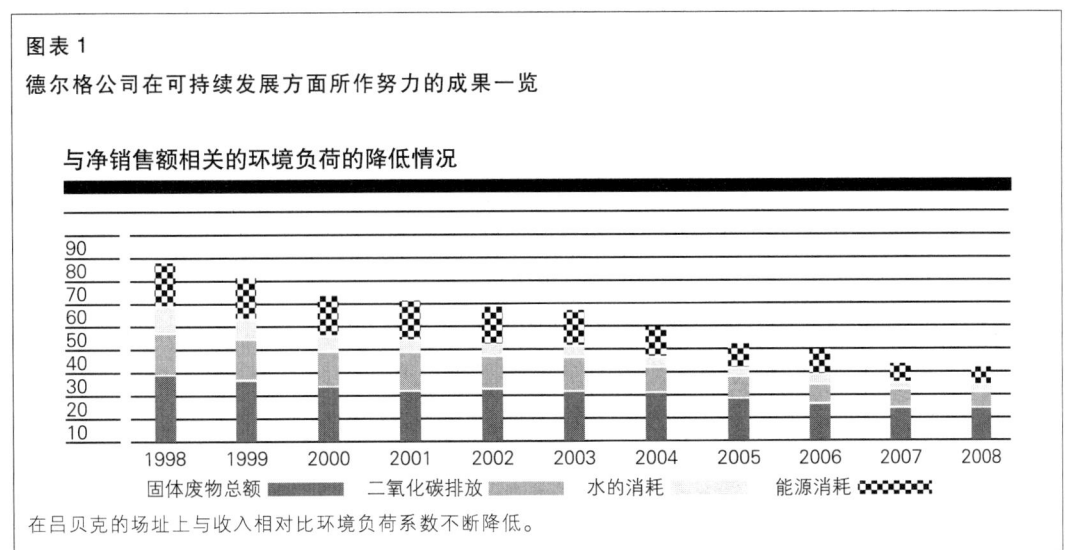

图表 1
德尔格公司在可持续发展方面所作努力的成果一览

与净销售额相关的环境负荷的降低情况

固体废物总额　　二氧化碳排放　　水的消耗　　能源消耗

在吕贝克的场址上与收入相对比环境负荷系数不断降低。

---

⑥ "Commuter" 直译为通勤者，指从家中往返工作地点的人。这里比喻外部包装像通勤者一样，往返于供应商、生产、物流以及客户之间。——译者

## 挑战……还是机遇

2003 年当德尔格公司与"西门子医疗系统"集团⑦组成合资企业时,丹佛斯厂成为了德尔格公司的经营基地之一。在组成合资企业时,德尔格公司的管理层考虑关闭丹佛斯厂,并把监护仪的生产迁移到德尔格公司在宾州泰尔福特区(Telford, PA)现有的机构中去,或者把这部分生产外包给亚洲的第三方去做。当时,公司管理层选择了把监护仪的生产移往丹佛斯厂的方案。这样做的理由之一是,在生产差异产品(系列产品)时,产品的整合与软件的整合成为生产中越来越重要的因素。这一决策——迁移到丹佛斯镇生产监护仪——还可使德尔格公司的生产邻近(~20 英里)它在马萨诸塞州安多弗镇的办事处。安多弗厂有研究与开发、生产管理、营销和软件工程人员,包括监护仪在内的许多产品正是由这些员工负责。安多弗厂也设计和开发在丹佛斯生产分部中使用的监护仪测试工作站。

丹佛斯的工作人员觉得,公司管理层对他们的工厂常有前景渺茫之感,工作人员间也笼罩着工厂寿命不可预测的气氛。2007 年一位新的营运主管夫瑞克(Fehrecke)博士就任,再一次把重点放在生产和产品设计的有效性和效率上。夫瑞克访问了丹佛斯工厂,并指定由管理层组成一个工作小组来研究各种迁移方案。夫瑞克博士宣称,留在丹佛斯并不可取。丹佛斯的设施租约即将到期,德尔格公司的管理层并不想要继续租用这些外部的过时的设施。从目前经营情况来看,丹佛斯并未体现公司所主张的生产效率高、机构精简的经营理念。经营的现状反映了 20 世纪 90 年代后期该行业产能利用的普遍情况,而不是德尔格公司世界各地的工厂所追求的最先进的生产经营。因此,毫无疑问,这一任务组的责任是要确保,它所提出的建议必须在流程的产能和经营的绩效方面有显著的进步。衡量新设施的一项重要标准在于,它必须少投入、多产出。迁离丹佛斯是解决这一问题的途径之一。从图表 2 和图表 3,可以分别看到丹佛斯厂的场地分配和布局的概略情况。

主要的备选方案有三。在 2003 年,本可以把监护仪的生产迁去泰尔福,或外包给亚洲地区。不过,这两个方案都会导致生产、工艺工程师、IT 集成者和产品工程师这几者之间具有战略重要性的沟通变得困难。如果可行并且经济合理,显然应该把这些职能设置在同一个地点。方案三,把监护仪的生产迁往安多弗,这也可以使三个职能设置在同一个地点。开始的时候,并不明确这种做法是否可行;即使可行,其结果是否能令人满意地降低营业总成本,亦尚不可知。

---

⑦ Siemens Medical Solutions 的直译。这是成立于 1877 年的一家德国的家庭所有的小企业,于 2000 年并入西门子公司,2001 年改成此名,在 2008 年再次重组时改名为"西门子医疗保健"(Siemens Healthcare)。——译者

**图表 2**
**当前丹佛斯市厂的面积分配情况**

| 接收 | 1 521 平方英尺 |
|---|---|
| 原材料操作 | 1 222 平方英尺 |
| 1 号库房 | 511 平方英尺 |
| 2 号库房 | 7 977 平方英尺 |
| 3 号库房 | 2 456 平方英尺 |
| 包装 | 1 491 平方英尺 |
| 发运 | 2 773 平方英尺 |
| 生产区 1 | 832 平方英尺 |
| 生产区 2 | 1 152 平方英尺 |
| 生产区 3 | 1 100 平方英尺 |
| 生产区 4 | 589 平方英尺 |
| 生产区 5 | 721 平方英尺 |
| 生产区 6 | 931 平方英尺 |
| 返工和修理 | 1 237 平方英尺 |
| 第 2 道返工和修理 | 540 平方英尺 |
| 检测实验室 | 547 平方英尺 |
| 校正实验室 | 225 平方英尺 |
| 办公室 | 2 178 平方英尺 |
| 通道 | 5 249 平方英尺 |
| **总面积** | **33 252 平方英尺** |

**图表 3**
**丹佛斯厂目前的布局图（约 33 000 平方英尺）**

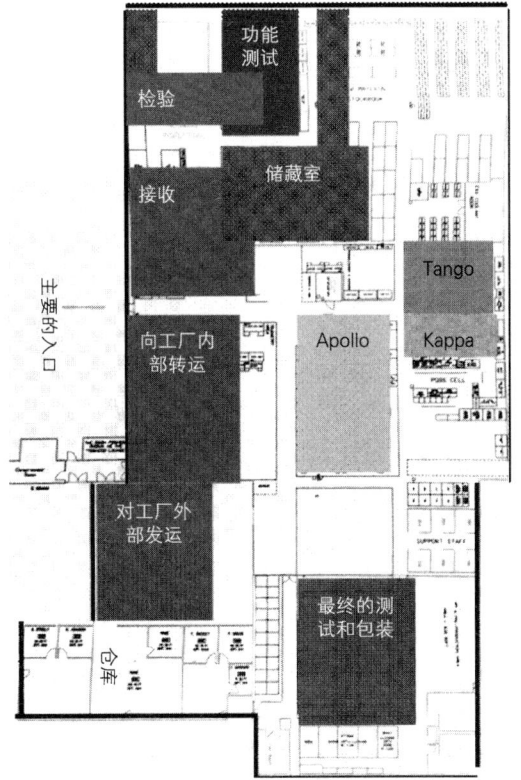

德尔格公司的安多弗厂尚有闲置的场地。德尔格公司曾考虑将闲置场地出租，但又随即否决了这项意见，因为公司希望严密控制将迁入该闲置场地的经营品种。邻近的一家企业（非德尔格公司的）排放出的化学品，引起公司格外关注这个问题。德尔格公司希望控制将设在安多弗的企业经营何种行业，但把场地分租出去会剥夺它对此的控制能力。过去，公司管理层从未考虑过把丹佛斯的经营迁移到此地是一项可行的方案，因为安多弗闲置场地的面积比丹佛斯现在的经营场地小得多（只有 45%）。工作小组决定重新审查这一方案，因为公司致力于一项新的名为 PRIME 的改进流程的项目，通过该项目流程得到了改进。PRIME（Production Improvement and Manufacturing Excellence，生产进步和制造卓越）是一项较新的创议，重点在于流程创新和采用精益管理的概念。工作小组的成员们认为，通过采用 PRIME 的各项原则可以显著减少需要的场地面积，因而使迁往安多弗的方案成为可行。

工作小组与一个第三方的咨询事务所合作，完成了对德尔格公司经营情况的详细评估。他们的研究指出，流程中的多处有待改进。监护仪的组装和测试多数（然而不是全部）都是单项作业——也就是说，虽然同时在流水线上移动的一批工件数量比较大（达 60 件），但每一个工人在一个时间内只对一件工作对象进行操作。这就意味着，对有 60 个工件的订单在一道生产步骤上要全部完成，才能移送到下一道工作站。工作小组和咨询事务所认为，这一情况与精益生产的原则相悖，并认为应该改用更加准时的适时生产（Just in Time，JIT）。在流动的生产线上应采用单一工件生产的原则，这才能节约经营场地，把闲置的场地充分利用起来。于是，工作小组设计了一种流程，使监护仪能够一个、一个地在生产线上向前移动，从而消除因 60 个单位的生产批量所需要额外占用的场地面积。

工作小组明白，要重新布置生产过程，必须在不打乱现有的监护仪供应链的前提下进行。监护仪的供应链相对比较简单，工作小组相信，把它迁往安多弗生产不会对此产生重大影响。目前，丹佛斯工厂的原材料和零部件来源于多处。其中有些供应商已经把产品运往安多弗了。就向外运送产品而言，丹佛斯厂每天都向外运送产成品。丹佛斯厂并不直接把产成品运送给客户。在丹佛斯生产的监护仪，首先运送到在德国吕贝克的德尔格公司的总厂。在吕贝克的工厂中，最终需要使产品到达客户定制的要求，并作整体测试。客户定制的要求包括贴上标签、软件集成、按 22 种不同的语言配置说明书、配齐各种配件、并作最后的包装。整体的测试包括对监护仪系统和附加在发运给最终消费者的产品上的德尔格公司其他产品的测试。德尔格公司的美国市场份额相对较小，在丹佛斯生产的监护仪中，大约 80% 最终运给美国境外的客户。因此，把监护仪运往德国，并未引起过多额外的或不必要的运送费用。德尔格公司希望在近期扩大其在美国的市场份额，并考虑将来把满足客户定制的工作、整体测试、附件的配套、发运产品等工作都迁往安多弗的工厂。这项变化，只包括为北美（美国和加拿大）市场所生产的监护仪。德尔格公司会继续把非北美客户所定购的全部监护仪都运往吕贝克完成最后的步骤,然后向客户发货。

## 现行的和建议的操作系统设计

德尔格公司丹佛斯厂实行一班制生产,每周工作五天。德尔格公司遵守公司的作息标准——生产的工作日为 7：30—4：30,午休一小时(不带薪),另外有两次各 15 分钟(带薪)的休息时间。公司现在不允许加班,也不打算实施两班制生产。对加班和两班制生产的限制规定,符合公司管理层在全球范围内实施的经营政策,并且不允许违反。每年的工作日是 250 天,但全体员工都享受全年的工资,包括 10 天的带薪假期,即每年按 260 个工作日计酬。

丹佛斯工厂生产多种型号的监护仪,每一种型号构成一个产品系列。这些型号包括 Tango、Kappa 和 M300[⑧]。Apollo 系列产品是丹佛斯厂生产的产量较高的产品。尼克森认为,Apollo 系列的生产系统代表了丹佛斯厂总的生产。Apollo 这一系列产品包括 Apollo Delta(见图表 4)和 Apollo Delta XL(见图表 4a)两个型号。因而,工作小组一开始就把注意力集中于对 Apollo 生产线的流程进行评估、重新设计和新流程的 Beta 测试。图表 5 对 Apollo 监护仪的七道生产工序进行了详细的说明。(图表 6 是现有流程的布局情况。)目前,对 Apollo 系列的监护仪(Delta 和 Delta XL)的需求平均每天为 64 台,德尔格公司并未储有大量产成品存货。因此,在 2008 年时,Apollo 系列产品的生产计划就定为每天 64 台。德尔格公司预期短期内不会有重大变化,因而 2009 年也就打算维持每天 64 台的数量。

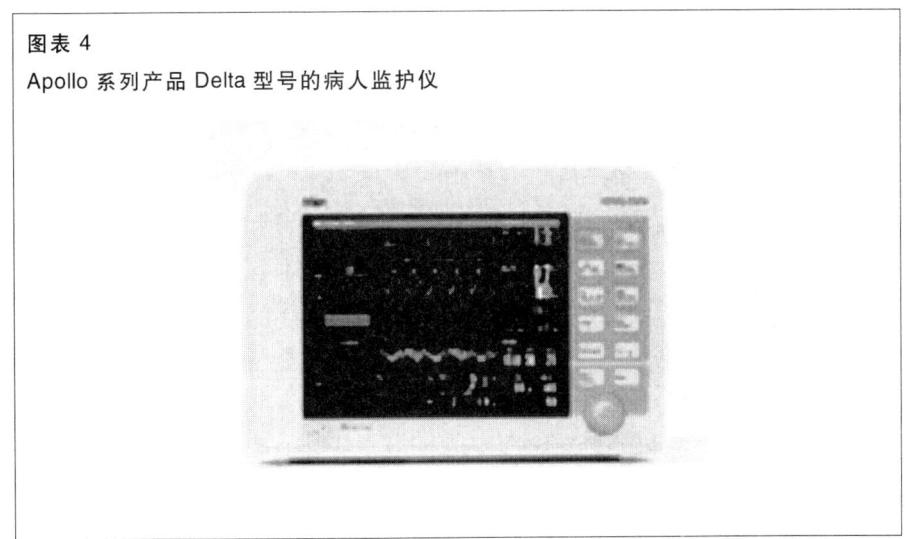

**图表 4**
Apollo 系列产品 Delta 型号的病人监护仪

---

⑧ Apollo 和 Tango 都是公司内部对某些系列产品的称呼。例如 Apollo 系列产品包括以 Delta、Delta XL、Vista XL 命名出售的各种监护仪。——原注

**图表 4a**
Apollo 系列产品 Delta XL 型号的病人监护仪

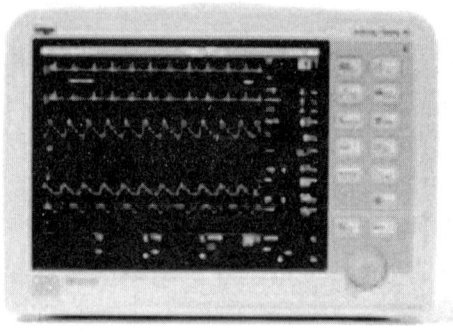

**图表 5**
**丹佛斯厂的流程说明\***

1. **监护仪组装**：这一道工序是把关键性零部件装入监护仪的外壳。这道工序关键在于准确地把各项零部件装入监护仪的适当位置，以使监护仪的显示板达到期望的亮度（明亮度）。Apollo 监护仪有两种不同的构造，在这道工序上所需的操作时间不同。占需求量 55% 的标准型监护仪（即 Delta 型号的产品）在这一道工序上每件产品的准备时间为 4 分钟，操作时间为 6 分钟。需求量占其余 45%、新型的"Delta XL"型号监护仪，每台的准备时间为 5 分钟，操作时间为 10 分钟。这一道工序共有独立操作的工人两名和机器两台。产品按需求流转，因而两个工人都以 55% 的时间处理 Delta 型监护仪，另 45% 的时间处理 Delta XL 型监护仪。

2. **初次环境测试（室温下的初次测试）\*\*** 室温下的初次测试是对组装的监护仪及其装配零部件在室温下所作的长时间的测试。工人以六台监护仪为一批进行测试。每台监护仪需要花费八分钟的时间为测试做准备（把零部件与测试设备连接起来）。将六台监护仪都与测试设备连接好以后，需要 240 分钟进行室温下的（运转）测试。共有十个测试工作站，每个工作站能够同时测试六台监护仪，在这一道工序上有两名工人（各自独立操作）。该工序上需要人工的只有准备工作而已。一旦准备就绪，进行测试时就不再需要工人（人工）了。在一项测试完成时，测试设备会自动关闭。因此，你可以假设工人们整天只是做准备和启动测试的工作。（换言之，没有必要人工结束初测，工人在启动测试后就可以于下午 4：30 工作日结束时离开。）

3. **环境复原**：环境复原是在环境测试终了时进行，需花费 1 分 48 秒。这项工作包括切断监护仪与测试工作站之间的连接，并把监护仪移到货架上去。当货架装满（60 台监护仪）时，工人就把货架移往下一道生产工序。上述 1 分 48 秒是每台监护仪所花费的时间，因为工人切断监护仪的全套零部件与测试设备的连接并将其移送是逐台进行的。该工序配备了一名工人，不需要机器。

4. **前端参数测试**：前端平行连接工序需要 10.5 分钟的操作时间。在这道工序有两名工人和两台机器，均独立操作。

5. **贴标签和最终的组装**：在贴标签和最终组装工序配有一名工人和一台机器。每台监护仪在贴标签和最终组装上需要花费五分钟的操作时间。

6. **最终检验**：最终检验工序需要 1 分钟的准备时间和 3.3 分钟操作时间。在这道工序一名工人和一台机器。

7. **包装**：包装的操作时间需要两分钟。包装包括把监护仪装箱，并把它置于供装船用的货板上，运往吕贝克。这道工序有一名工人和一台机器。

\* 原注：因竞争和保密的需要，生产步骤、操作时间和资源分配的情况都作了伪饰，但仍反映了德尔格公司的实际情况。

\*\* initial ambient test，这第一项测试是在室温下进行的。电子器皿在运行时往往会提高温度，这一项测试的目的是确定在室温下监护仪是否会因温度升得过高而不能正常运转，其目的是要找出制造过程中造成的、在若干小时的运转中可能暴露出来的缺陷。直译为"最初环境测试"其含义为"室温下的初次测试"。——译者

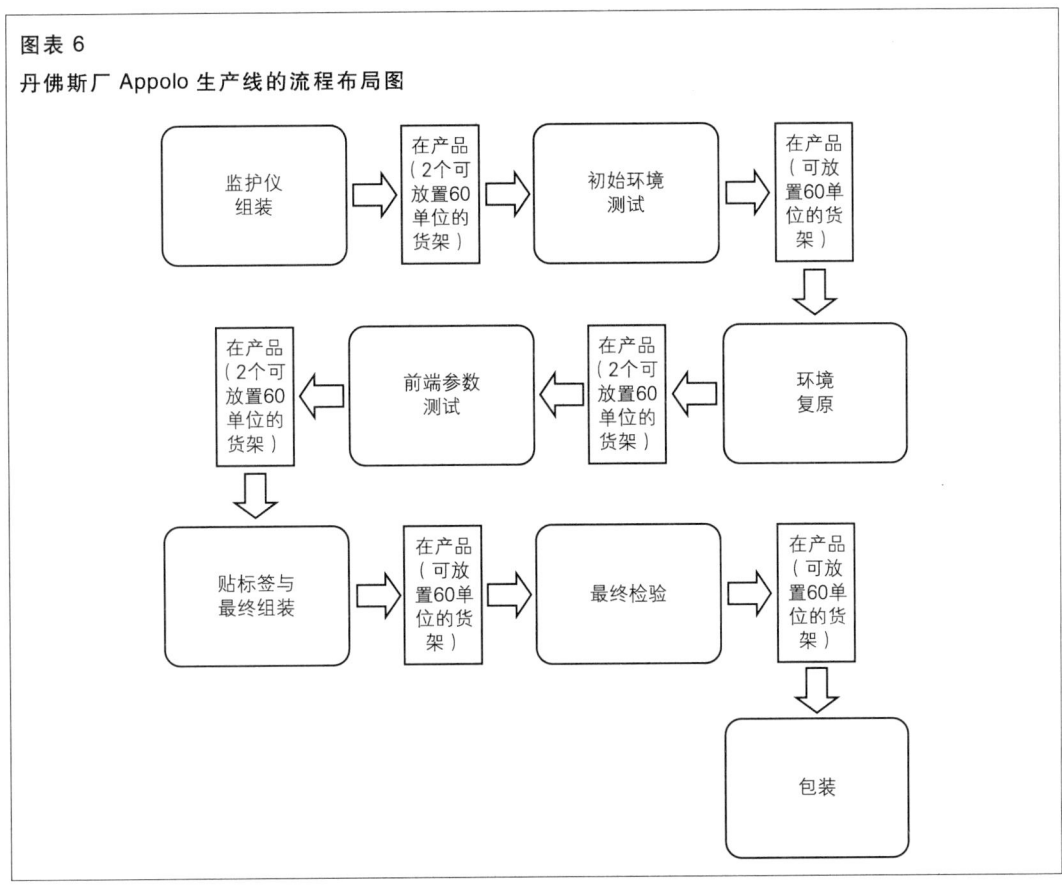

图表 6
丹佛斯厂 Appolo 生产线的流程布局图

图表 7 列示了建议的安多弗厂生产流程六道工序的设计。丹佛斯现有的工作时间制和不得加班、不得开第二班的限制，也将在安多弗的经营中实施。德尔格公司的管理层预期，在 2010 年及以后的年份，对包括 Apollo 系列在内的所有的监护仪的需求将会有所增加。在美国的市场份额的提高也会增加需求，这就要求安多弗厂在未来有更高的产量。吕贝克的管理层也对 2008 年丹佛斯工厂的订单周转时间表示担心。寄往丹佛斯的订单常常在订单下达之后的 8～10 天才送达吕贝克。这一拖延看来毫无道理，因为丹佛斯是每天都（以隔夜航空送达服务）发运所有的产成品的。工作小组面对的关键性流程设计问题是简单直接的：我们能不能在一个只及现有设施面积 45% 的场地上维持或提高监护仪的产量，并缩短我们的生产周转时间？而要回答这个问题，就不是那么简单、也不是那么简单直接了。

> **图表 7**
> **安多弗厂的流程说明\***
>
> 1. **生产准备**：新的流程始于把各项零部件从接收区直接送到生产线上，准备生产。这包括把监护仪所有的零部件事先都集中起来、各就其位，准备组装。担任这项工作的工人有一名，不需要机器。完成这道工序的操作时间为 4.9 分钟。
> 2. **监护仪组装**：在新的流程和设备下，工人可以在四分钟内完成把零部件装入监护仪外壳的准备工作，六分钟的时间完成操作。各种型号的监护仪在这道工序上的准备和操作时间相同——不同型号的监护仪（即 Delta 型号和 Delta XL 型号）的操作时间不再有所区别。在这道工序上，有两名工人和两台机器，均独立操作。
> 3. **环境测试**：在新的流程下，环境测试有 50 个单个的测试连接点，每一个连接点可测试一台监护仪。在这道工序只有一名工人，他负责把零部件准备好以供测试（3.5 分钟）；在测试结束时，切断零部件的连接点（1 分钟），以便转送到下一道生产工序（工序#4）\*\*。环境测试需要花费 240 分钟——其操作时间与丹佛斯厂的流程相同。和丹佛斯厂的情况一样，在这个长达 240 分钟的运作时间中不需要有操作工人，完成测试时机器会自动关闭。因此整个工作日内，有一名工人就能够启动全天所有的检验。
> 4. **初始化和前端参数测试**：这一道工序结合了初始化和前端（FE）的平行连接，初始化是对零部件的最终测试。操作时间为 10.1 分钟。这道工序有两名工人和两台机器，均独立操作。
> 5. **贴标签和最终组装**：贴标签和最终组装需要 5.1 分钟的操作时间。这道工序有一名工人和一台机器。
> 6. **最终检验和包装**：每台监护仪在最终检验和包装工序中需要 4.8 分钟。检验只是对监护仪（外表）作一目测；包装包括把监护仪装箱，并把它置于供装船的货板上，运往吕贝克。这道工序有一名工人和一台机器。
>
> \* 原注：因竞争和保密的需要，生产步骤、操作时间和资源分配的情况都作了伪饰，但仍反映了德尔格公司的实际情况。
>
> \*\* 原文此处为"工序#3"，大约是打印错误，在翻译时改为"工序#4"。——译者

## 评估迁址的财务效益[9]

从概念上讲，迁往安多弗是极好的方案；但同时也还有其他选择。例如，可将全部组装工作外包。最终，关于监护仪的生产的决定还是要取决于各方案的盈利性。迁往安多弗是否会提高财务业绩？当然，这一迁移需要一些投资，引起一些搬迁费用。搬迁之后可带来的成本节约，必须足以较快地偿付这笔费用。

从根本上来说，在丹佛斯的组装工厂的任务是按需要的数量生产出高质量的产品，并对成本进行管理。然而，德尔格医疗公司的管理层还希望每一家工厂都充分利用其资产。因此，丹佛斯工厂是被看作为一个投资中心。公司的管理层对每一种型号的监护仪制定具体的转移价格。将按转移价格算出的收入减去当年的营业费用，可算出该工厂的毛利。从工厂毛利中减去资本费用，得出"工厂经济利润"。资本成本率乘以工厂固定资产和存货的总额，可得资本费用；因为只有这些（固定资产和存货）才是工厂经理可控制的资产（除存货以外的流动资产和负债由公司总部管理）。对减去资本费用后的销售回报率设定 12% 为目标。其据以作出如此两重考核，显然出于

---

[9] 为了保密以及提高教学效果起见，已对本节的某些细节作了修饰。——原注

以下的理由：

工厂所有的费用最终都成为我们产品的制造成本。因此，工厂的所有成本都会计入产成品的存货价值，然后转入销货成本。工厂需要获得利润来抵偿其本身的投资，然后还要致力于抵付整个公司的行政费用。12%的经济贡献额，是制造核心仪器所创造的基本价值。在吕贝克，德尔格根据客户要求对产品进行设置、安装软件和搭配附件，这些为最终发运出去的产品额外增添了价值。

图表8列示了丹佛斯2008年的营业业绩。

**图表 8**
**丹佛斯组装经营单位的利润表** *

| | | |
|---|---:|---:|
| 销售收入 | $ 37 540 000 | 100% |
| 减变动成本： | | |
| 直接材料 | $ 27 302 000 | 73% |
| 变动制造间接费用 | 357 000 | 1% |
| 变动的辅助与物流间接费用 | 4 925 | 0% |
| 贡献毛益 | $ 9 876 075 | 26% |
| 减固定成本： | | |
| 组装人工 | 1 872 000 | |
| 辅助与物流人工 | 1 144 000 | |
| 工厂管理费用 | 480 000 | |
| 占用费用 | 928 000 | |
| 折旧——组装所用设备 | 456 000 | |
| 折旧——家具与固定装置 | 259 800 | |
| 折旧——管理用资产 | 4 800 | |
| | $ 5 144 600 | 14% |
| 厂毛利 | $ 4 731 475 | 13% |
| 资本费用（资本成本 = 10%） | $ 1 805 600 | |
| 工厂经济利润 | $ 2 925 875 | 8% |

*注：为保密起见，图表8至图表10的数字均经伪饰；但仍代表德尔格公司的实际情况。——原注

2006年全年，丹佛斯厂的产品需求量比前一年以两位数的速度增加，但2007年比2006年的需求增长数量，却骤跌了5%。工厂的毛利也随之下降。这一结果可能由多项原因引起。总体的经济状况使得近年的需求缩减，因为各医院和其他医疗保健机构决定推迟新设备的购置。随着市场价格下降，2008年的需求量有所恢复，但工厂的毛利未见改善。市场价格下降，促使丹佛斯降低其转移价格，导致毛利减少。对丹佛斯厂的新安排，不仅必须适应价格下降的情况，并且如果工厂毛利对需求变化的敏感程度有所降低

的话，还会对工厂带来好处。

比尔·尼克森的 PRIME 工作小组对建议的迁移可能会带来的各种结果进行了一系列的考量。图表 9 列示了预期的员工人数的变化；图表 10 则为工作队的书面报告中与成本和节省有关的摘录。

**图表 9**
**PRIME 的规划对人数变化的估计**

|  | 丹佛斯的现状 | 对安多弗厂的预期 |
| --- | --- | --- |
| 装配工 | 30 | 24 |
| 辅助与物流人员 | 22 | 12 |
| 工厂管理部门 | 4 | 4 |
|  | 56 | 40 |

**图表 10**
**关于迁往安多弗潜在的成本和节约的报告书摘录**

有一部分与迁移有关的成本和节约是显而易见的。当然，迁移到安多弗会消除每年在丹佛斯所必须支付的租金 $400 000。丹佛斯厂的维护、取暖、空调和保安费用也必因迁移而省下了。如果组装工作能够在安多弗现有的场地上顺利进行，则安多弗厂现有的占用成本会有一部分分配给监护仪。根据被占用的面积，我们估计安多弗的组装成本会减少了 $499 000，即分配出去的一部分占用成本。

为使安多弗厂能够容纳组装工序，必须进行一些投资（包括设备的改装）。主要的费用是安装新的环境测试系统。整套系统包括一个服务器和 50 个测试站，其建造和安装成本为 $600 000。到 2008 年年底时，老的测试机器都已足额提取折旧并以净残值售出，不会产生废弃损益。我们估计这些系统的经济寿命为 10 年。目前在丹佛斯厂的家具和固定装置中，约有半数还可以迁移到安多弗的新厂继续使用。其他的固定装置属于对建筑物的装修，是不可迁移的。那一部分固定资产必须销账；好在到 2008 年年底时，资产都已足额提取折旧了。我们必须花费 $100 000 于丹佛斯厂的新家具和固定装置，为迁入组装工序准备。按公司政策，在租赁资产上所作的装修应在 10 年内折旧完毕。我们可以把所有行政和管理用的资产（主要是办公桌、电脑和其他办公家具）迁往新址。这些都是新近添置的，因而每年所提取的折旧费将保持不变。

我们计划把迁移的物流工作在三天的周末休假*内完成。这就不会损失生产时间。不过，这还是需要几个周末的时间来做好准备工作。因迁移而发生的现金支付额约为 $157 000。

这一迁移将节省在安多弗的开支。可以立即见效的是不再需要在安多弗和丹佛斯之间来回接送工程师、搬运零部件和设备了。我们估计每年可因此节省的现金支付额和工程师损失的时间，价值共计 $300 000。其中现金支付额包括通勤面包车驾驶员的工资（满负荷的年薪为 $35 000），以及面包车的租金、维修和运行成本。这些费用每年总共为 $10 000。安多弗厂的另一节约来自计入现有业务的场地占用成本将有一部分分配给组装工序。在本报告书前面已经详细说明，这部分重新分配给组装工序的成本估计每年为 $499 000。

\* 周末只有两天假，美国往往把节日调到星期一或星期五，形成一个"长周末（long weekend）"，这个情况和我们相似。——译者

# Dräger Medical Systems, Inc. : Technology for Life

*Paul Mulligan*
*Babson College*

*Alfred J. Nanni, Jr.*
*Babson College*

## INTRODUCTION

Bill Nicholson, Strategic Operations Manager for Dräger Medical Systems, Inc., faced a daunting task...or was it a great opportunity? Dräger management recently announced plans to close the company's Danvers, MA, production facility and move the patient monitoring production operations currently in Danvers to its Monitoring and IT Product headquarters in Andover, MA, if possible while meeting desired criteria. In announcing this decision, management noted the many benefits associated with co-location of R&D and production operations. Bill also knew that management anticipated significant cost savings after absorbing the consolidation costs. Cost savings, co-location benefits, all good news...so where was the challenge?

For starters, the Danvers site was a 33 000 sq. ft. production facility and Andover had approximately 18 000 sq. ft. of available space. Despite the reduction in space, management also made it clear that the new facility must be capable of producing the same output volume as the Danvers production site. In fact, management also anticipated that the new facility would be positioned to meet higher production volumes if market demand grew. Bill wondered aloud, *"We're operating at a high utilization level today. There's simply no slack in the system. And, we have no extra space here in Danvers. How can we move the entire production system to a facility with 45% less space and maintain or expand our capacity? Of course, if we can do this, we could serve as a model for operating system design and redesign for other Dräger facilities."*

---

\* *The authors are grateful to Drager Strategic Operations Manager Bill Nicholson and Drager's Manager of Production Engineering, Mahesh Lawande, for their cooperation and assistance in the preparation of this case.*

## COMPANY PROFILE

Dräger, headquartered in Lübeck Germany, is an international leader in medical and safety technology. Founded in 1889, Dräger is now a fifth generation family-run business. The Dräger website[①] attributes the organization's long-term success to an ongoing commitment to "a value-oriented corporate culture with four central strengths: close collaboration with our customers, the expertise of our employees, continuous innovation and outstanding quality. Technology for Life is our guiding principle and our mission. Wherever they are deployed-in clinical settings, industry, mining or emergency services-Dräger products protect, support and save lives."

Dräger's two main business units are safety products and medical products. The Safety Division provides its customers with complete hazard management solutions with a special focus on personal safety and protecting production facilities. The current product portfolio includes stationary and mobile gas detection systems, respiratory protection, firefighting equipment, professional diving gear, and alcohol and drug-testing instruments.

The Medical Division's product suite encompasses anesthesia workstations, ventilation equipment for both hospital-based intensive care and home care, emergency and mobile ventilation units, warming therapy equipment for infants, patient monitoring equipment, and clinical IT and software solutions. Dräger's customers are increasingly interested in purchasing integrated solutions as opposed to individual products; therefore, the monitors produced today in Danvers must be viewed as a component to a solution, rather than a discreet product. This focus on integrated solutions is also raising the importance of Dräger's clinical IT and software products. In the past, monitors typically captured and displayed information related to one aspect of patient care. Many of today's monitors assimilate data from multiple patient tracking devices and display an amalgam of synthesized patient information.

## SOCIAL RESPONSIBILITY AND ENVIRONMENTAL PROTECTION

Dräger management stresses that all employees carry the responsibility of protecting lives, noting that "*whenever our products are used, people entrust us with their most valued possession—their life. That's why we get involved in issues far beyond the boundaries of our company grounds—for our customers, our employees, our investors, and for society as a whole.*"

---

① www.draeger.com

Dräger's strategy encourages the design of processes with sustainability in mind and a goal to utilize all resources sparingly. Since 1998, all operations at the Lübeck site have been certified in accordance with DIN EN ISO 14001[②]as part of a group certification. In the future, this certification will be continuously extended to all Dräger subsidiaries. The company focuses considerable attention on waste prevention and recycling, reducing water consumption, and redesigning production lines to meet high environmental standards. In addition, the company regularly pursues projects dedicated to reducing carbon dioxide emissions. Examples of these projects include:

- Implementing a cogeneration power plant: Dräger developed a gas-powered cogeneration power plant in Lübeck. This plant entered service in 2008, generating electricity with the most modern combined heat and power generation technologies while simultaneously producing heat, which reduces energy consumption and carbon dioxide emissions.
- Implementing reusable packaging systems: Dräger has been using "commuter" packaging systems for many years. These environmentally friendly reusable packaging solutions "commute" between suppliers, production, logistics, as well as customers—helping Dräger to avoid large amounts of wood and cardboard waste. This also results in less exposure to dust, preserves the health of employees through ergonomic design and, due to its long life cycle, reduces both packaging and handling costs.
- Activated carbon production: Dräger's activated carbon production facilities play a major role in helping to reduce air emissions and guarantee effective explosion protection and high safety standards when dealing with chemicals. By effectively cleaning the dust-laden flue-gas, state-of-the-art flue gas scrubbers, integrated gas measuring and control technology, as well as numerous high performance filters, ensure environmentally compatible and fail-safe operations of production facilities.

See Exhibit 1 for summary results of Dräger's sustainability efforts.

---

[②] The ISO 14000 standards are practical tools for the manager who is not satisfied with mere compliance with legislation – which may be perceived as a cost of doing business. They are for the proactive manager with the vision to understand that implementing a strategic approach can bring return on investment in environment-related measures. Source: ISO Web site.

**Exhibit 1**
Summary Results of Dräger's Sustainability Efforts

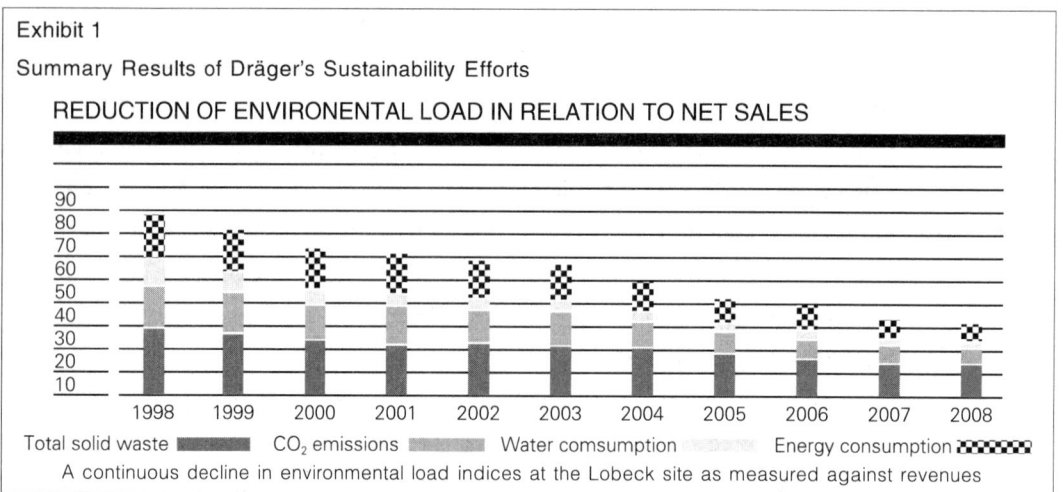

A continuous decline in environmental load indices at the Lobeck site as measured against revenues

# THE CHALLENGE...OR OPPORTUNITY

The Danvers facility became part of the Dräger operating infrastructure when the company entered into a joint venture with Siemens Medical Solutions in 2003. Upon entering this joint venture, Dräger management considered closing the Danvers facility and either moving monitor production to an existing Dräger facility in Telford, PA, or outsourcing production to a third party located in Asia. At the time, management opted to keep monitor production in the Danvers facility. One reason for this was that product integration and software integration were becoming increasingly important factors in creating differentiated products. The decision to keep production in Danvers allowed Dräger to maintain a production presence in close proximity (~20 miles) to its nearby Andover, MA, offices. The Andover facility housed research and development, product management, marketing, and software engineering personnel who were responsible for a variety of Dräger products, including monitors. Andover also designed and developed the monitor testing stations used in the Danvers production facility.

For the Danvers workforce, management's commitment to their facility always felt tenuous, and considerable uncertainty as to the longevity of the plant enveloped the workforce. The 2007 arrival of new operations chief, Dr. Fehrecke, marked a renewed focus on effectiveness and efficiency in both production and product design. Dr. Fehrecke visited the Danvers plant and directed management to form a task force to study relocation options. Dr. Fehrecke declared that remaining in Danvers was not an option. The lease on the Danvers facility was coming due for renewal and Dräger management did not want to extend the lease for extraneous, outdated facilities. As currently constituted, the Danvers operation did not reflect the corporate commitment to highly productive, lean operations. The current operations reflected the state of the capabilities prevalent in the industry during late 90s, not the state-of-the-art that Dräger strove to achieve throughout its global operating facilities. It was no surprise, therefore, that the charge for this task force also stipulated that proposed solutions must incorporate significant improvements in process capabilities and operational performance. An important criterion for the new operations facility was that it should be able to do more with less. Leaving Danvers was one way to force the issue. Space allocation and a high-level footprint for the Danvers facility can be found in Exhibit 2 and Exhibit 3 respectively.

Three primary alternatives were available. As in 2003, monitor production could have been relocated to Telford or outsourced to Asia. Both of those options, however, made the strategically important connection between production, process engineers, IT integrators, and product engineers difficult. Co-location of these functions was clearly the preferred alternative, if feasible and financially advantageous. The third option, moving the monitor production to Andover, would allow co-location. It was unclear at the outset whether this could be done, however, and, if so, whether satisfactory reductions in total operating costs would be realized as a result.

Dräger's Andover facility had available unused space. At one time, Dräger considered subletting this space but rejected the idea based on a desire to closely

Exhibit 2

current danvers Space Allocation (square feet)

| | | |
|---|---|---|
| Receiving | 1 521 | Sq. feet |
| Raw materials processing | 1 222 | Sq. feet |
| Stock room 1 | 511 | Sq. feet |
| Stock room 2 | 7 977 | Sq. feet |
| Stock room 3 | 2 456 | Sq. feet |
| Packing | 1 491 | Sq. feet |
| Shipping | 2 773 | Sq. feet |
| Production area 1 | 832 | Sq. feet |
| Production area 2 | 1 152 | Sq. feet |
| Production area 3 | 1 100 | Sq. feet |
| Production area 4 | 589 | Sq. feet |
| Production area 5 | 721 | Sq. feet |
| Production area 6 | 931 | Sq. feet |
| Rework and repair | 1 237 | Sq. feet |
| 2nd Rework and repair | 540 | Sq. feet |
| Test Lab | 547 | Sq. feet |
| Calibration Lab | 225 | Sq. feet |
| Ofices | 2 178 | Sq. feet |
| Aisles | 5 249 | Sq. feet |
| **TOTAL SQUARE FOOTAGE** | **33 252** | Sq. feet |

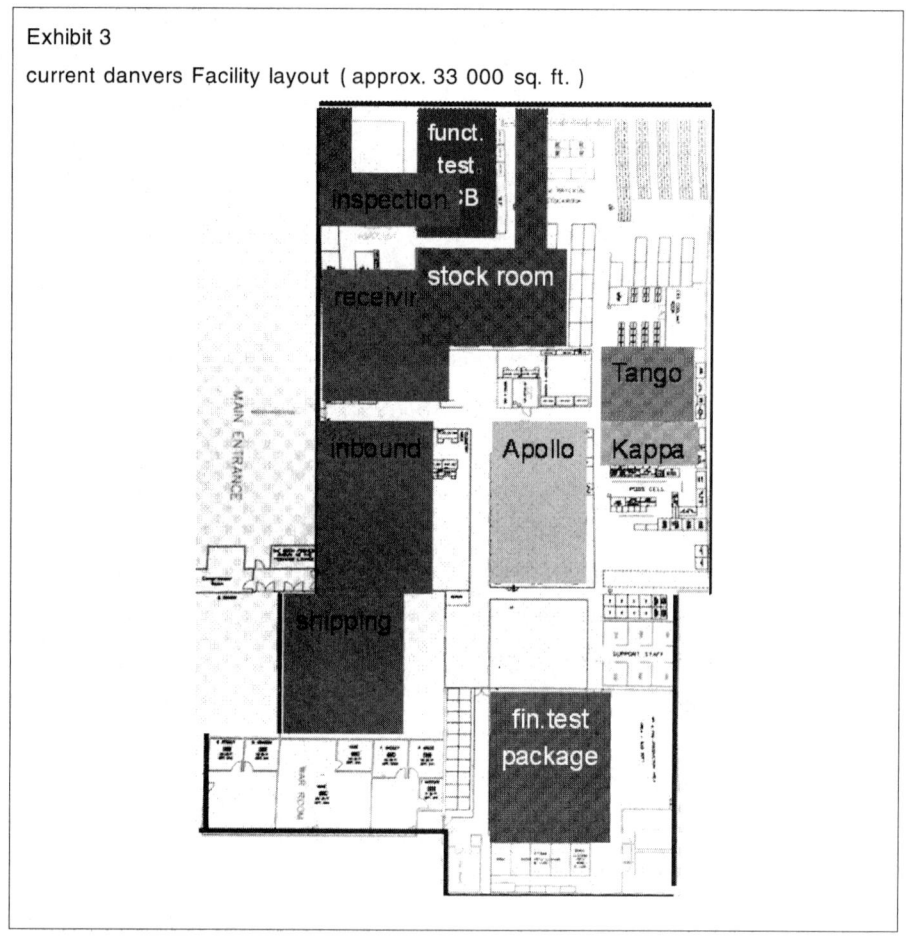

Exhibit 3
current danvers Facility layout ( approx. 33 000 sq. ft. )

control the type of operations that would fill the space. A chemical spill at a neighboring ( non-Dräger ) facility only heightened these concerns further. Dräger wanted to control the types of operations that would be present in Andover, and subletting the available space would strip the company of this control. In the past, management never considered moving the Danvers operation to this location to be a viable option because the space available was significantly smaller (45%) than the current Danvers operation. The task force opted to revisit this alternative, based upon their observation of process improvements created through the company's commitment to a new process improvement program entitled PRIME. PRIME ( Production Improvement and Manufacturing Excellence ) was a relatively new initiative focused on process innovation and the adoption of lean processing concepts. Task force members believed that improvement generated through the adoption of PRIME principles could include substantial reduction in space requirements, thus making relocation to Andover a viable option.

The task force, in collaboration with a third party consulting firm, completed a detailed assessment of the Danvers operation. Their analysis identified numerous opportunities for process improvement. Monitor assembly and testing was largely, though not entirely, a single unit operation – i. e. , each worker completing his/her task on one unit at a time. Yet the production units moved through the system in relatively large (60 - unit) production lots. This meant that each production step completed an order lot of 60 production units prior to moving that lot on to the next production station. The task force and the consulting partners observed this to be quite contrary to lean production principles and believed that transitioning to a more JIT (Just in Time) single-unit production philosophy for moving units through the system could generate a considerable portion of the space savings necessary to fit the operation into the available space. As a result, the task force designed a process that would eliminate the use of those 60 – unit production lots and allow monitors to flow through the system as individual units.

The task force knew that it was important to complete any process relocation without causing any disruption in the existing monitor supply chain. The monitor supply chain was relatively straightforward, and the task force believed that it would not be significantly impacted by a move to Andover. The Danvers plant currently received raw materials and components from a variety of sources. Several of these suppliers already shipped product to Andover. On the outbound side, Danvers shipped all finished product daily. Danvers did not ship finished goods directly to customers. Monitors produced in Danvers first went to Dräger's main facility in Lübeck, Germany. The Lübeck site performed final customization and integration testing. Final customization included labeling, software integration, documentation to support 22 different languages, consolidation with accessories, and final packaging. Integration testing involved system testing the monitors together with additional Dräger products that comprised the final, complete product shipment to end customers. Dräger's U. S. market share was relatively small, with approximately 80% of the monitors produced in Danvers ultimately shipped to customers outside of the U. S. , so sending monitors to Germany did not create significant excess or unnecessary shipping expenses. Dräger hoped to expand its U. S. presence and market share in the near future and may consider shifting customization, integrative testing, component kitting, and customer shipment responsibility to the Andover facility in the future. This shift would only apply to monitors destined for the North American (U. S. and Canada) market. Dräger would continue to ship all monitors ordered by non-North American customers to Lübeck for final processing and customer shipment.

## CURRENT AND PROPOSED OPERATING DESIGN

Dräger's Danvers facility operates one production shift that works five days per week. Dräger conforms to company standards that define work schedules-the production workday is 7: 30 – 4: 30 with a one-hour (unpaid) lunch break and two (paid) 15 – minute breaks. The company does not currently allow overtime and does not wish to implement a second production shift. These constraints on overtime and second shifts are consistent with corporate management's global operating policies and cannot be violated. There are 250 workdays per year, but all personnel are paid for a full year, including 10 paid holidays; therefore payment is computed for 260 days.

The Danvers plant produced multiple monitor types, each a product platform. These monitor types include Apollo, Tango, Kappa, and the M300.③ The Apollo platform is among the higher volume products produced in Danvers, and Nicholson believed that the Apollo production system was representative of the overall production environment at Danvers. Apollo is a product platform that includes the Apollo Delta (see Exhibit 4) and Apollo Delta XL (see Exhibit 4a) models. The task force therefore focused initial process assessment, redesign, and new process beta testing efforts on the Apollo line. Exhibit 5 contains a detailed description of the seven-step production process for Apollo monitors. (Exhibit 6 presents a process flow for the current process) Current demand for all Apollo monitors (Delta and Delta XL) averages 64 units per day, and Dräger does not store any significant finished goods inventory. Therefore, the production rate for the Apollo product was set at 64 units per day in 2008. Dräger did not anticipate significant short-term change in Apollo demand and planned to maintain the production rate at 64 units per day in 2009.

Exhibit 4
Apollo Platform delta Model Patient Monitor

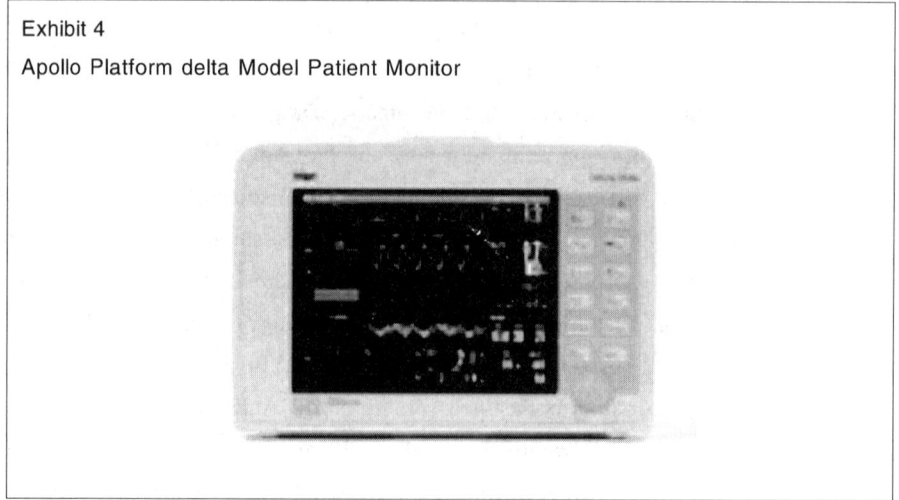

---

③ Apollo and Tango are internal references to a family of products. For example, the Apollo family includes the monitors sold under the product name Delta, Delta XL, and Vista XL.

### Exhibit 4a
### Apollo Platform delta XL Model Patient Monitor

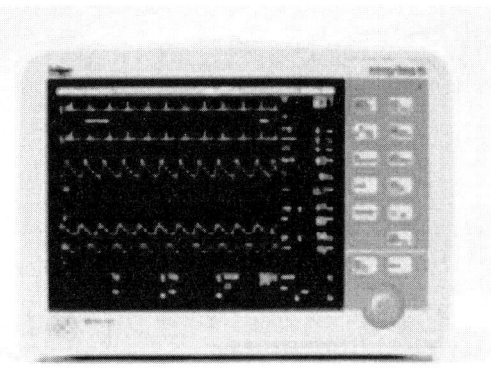

### Exhibit 5
### Process Description for Danvers Facility[5]

1. **Monitor assembly:** This step fits critical components into the housing of the monitor. It is critical to properly align components in the monitor in order to achieve the desired luminance (brightness) of the monitor's display panel. There are two different configurations for Apollo monitors and each requires a different amount of processing time at this step. The standard monitor or Delta product, which represents 55% of demand, requires 4 minutes of set-up time per monitor and 6 minutes of processing time. The newer "Delta XL" monitor, which comprises the other 45% of demand, requires 5 minutes of set-up time per monitor and 10 minutes of processing time. There are two workers and two machines, each working independently, at this process step. The flow of product is based upon demand, so both workers process a mix (55% & 45%) of Delta and Delta XL monitors.

2. **Initial ambient test:** The ambient test is an extended run in test of the assembled monitor and its assembled components at room temperature. Workers test monitors in batches of six. It requires eight minutes of set-up time per monitor to prepare a unit for testing (connecting components to test equipment). Once the six monitors are connected to the testing equipment it then requires 240 minutes of ambient (run) test time. There are ten testing stations, each capable of supporting six monitors, and two workers (working independently) at this stage. The only labor requirement at this stage is for the set-up time. Once the set-up is complete, the test runs with no worker (labor) involvement. The testing equipment will automatically shut down upon completion of a test, so you can assume that workers set-up and initiate tests for the full workday. (In other words, it is not necessary to stop initiating tests so that all tests are completed by 4:30 pm-the end of the workday.)

3. **Ambient offset:** The ambient offset step is a 1 - minute 48 - second process that occurs upon completion of the ambient test. This task involves disconnecting the monitor from the testing station and moving the monitor to the lot rack. When the rack is full (60 units) the worker moves the rack to the next production step (Step 3). The 1 - minute and 48 - second time is a per-unit time, as the worker disconnects and moves one set of components at a time. There is one person assigned to this step and there are no machinery requirements.

4. **Front-end parameter testing:** The FE parallel connection step requires 10.5 minutes of processing time. There are two workers and two machines, each working independently, at this process step.

5. **Label and final assembly:** There is one worker and one machine at the labeling and final assembly step. In total, labeling and final assembly requires five minutes of processing time per monitor.

6. **Final inspection:** The final inspection step requires 1 minute of set-up time and 3.3 minutes of processing time. There is one worker and one machine at this processing step.

7. **Packaging:** Packaging requires two minutes of processing time. Packaging involves boxing the monitor and adding it to the pallet for shipment to Lübeck. There is one worker and one machine at this processing step.

[5] Production steps, process times, and resource allocation, while representative of actual processes at Dräger, are disguised for competitive and confidentiality purposes.

**Exhibit 6**
Process Layout for Appolo Line at danvers Facility

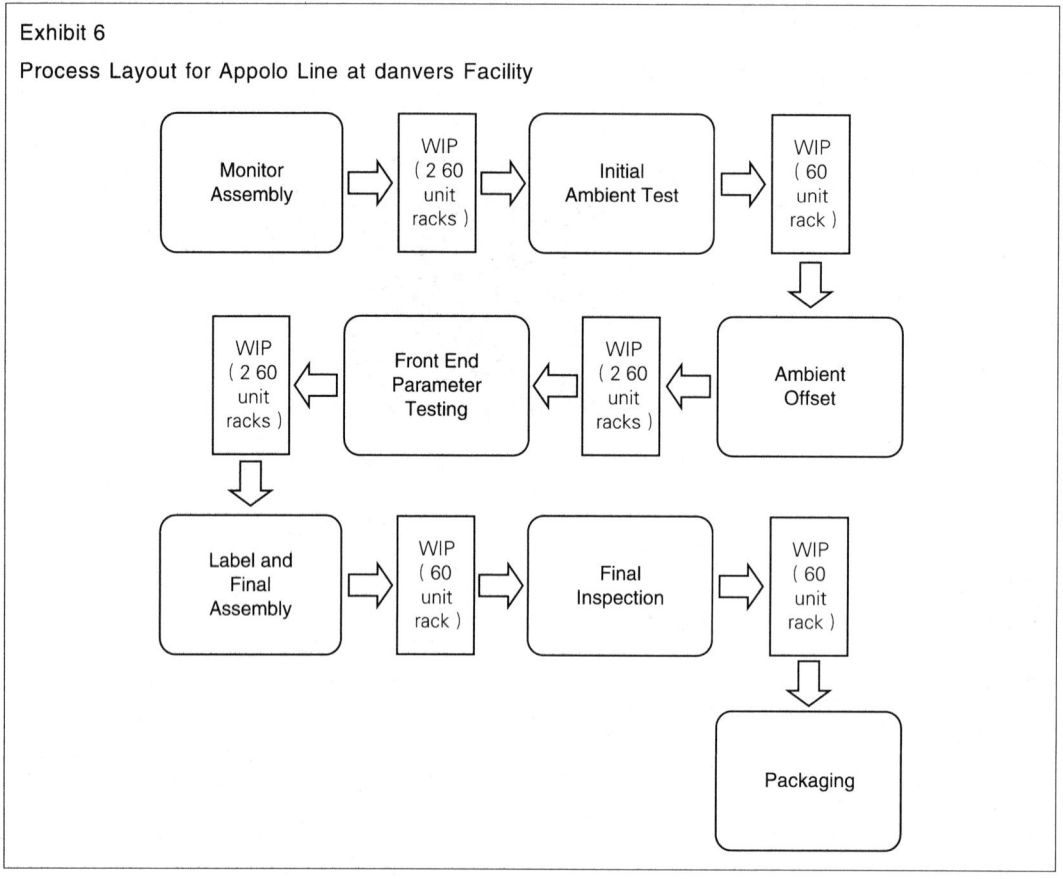

Details of the proposed design for the new 6 - step Andover production process can be found in Exhibit 7. The work schedule and constraints on overtime and second shifts that exist in Danvers will also be applied to the proposed Andover operation. Dräger management anticipates growth in demand for all monitors, including Apollo, in 2010 and beyond. The expansion of U. S. market share would also add to demand growth and require that the Andover facility be capable of producing at higher volumes in the future. Management in Lübeck also expressed concerns with order turnaround performance for 2008 at the Danvers plant. Orders sent to Danvers often arrived in Lübeck 8 - 10 days after order placement. This appeared illogical, given that Danvers shipped (overnight air) all finished goods daily. The critical process design question before the task force remains simple and straightforward: Can we produce similar or possibly higher volumes of monitors in a facility that is 45% smaller than our current site and improve our turnaround times? The answer to that question is less simple, and perhaps not so straightforward.

### Exhibit 7

### Process Description for Andover Facility[6]

1. **Production set-up:** The new process begins with components coming direct to the line from the receiving area and prepared for production. This includes collecting and aligning all components for the monitor in advance of assembly. There is one worker assigned to this task and no machinery requirements. It requires 4.9 minutes of process time to complete this step.

2. **Monitor assembly:** The new process and equipment allows workers to complete the fit housing process with four minutes of set-up time and six minutes of processing time. These processing times apply to all monitors – there is no longer a need to have different process times based upon the monitor type (i.e. Delta vs. Delta XL). There are two workers and two machines, each working independently, at this process step.

3. **Ambient test:** The new process for ambient test has 50 single-unit testing connections and each connection supports the testing of one monitor. There is one worker at this step. This worker is responsible for setting up the components for test (3.5 minutes) and, upon test completion, disconnecting components (1 minute) to facilitate movement to the next production step (Step #3). The ambient test is a 240 – minute process – same running time as the Danvers process. As was true in Danvers, there is no labor requirement during the 240 – minute test period and test equipment will automatically shut down upon completion, so the worker can initiate tests for the entire workday.

4. **Initialization and front-end parameter testing:** This combined step of initialization, a form of final component test, and FE parallel connection requires 10.1 minutes of processing time. There are two workers and two machines, each working independently, at this process step.

5. **Label and final assembly:** The labeling and final assembly process requires 5.1 minutes of processing time. There is one worker and one machine at this processing step.

6. **Final inspection and packaging:** The final inspection and packaging step requires 4.8 minutes per monitor. The inspection is simply a visual (external) check of the monitor, and packaging involves boxing the monitor and adding it to the pallet for shipment to Lübeck. There is one worker and one machine at this processing step.

[6] Production steps, process times, and resource allocation, while representative of actual processes at Dräger, are disguised for competitive and confidentiality purposes.

# ASSESSING THE FINANCIAL BENEFITS OF THE MOVE[4]

While the move to Andover was conceptually appealing, other options were available. For example, the entire assembly operation could be outsourced. Ultimately, the decision about the fate of the monitor production operation would be determined based on profitability criteria. Would the move to Andover produce improved financial performance? Certainly, the move would require some investment and some moving cost. Any savings realized in the operations would have to pay that cost back relatively quickly.

Basically, the job of the assembly plant in Danvers was to manage costs

---

[4] Some speciic details in this section have been modiied for the purposes of conidentiality and to permit increased pedagogical effectiveness.

while producing high-quality product in requisite volume. Dräger Medical management, however, wanted to make sure that each plant utilized its asset base well, too. Therefore, the Danvers plant was treated as an investment center. Corporate management set specific transfer prices for each of the monitor models. Annual plant operating expenses were subtracted from the transfer price revenues to determine a measure of plant margin. A capital charge was subtracted from plant margin, resulting in "plant economic income." The capital charge reflected the cost of capital multiplied by total fixed plant assets plus inventory, since only these assets were under control of the plant manager. (Current assets and liabilities other than inventory were all managed at corporate headquarters.) There was a target return on sales of 12% after the capital charge. The rationale of this apparent double-hurdle was explained as follows:

*All of the plant expenses become part of the final manufacturing costs for our products. Therefore, all of the plant costs pass through finished goods inventory and are expensed as cost of goods sold. The plant needs to generate income to cover its own investment, but then has to contribute to covering the overall corporate administrative costs. The 12% economic contribution accounts for the basic value created in the manufacture of the core instruments. Configuration, software loading, and accessory bundling in Lübeck contribute the remainder of the value of the final delivered product.*

The performance results for 2008 operations in Danvers are shown in Exhibit 8.

Demand volume in units at Danvers had risen by double-digit rates through 2006, but tumbled by 5% in 2007. Plant margin had fallen. There was a variety of factors that may have accounted for this. General economic conditions had led to diminished demand recently as hospitals and other health care facilities decided to defer purchases of new equipment. Lower market prices had restored demand volume in 2008, but not plant margin. Those lower market prices had, in turn, pushed back the transfer prices for Danvers, resulting in a drop in margins. Not only would the new arrangement in Andover have to cope with the lower prices, but it would also be beneficial if the plant margin were less sensitive to changes in demand.

Bill Nicholson's PRIME team reviewed a wide array of effects that the proposed move would have. Exhibit 9 contains a table specifying the expected headcount reductions. Exhibit 10 contains some excerpts from the team's written report related to costs and savings.

## Exhibit 8
### Income Statements for Danvers Assembly Business Unit[7]

| | | |
|---|---:|---:|
| Revenue | $ 37 540 000 | 100% |
| Less Variable Costs: | | |
| Direct Materials | $ 27 302 000 | 73% |
| Variable Manufacturing OH | 357 000 | 1% |
| Variable Support & Logistics OH | 4 925 | 0% |
| Contribution Margin | $ 9 876 075 | 26% |
| | | |
| Less Fixed Costs: | | |
| Assembly Labor | 1 872 000 | |
| Support & Logistics Labor | 1 144 000 | |
| Plant Administration and Management | 480 000 | |
| Occupancy | 928 000 | |
| Depreciation-Assembly Equipment | 456 000 | |
| Depreciation-Furnishing and Fixtures | 259 800 | |
| Depreciation-Administration Assets | 4 800 | |
| | $ 5 144 600 | 14% |
| Plant Margin | $ 4 731 475 | 13% |
| Capital Charge (cost of capital = 10%) | $ 1 805 600 | |
| Plant Economic Income | $ 2 925 875 | 8% |

[7] The quantitative data in Exhibits 8 through 10, while representative of actual observations at Dräger, have been disguised for competitive and confidentiality purposes.

## Exhibit 9
### Estimates of Headcount Changes from PRIME Reconfiguration

| | Current/Danvers | Projected/Andover |
|---|---:|---:|
| Assembly Labor | 30 | 24 |
| Support & Logistics Labor | 22 | 12 |
| Plant Administration and Management | 4 | 4 |
| | 56 | 40 |

## Exhibit 10

### Excerpts from the Report on Potential Costs and Savings from Move to Andover

Some of the costs and savings related to the move are obvious. Certainly, a move to Andover would eliminate the need to pay the $400 000 per year lease in Danvers. Additionally, the costs of maintaining, heating, cooling, and securing the Danvers facility would be eliminated by the move. If the assembly operation could be successfully fit into the available space in Andover, it would simply be allocated a share of the current Andover facility occupancy costs. Based on space occupied, we estimate the assembly operation's share of Andover's occupancy cost to be $499 000 per year.

There will have to be some investment in preparing the Andover facilities to house an assembly operation, including some equipment modification. The major expenditure will be for new ambient testing systems. Each system, consisting of a server and 50 test stations, will cost $600 000 to build and install. All of the old testing machines will be fully depreciated by the end of 2008 and sold for their salvage value for a net effect of no gain or loss. We estimate the economic life of these systems to be 10 years. We can move and reuse about half of the furnishings and fixtures currently in Danvers in the new facility in Andover. The remaining fixtures are leasehold improvements made to the building and cannot be moved. Those assets would have to be written off, except, luckily, they will be fully depreciated at the end of 2008. In Andover, we will have to spend $100 000 on new furnishings and fixtures to prepare the building for the assembly operation. Following company policy, those new leasehold improvements will be depreciated over 10 years. We can move all of the administration and management assets, which are primarily desks, computers, and other office furnishings. These were all replaced recently, so annual expenses related to their depreciation will remain unchanged.

We have planned the logistics on the move itself to be possible to execute over a three-day holiday weekend. There should be no loss of productive time. This will require several weekends of preparation and planning, however. There will be an out-of-pocket cost of $157 000 attached to the move.

The move will create savings in Andover. One immediate effect will be the removal of the need to shuttle engineers, parts, and equipment back and forth between Andover and Danvers. We estimate this savings to be $300 000 per year in combined out-of-pocket costs and recovery of lost engineer's time. The out-of-pocket costs are the shuttle driver, whose fully-loaded annual cost is $35 000, and the annual lease, maintenance, and operating costs of the van. These costs are $10 000 per year. Another savings in Andover will come from the reassignment of occupancy costs currently covered by the existing business to the assembly operation. As detailed elsewhere in this report, we estimate that $499 000 per year will be reallocated to the assembly operation.

# 战略实施
## Strategy Implementation

# 医疗保健网络联盟：利用平衡计分卡促进变革

Anne M. A. Sergeant
Grand Valley State University

Paulette Ratliff-Miller
Grand Valley State University

## 简介

阿利森·斯拜（Alison Spier），医疗保健网络联盟（Alliance Healthcare Network，简称 AHN）[①] 的主席兼 CEO，很快将与董事会成员会面，回顾过去的十年并设定未来五年的愿景。当她坐在办公室等待人力资源部主管乔瑟夫·贝克（Joseph Baker）时，她思索着未来。对医疗保健网络联盟（AHN）过去十年形成的竞争优势，她感到欣慰，但是她也担心，在快速变化的医疗保健环境中，医疗保健网络联盟（AHN）必须具有前瞻性，才能保持其领导地位。

此外，阿利森一直在思考新的医疗保健法规将对医疗保健网络联盟（AHN）的经营产生怎样的影响。2009 年 2 月，奥巴马总统签署了美国复苏与再投资法案(the American Recovery and Reinvestment Act，ARRA)。作为 ARRA 法案的组成部分，拟订经济和临床健康信息技术法案（the Health Information Technology for Economic and Clinical Health，简称 HITECH）的一个具体动机就是：加速实施电子健康档案（electronic health record，简称 EHR）系统。这些系统创建了一个病人信息数据库，医院、诊所、医生和药房可利用这一数据库更好地治疗病人，不复存在病历记录不清或抄写错误的情况。尽管医疗保健网络联盟（AHN）已经建立了电子健康档案（electronic health record，简称 EHR）系统，但是它并没有被联盟内的所有机构和医生使用。阿利森想知道，她要如何说服医师们使用计算机化医嘱录入系统（computerized physician order entry，简称 CPOE），从而实现该系统的全部效益。

**阿利森**：嗨，乔，谢谢你能过来。我希望在关于医疗保健网络联盟（AHN）未来方向的董事会会议召开之前，我们能够进行一场头脑风暴。正

---

\* 本篇译者为赵澄，校订者为胡金凤、余辉。
[①] 案例所述情境以一家真实公司的情况为基础；但对公司的名称、地址和业务数据都作了伪饰。——原注

如你所知，在联盟的各个岗位上，我们都拥有杰出的人才。如果我们要保持竞争力，我们必须留住这些人。我希望我们团队拥有突出的工作经验，这样他们能够为我们的病人提供非凡的护理服务。我们已经能够将我们的信息技术设备和流程系统化，从而大大提高我们的效率和质量。我们已开发出了最先进的档案系统，但只有在每一个人接受和使用这个系统的情况下，它才能发挥最大的作用。

**乔瑟夫**：说得对。从制造业转入到医疗保健行业后，我发现在管理员工的方式上有很大的不同。这个行业都是自我导向的职业而不是经理和生产员工导向，从而形成了一个非常不同的氛围。

**阿利森**：我同意，但是，如果我们要在降低经营成本的同时继续提高我们的服务质量，我们必须在已有的接受我们服务的整个社区和新获得的区域内，采用全面化的系统操作。我发现抗拒变化是人的天性，但是我认为将程序标准化能够使我们保持竞争力，同时有助于我们达到新的医疗保健要求。

**乔瑟夫**：所以，你想找一种方法来说服系统内的所有医师使用计算机化医嘱录入（computerized physician order entry，简称 CPOE）吗？我有一些想法。我立刻想到的就是使用平衡计分卡方法。在制造业，平衡计分卡被用来连接战略、目标、绩效考核、激励和行动，已经多年。

**阿利森**：这听起来是讨论我们这个问题的一个很有趣的出发点。我们应该首先辨别出我们每个机构的最佳实践的目标，并制定衡量成功实现目标的考核方式。当然，这些目标必须支持我们的使命，并与联盟文化相适应……或者我们要找到一种方法来"适应"我们的文化。新颁布的经济和临床信息技术法案（HITECH）的要求，包括使用电子健康记录系统。我应该将此作为我们的目标之一。一些医师们一直不情愿使用计算机化医嘱录入（CPOE）系统来做记录，因为这不是他们已经习惯的工作方式。我们也要解决这个问题，并找到一种方式激励每个人在工作中使用这个系统。平衡计分卡可以既激励员工又考核绩效吗？

**乔瑟夫**：我认为可以。给我几天的时间准备一个备忘录，我会再来找你。

## 医疗保健网络联盟（AHN）的背景

佐治亚州亚特兰大的医疗保健网络联盟（AHN）是一家以诚信为本的公司，致力于协调非营利性医疗机构、医疗保健服务和其他机构的综合医疗服务网络部门。它的核心价值理念包括：尊重、社会公正、慈悲、为得不到充分服务的人群提供治疗，及追求卓越。医疗保健网络联盟（AHN）为每一个人，特别是穷人和社会最弱势群体，提供身体、心灵和精神的治疗。为了提供最好的服务，公司在可承受的成本结构内，致力于提供高品质、综合性的、为整个社区提供医疗保健服务。

10 年前，当两个医疗系统合并时，医疗保健网络联盟（AHN）成立，并通过兼并已发展了 40 多家医院，拥有超过 8 000 多名现役医师。在最初合并之时，医学研究所（Institute of Medicine）正倡导减少用药失误[2]，而医疗保健网络联盟（AHN）选择了建设更加安全的健康体系，积极地追求这一目标。被再三引述的导致医疗事故的一个问题，就是分散化和分割化的医疗服务体系，包括病人的医疗档案。公司相信，要实现医疗保健的质量目标，就需要实施一个全面的电子健康档案系统（EHR），并在整个治疗中连续使用。考虑到几乎没有医院在使用电子健康档案系统（EHR），这是一个大胆的经营决策。

为了实现卓越的病人治疗这一核心价值，医疗保健网络联盟（AHN）决定创建一个医疗保健网络，这个网络拥有最佳临床知识和能够帮助临床医师为所服务的每一个社区提供更好的健康服务的在线工具。AHN 雇用了最称职的员工，并实施最先进的信息技术应用程序，包括为临床医师提供完整的病人档案的电子健康档案（EHR）。在 EHR 系统内，AHN 合并了计算机化医嘱录入系统（CPOE）。这不但提供了医嘱生成的方式，而且为临床医师在进行特定诊断时，提供建议的方案并提醒潜在的并发症。在它们开发之初，电子健康档案（EHR）和计算机化医嘱录入（CPOE）在医疗保健中都没有被广泛使用。计算机化医嘱录入系统（CPOE）通过向从业者提供提示和警告减少了医疗失误，从而提高医疗服务质量，而电子健康档案（EHR）则减少了因病人信息缺失所造成的失误。AHN 相信，在众多的医疗机构中使用标准化、高质量的信息系统，将在可承受的成本范围内，促进卓越的医疗服务。

## 医疗保健网络联盟（AHN）的文化变革

随着新的医疗系统的引入，必须重塑其运行流程和文化，来反映医疗保健网络联盟（AHN）的企业文化。这需要时间和精力。高级管理层能够理解这一变化是必要的，但是必须让一般员工也认同。AHN 面临的挑战就是，让每个新机构内的每个新人相信：标准化、集中化的信息技术系统对每一个人来说都更好，并且一旦实施这个系统，用户操作起来更加容易，并且会对它感到满意。

变革总是困难的，对那些已经习惯自主行医的医师们来说，尤其如此。首先，一个标准化的系统指定了医师的选择范围，从而限制其自主性，即使是经过临床已证实的方法，如果不在规定的范围之内，也不得选用。这对于一些人来说很难接受；当系统所规定的方法与医师所习惯的做法不一致时，尤其如此。简单的事情（例如对比四种颜色的尿液，而非先前的五种颜色）对医疗工作者来说也会是困难的。

其次，一些医师可能不喜欢使用电脑。年纪大的医师在计算机开始使用之前就已经学习开药了。很多年来，一些医师将处方口述给护士，再由护士

---

[2] 1999 年，美国医学研究所的保健质量委员会出版了"人非圣贤孰能无过：建设更加安全的健康体系"要求医疗保健提供者提高安全用药的水平。——原注

将处方抄写给其他人使用。当由其他人而非医师将处方输入系统时，计算机化医嘱录入系统（CPOE）反而会使原先所指望的减少失误的优点，实现不了。因此，事实上由医师亲自将处方录入系统，是非常重要的。为了解决这个问题，这会导致医师们超负荷工作，至少在学习使用新系统时，令人烦恼不堪。因此，医疗保健网络联盟（AHN）特别注意鼓励和培训医师们快速、有效地使用电子健康档案（EHR）和计算机化医嘱录入（CPOE）。医疗保健网络联盟（AHN）训练了一批"超级使用者"，然后由他们向其他医师们推广这个系统。来自同事的压力和充分的支撑服务被认为是改变医师行为的关键。

## 医疗保健网络联盟（AHN）未来的方向

目前，约60%的医疗保健网络联盟（AHN）所属机构实施了标准化的信息技术服务。鉴于这个成功，AHN正积极推进标准化于其他流程，如收入项目、供应链管理、应付账款、人力资源和其他服务与临床技能。每一个机构仍可以决定为特定社区提供所需的独特的医疗保健服务。管理层希望利用集中化支持服务的效率优势，继续在可承受成本内提供最佳的医疗服务。AHN仍然致力于提供卓越的医疗服务，特别是为穷人和最弱势的社会群体。

## 医疗保健信息的技术趋势

经济和临床信息技术法案（HITECH）的设计初衷之一就是加速实施电子健康档案系统（EHR）。医疗服务提供者采用了电子健康档案（EHR）并以一种有意义的方式使用该系统改善医疗服务，他们将从2011年1月开始到2014年终止的一个计划中得到奖励。那些未采用电子健康档案（EHR）的提供者，不仅不能获得采用系统的激励，而且从2015年开始将会受到处罚。

电子健康档案系统（EHR）是一个拥有丰富的患者的具体数据资料，这些数据由医疗保健机构内生成并维护，但是获得授权的其他人也能够使用这些文档。电子健康档案系统（EHR）被看作是保管病人信息的容器，它也被看作是为二次使用而汇总临床数据的辅助工具。当病人需要在其他机构获得服务时，他们的记录能够被系统内的其他医疗保健提供者获得。这为治疗提供了更好的连续性和综合性。

药物整合是反映电子健康档案（EHR）有用性的一个实例。当一个病人入院后，最大的难题之一就是收集病人在家服用药物的信息。电子健康档案（EHR）将大大减少这个协调问题。医疗保健服务提供者可不再仅仅依赖病人或病人家属所报告的信息。电子健康档案（EHR）能涵盖来自医师们的记录、以前的出院医嘱，甚至是药店记录。这些连同病人信息，可为将要采用的药物治疗提供更好的参考。进一步来说，在病人转院或出院之后，其他机构将获得药物治疗处方的详细记录。

除了储存病人数据，一个综合性的电子健康档案系统（EHR）还为医疗保健服务提供者提供更广泛的临床信息和专业知识。有权使用这个系统的医师们或临床医生能够利用成百上千的有据可依的处方集。他们还可以利用在线支持工具，获得最新的医药证据，链接其他的工具和文献以及特定的规则、警示和对策，以确保服务质量和病人的安全。这些工具是计算机化医嘱录入系统（CPOE）的组成部分。计算机化医嘱录入（CPOE）的主要功能，就是为电子化生成处方、传递和按适当的用量执行处方提供一个媒介工具。

在输入处方的过程中，一个完善的系统也会向使用者提示安全性和有效性的问题。一般的警示包括：过敏、错误剂量、重复的处方、潜在的不良药物反应和其他禁忌症状。这些警示将会防止一些可避免的并发症。进一步来说，计算机化医嘱录入系统（CPOE）为常见症状储存了一些合适的处方，这有助于确保对病人的治疗与最佳治疗的标准一致，进而提高安全性[3]。这些处方的汇总提供了一个良好的出发点，医师的效率提高了，因为只有非常规性变化才必须记录。工时—动作研究学表明计算机化医嘱录入（CPOE）减少了医师们开处方的时间[4]。计算机化医嘱录入（CPOE）是一个强大的工具；它既能提供操作功效，又能提高效率。

计算机化医嘱录入（CPOE）的实施是富有挑战性的。它不仅需要开发系统和把技术付诸实施，它还需要培训用户。最初建立这样的协议可能比较困难，因为每一个用户都想要将他或她自己的程序作为标准。标准化的系统可能与一直以来能够自由决定药方的临床医生的实践操作相反。医师们在开出药方时有他们偏好的独特方式，并且每个医师的要求和工作流程可能都不一样。标准化的系统迫使他们使用他们可能不常用的选择。这样的看法可能出现，认为是信息技术，而不是医疗护理在决定这些选择。

其次，更难的问题是：为让计算机化医嘱录入系统（CPOE）及其临床支持工具有效，医师们必须录入他们自己的药方。这是医师、护士和其他工作者的工作流程中的一个巨大变化。培训是关键。为了让医师们正确地使用该系统，他们必须接受充分的培训，并且在他们形成必要的技能和信心的过程中必须有足够的支持。一些医生对使用计算机化医嘱录入系统（CPOE）保持沉默。首先，处方录入被视为一项应该由单位内秘书或护士来完成的卑微工作。其次，一些医师缺乏电脑等现代技术知识。他们从没学过使用现代技术，并且不愿意使用现代技术。他们不想投入时间和精力学习一个新系统。许多医生认为学习如何使用计算机化医嘱录入（CPOE）是他们已有的繁重工作外一项额外负担。为了优化计算机化医嘱录入（CPOE）的价值，医师们必须对系统感到满意并相信它能改进他们所做的工作。

---

[3] E. 德兰森、B. 吉伯德、J. 梅兹格和 E. 韦勒波博（2009），《挽救生命，节省治疗费用：马萨诸塞州医院的计算机化医嘱录入系统战略》，马萨诸塞州技术合作与新英格兰医疗保健协会（web3.streamhoster.com/mtc/cpoe2009.pdf-downloaded 5/11/2011）。

[4] A. A. 阿姆森、S. 唐格、S. 斯皮戴和 A. 莫林（2008），《评价电子病历（EMR）和计算机化医嘱录入（CPOE）的实施对医师效率影响的一则工时—动作研究》，医疗保健信息管理期刊，22（4）：31-37。

尽管电子健康档案和计算机化医嘱录入系统已使用30多年了，但迄止2006年，只有不足10%的医院使用了完备的综合系统[5]。纸质版的记录仍然是大多数美国医院偏好的记录方式[6]。目前由于经济和临床信息技术（HITECH）法案的奖励和惩罚的实施正在逼近，计算机化医嘱录入（CPOE）的实施不只是作为一个选择。到2015年，除了实施各种电子健康档案（EHRs）系统外，医院将没有其他的现实选择。他们越晚开始实施这个系统，无法获得全部财务激励的可能性就越大，而受到不利诱因（被处罚）的可能性就越大。医院要获得奖励金，必须证明他们实施了一个有效的系统，这个系统也按照计划在使用，并且实现了预期结果。有文件证明，对未来几年内系统的"有效使用"制定了严格的时间安排。长远的现实就是：无论"医疗保健改革"成什么样，真正有效的使用系统绝对是未来所要求。

## 有效的使用

美国复苏与再投资法案（ARRA）的经济和临床信息技术（HITECH）部分具体指出：应该激励医疗保险和医疗补助计划提供者，但不是对采用EHR进行奖励，而是对"有效的使用"各种电子健康档案（EHRs）进行奖励。在2010年7月，美国卫生与公众服务部（Department of Health and Human Services，HHS）公布了项目的最终条例，界定了"有效的使用"的阶段1。"有效的使用"的三个主要构成要求是：实施的系统必须以有效的方式进行使用（如电子处方）；必须用于健康信息的电子交流来改善医疗质量；必须用来提高临床质量和其他考核。

"有效使用"激励分为：提高质量、安全性与效率，缩小医疗健康服务的差异，履行对病人及其家属在治疗中的承诺，改善医护协调、提高人口和公众健康，以及确保充分的隐私权和安全性。阶段1的核心要求和要求目录，列示于表1。阶段2和阶段3[7]主要包括逐渐提高阶段1所要求的使用程度。例如，在阶段1，至少30%的药物治疗处方必须由提供者录入计算机化医嘱录入系统（CPOE），然而到了阶段3，要求至少达到80%。"有效的使用"的标准，随着立法解释而得到继续发展；但是，有一件事是不变的，医院要获得奖励金和避免处罚，服务的提供者就必须使用精密的电子健康档案。显然，医疗服务提供者要获得奖励金（和避免处罚），则必须采用和使用精密的电子健康档案记录。

---

[5] D. 斯麦兹和 E. 伯纳（2007），电子健康记录操作指南，健康管理出版社，第3页。
[6] 美国医院电子健康记录的使用，新英格兰药学日报，2009年3月25日。
[7] http://healthit.hhs.gov/media/faca/MU_RFC%20_2011-01-12_final.pdf（August 9, 2011）.

**表 1**
**阶段 1——关系到有效使用的要求**[8]

**核心指标**

1. 使用计算机化医嘱录入药物处方。
2. 实施一种药物对另一种药物和药物对过敏反应的检测。
3. 保存和不断更新有关当前的有效诊断（active diagnoses）的最新问题清单。
4. 电子化生成并传递获得允许的药方。
5. 维护不断更新在用药物清单。
6. 维护在用药物过敏反应的清单。
7. 记录人口统计资料（语言、性别、种族、民族、生日）。
8. 记录和绘制生命体征变化（身高、体重、血压、身体质量指数（BMI）[9]、儿童生长发育）。
9. 记录烟龄在 13 年及以上的病人。
10. 向内容管理系统（CMS）[10] 或各州报告门诊临床质量指标。
11. 实施一个临床决策支持的规范。
12. 根据要求，向病人提供其健康信息的电子复印件。
13. 每一次巡查时向病人提供临床总结。
14. 在提供者和病人授权的单位之间有电子交换关键临床信息的能力。
15. 保护电子健康信息（隐私和安全）。

**设定指标的项目清单**

1. 实施药物规定检测。
2. 将临床实验室测试的结果作为结构化数据纳入电子健康档案（EHR）中。
3. 根据特定情况生成患者清单，用于改善质量、减少差异、研究和扩大服务范围。
4. 向病人发送预防性/后续治疗的提醒事项。
5. 通过电子网络向病人及时提供他们的健康信息（包括实验室测验结果、问题清单、药物治疗清单、过敏症）。
6. 利用注册的电子健康档案（EHR）识别供特定病人的教育资源，如果合适则提供给病人。
7. 进行相关的药物治疗协调。
8. 为转院治疗或转诊病人提供治疗汇总记录。
9. 具有向免记录登记处提交电子数据或实际文本的能力。
10. 能够向公众健康机构和实际下属机构提交电子的症状监测数据。

因为 AHN 已经实施电子健康档案多年了，并且在它的很多医院都拥有运行系统，该组织在计算机化医嘱录入（CPOE）执行方面为行业的领导者。当然，如果提供者不采用该系统，那么再好的系统也没有意义。一些医师不想直接将自己的处方录入到计算机化医嘱录入系统（CPOE），他们可以将处方口述给护士，由护士将其录入系统。当护士录入处方并出现警示时，护士必须就警示的性质与医师进行沟通，医师必须决定是否有必要变更

---

[8] https://www.cms.gov/Regulations-and-Guidance/Legislation/EHRIncentivePrograms/downloads/MU_Stage1_Req Overview.pdf.

[9] BMI 指数（Body Mass Index），是用体重公斤数除以身高米数平方得出的数字，简称体质指数或体重指数。——译者

[10] CMS 是 Content Management System 的缩写，意为"内容管理系统"，是一个很广泛的称呼，从一般的博客程序、新闻发布程序，到综合性的网站管理程序都可以被称为内容管理系统。来源于百度资料。——译者。

处方。如果医师自己直接将处方录入系统，警示会马上反映给医师本人。系统的设计也适用于非医师录入处方的情况，当医师无法进入计算机系统时，他们可以通过电话完成处方的录入。这种情况预期会很少。非医师录入的处方的比例是"有效使用"的重要组成元素，并且由计算机化医嘱录入系统（CPOE）来监控。

## 要求

医疗保健网络联盟（AHN）要确保遵守经济和临床信息技术（HITECH）法案以获取尽可能多的奖励金。因此，医师们使用系统非常重要。乔瑟夫·贝克已经着手开发平衡计分卡，并要求你帮助开发受雇医师的绩效考核。为乔瑟夫·贝克及阿利森·斯拜等人，编制一个内部备忘录[11]。在备忘录中你应该：

a. 讨论如何利用平衡计分卡激励医师们使用计算机化医嘱录入系统（CPOE）。

b. 解释你为医师团队开发平衡计分卡的过程。

c. 为医师团队编制一份计分卡的样本。

d. 创建一个战略路径图，展示你开发的学习和成长的方法（在 C 部分中）如何与平衡计分卡的其他三个指标计分卡（过程、客户、财务）相联系。

e. 深刻讨论你为医师团体制定的公司战略、目标和方法是如何联系在一起的。

## 讨论题

1. **公司战略**：请描述医疗保健网络联盟（AHN）使用的整体战略，以及 AHN 如何在其信息技术服务上实施这一战略。在运用这一信息战略时，AHN 将面临哪些具体问题？如果医师们拒绝使用 CPOE，并继续以他们习惯的方式做事，可能会产生什么样的战略和经济结果？

2. **对医师们的激励**：激励医师们应该使用什么奖励？医师们和其他医疗保健工作者之间的激励因素是否存在差异？医师的年龄会如何影响必要的激励？

3. **医师们的计算机化医嘱录入（CPOE）工作流程**：CPOE 系统如何影响医师的工作流程？当计算机化医嘱录入系统（CPOE）存在时，医师们能否避开计算机化医嘱录入系统（CPOE）？如果医师们不录入自己的处方，对质量可能有什么影响？医院将如何促使所有的医师录入他们自己的处方？

4. **医药行业对比制造业**：医药业环境与制造业环境有何相似？他们又

---

[11] Internal memorandum，指供公司内部人员阅读或涉及内部问题的备忘录。与此相对的是 external memorandum（外部备忘录），供公司外部人员阅读，通常措辞比较正式、友好，传递公司的正面信息。——译者

有何区别？例如，从收入来源、组织结构、经营等方面来看。

5. **平衡计分卡**：一个医院为什么可能使用平衡计分卡体系？一家非营利医院的平衡计分卡如何区别于一家营利性企业？如何利用平衡计分卡体系进行激励？

# Alliance Healthcare Network: Using a Balanced Scorecard to Motivate Change

Anne M. A. Sergeant
Grand Valley State University

Paulette Ratliff-Miller
Grand Valley State University

## INTRODUCTION

Alison Spier, president and CEO of Alliance Healthcare Network (AHN)[1], would soon be meeting with the board of directors to review the past ten years and to develop a vision for the next five years. As she sat in her office waiting for Joseph Baker, the director of human resources, she pondered the future. She was pleased with the competitive advantage AHN had developed over the past ten years, but was concerned that in the rapidly changing healthcare environment, AHN would have to be proactive to remain a leader.

In addition, Alison had been thinking about how new health care regulations would affect AHN operations. In February of 2009, President Obama signed the American Recovery and Reinvestment Act (ARRA) into law. As part of the ARRA, the Health Information Technology for Economic and Clinical Health (HITECH) Act contains specific incentives designed to accelerate the adoption of electronic health record (EHR) systems. These systems create a database of patient information, which can be used by hospitals, clinics, doctors, and pharmacies that treat the patient without duplication of records or transcription errors. While AHN has developed an EHR, it is not being used at all of its facilities or by all of its physicians. Alison wondered how she was going to convince the physicians to use the computerized physician order entry (CPOE) system so that full benefits could be achieved.

Alison: Hi, Joe. Thanks for coming in. I was hoping we could do a little brainstorming before the board meeting about the future direction of AHN. As

---

[1] The situation is based on a real company; however, the company's name, location, and business data have been disguised.

you know, we have exceptional talent working at all levels at Alliance. If we are going to remain competitive, we need to keep these folks. I want our associates to have an extraordinary work experience so they can create an extraordinary care experience for our clients. We have been able to systematize our IT equipment and procedures to capitalize on tremendous efficiency and quality gains. We have developed state-of-the-art record systems, but the best systems can only work if they are accepted and used by everyone.

Joseph: That's true. Since moving from manufacturing into the healthcare industry, I have noticed a lot of differences in the ways that people are managed. Here we have self-directed professionals instead of managers and production workers, which leads to a very different atmosphere.

Alison: I agree, but if we are going to continue to improve the quality of our services while reducing operating costs, we are going to have to adopt system-wide practices that will be used throughout our existing community as well as in newly acquired locations. I realize that it is human nature to resist change, but I think that having standardized procedures can keep us competitive as well as helping us to meet the new healthcare requirements.

Joseph: So, you want to find a way to convince all of the physicians in the system to use the CPOE? I have a few ideas. One thing that comes to mind immediately is using a balanced scorecard approach. In manufacturing, balanced scorecards have been used for years to link strategy, objectives, performance measures, incentives, and actions.

Alison: That sounds like an interesting place to start. We should start by identifying the objectives for best practices from each of our facilities and develop ways to measure our success in achieving them. Of course, these objectives must support our mission and be compatible with Alliance's culture... or we're going to have to find a way to "adjust" our culture. The new HITECH requirements include the use of electronic health records. We should include this as one of our objectives. Some of our physicians have been reluctant to use the CPOE system, which feeds into the records, because it's not how they're accustomed to working. We need to address this concern as well and find a way to motivate everyone to work within the system. Can the scorecard be used to motivate as well as measure performance?

Joseph: I expect so. Give me a few days to prepare a memo and I'll get back with you.

# AHN BACKGROUND

Alliance Healthcare Network (AHN) of Atlanta, Georgia, is a large faith-based organization devoted to the ministry of healing through an integrated health delivery network of nonprofit hospitals, healthcare services, and other agencies. Its core values include: respect, social justice, compassion, providing care for the underserved, and excellence. AHN provides healing services for body, mind, and spirit to everyone, especially the poor and most vulnerable of society. To best serve all, the company strives to provide high-quality, integrated, community-based healthcare within an affordable cost structure.

AHN was founded 10 years ago when two health systems merged, and has grown through acquisitions to over 40 hospitals with more than 8 000 active staff physicians. At the time of the initial merger, the Institute of Medicine was advocating reducing errors in medicine,[②] and AHN chose to aggressively pursue the goal of building a safer health system. One oft-cited problem leading to medical errors is the decentralized and fragmented nature of the healthcare delivery system, including the patient medical records. The company believed that to achieve the goal of quality healthcare, it would need to implement a system-wide electronic health record (EHR) system and use it across a continuum of care. This was a bold business decision, given that few hospitals were using EHR.

To achieve the core value of excellence in patient care, AHN was determined to create a healthcare network with the best clinical knowledge and online tools that would enable clinicians to provide the superior healthcare to every community served. AHN hired the most competent staff available and implemented state-of-the-art IT applications, which included EHR to provide clinicians with complete patient records. Within the EHR, AHN incorporated computerize physician order entry (CPOE). This not only provides the means to issue orders, but also provides clinicians with recommended protocols for specific diagnoses and alerts for potential complications. At the time they were initiated, neither EHR nor CPOE were widely used in healthcare. CPOE systems reduce medical errors by providing cues and alerts for practitioners that enhance the quality of medical care provided, while EHR reduces errors from incomplete patient information. AHN believed that using a standardized, top-quality IT system across a number of facilities would promote excellent care at an affordable cost.

## CHANGING CULTURE AT AHN

As new health systems are brought into the organization, their operating procedures and culture must be remolded to reflect the AHN culture. This takes

---

[②] In 1999, the Institute of Medicine's Committee on Quality of Health Care in America published "To Err Is Human: Building a Safer Health System," which charged healthcare providers with elevating the level of safety in medicine.

time and effort. Top management may understand the changes that are needed, but the rank-and-file must also buy in. The challenge for AHN is to convince each new person at each new facility that the standardized, centralized IT system is better for everyone and will be easier to operate once it is implemented and users are comfortable with it.

Change can be difficult, particularly on physicians who have been used to independence in how they practice medicine. First, a standardized system limits independence by dictating choices to physicians, albeit clinically proven choices. This can be hard for some to accept, particularly if the system does not correspond to what the physician is accustomed to doing. Simple things, such as comparisons to four colors of urine rather than the previously available five choices, can be difficult on practitioners.

Second, some physicians may not be inclined to use computers. Older physicians learned to practice medicine prior to the use of computers. For years, some of these individuals have given verbal orders to nurses who then transcribed the orders for use by others. A CPOE system loses much of its error-reduction value when someone other than a physician inputs orders into the system. Thus, it is critical that the physician actually enter the order into the system. To compound the problem, physicians tend to be overworked, and the prospect of learning to use a new system can be disturbing at the least. Thus, AHN devotes special attention to encouraging and training physicians in an efficient and effective use of EHR and CPOE. AHN trains a set of "super users" who then promote the system to other physicians. Peer pressure and adequate support services have been found to be the key to changing physician behavior.

## FUTURE DIRECTION FOR AHN

Currently, about 60 percent of AHN facilities have implemented the standardized IT services. Given this success, AHN is moving into standardizing other procedures, such as revenue programs, supply chain management, accounts payable, human resources, and other service and clinical skills. Each facility will still determine the unique healthcare services needed in its specific community. Management hopes to capitalize on efficiencies of centralized support services to continue to provide the best quality care at an affordable cost. AHN remains committed to providing excellent healing services, especially for the poor and most vulnerable of society.

## HEALTHCARE INFORMATION TECHNOLOGY TRENDS

The HITECH Act contains incentives specifically designed to accelerate the adoption of electronic health record (EHR) systems. Healthcare providers who adopt EHRs and use them in a meaningful way to improve patient care are rewarded through a program that began in January 2011 and terminates at the end of 2014. Those providers who do not adopt EHR will not only fail to receive the incentives for adoption, but will be penalized as well starting in 2015.

An EHR is a rich source of patient specific data generated and maintained within a healthcare institution, but which is accessible by others authorized to use the documents. The EHR can be thought of as a container holding patient information and as a tool for aggregating clinical data for secondary use. When patients need services at other facilities, their records are easily accessible by providers within the system. This provides greater continuity and integration of care.

One example of the usefulness of the EHR is with medication reconciliation. When a patient is admitted to the hospital, one of the biggest challenges is assembling information about medications being taken at home. The EHR is intended to significantly reduce this coordination problem. No longer will healthcare providers have to rely solely on information reported from the patient or the patient's family. The EHR is intended to contain records from physicians, former discharge orders, and even pharmacy records. These, along with patient information, will provide a far superior picture of medications being taken. Moreover, after the patient is transferred or discharged, other facilities will have a detailed record of prescribed medications.

In addition to storing patient data, a comprehensive EHR system provides extensive clinical intelligence and expertise for the provider. Physicians or clinicians with access to the system can use hundreds of evidence-based order sets, as well as online support tools that provide current medical evidence, links to other tools and literature, and specific rules, alerts, and strategies that assure patient safety and quality. These tools are part of a computerized physician order entry (CPOE) system. The primary function of CPOE is to provide a vehicle for electronically issuing orders and transmitting and executing them by the appropriate unit.

In the process of entering the order, a well-developed system will also prompt users for safety and effectiveness. Common alerts include allergies, incorrect dosage, duplicated orders, potential adverse drug interactions, and other contraindications. These alerts are intended to prevent avoidable complications. Moreover, CPOE systems store sets of appropriate orders for common conditions, which helps ensure that the patient's treatment complies with standards for best practice, further enhancing safety.[3] Given that these order sets provide a well-developed starting point, physician efficiency is increased because only non-routine changes must be recorded. Time-motion studies have shown that CPOE reduces the time physicians spend on orders.[4] CPOE is a powerful tool; it provides both operational efficacy and efficiency.

Implementing CPOE can be challenging. It requires not only developing the system and implementing the technology, but it also requires training the users. Initially establishing the protocols can be difficult because each user wants his or her own procedures as the standard. A standardized system can be contrary to the practices of clinicians, who historically have had freedom to determine order parameters. Physicians have particular ways in which they like to structure orders, and each physician's desires and workflow can be different. A standardized system forces them to use choices they may not typically use. The perception can be that IT is driving these choices, not medical care.

A second, more difficult problem is that for the CPOE system and its clinical support tools to be effective, physicians must enter their own orders. This can be a drastic change in workflow for physicians, nurses, and others. Training is critical. For physicians to use the system properly, they must be adequately trained and must have sufficient support in place as they develop the necessary competencies and confidences. Some doctors have been reticent to use CPOE systems. First, order entry was viewed as a menial task, to be done by unit secretaries or nurses. Second, some physicians are technologically incompetent. They have never learned to use current technology and feel uncomfortable doing so. The investment in time and effort to learn a new system is more than they want to devote. Many doctors view learning how to use CPOE as an additional burden to their already busy schedules. In order to optimize the value of CPOE, physicians have to be comfortable with the system and believe it enhances the work they do.

Even though electronic health records with computerized physician order entry systems have been available for more than 30 years, as of 2006 fewer than 10 percent of hospitals used a fully integrated system.[5] Paper-based recording is still the preferred means of charting for most U. S. hospitals.[6] But with the HITECH Act rewards and penalties looming on the horizon, implementation of

---

[3] Drazen, E., B. Gilboard, J. Metzger, and E. Welebob. 2009. Saving Lives, Saving Money in Practice: Strategies for Computerized Physician Order Entry in Massachusetts Hospitals. Massachusetts Technology Collaborative and New England Healthcare Institute. (web3. streamhoster. com/mtc/cpoe2009. pdf- downloaded 5/11/2011)

[4] Amusan, A. A., S. Tongen, S. Speedie, and A. Mellin. 2008. A Time-Motion Study to Evaluate the Impact of EMR and CPOE Implementation on Physician Efficiency. Journal of Healthcare Information Management 22 (4): 31 – 37.

[5] Smaltz, D., and E. Berner. 2007. *The Executive's Guide to Electronic Health Records*. Health Administration Press. p. 3.

[6] *Use of Electronic Health Records in U. S. Hospitals*. New England Journal of Medicine, March 25, 2009.

CPOE is not merely an option. Hospitals have no realistic choice but to implement EHRs by 2015. The longer they delay getting started, the greater the likelihood of recouping less than the full financial incentives and becoming subject to the disincentives (penalties). To receive stimulus money, hospitals must demonstrate that they have implemented a meaningful system, that the system is being used as it was intended, and that the desired results are being achieved. A strict time schedule has been established to document "meaningful use" over the next few years. The longer-term reality is that truly meaningful use is an absolute requirement for the future, regardless of what emerges as "healthcare reform."

## MEANINGFUL USE

The HITECH portion of the American Recovery and Reinvestment Act (ARRA) specifically mandates that incentives should be given to Medicare and Medicaid providers, not for EHR adoption, but for "meaningful use" of EHRs. In July of 2010, the U. S. Department of Health and Human Services (HHS) released that program's final rule, defining stage 1 of "meaningful use." The three main components of "meaningful use" require that the system implemented must be used in a meaningful manner (for example, e-prescribing), must be used for electronic exchange of health information to improve quality of care, and must be used to submit clinical quality and other measures. The "meaningful use" incentives categories are improvement in quality, safety, and efficiency and reduction in healthcare disparities, engagement of patients and their families in their care, improvement in care coordination, improvements in population and public health, and assurance of adequate privacy and security. A list of stage 1 core requirements and menu requirements is found in Table 1. Stages 2 and 3[7]typically involve ratcheting up the required usage found in stage 1. For example, at stage 1, at least 30% of medication orders must be provider entered in the CPOE system, whereas by stage 3, at least 80% is required. "Meaningful Use" criteria continue to evolve as the legislation is interpreted; but, one thing is consistent, providers must use a sophisticated electronic health record for hospitals to receive stimulus money and avoid penalties. Clearly, to receive stimulus money (and avoid penalties), healthcare providers must adopt and use a sophisticated electronic health record.

---

[7] http://healthit.hhs.gov/media/faca/MU_RFC%20_2011-01-12_final.pdf (August 9, 2011).

| Table 1 |
|---|
| Stage 1 – Meaningful Use Requirement[8] |
| Core Measures |

1. Use computerized order entry for medication orders.
2. Implement drug-drug and drug-allergy interaction checks.
3. Maintain an up-to-date problem list of current and active diagnoses.
4. Generate and transmit permissible prescriptions electronically.
5. Maintain active medication list.
6. Maintain active medication allergy list.
7. Record demographics (language, gender, race, ethnicity, date of birth).
8. Record and chart changes in vital signs (height, weight, blood pressure, BMI, child growth).
9. Record smoking status for patients 13 years old or older.
10. Report ambulatory clinical quality measures to CMS or the states.
11. Implement one clinical decision support rule.
12. Provide patients with an electronic copy of their health information upon request.
13. Provide clinical summaries to patients for each office visit.
14. Capability to exchange key clinical information electronically among providers and patient authorized entities.
15. Protect electronic health information (privacy and security).

| Menu Set Measures |
|---|

1. Implement drug-formulary checks.
2. Incorporate clinical lab-test results into EHR as structured data.
3. Generate lists of patients by specific conditions to use for quality improvement, reduction of disparities, research, and outreach.
4. Send patient reminders for preventive/follow-up care.
5. Provide patients with timely electronic access to their health information (including lab results, problem list, medication lists, allergies).
6. Use certified EHR to identify patient-specific education resources and provide to patient if appropriate.
7. Perform medication reconciliation as relevant.
8. Provide summary care record for transitions to care or referrals.
9. Capability to submit electronic data to immunization registries and actual submissions.
10. Capability to submit electronic syndromic surveillance data to public health agencies and actual submission.

[8] https://www.cms.gov/Regulations-and-Guidance/Legislation/EHRIncentivePrograms/downloads/MU_Stage1_ReqOverview.pdf

Because AHN has been implementing an electronic health record for many years and has operational systems in many of its hospitals, the organization leads the industry in CPOE implementation. Still, even the best system is worthless if the providers do not use the system. Physicians who do not want to enter their own orders directly into the CPOE system can dictate their orders to a nurse, who then enters them into the system. When a nurse is entering the orders and an alert is triggered, the nurse must then communicate with the physician the nature of the alert and the physician must decide if a change in the order is necessary. If the physician were directly entering the order in the system, the alert would immediately reach the intended individual. The systems are designed to accommodate non-physician order entry to allow physicians to complete an order via the phone when computer access is unavailable. This situation is expected to be rare. The percentage of non-physician orders is a significant element of "meaningful use" and is monitored by the CPOE system.

## REQUIRED

AHN would like to insure compliance with HITECH to receive the most stimulus money possible. Therefore, it is important that physicians are using the system. Joseph Baker has begun to develop a balanced scorecard and has asked your help in developing performance measures for the physician employees. Prepare an internal memorandum from Joseph Baker to Alison Spier. In it you should:

a. Discuss how a balanced scorecard could be used to motivate the physicians to use the computerized physician order entry (CPOE) system.

b. Explain the process you would use to develop a balanced scorecard for the physician group.

c. Prepare a sample scorecard for the physician group.

d. Create a strategy map to show how the learning and growth measure(s) you developed in part c are related to the other three balanced scorecard perspectives (process, customer, and financial).

e. Discuss in depth how the company strategy, objectives, and measures you developed for the physician group are linked together.

## DISCUSSION QUESTIONS

1. **Company strategy.** Describe the overall strategy used by AHN and how AHN operationalizes this strategy with its IT services. What specific problems does AHN face using this IT strategy? What strategic and economic consequences might there be if physicians refused to use the CPOE and continued doing things as they always have?

2. **Motivation for physicians.** What rewards can be used to motivate physicians? Do the incentives differ between physicians and other healthcare professionals? How might physician age affect the required incentives?

3. **CPOE workflow for physicians.** How does a CPOE system affect the workflow for the physician? Can physicians avoid using a CPOE system when it is in place? What might be the effects on quality if physicians do not enter their

own orders? How can hospitals facilitate all physicians to enter their own orders?

4. **Hospital versus manufacturing.** How is a hospital environment similar to a manufacturing environment? How do they differ? For example, consider revenue generation, organizational structure, operations, etc.

5. **Balanced Scorecard.** Why might a hospitals use the balanced scorecard framework? How would the balanced scorecard of a nonprofit hospital differ from a for-profit business? How can a balanced scorecard framework be used to motivate?

# 编制计划与预算
Planning & Budgeting

# 会计师有时未能预算

*Gail Hoover King*
*Purdue University Calumet*

*Jane Saly*
*University of St. Thomas*

编制预算在所有组织中都很重要,对非营利组织尤其如此,因为这些组织每年的收入来源都不相同。非营利组织的领导对年度实际收入和成本之间的差异负有监督责任,并需要做出经营决策以确保该组织的生存和发展。

## 简介

2003 年 8 月,美国会计学会中西部地区(american accounting association midwest Region,AAA-MW)的督导委员会(Steering Committee)发现,2003 年年会出现的净损失达 24 232 美元,使账面余额低于 50 000 美元。这还没有把前一年 13 264 美元的亏损计算在内。考虑到未来可能出现的不良趋势,董事会设置了司库[①]一职,并要求司库对这些损失进行调查研究。

## 组织

该督导委员会完全由志愿者组成,其任务是组织和召开每年一次的年会,以居住在伊利诺伊、印第安纳、爱荷华、堪萨斯、密歇根、明尼苏达、北达科他、南达科塔、内布拉斯加和威斯康星等各州的美国会计学会会员为与会对象。美国会计学会(AAA)是一个非营利组织,其会员主要是会计学者。该组织"旨在促进全世界会计教育、研究和实务工作的卓越发展。1916 年成立时,名为美国高校会计教师协会(american association of university instructors in accounting);于 1936 年采用现在这个名称。该学会将学术界人士组织起来,以推进会计教育以及促进会计工作的纪律和专业化。"(《美国会计学会:我们的共同使命》,http://aaahq.org/about/AAAShareVisionDocumentJan08fnl_4_.pdf,2008,p 6。)

督导委员会每年召开两次会议,春季召开 AAA-MW 地区会议,8 月召开美

---

\* 本篇译者为杨继良,校订者为胡金凤、赵澄。
① treasurer,或译"财务主管"。——译者

国会计学会全国年度大会。下面所述为典型的 AAA-MW 年会组织过程：

1. 在会议召开的十八个月前（通常是在 8 月份 AAA 的全国会议这个时候），督导委员会就要决定在中西部地区的哪一个城市召开会议，并向 AAA 全国办公室呈递一份申请，要求寻找确定会议地址。

2. 会议主持者是督导委员会的一位志愿者，每年由不同的（新）人担任。

3. 会议事项的协调人（AAA 全国办公室聘用的第三方）将与会议所在城市的各酒店联系，并向 AAA-MW 督导委员会提供一份清单，列出候选的各个酒店名称及其房价和停车费率。

4. 在上一年的 AAA-MW 春季地区性会议期间，督导委员会根据各个酒店的位置和房间费率，为本次年会选定一家酒店。

5. 会议事项的协调人负责与酒店协商最终合同，合同由 AAA 的常务董事签署，AAA 总部将保留一份副本。

6. 据此，新任的 AAA-MW 地区会议主持者负责组织这一会议。

对于正式流程一般没有太多限制，因此会议主持人需确定他/她要如何开展会议。按照惯例，会议要收取注册费，以支付食品、视听设施和会议室费用。会议主持者和其他一些志愿者一起组织征集论文、审查论文、会议发言人、接待以及与地区分会会员的通信联系。通常，会议有几次职业继续教育（CPE）的讲习会，并提供星期五和星期六的早餐、星期五的午餐、星期五和星期六早上和星期五下午的点心以及星期四和星期五这两天的晚宴。筹备这一切是很费力的，会议主持者通常必须全身心投入。所有的现金收入和支出都由 AAA 雇员经手。他们收集注册费、支付酒店账单等，在区域组织的账户上收支款项。AAA-MW 的督导委员会主席会定期收到各项活动的报告书。2002 年以前，AAA-MW 的各次会议通常都会有结余，督导委员会很少担心财务问题。

# 背景

在 2002 年 8 月 AAA-MW 督导委员会的会议上，委员会得知 2002 年春季的地区会议亏损了 14 389.13 美元。图表 1 列示了 2001 年与 2002 年的对比情况。2002 年 AAA-MW 的地区性会议是 3 月份在密尔沃基举行的，出席人数为 170 人。出席人数比前一年在圣路易斯举行的会议骤降了 30.6%，这是最近几年的历史上，出席人数少于 200 人的不多的几次之一。委员会认为，出席人数低的主要原因是人们不愿意乘坐飞机（旅行），因为此时"9·11"恐怖袭击刚发生不久。此外，委员会还认为会议的地址（威斯康星州的密尔沃基市）在早春时节旅行不便、不具吸引力。因此，委员会确信 2002 年的会议出现现金净流出是个反常现象，不需要做进一步的调查研究。于是，委员会接着开始讨论明年春季将在圣路易士市的千禧大酒店（Millennium Hotel）召开的 2003 年 AAA-MW 年会。中西部地区分会通常都是每隔一年便在圣·路易士市召开一次年会，因为该市处在中心位置、春季气候宜人，参加的人总是特别多。为此，委员会并不担心 2003 年的会议会出现亏损的结果。

**图表 1**

**2001 年与 2002 年的对照表**

**财务报告**

**AAA 中西部地区分会**

截止于 2001 年 9 月 30 日和 2002 年 9 月 30 日的会计年度

|  | 09/01 – 08/02 | 09/00 – 08/01 |
|---|---|---|
| 出席人数 | 170 | 245 |
| **现金流入** |  |  |
| 年中会议 |  |  |
| 注册费 | $ 14 835.00 | $ 20 125.00 |
| 捐款 | 0.00 | 1 990.00 |
| 展费收入 | 4 200.00 | 4 500.00 |
| 职业继续教育（CPE） | 2 400.00 | 3 270.00 |
| 会议总收入 | $ 21 435.00 | $ 29 885.00 |
| 利息 | 1 313.29 | 4 312.20 |
| 现金收入总额 | $ 22 748.29 | $ 34 197.20 |
| **现金流出** |  |  |
| 年中会议 |  |  |
| 印刷 | $ 2 890.55 | $ 2 425.52 |
| 邮件 | 752.35 | 470.17 |
| 展费支出 | 354.82 | 460.00 |
| 食品/饮料 | 28 527.36 | 18 490.63 |
| 视听设施 | 0.00 | 2 965.85 |
| 扬声器 | 469.76 | 1 477.92 |
| 会议事项协调员 | 2 231.05 | 0.00 |
| 邮寄费 | 55.97 | 0.00 |
| 差旅费 | 0.00 | 184.79 |
| AAA 员工 | 154.00 | 105.00 |
| 职业继续教育旅行 | 350.00 | 1 990.00 |
| 会议总支出 | $ 35 785.86 | $ 28 569.88 |
| 行政管理费用 | 1 351.61 | 1 590.02 |
| 现金支出总额 | $ 37 137.47 | $ 30 159.90 |
| 资产净变动额 | $ (14 389.18) | $ 4 037.30 |
| 期初现金余额 | 88 783.55 | 84 746.25 |
| 期末现金余额 | $ 74 394.37 | $ 88 783.55 |

2003年3月，AAA-MW会议按为期两天半的惯例安排进行，与会者参加了几个包括在注册费中的职业继续教育讲习会和一些其他的活动。图表2列示了2003年AAA-MW年会的日程安排。

会议一结束，在星期六督导委员会的午餐会上，新任AAA-MW主席（2003年会议主持者）主持了会议。和往常一样，会议事项协调人出席会议并报告了最终出席的人数。出席人数为185人，比前一年170人多，但仍低于200人的最低预期数。督导委员会还未掌握该次会议的任何财务数据，并不认为出席人数少就会造成亏损。因此，会议的其余时间就用于讨论将在堪萨斯市召开的2004年会议和回到圣路易士市召开的2005年会议。

2003年8月，在AAA全国会议上，督导委员会又一次相聚。此时已从AAA总部的职员处获得了有关2003年3月会议的财务信息（见图表3）。委员会非常震惊，因为春季会议的亏损额几乎为2002年亏损额的一倍。如果这一情况继续下去，中西部地区分会将在几年内破产。在这一担心之下，委员会决定任命一位司库。该司库正式的职责是从AAA获取AAA-MW的月度财务报告，并就AAA-MW地区分会的财务状况在督导委员会的会议和年会上进行报告。不过，这位司库首先需要对2003年的亏损进行调查研究。

## 要求

1. 作为司库，请确定你还需要哪些补充资料。
2. 请对信息进行分析，并编制一份报告，说明各项亏损的原因。
3. 请向督导委员会建议如何避免未来会议的损失。

**图表 2**

**AAA 中西部地区年会、日程安排**

| 日期 | 时间 | 会议议程 | 督导委员会活动 |
|---|---|---|---|
| 星期四 | 下午 | 红雀队棒球体育馆之旅 | |
| | 晚上 | 美味的欢迎酒会和开放酒吧。欢迎酒会部分由教科书出版商赞助 | |
| 星期五 | 晚上7:00 | 自助早餐:大陆卷、麦片、烤面包、酸奶、水果、咖啡、牛奶和茶 | 督导委员会在早餐会议上收集参与信息和需要解决的各种问题及问及尚未确定的下一年会召开的最终选址和其他细节问题 |
| | 上午8:30~10:00 | 五场同时进行的职业继续教育课程 | |
| | 上午10:00~10:30 | 上午休息时供应各种食物和饮料(咖啡、瓶装水和果汁) | |
| | 10:30~中午 | 7场同时进行的职业继续教育课程 | |
| | 中午~下午1:30 | 与发言人共进午餐 | 颁发论文奖状和终身会员奖 |
| | 下午1:45~3:15 | 7场同时进行的职业继续教育课程 | |
| | 下午3:15~3:45 | 下午休息时间,供应咖啡/苏打水和零食 | |
| | 下午3:45~5:15 | 7场同时进行的职业继续教育课程 | |
| | 晚上6:00~7:30 | 晚宴在两个指点地点供应各类冷暖开胃小吃,包括烤牛肉、烤火鸡、各类蔬菜、蛋类、薯片和酱……以及一个开放酒吧 | |
| | 晚上7:30~9:00 | 冰淇淋联谊会由美国会计学会教学组与课务组赞助 | |
| 星期六 | 上午7:30~9:00 | AAA*-MW 事务会议 | AAA-MW主席和会议主持负责主持会议,提名和选举新的督导委员会成员 |
| | 上午9:00~10:30 | 美国会计准则委员会最新情况通报和2场同时进行的职业继续教育课程 | |
| | 上午10:30~11:00 | 上午休息时间供应咖啡和各种小食品 | |
| | 上午11:00~12:30 | 5场同时进行的职业继续教育课程 | |
| | 下午12:30~2:00 督导委员会议 | 无事件;会议结束 | 督导委员会午餐会;会议主持成为下一届主席并主持会议 |

* AAA 为美国会计学会(American Accounting Association)的缩写。

## 图表 3

### 向督导委员会提供的 AAA-MW 的财务资料(2002~2003 年)

| 日期 | 9-02 | 10-02 | 11-02 | 12-02 | 1-03 | 2-03 | 3-03 | 4-03 | 5-03 | 6-03 | 7-03 | 8-03 | 合计 | 去年 |
|---|---|---|---|---|---|---|---|---|---|---|---|---|---|---|
| 期初现金余额 | 70 394.37 | 75 500.56 | 75 568.03 | 74 529.07 | 74 562.27 | 76 392.44 | 79 251.84 | 92 040.53 | 91 981.19 | 53 269.27 | | | | |
| **年中会议现金收入** | | | | | | | | | | | | | | |
| 广告费 | | | | | | | | | | | | | 0.00 | |
| 注册费 | | | | | | 1 032.00 | 12 477.00 | 2 919.00 | | | | | 16 428.00 | 14 835.00 |
| 捐款 | | | | | | | | | | | | | 0.00 | 0.00 |
| 展览会收入 | | | | | 1 800.00 | 1 800.00 | 600.00 | | | | | | 4 200.00 | 4 200.00 |
| CPE | | | | | | | | | | | | | 0.00 | |
| 注册费 | | | | | | | | | | | | | 0.00 | 2 400.00 |
| 年中会议合计 | 0.00 | 0.00 | 0.00 | 0.00 | 1 800.00 | 2 832.00 | 13 077.00 | 2 919.00 | 0.00 | | | | 20 628.00 | 21 435.00 |
| **其他收入** | | | | | | | | | | | | | | |
| 捐款 | | | | | | | | | | | | | — | — |
| 利息收入 | | 67.47 | 67.83 | 33.80 | 30.77 | 30.59 | 26.53 | 33.73 | 28.76 | 13.36 | | | 332.84 | 1 313.29 |
| 收入合计 | 0.00 | 67.47 | 67.83 | 33.80 | 1 830.77 | 2 862.59 | 13 103.53 | 2 952.73 | 28.76 | 13.36 | — | — | 20 960.84 | 22 748.29 |
| **年中会议支出** | | | | | | | | | | | | | | |
| 印刷 | | | | | | | 2 716.25 | | | | | | 2 716.25 | 2 890.55 |
| 复印 | | | | | | | | | | | | | 0.00 | |
| 邮件 | | | | | | | | | | | | | 0.00 | 752.35 |
| 注册费用 | | | | | | | | | | | | | 0.00 | |
| 展览会费用 | | | | | | | | | | | | | 0.00 | 354.82 |
| 酒店房间/食物/饮料 | | | | | | | | | 34 010.36 | (40.00) | | | 33 970.36 | 28 527.36 |
| 酒店视听设施费用 | | | | | | | | | 3 983.40 | | | | 3 983.40 | — |
| 会议娱乐 | | | | | | | | | 84.00 | | | | 84.00 | — |
| 扬声器 | | | | | | | | | 662.32 | 507.35 | | | 1 169.68 | 469.76 |
| 会议协调员费用 | | | 1 106.19 | | | | | | | | | | 1 244.59 | 2 231.05 |
| 邮费 | (1 106.19) | | | | | | | | 1 244.59 | | | | 0.00 | 55.97 |

表 3 转下一页

接上页

| 日期 | 9-02 | 10-02 | 11-02 | 12-02 | 1-03 | 2-03 | 3-03 | 4-03 | 5-03 | 6-03 | 7-03 | 8-03 | 合计 | 去年 |
|---|---|---|---|---|---|---|---|---|---|---|---|---|---|---|
| 物料 | | | | | | | | 105.00 | | | | | 105.00 | — |
| 电话费 | | | | | | | | | | | | | 0.00 | — |
| 差旅费 | | | | | | | | | | | | | 0.00 | — |
| AAA 职员提供支援 | | | | | | | | | | | | | 0.00 | 350.00 |
| 杂项费用 | | | | | | | | | | | | | 0.00 | 154.00 |
| CPE | | | | | | | | | | | | | 0.00 | 0.00 |
| 酒店房间/食物/饮料 | | | | | | | | | | | | | — | — |
| 酒店视听设施费用 | | | | | | | | | | | | | — | — |
| 杂项费用 | | | | | | | | | | | | | — | — |
| 扬声器 | | | | | | | | | | | | | — | — |
| 会议合计 | (1 106.19) | 0.00 | 1 106.19 | 0.00 | 0.00 | 0.00 | 0.00 | 2 821.25 | 38 740.08 | 1 711.94 | 0.00 | 0.00 | 43 273.28 | 35 785.86 |
| 行政管理费用 | | | | | | | | | | | | | | |
| 邮费 | | | 0.60 | 0.60 | 0.60 | 3.19 | 58.04 | 78.32 | 0.60 | 0.60 | | | 142.55 | 86.11 |
| 杂项费用 | | | | | | | | | | | | | 0.00 | — |
| 会议室费用 | | | | | | | | | | | | | 0.00 | 1 000.00 |
| 奖品 | | | | | | | 256.80 | 112.50 | | | | | 369.30 | 265.50 |
| 行政费用合计 | 0.00 | 0.00 | 0.60 | 0.60 | 0.60 | 3.19 | 314.84 | 190.82 | 0.60 | 0.60 | — | — | 511.85 | 1 351.61 |
| 委员会高级职员 | | | | | | | | | | | | | | |
| 酒店房间/食物/饮料 | | | | | | | | | | | | | — | — |
| 差旅费 | | | | | | | | | | | | | — | — |
| 杂项费用 | | | | | | | | | | | | | — | — |
| 委员会高级职员合计 | (1 106.19) | 0.00 | 1 106.79 | | | 3.19 | 314.84 | 3 012.07 | 38 740.68 | 1 712.54 | — | — | 43 785.13 | 37 137.47 |
| 支出合计 | 75 500.56 | 75 568.03 | 74 529.07 | 74 562.27 | 76 392.27 | 76 392.44 | 79 251.84 | 92 040.53 | 91 981.19 | 53 269.27 | | | | |
| 期末现金余额 | | | | | | | | | | 51 570.09 | | | | |

# Sometimes Accountants Fail to Budget

Gail Hoover King
Purdue University Calumet

Jane Saly
University of St. Thomas

> Budgeting is important in all organizations, but it is especially in nonprofit organizations where revenue sources are often inconsistent from year to year. Nonprofit leadership has a fiscal responsibility to monitor the variances between actual revenues and cost and make operating decisions to ensure the organization's viability and success.

## INTRODUCTION

In August 2003, the Steering Committee of the American Accounting Association Midwest Region (AAA-MW) discovered that its 2003 annual meeting had a net loss of $ 24 232, leaving a net account balance at less than $ 50 000. This was on top of a loss of $ 13 264 the previous year. Concerned about a possible trend, the board created a treasurer position and asked the treasurer to investigate these losses.

## THE ORGANIZATION

The steering committee is an entirely volunteer board whose task is to organize and run an annual conference targeting members of the American Accounting Association who reside in the states of Illinois, Indiana, Iowa, Kansas, Michigan, Minnesota, Missouri, North Dakota, South Dakota, Nebraska, and Wisconsin. The American Accounting Association (AAA) is a not-for-profit organization whose members are primarily accounting academics. The organization " promotes worldwide excellence in accounting education, research and practice. Founded in 1916 as the American Association of University Instructors in Accounting, its present name was adopted in 1936. The Association brings together the academic community to further accounting education and to advance the discipline and profession of accounting. "

(*American Accounting Association Our Shared Vision*, http://aaahq.org/about/AAAShareVisionDocumentJan08fnl_ 4_ .pdf, 2008, p 6)

The steering committee meets twice a year; every spring at the annual AAA-MW Region meeting and in August at the national meeting of the American Accounting Association. The typical process for organizing the AAA-MW annual meeting was as follows:

1. Eighteen months prior to the meeting (usually at the August AAA national meeting), the steering committee determines in which city within the Midwest region to hold the meeting and submits a meeting site search request to the AAA national office.

2. The program chair for the meeting is a volunteer of the steering committee and is a different (and new) person each year.

3. The event coordinator (a third party hired by the AAA national office) contacts hotels in the chosen city and provides the AAA-MW steering committee with a list of hotels, room rates, and parking rates.

4. At the spring AAA-MW regional meeting, one year prior to the next meeting, the steering committee chooses a hotel based on its location in the city and room rates offered.

5. The event coordinator negotiates the final contract, it is signed by the AAA executive director, and a copy is kept in the AAA headquarter files.

6. The new AAA-MW regional meeting program chair is then responsible for organizing the meeting.

There was little in the way of a formal process, so each program chair would determine how he/she wanted to run the meeting. There was a tradition of charging a registration fee that covered food, audiovisual needs, and meeting rooms. The program chair, working with a few other volunteers, would organize the call for papers, review of papers, program speakers, receptions, and communication with members within the region. Typically, the meeting had multiple continuing professional education (CPE) sessions, offered breakfast on Friday and Saturday, lunch on Friday, snack breaks on Friday and Saturday morning and Friday afternoon, and evening receptions on both Thursday and Friday. All of this planning was a significant amount of effort and generally consumed the program chair's attention. All cash inflows and outflows were handled by the AAA staff members. They collected registration fees, paid the hotel bills, etc., charging or crediting the region's accounts. The AAA-MW steering committee president would receive periodic account activity reports. Prior to 2002, the AAA-MW meetings had generally resulted in an increase in cash flow and the steering committee had little need to worry about finances.

## BACKGROUND

At the August 2002 meeting of the AAA-MW steering committee, the committee learned that the spring 2002 regional meeting showed a loss of $14 389.13. The comparison of 2001 and 2002 is shown in Exhibit 1. The 2002 AAA-MW regional meeting had been held in Milwaukee in March and the attendance at that meeting was 170. This was a 30.6 percent drop from the previous year's meeting held in St. Louis, and one of the few times in the region's recent history that the meeting attendance was below 200 attendees. The committee believed the main reason for the low attendance was reluctance to fly (travel) so soon after the after the 9/11 terrorist attack. In addition, the committee believed the location (Milwaukee, Wisconsin) in early spring was difficult to travel to and may not have been appealing. Therefore, the committee was satisfied that the net cash outflow for the 2002 meeting was an anomaly and there was no need for more investigation. As such, the committee proceeded to discuss the plans for the 2003 AAA-MW annual meeting, which was to be held the following spring at the Millennium Hotel in St. Louis. The Midwest region had the policy of holding the annual meeting in St. Louis every other year and, because of the central location and more favorable spring weather, the St. Louis meetings had always been well attended. For that reason, the committee was not concerned that the 2003 meeting might result in a loss.

The March 2003, AAA-MW meeting was held and followed the typical two-and-a-half-day format, with participants attending a number of CPE sessions and other activities included in their registration fee. The schedule of events for the 2003 AAA-MW annual meeting is shown in Exhibit 2.

Immediately after the meeting, during the Saturday steering committee luncheon meeting, the new AAA-MW president (the 2003 program chair) presided over the meeting. As normal, the event coordinator attended and reported the final attendance numbers. The attendance was 185, which was higher than the previous year's attendance of 170, but still lower than the 200 or more expected. The steering committee, not yet having any financial figures from the meeting, did not consider that the low attendance might result in a loss. Therefore, the remainder of the meeting was spent discussing the plans for the 2004 meeting in Kansas City and the plan for the 2005 meeting, which would be back in St. Louis.

## Exhibit 1
## Comparison of 2001 and 2002

Financial Report
AAA Midwest Region
For years ending September 30, 2001, and September 30, 2002

|  | 09/01 – 08/02 | 09/00 – 08/01 |
|---|---:|---:|
| Attendance | 170 | 245 |
|  |  |  |
| INFLOWS |  |  |
| Mid-year Meeting |  |  |
| Registration | $ 14 835.00 | $ 20 125.00 |
| Contributions | 0.00 | 1 990.00 |
| Exhibitor Fees | 4 200.00 | 4 500.00 |
| CPE | 2 400.00 | 3 270.00 |
| Total Meeting | $ 21 435.00 | $ 29 885.00 |
| Interest | 1 313.29 | 4 312.20 |
| Total Inflows | $ 22 748.29 | $ 34 197.20 |
|  |  |  |
| OUTFLOWS |  |  |
| Mid-year Meeting |  |  |
| Printing | $ 2 890.55 | $ 2 425.52 |
| Mailing | 752.35 | 470.17 |
| Exhibitor Expense | 354.82 | 460.00 |
| Food/Bev | 28 527.36 | 18 490.63 |
| Audio Visual | 0.00 | 2 965.85 |
| Speakers | 469.76 | 1 477.92 |
| Mtg Coord | 2 231.05 | 0.00 |
| Postage | 55.97 | 0.00 |
| Travel | 0.00 | 184.79 |
| AAA Staff | 154.00 | 105.00 |
| CPE travel | 350.00 | 1 990.00 |
| Total Meeting | $ 35 785.86 | $ 28 569.88 |
| G&A | 1 351.61 | 1 590.02 |
| Total Outflows | $ 37 137.47 | $ 30 159.90 |
|  |  |  |
| Net change in assets | $ (14 389.18) | $ 4 037.30 |
| Beginning Cash | 88 783.55 | 84 746.25 |
| Ending Cash | $ 74 394.37 | $ 88 783.55 |

## Exhibit 2
### Midwest Region of the American Accounting Association 2003 Meeting Program

| Day | Time | Participant Events | Steering Committee Activities |
|---|---|---|---|
| Thursday | Afternoon | Tour of Cardinals Baseball Stadium | |
| | Evening | Welcome reception with appetizers and open bar. Reception was sponsored in part by the textbook publishers | |
| Friday | 7:00 pm | Buffet breakfast continental rolls, cereal, toast, yogurt, fruit, coffee, milk, tea | Steering committee breakfast meeting to receive information on meeting attendance and issues that needed to be addressed and finalize location or other details not yet decided for next year's event. |
| | 8:30–10 am | 5 concurrent CPE sessions | |
| | 10–10:30 pm | Morning reception with food and drink (coffee, bottled water, and juice) | |
| | 10:30–noon | 7 concurrent CPE sessions | |
| | Noon–1:30 pm | Luncheon with speaker | Awards for papers and lifetime members |
| | 1:45–3:15 pm | 7 concurrent CPE sessions | |
| | 3:45–5:15 pm | Afternoon refreshment break with coffee/soda and snack | |
| | 3:45–5:15 pm | 7 concurrent CPE sessions | |
| | 6–7:30 pm | Reception with hot and cold hors d'oeuvres including two carving stations (roast beef and turkey) as well as vegetables, egg rolls, chips and dips…and an open bar | |
| | 7:30–9:00 pm | Ice cream social sponsored by the Teaching and Curriculum Section of the AAA* | |
| Saturday | 7:30–9:00 am | AAA-MW business meeting | President and program chair preside over the meeting; Nominate and vote on new steering committee members |
| | 9–10:30 am | FASB update and 2 other concurrent CPE sessions | |
| | 10:30–11:00 am | Morning break with coffee and snacks | |
| | 11–12:30 pm | 5 concurrent CPE sessions | |
| | 12:30–2:00 pm Steering Committee Meeting | No events; conference has ended | Steering committee luncheon and meeting; the program chair becomes the president and presides over the meeting |

* AAA stands for American Accounting Association

The steering committee met again in August 2003 at the AAA national meeting and received from AAA headquarters' staff the financial information about the March 2003 meeting. (See Exhibit 3.) The committee was shocked to find that the spring meeting had resulted in a loss that was almost twice the loss incurred in 2002. If this pattern continued, the Midwest region would be bankrupt within a couple of years. Concerned, the committee decided to appoint a treasurer. The official duties of the treasurer would be to receive monthly financial reports of the AAA-MW from the AAA and report on the AAA-MW region's financial situation at steering committee meetings and the annual meeting. First, however, the treasurer would need to investigate the 2003 loss.

## REQUIRED

1. As treasurer, determine what additional information you would like.

2. Analyze the information and prepare a report for the steering committee explaining the losses.

3. Provide suggestions to the steering committee on how to avoid future meeting losses.

## Exhibit 3
### AAA-MW Financial Information Provided to Steering Committee for 2002 – 2003

| | Sep-02 | Oct-02 | Nov-02 | Dec-02 | Jan-03 | Feb-03 | Mar-03 | Apr-03 | May-03 | Jun-03 | Jul-03 | Aug-03 | TOTAL | Prior Year Totals |
|---|---|---|---|---|---|---|---|---|---|---|---|---|---|---|
| Beginning Cash Balance | 74 394.37 | 75 500.56 | 75 568.03 | 74 529.07 | 74 562.27 | 76 392.44 | 79 251.84 | 92 040.53 | 91 981.19 | 53 269.27 | | | | |
| *INFLOW* MID-YEAR MEETING | | | | | | | | | | | | | | |
| Advertising | | | | | | | | | | | | | 0.00 | 0.00 |
| Registration Fees | | | | | | 1 032.00 | 12 477.00 | 2 919.00 | | | | | 16 428.00 | 14 835.00 |
| Contributions | | | | | | | | | | | | | 0.00 | 0.00 |
| Exhibitor Fees | | | | | 1 800.00 | | 600.00 | | | | | | 4 200.00 | 4 200.00 |
| CPE | | | | | | | | | | | | | 0.00 | 0.00 |
| Registration Fees | | | | | | | | | | | | | 0.00 | 2 400.00 |
| Total Mid-year Meeting | 0.00 | 0.00 | 0.00 | 0.00 | 1 800.00 | 1 032.00 | 13 077.00 | 2 919.00 | 0.00 | 0.00 | | | 20 628.00 | 21 435.00 |
| OTHER INCOME | | | | | | | | | | | | | | |
| Contributions | | | | | | | | | | | | | — | — |
| Interest Income | | 67.47 | 67.83 | 33.80 | 30.77 | 30.59 | 26.53 | 33.73 | 28.76 | 13.36 | | | 332.84 | 1 313.29 |
| Total Inflow | 0.00 | 67.47 | 67.83 | 33.80 | 1 830.77 | 2 862.59 | 13 103.53 | 2 952.73 | 28.76 | 13.36 | | | 20 960.84 | 22 748.29 |
| *OUTFLOW* MID-YEAR MEETING | | | | | | | | | | | | | | |
| Printing | | | | | | | | 2 716.25 | | | | | 2 716.25 | 2 890.55 |
| Copying | | | | | | | | | | | | | 0.00 | 0.00 |
| Mailing | | | | | | | | | | | | | 0.00 | 752.35 |
| Registration Expense | | | | | | | | | | | | | 0.00 | 354.82 |
| Exhibitor Expense | | | | | | | | | | | | | 0.00 | — |
| Hotel-Rooms/Food/Bev | | | | | | | | | 34 010.36 | (40.00) | | | 33 970.36 | 28 527.36 |
| Hotel-Audio Visuals | | | | | | | | | 3 983.40 | | | | 3 983.40 | — |
| Mtg. Entertainment | | | | | | | | | 84.00 | | | | 84.00 | — |
| Speakers | | | | | | | | | 662.32 | 507.35 | | | 1 169.68 | 469.76 |
| Mtg. Coord. - Exp. | (1 106.19) | | 1 106.19 | | | | | | | 1 244.59 | | | 1 244.59 | 2 231.05 |
| Postage | | | | | | | | | | | | | 0.00 | 55.97 |

Table 3 continues on next page

## Panel B-General Ledger Data

| | Sep-02 | Oct-02 | Nov-02 | Dec-02 | Jan-03 | Feb-03 | Mar-03 | Apr-03 | May-03 | Jun-03 | Jul-03 | Aug-03 | TOTAL Year | Prior Year Totals |
|---|---|---|---|---|---|---|---|---|---|---|---|---|---|---|
| Supplies | | | | | | | | 105.00 | | | | | 105.00 | — |
| Telephone | | | | | | | | | | | | | 0.00 | — |
| Travel | | | | | | | | | | | | | 0.00 | — |
| AAA Staff Support | | | | | | | | | | | | | 0.00 | 350.00 |
| Misc. | | | | | | | | | | | | | 0.00 | 154.00 |
| CPE | | | | | | | | | | | | | 0.00 | — |
| Hotel-Rooms/Food/Bev | | | | | | | | | | | | | 0.00 | — |
| Hotel. Audio Visuals | | | | | | | | | | | | | — | — |
| Misc. | | | | | | | | | | | | | — | — |
| Speakers | | | | | | | | | | | | | — | — |
| Travel | | | | | | | | | | | | | — | — |
| Total Meeting | (1 106.19) | 0.00 | 1 106.19 | 0.00 | 0.00 | 0.00 | 0.00 | 2 821.25 | 38 740.08 | 1 711.94 | 0.00 | 0.00 | 43 273.28 | 35 785.86 |
| GENERAL/ADMIN. | | | | | | | | | | | | | | |
| Postage | | | | 0.60 | 0.60 | 3.19 | 58.04 | 78.32 | 0.60 | 0.60 | | | 142.55 | 86.11 |
| Misc. | | | | | | | | | | | | | 0.00 | — |
| Council Fee | | | | | | | | | | | | | 0.00 | 1 000.00 |
| Awards | | | | | | | 256.80 | 112.50 | | | | | 369.30 | 265.50 |
| Total General | 0.00 | 0.00 | 0.00 | 0.60 | 0.60 | 3.19 | 314.84 | 190.82 | 0.60 | 0.60 | | — | 511.85 | 1 351.61 |
| COMMITTEES/OFFICERS | | | | | | | | | | | | | | |
| Hotel-Rooms/Food/Bev | | | | | | | | | | | | | — | — |
| Travel | | | | | | | | | | | | | — | — |
| Misc. | | | | | | | | | | | | | — | — |
| Total Committee/Officers | | | | | | | | | | | | | | |
| Total Outflow | (1 106.19) | 0.00 | 1 106.79 | 0.60 | 0.60 | 3.19 | 314.84 | 3 012.07 | 38 740.68 | 1 712.54 | — | — | 43 785.13 | 37 137.47 |
| Ending Cash Balance | 75 500.56 | 75 568.03 | 74 529.07 | 74 562.27 | 76 392.44 | 79 251.84 | 92 040.53 | 91 981.19 | 53 269.27 | 51 570.09 | | | | |

# SEWMEX 公司：国际背景下的短期利润规划

Gus Gordon
University of Texas at Tyler

David E. Stout
Youngstown State University

Sarah Hartzog, Student
Former Student, Millsaps College

Matt Lusty, Student
Former Student, University of Texasat Tyler

Jay Nelson, Student
FormerStudent, University of Texasat Tyler

## 简介

　　SEWMEX 公司是一家新成立的制衣厂，位于墨西哥。它原是一家美资企业，在墨西哥经过合并成为一家墨西哥公司，并且加入了墨西哥的美墨联营工厂项目（maquiladora program）[1]。依照合同，美国母公司，缝纫股份有限公司（SEWInc.，下文简称为 SEW），购买 SEWMEX 制衣厂的所有产成品。SEW 向 SEWMEX 制衣厂提供所有原材料。这些交易在美墨联营体系内进行，并且符合北美自由贸易协议（North American Free Trade Agreement，简称 NAFTA）规定，这样一来，这些交易就不需要缴纳进口或出口关税。因此，美墨联营工厂只负责将原材料组装成完工产品，接着将完工产品运回美国的 SEW 公司。于是，SEWMEX 没有原材料成本。不过，考虑到有些紧急订单等不及进口原材料，SEWMEX 也留有少量产成品的存货。

---

　　* 本篇译者为赵澄，校订者为陈秀云、胡金凤。
　　[1] Maquiladora，马基拉多拉，原为一家墨西哥工厂的名字，这家工厂的最主要目的是将原材料装配成最终产品，再将最终产品出口到原材料原产国家（如美国）。马基拉朵拉（或简称马基拉）工厂对运入的原材料和产出的产品并没有所有权，因为原材料只是以契约形式暂时性进口的，并且依法必须将其用于组装最终产品，接着出口回原出口国，这则案例中 SEW 就是这样一家工厂。——原注（SEW 是一家美国的公司，它在墨西哥的子公司为 SEWMEX，其中 MEX 即代表墨西哥。——译者）

除了SEWMEX制衣厂，SEW在美国东南部还有其他几家工厂。其中一家工厂（位于密西西比州东南部）还是配送中心和中心仓库：来自其他工厂的所有完工商品被存储在这里并最终被运走。SEW通过这个配送中心向美国50个州以及加拿大的所有顾客供应商品。

在与公司董事长的一次意见不合之后，SEW公司的总会计师最近突然辞职了。在他离职后，他为公司所作的许多核算资料也神秘地不知所踪。考虑到美国工厂的劳动力成本较高，SEW公司董事长打算未来利用SEWMEX生产更多的产品。然而，SEWMEX毕竟是个新厂，尚未盈利。因此，SEW和SEWMEX可以通过实施利润规划共同受益。

假设你是总会计师助理，首先，董事长希望你发挥自己的能力为SEWMEX工厂开发一套本量利（成本—产量—利润）模型，用来处理一些短期利润规划问题。董事长特别希望能更加确切地了解需要多少的产出量，才能使SEWMEX在短期内盈利（假定按照目前的产品组合），需要采用什么样的长期战略改善经营进而获利。董事长还想知道：外汇汇率问题到底会不会使利润规划过程变得复杂。因此，在他寻找新任总会计师的同时，他请你负责构建SEWMEX公司的本量利模型。为了能给董事长留下好印象，你非常愿意接受这项任务。

## 设备管理控制与时间调度程序（FACTS[②]）

在你刚进SEW时，公司总会计师曾向你解释，制衣行业通常以生产单件服装所需的"标准工时"[③]（standard allowedminutes，简称SAMs）为基础进行服装的成本与定价核算。事实上，在制衣行业，产品通常以这类标准进行计量，而不是按完工产品的件数进行计量。总会计师告诉你："标准工时"是根据生产工程师的估计得出的，他们先估算出完成每项缝制工序所需的时间，进而推算出生产一款衣服所需的全部时间。这种估算方法来自于工时与动作研究（也就是工业工程研究），并且考虑了很多变量，包括：每种缝纫机完成同一道工序的速度、每位操作员的教育/培训，以及SEWMEX装配工人现在使用的技术。

### 预计售价

在安排你完成这项工作时，SEW董事长给了你一份单位产品售价的数据，如表1[④]。表1列示的价格来自公司市场部，它们以美元（USD）为单

---

[②] FACTS，即Facilities Administration Control and Time Schedule的缩写。——译者
[③] 标准工时（SAMs）和标准人工时间（standardlabor times）同义，用来将直接人工成本计入半成品存货（和完工产品存货），并用来计算标准成本系统下的直接人工差异。——原注（注意：这里的标准工时，即标准工作时间，是以分钟为单位的。——译者
[④] 如后文所释，表1列示的价格是每一系列产品的平均价格，是基于假定的各种产品系列组合和选项得出的平均价格。——原注

位，以内部调拨价格⑤为基础，该调拨价格是每件衣服和初始的产品销售组合价格的决定因素。在与该公司的审计事务所讨论之后，他们认为表1列示的销售价格可用于计算美国的所得税。并且，假设这些价格在短期的计划期限内是有效的，你在建立本量利模型时可以使用。

**表1**
**SEWMEX——单件成衣的平均合同售价（以产品系列分类）**

| 产品系列 | 单件产品平均售价 |
| --- | --- |
| 裤子 | $ 7.00 |
| 衬衫 | $ 6.00 |
| 夹克 | $ 25.00 |
| 其他 | $ 3.00 |

（注：SEW 与 SEWMEX 之间的合同明确表明，SEW 以美元对 SEWMEX 进行结算。另外，表中的单件售价是在考虑每一产品系列中各个款式之后算出的各产品系列的平均售价。）

### 计划生产/销售组合

表2⑥列示了 SEWMEX 对各产品系列制定的月度基础生产/销售水平。这是 SEW 董事长给你的。表中的"标准工时"值表示制造每种衣服所需的平均标准时间。如前文所释，这些是根据现有生产工艺和装配水平估算出的。从表2可以看到，每月的总生产量按"标准工时"表示，目前计划需要 2 500 000 分钟。因为"标准工时"的意思是生产各种衣服所需的标准劳动时间，其反映了 SEWMEX 工厂装配部门的特定效率水平。⑦

**表2**
**SEWMEX 当前各产品系列的月度生产计划及合计数（单位：分钟［SAMs，标准工时］）**

| 产品系列 | 单位产品的平均标准工时（单位：分钟） | 月度计划生产水平（单位：分钟［SAMs，标准工时］） |
| --- | --- | --- |
| 裤子 | 50 | 1 200 000 |
| 衬衫 | 40 | 1 000 000 |
| 夹克 | 90 | 200 000 |
| 其他 | 20 | 100 000 |
| 合计 | | 2 500 000 |

---

⑤ 内部调拨价格是指产品或劳务在公司内部跨部门转移时的定价。该价格表示销售部门的"销售收入"和采购部门的"成本"。因此，他们可以用在评估这两个部门的财务业绩（例如，投资回报率）上。在编制合并财务报表时，如案例中的 SEWMEX 和 SEW，任何的公司内部交易效果将被抵销，这样报告只反映与外部利益人之间的交易利润额。——原注

⑥ 董事长判断，表2列示的销售组合在近期相对稳定，因此适合用来构建本量利模型。——原注

⑦ 在 SEWMEX 的经营环境下，"效率"可以看成是每月的标准工时数（产出），以总工时的百分比来表示。因此，提高效率即反映为增大每月的产出（以标准工时表示），相对表2中的总标准工时而言。——原注

### 一些简化的假设

在你和董事长的讨论中,他向你强调这一点:单件服装的销售价格(表1)和其对应的平均标准工时(表2)代表的是每一产品系列中大概的平均数字。事实上,SEW生产的裤子和衬衫有200多种款式,夹克衫有50多种,其他产品系列也大约有50种款式。例如,表2中每条裤子所需的平均标准工时是50分钟。然而,依据工程师的估计,这一系列的某一款裤子的标准工时很可能不是50分钟。因此,表1、表2列示的数据应看成每一系列所有产品的加权平均数,其中平均数的权重是以假定的服装组合为基础确定的。例如,假设在裤子产品系列中,款式1的裤子产量占一定的比例,款式2的裤子产量占一定的比例,等等。

接下来,表2反映的计划生产水平(如:每月所需的2 500 000标准工时在各个产品系列间的分配)是在不同产品系列类别中既定生产/销售组合下的反映。看到表1、表2列示的信息,你首先会想到两个方面:(1)你负责建模的利润规划环境,肯定要比你在课堂内所解决过的那些问题要复杂得多;(2)这则案例中的产品/产出组合很多,看上去让人头疼。毕竟,一项假定的标准销售组合既包括同一产品系列内的组合,又包括不同产品系列间的组合。因此,你不知道到底能否解决手头的问题。

不过,在与SEW董事长进一步交谈后,你松了一口气。因为你俩一致同意:在可预见的未来,表1和表2反映的数据组合很可能是稳定的,你可以把这些数据用在你要建立的短期利润规划模型(如,本量利)中。因此,你可以假定,在你为SEWMEX初步构建本量利模型时,可以有效利用表1、表2所列示的数据。

### 工厂分布

如图1所示,SEW有6家工厂,5家在美国,1家在墨西哥(SEWMEX)。SEW主要采用专业化生产模式。在美国的5家工厂中,有4家只生产单一的产品系列:两家工厂生产裤子,其他两家生产衬衫。而第五家生产夹克。第四条产品线(被称为"其他")生产的服装准确来说不是夹克,但与夹克设计类似;这些服装在夹克工厂内生产。相比之下,SEWMEX生产所有这四种产品系列,因此,可以和SEW公司内的其他5家工厂区别开来。

SEW的专业化模式的实践表明超过125人的劳动力的工厂会产生规模不经济,而低于125人的工厂又达不到最优效率。然而,SEWMEX采用完全不同的经营模式——在同一家较大型的工厂里,用同样的设备生产所有产品。由于文化的差异和SEWMEX采纳的非专业化的生产方法,SEW董事长不确定这种经营模式是否影响装配的劳动生产效率,进而影响SEWMEX工厂的盈利性。

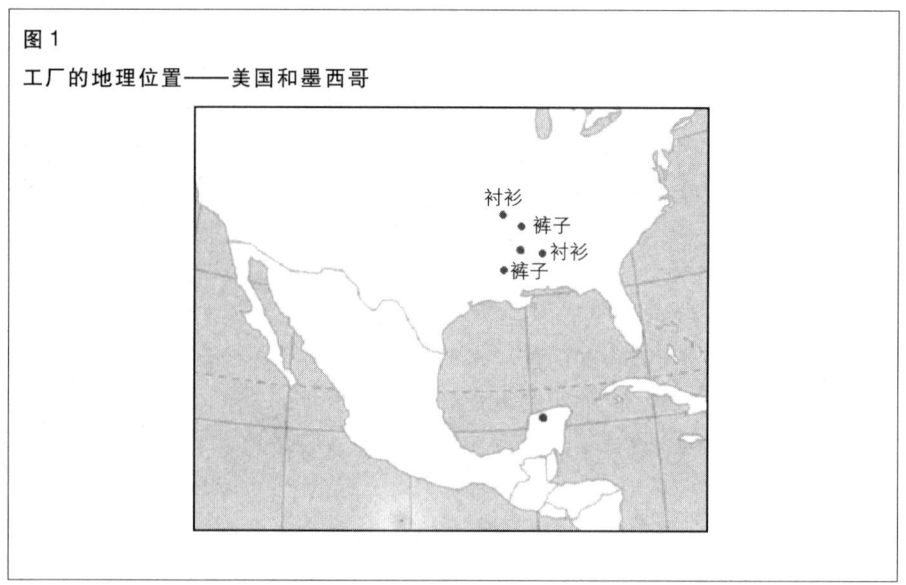

**图 1**
**工厂的地理位置——美国和墨西哥**

## 效率对 SEWMEX 的财务成功所起的战略重要性

你已经意识到，考虑到公司的产品特性和相关的生产流程，劳动效率是盈利的关键。毕竟，效率实际上是生产能力的另一计量指标：生产能力越大，既定劳动力的产出量越大，二者是等价的。

你还会意识到，在开发 SEWMEX 的短期利润规划模型时，理解制造流程的效率非常重要。如果装配工人在某个月里根据表 2 反映的标准工时进行生产，我们就说他们按计划、预期效率进行工作。如果装配工人在某个月里，生产的标准工时比计划数更多（假设当月组装员工人数保持不变），那么就说效率比计划更高，反之亦然。更高的劳动效率（生产率）会带来更多的经营收入/利润。

在查看 SEW 旗下每家工厂以前期间生产报告的基础上，你会发现美国 5 家工厂的平均效率为 85%。假定在美国每周的工作时间为 40 小时，一个操作者以 100% 的（即：标准）效率生产，则每周可以生产的产品为 2 400 标准工时（即：40 小时/周 × 60 分钟/小时）[⑧]。这 5 家工厂为 85% 的效率就意味着，每位 SEW 美国工厂的操作工人平均每周产出约为 2 040 标准工时（即 2 400 × 85%）。

对效率和产出之间的联系考虑的越多，你越会发现，实际上，你可以计算出 SEWMEX 工厂在一定期间内（比如 1 个月）的计划效率，方法与前面列示的对美国工厂的计算相似。表 2 列示的标准工时表示的是某月计划的总产出水平和计划的产品组合。

作为 SEWMEX 管理信息系统的一部分，每位生产工人在每天工作结束时上交一份表格，表中包含记录该工人当天的操作情况的条码。同时，可以

---

⑧ 根据定义，这个产出水平独立于产品组合。案例下文提到这一部分的名称："人工成本的性质：美国与墨西哥对比"。——原注

使用该条码找出该工人当天生产的产品系列。简而言之，这些表格包含了产出、标准工时、产品系列、生产指令等信息。一天结束时，使用光学识别器读出条码。利用这种方式获得的信息来确定操作员、产品系列以及整个工厂的效率水平。

### SEWMEX 的成本数据

董事长向你提供了预计的月度成本数据（表3），这些数据是董事长和 SEW 前任总会计师的最后一次会议后保留下来的。董事长提醒你，装配工人的操作用标准工时的值表示，只有他们的工作被视为直接人工，并且他和前任总会计师都认为要达到 SEWMEX 的计划生产水平（表2），大约需要 400 个机器操作工人。表 3 的数据便是按照机器操作工人 400 人、总员工 500 人算出的。[9]

### 劳动生产率/效率

在墨西哥，不付加班费的话，一周最多允许工作 48 小时。另外，在与董事长的交谈中你了解到，得益于学习曲线和其他变量，SEWMEX 有望按美国工厂装配工人的平均劳动生产率开始生产。因此，根据 SEWMEX 最初的计划目标，你和董事长都同意按每位工人每天工作 500 分钟为基础来计算 SEWMEX 工厂装配工人的工作效率（劳动生产率）[10]。另一方面，假设按每位操作员一周不加班的最长工作时间为 48 小时（周一至周五）。你会发现你们的估计不够准确，实际上，在墨西哥每个工作日不加班的最长工作时间是 576 分钟（即：48 小时/周 ÷ 5 天/周 × 60 分钟/小时）。此外，你同意董事长的观点，为了简化计划，按每月有 20 个工作日，并且不考虑任何加班工时来编预算。

董事长告诉你，在当前汇率下，缝纫工的劳动力成本是每天 14 美元，包括所得税和其他一些法律要求的福利。因此，每个操作工人在不加班的情况下全勤工作一周的成本是 70 美元。

### 劳动力成本的性质：美国和墨西哥的对比

接下来，你与董事长讨论了美国和墨西哥劳动法的重大差异。你们讨论了服装行业存在的这样一个事实：需求低迷期后紧随着需求高峰期，这一现象时常出现。SEW 美国的工厂，在需求下降时，通过（暂时性）裁减生产工人来解决这一问题。不过，董事长提醒你，在墨西哥这种情况更为复杂，因为墨西哥劳动法不允许这样的裁员。墨西哥当前法律要求：雇主如果要终

---

[9] 由于 SEWMEX 这家工厂里要生产所有产品系列（与 SEW 的专业化模式对比），与美国 SEW 采用的所谓的最优专业化模式相比，SEWMEX 雇佣更多的工人。——原注

[10] 例如，假定一个装配工人花费 500 分钟一天。要评估这个工人的生产率（效率），我们需要知道这个工人生产了多少产品（以标准工时表示）。如果该工人当天的产出（以标准工时计量）是 500，那么这个工人的工作效率是 100%。如果这个工人生产的产出超过 500，那么就是这个工人工作效率高于 100%。而 SEW 美国工厂的平均效率为 85%。——原注

止与雇员的劳动合同，即使雇主有计划在不久的将来再次雇佣员工[11]，雇主仍需支付三个月的工资作为解雇费。你不确定的是，劳动法和公司政策的差异对 SEWMEX 的本量利分析（特别是，变动成本和短期固定成本的组合）是否产生影响以及产生什么影响，但是你担心会产生影响，且这个想法挥之不去。

在与你讨论这部法律影响的时候，董事长指出，采用需求低迷期不解雇员工的政策对 SEWMEX 最有利。这样能节省解雇费用，也会建立更高的员工忠诚度。对一个刚起步的公司来说，员工忠诚度非常重要。在 SEWMEX 处于需求低迷期时，公司不会招聘新的员工来替代辞职的员工。不过，他认为辞职的员工数量实际非常有限。董事长指出，由于市场需求的波动，或许隔一段时间就需要对一个或多个产品系列的生产水平作出调整。董事长还解释到，SEWMEX 要对所有操作工人进行轮岗培训，这样员工就能在产品线内部以及不同产品系列间轮岗，在这种情况下，就能更灵活地应对市场需求的变化。

董事长接着说道，他和前任总会计师达成共识：在对利润规划做计算时，假定 SEWMEX 所有产品系列的效率相同。也就是说，由于所有的操作员工都接受了轮岗培训，假定他们的（计划）劳动生产率水平是相同的，操作员工在不同产品系列间的岗位变动，不会影响特定产品的生产率。另外，如果需要分配成本的话，表 3 列示的"生产"成本要按照不同产品系列的标准工时分配到各产品系列中。从本质上来说，这些成本表示可追溯到每一产品系列或每一件服装产品上的成本。

### 外汇汇率

会议中，董事长指出，在过去的几个月里，比索的汇率已经开始大幅波动。他自忖，这些波动可能是利润规划中要考虑的一个复杂因素，因为 SEWMEX 的收入以美元计算，而付出的成本费用却以比索计算。去年一年的汇率（比索对美元）在 12∶1 和 15∶1 之间波动。你和他都同意，为了实现表 3 所示的初始利润规划目标，假定比索对美元的汇率为 13∶1。

---

[11] 然而，如果员工自动离职，解雇费就不需要支付了。——原注

### 表 3
SEWMEX 的月度成本预算，按表 2 列示的计划生产水平计算，单位：比索（假定汇率为比索：美元 = 13 : 1）

| 部门成本统计 | 金额（单位：比索） |
| --- | --- |
| 裁剪和捆扎： | |
| 　间接人工 | 255 000 |
| 　物料 | 50 000 |
| 生产： | |
| 　直接人工 | 1 200 000 |
| 　间接人工 | 300 000 |
| 　物料 | 500 000 |
| 质量⑫： | |
| 　人工 | 125 000 |
| 　物料 | 5 000 |
| 维护： | |
| 　人工 | 200 000 |
| 　零部件 | 160 000 |
| 运输： | |
| 　人工 | 60 000 |
| 　其他* | 50 000 |
| 　额外关税^ | 40 000 |
| 人力资源： | |
| 　人工 | 40 000 |
| 　其他* | 10 000 |
| 行政费用： | |
| 　一般管理费用* | 750 000 |
| 　公共事业费 | 250 000 |
| 　其他 | 100 000 |
| 杂项： | |
| 　人工 | 40 000 |
| 　其他* | 5 000 |
| 合计 | 4 140 000 |

*假定在计划产量的相关范围内，这些成本是固定的。依据所做假设，可能还有其他一些成本，也可以看作是固定的。

^收发集装箱、报关和雇佣码头工人需要特定的额外费用，金额为 5 000 比索。在当前计划 2 500 000 标准工时的生产水平下，每周所需的运输量为收、发各一个集装箱（每月运输 8 次）。也就是说一个发货集装箱装有价值 625 000 个标准工时的产品（即 2 500 000/4，译者）。实际中存在一些量不大的收发，这里假定未装满的容器不会发出，在整个特定范围内这项成本将是固定的。

## 案例问题

（注意：请与你的老师讨论决定是否需要做第 7 和第 8 两道备选题。）

1. 讨论什么是本量利分析，以及在什么方式下本量利分析可以用作管理工具？考虑所有影响本量利假设的定量因素，特别是与 SEWMEX 有关的。

---

⑫ 根据 ISO9000 系列国际标准，质量成本的定义是：将产品质量保持在规定的质量水平上所需的有关费用。它是企业生产总成本的一个组成部分。质量成本由两部分构成，即运行质量成本和外部质量保证成本。——译者

2. **成本性态问题**：定义"变动成本"和"固定成本"。按照案例列出的实际情况，识别表3列示的所有固定和变动成本。为进行成本分类，假定相关作业变量（成本动因）是标准工时（或约当产量，生产的产品数量）。进一步假定表3列示的每种产品系列的成本可以依据标准工时（生产的产品数量）的变动划分为"固定"或"变动"。如果你认为列示的成本属于"混合"成本性态（即，由固定成本和变动成本两部分组成），根据你所认为的主要成本性态，做出分类决定：归类为变动成本或固定成本。并将金额以比索和美元同时列示。

3. **利润规划模型**

   a. 设计一个方程式，使其能恰当地反映本量利关系以及SEWMEX工厂的短期盈利性（税前）。[提示：你的等式应该把每月的税前利润 $\pi_B$ 表示成每月固定成本水平（FC）、每月的总销量X、单位产品边际贡献（sp-vc）以及表2所列生产/销售组合的函数。根据表1所给的单位产品销售单价数据和上述问题2中变动成本的分类，你应该能够根据表2反映的生产/销售组合数据，计算单位加权平均边际贡献率和/或加权平均边际贡献，来用于利润规划的目的。]

   b. 建立起短期税前利润等式（$\pi_B$），便可使用Excel编制SEWMEX工厂的利润-销量（PV）图。也就是说，生成一幅以每月税前利润（$\pi_B$）为因变量、以每月销售量（X）为自变量的函数图。清晰地标出X、Y轴、X轴截距、Y轴截距以及税前利润函数斜率。为了生成函数图，你需要使用在当前生产/销售组合（表2中列示）下的单位加权平均边际贡献率。图中应反映下列X值（月销量）对应的税前利润（$\pi_B$），X值范围为0到70 000，以5 000件为增量。

4. **盈亏平衡计算**

   a. 在问题3中用到单位加权平均边际贡献这个指标，该指标体现了当前的生产/销售计划，请通过该指标为整个SEWMEX工厂计算盈亏平衡点，请分别按以总标准工时和总产量（产出的数量）两种形式表达，并写出计算过程。[提示：为得到盈亏平衡点，可使用你在问题3a中建立的税后利润 $\pi_B$ 等式。由于收入以美元表示，并且美元是更稳定的货币，以美元为基础计算所有盈亏平衡点。] 你计算过程中进行的所有假设都应注明。

   b. 如果将SEWMEX作为分析的总体，根据反映当前生产/销售计划（表2）的加权平均边际贡献率，该厂的盈亏平衡点（以金额表示）为多少？请列示计算过程。

   c. 给定当前的生产/销售计划（表2），利用Excel中的**规划求解**程序计算整体的盈亏平衡点（每月的产品总量，X）。

   d. 在案例中表2列示的生产/销售组合基础上，计算各产品系列的盈亏平衡点（分别以每月的销量和金额表示）。

5. **效率相关问题**

   a. 根据案例（如表2）所提供的数据，工厂的计划效率（如，每月计划产出的总的标准工时，以及相对应的SEWMEX所有装配员工的总的分钟数）大约在什么水平?

b. 根据当前的生产/销售组合,以月份为基础,SEWMEX 实现盈亏平衡时,整体（或平均）效率水平为多少。

c. 编制一张表格,列示每月的税前利润 $\pi_B$,该数据来自于工厂效率的变动（正如前文（a）所定义的）：从 50% 到 100%,每一增量为 10%。为计算这个问题,假定需求的变化是由每月的生产变化所引起的,并且 SEW 将继续购入 SEWMEX 的所有产品。还假定 SEWMEX 工厂的装配工人的总数不变。

d. 假定每小时和总的人工成本保持不变,引起 SEWMEX 工厂效率变化的原因有哪些？也就是说,根据上述（c）部分所编制的表,你认为什么因素会引起 SEWMEX 的效率变化。

6. **总结报告**：在前述的结果和分析基础上,根据你所完成的利润规划的相关练习,以 SEW 董事长为报告对象,总结一份关于核心观点、问题、建议和风险的书面报告。你的报告从某种意义上来说应该是一份咨询报告,应尽量清晰、切题、精炼。

7. （选做题）：**外汇汇率和汇率风险**

a. 什么是"外汇汇率"？总的来说,一段时间内哪些因素会影响外汇汇率的变化？

b. 外汇汇率的变化将有利于还是不利于跨国经营的美国公司？

c. 既然与货币汇率相关的不确定性是固有的,那么,是否可能降低这种不确定性？也就是说,有哪些有效的方法能够用来控制或至少处理这种风险？就外汇风险问题,你会向 SEW 董事长提出什么建议？

d. 考虑到 SEWMEX 公司收到的货款为美元,支付的费用为墨西哥比索,就外汇汇率而言,SEWMEX 公司的最大风险是什么？

8. （选做题）：**外汇汇率——敏感性分析**：如果汇率变为 15∶1,在保持销售组合、生产力（即总产出）和销售价格不变的情况下,月度盈亏平衡点（以美元表示）是多少？如果汇率为 11∶1,月度盈亏平衡点（以美元表示）又将是多少？假定工厂产出和销售组合如表 2 所示,并且销售价格如表 1 所示,则在 15∶1 和 11∶1 这两种汇率下税前利润或损失（以美元表示）分别为多少？编制一张表格将这些结果与根据案例基础假设（即汇率为 13∶1）得到的结果进行对比。根据你所做的这些敏感性分析,能够得出哪些主要观点？

# SEWMEX: Short-Term Profit Planning in an International Setting

*Gus Gordon*
*University of Texas at Tyler*

*David E. Stout*
*Youngstown State University*

*Sarah Hartzog, Student*
*Former Student, Millsaps College*

*Matt Lusty, Student*
*Former Student, University of Texas at Tyler*

*Jay Nelson, Student*
*Former Student, University of Texas at Tyler*

## INTRODUCTION

SEWMEX is a newly formed sewing factory located in Mexico. SEWMEX, owned by an American company, is incorporated in Mexico as a Mexican company, and is enrolled in the *maquiladora* program[1] in Mexico. By contract, the American parent company, SEW Inc. (henceforth referred to as SEW), purchases all of SEWMEX's output. SEW provides all raw materials to SEWMEX. These transactions occur under the *maquiladora* system and North American Free Trade Agreement (NAFTA) rules so that no import or export duties are required on these transfers. Because of this, the *maquiladora* is responsible only for assembling the raw materials into finished products and then shipping the completed products back to SEW in the U.S. As a result, SEWMEX has no raw materials cost. To be able to meet rush orders without waiting for materials to be imported, however, SEWMEX does maintain a small

---

[1] *Maquiladora* is the name for a Mexican factory whose primary purpose is to assemble raw materials into a final product and then export that final product to the country of origin (e.g., the U.S.). The *maquiladora* (or *maquila*) is not the owner of record of the raw materials or any inventory, as the raw materials are imported temporarily under bond and must, by law, be used to assemble a final product and then be exported back to the owner of record, in this case SEW.

inventory of finished product.

In addition to SEWMEX, SEW has several other factories located in the southeastern part of the U.S. One of the factories (located in southeastern Mississippi) also serves as a distribution center and central warehouse where finished goods from all the other factories are stored and ultimately shipped. From this distribution center, SEW supplies customers in all 50 states and Canada.

The controller of SEW recently resigned unexpectedly after a disagreement with the president of the company. After his departure, many of his calculations concerning SEWMEX mysteriously disappeared. Given the cost of labor in the U.S. factories, the president of SEW would like to send as much future production to SEWMEX as possible. The SEWMEX operation is relatively new, however, and not yet profitable. Therefore, both SEW and SEWMEX could benefit from profit-planning exercises.

As a start, the president would like for you, in your capacity as assistant controller, to develop a cost-volume-profit (CVP) model for the SEWMEX facility, which model could be used to address a number of short-term profit-planning issues. In particular, the president would like to get a better handle on exactly what volume of output would be needed to make SEWMEX profitable in the short run (given the present mix of garments produced) and what strategies might be pursued longer term to improve operations and therefore profitability. The president also wonders how, if at all, the issue of foreign exchange rates might complicate the profit-planning process. Therefore, he has charged you with the responsibility of developing the CVP model for SEWMEX, while he looks for a new controller. As someone interested in making a positive impression on the president, you are eager to accept this assignment.

# FACTS

When you were hired by SEW, the controller of the company explained that in the sewing industry it is normal to cost and price garments on the basis of what is called "standard allowed minutes" (SAMs) associated with the production of each garment.[2] In fact, in the sewing industry, production is often measured in these terms rather than in units of finished product. The controller had explained to you that SAMs are based on production engineers' estimates of time needed to perform each sewing operation and therefore the total time required to complete a

---

[2] SAMs are the equivalent of standard labor times used to charge direct labor cost to work-in-process (WIP) inventory (and finished goods inventory) and to calculate direct labor variances under a standard cost system.

particular style garment. The estimates are derived from time-and-motion (i. e., industrial engineering) studies and take into account a number of variables, including the speed of each type of sewing machine required for a specific operation, the education/training of each operator, and existing technology used by the assembly workers at SEWMEX.

## BUDGETED SELLING PRICES

In preparing you for this project, the president of SEW provided you with the per-unit selling price data presented in Table 1.[3] The prices listed in Table 1 are expressed in U. S. dollars (USD) and are based on SEW's transfer price[4] determination for each garment and an initial sales mix of products obtained from the company's marketing department. On the basis of discussions with the company's audit firm, the selling prices represented in Table 1 were deemed acceptable for U. S. income tax purposes. Further, these prices are assumed to be valid within the short-term planning horizon associated with the construction of the CVP model you've been asked to develop.

Table 1
SEWMEX—Average Contracted Sales Prices per Garment, by product line

| Product Line | Average Selling Price per Unit |
| --- | --- |
| Pants | $ 7.00 |
| Shirts | $ 6.00 |
| Jackets | $ 25.00 |
| Other | $ 3.00 |

(Notes: The contract between SEW and SEWMEX explicitly states that SEW will pay SEWMEX in U. S. dollars, USD. Also, the above selling prices per unit represent averages within each product line, given an assumed mix of garments within each line.)

## BUDGETED PRODUCTION/SALES MIX

Information about planned production/sales levels on a monthly basis for

---

[3] As explained later, the prices listed in Table 1 are average prices of garments within each product line, based on an assumed mix of different styles and options within each of the four product lines.

[4] A "transfer price" is the amount assigned to interdivisional transfers of goods or services within a corporation. Such prices represent "sales revenue" to the selling division and "costs" to the purchasing division. As such, they can be used to evaluate the financial performance (e. g., ROI) of both divisions. When consolidated financial statements are prepared, as in the case here with SEWMEX and SEW, the effect of any intra-company transactions are eliminated so that the amount of profit reported reflects transactions with external parties only.

SEWMEX, by product line, is given in Table 2. ⑤This information was provided to you by the president of SEW. The SAM values reported in Table 2 represent the average number of standard minutes needed to make each type garment. As noted above, these estimates are based on the existing technology used in the manufacturing process as well as the current skill levels for assembly personnel. As can be seen from Table 2, total productive output, expressed on a monthly basis and in terms of SAMs, is currently planned at 2 500 000 minutes. Because SAMs are interpreted as standard labor times for the various garments manufactured, they reflect a particular level of efficiency on the part of assembly personnel at the SEWMEX plant. ⑥

Table 2
Current monthly production plan for SEWMEX (expressed in minutes [SAMs]), by product line and in total

| Product Line | Average SAM per Unit of Product (in minutes) | Monthly Planned Production Level (in minutes [SAMs]) |
| --- | --- | --- |
| Pants | 50 | 1 200 000 |
| Shirts | 40 | 1 000 000 |
| Jackets | 90 | 200 000 |
| Other | 20 | 100 000 |
| TOTAL | | 2 500 000 |

## SOME SIMPLIFYING ASSUMPTIONS

In your discussions with the president, he emphasized to you the point that the per-unit sales prices (Table 1) and average per-unit-of-output SAMs (Table 2) represent broad averages within each product line. In actuality, there are more than 200 different styles of pants, over 200 different styles of shirts, more than 50 different styles of jackets, and about 50 different styles in SEW's other product line. For example, as reported in Table 2, the SAM for the average pair of pants is 50 minutes. Based on engineering estimates, however, the SAM for a particular style of pants within this product line would likely be different from 50 minutes. Thus, the average figures reported in Tables 1 and 2 are to be interpreted as

---

⑤ The sales mix reflected in Table 2 is judged by the president of SEW to be relatively stable in the near term and therefore suitable for use in constructing a CVP model for SEWMEX.

⑥ In the context of the SEWMEX, "efficiency" can be interpreted as the number of SAMs (output) produced per month expressed as a percentage of the total time worked. Thus, increased efficiency would be reflected by output per month (measured in SAMs) greater than the total SAMs reflected in Table 2.

weighted averages within each product line, where the weights in determining the average are based on an assumed mix of styles. For example, in the pants product line, it is assumed that a certain percentage of output would be style #1, a certain percentage would be style #2, etc.

Further, the planned production levels reflected in Table 2 (i. e., allocation of 2 500 000 SAMs, per month, across product lines) are themselves reflective of an assumed production/sales mix across product lines. Your initial reaction to the information presented in Tables 1 and 2 is twofold: (1) the profit-planning context you were charged with modeling is certainly a lot more complex than the more straightforward problems you addressed in the classroom, and (2) in the present case there seems to be an almost bewildering array of combinations of products/outputs. After all, a standard sales mix is assumed both within and across product lines. You are unsure, therefore, whether the problem at hand is at all tractable.

You were relieved, however, that in further conversations with the president of SEW the two of you came to an agreement that you could assume for the foreseeable future that the mix reflected in Tables 1 and 2 would likely be stable and therefore appropriate to use in the short-term profit-planning (i. e., CVP) model you would be building. Thus, you can assume that the data presented in Tables 1 and 2 are valid for constructing your initial CVP model for SEWMEX.

## FACTORY CONFIGURATIONS

As indicated in Figure 1, SEW has a six factories, five in the U. S. and one in Mexico (SEWMEX). SEW has principally followed a model of specialization. Four of the five U. S. factories produce only a single product line: two of the factories produce pants, two others produce shirts, while the fifth U. S. factory produces jackets. The fourth product line (dubbed "other") consists of garments that are not precisely jackets but are similar in design to jackets; these garments are produced in the jackets factory. By contrast, SEWMEX produces all four product lines and therefore can be distinguished from the other five factories in the SEW family.

SEW's experience with its specialization model has shown that a workforce of more than approximately 125 people in the factory creates diseconomies of scale and that fewer than 125 does not allow for optimum efficiency. SEWMEX, however, embraces a different operating model-it is a large factory producing all products in the same facility. Due to cultural differences and the non-specialized approach to be followed at SEWMEX, the president of SEW is uncertain how this operating model will affect assembly labor productivity and therefore profitability of the SEWMEX factory.

Figure 1
Geographic Plant Locations—U. S. and Mexico

## THE STRATEGIC IMPORTANCE OF EFFICIENCY TO THE FINANCIAL SUCCESS OF SEWMEX

You have come to realize that given the nature of the company's products and the associated production process, *labor efficiency* is the key to profitability. After all, efficiency is really another measure of throughput: the greater the throughput, the greater the volume of output for a given amount of labor, all things equal.

You realize, then, that efficiency in the manufacturing process is important to understand in developing a short-term profit-planning model for SEWMEX. If the assembly workers in any given month produce according to the planned SAMs reflected in Table 2, we could say that they are working at planned, or expected, efficiency. In any given month, if more SAMs are produced than what was planned (assuming the same number of assembly workers employed during the month), then efficiency would be higher than what was planned (and vice-versa). Higher labor efficiency (productivity) should translate to greater operating income/profit.

Based upon prior experience in reviewing the production reports of each factory in the SEW family, you know that the five U. S. factories average about 85% efficiency. Assuming a 40-hour work week in the U. S., an operator at 100% (i. e., "standard") efficiency would be capable of producing output represented as 2 400 (i. e., 40 hours/week × 60 minutes/hour) SAMs for the week. [7] That means, on average, that each SEW operator in the U. S. is

---

[7] This output level is, by definition, independent of product mix. See also the section titled "The Nature of Labor Costs: The U. S. vs. Mexico" later in the case.

generating output per week of approximately 2 040 SAMs (i. e. , 2 400 × 0.85).

The more you thought about this idea of efficiencies and related output, the more you realized that you could actually compute the planned efficiency for the SEWMEX plant for a given time period (such as a month), similar to the U. S. calculation presented above. The SAMs reported in Table 2 represent a planned level of total output and planned product mix for a typical month.

As part of SEWMEX's management information system, each machine operator turns in, at the end of the day, a form that has a bar code for each operation performed during the day by that operator. As well, the bar code identifies the product line (or lines) worked on during the day by the worker. In short, these forms contain data on output, SAMs, product line, production order, and so forth. At the end of the day, the bar codes are read by optical readers; efficiency levels for operators, product lines, and the plant as a whole are determined using information obtained in this manner.

## COST DATA FOR SEWMEX

The president provided you with total monthly estimated cost data (Table 3), which were salvaged from the president's last meeting with the former controller of SEW. The president reminded you that only assembly labor that has SAM values for their operations are considered direct labor and that both he and the former controller had felt that to meet the planned production levels for SEWMEX (Table 2), about 400 machine operators would be required. The data in Table 3 are based on total employment of 500 workers, including 400 machine operators. [8]

## LABOR PRODUCTIVITY/EFFICIENCY

In Mexico, the allowable work week before paying overtime is 48 hours. Further, in conversations with the president you know that, due to the learning curve and other variables, SEWMEX would likely begin at the average level of assembly labor productivity that the U. S. plants enjoy. Thus, for initial planning purposes regarding the SEWMEX plant, you and the president agreed to use 500 minutes per worker per day as the basis for calculating assembly labor efficiency (productivity). [9] Further, you are to assume that 48 hours will be

---

[8] Since SEWMEX manufactures all product lines within one facility (in contrast to SEW's model of specialization), SEWMEX employs more people than SEW believes is optimal for its specialization model followed in the U. S.

[9] For example, assume that an assembly worker puts in 500 minutes in a day. To assess the level of this worker's productivity (efficiency), we need to know how much output (expressed in SAMs) this worker produced. If the output of the worker for the day (measured in SAMs) was 500, then that individual is said to have been working at 100% efficiency. If the worker produced output for which the SAMs exceeded 500, then the worker was working above 100% efficiency. Recall that the U. S. plants for SEW average 85% efficiency.

worked by each operator (Monday – Friday) without incurring overtime. You realize that this is not exactly accurate as each work-day in Mexico actually has 576 minutes (i. e., 48 hours/week ÷ 5 days/week × 60 minutes/hour) available per week. Furthermore, you agreed with the president that in order to simplify planning, a 20-work-day month would be used and that no overtime would be budgeted.

At the current exchange rate, the president reminded you that labor costs for sewing operators are currently 14.00 USD per day, including payroll taxes and other legally required benefits. Therefore, the cost for an operator who works a complete week without overtime is 70 (5 × $14.00) USD equivalent for the week.

## THE NATURE OF LABOR COSTS: U. S. VS. MEXICO

You then discussed with the president an important distinction between U. S. and Mexican labor laws. The two of you discussed the fact that in the sewing industry there are sometimes periods of low demand followed by periods of high demand. SEW has solved this problem in its U. S. factories by (temporarily) laying off production workers when demand drops. The president pointed out to you, however, that the situation in Mexico is more complicated because Mexican labor law does not allow for such layoffs. Current Mexican law requires employers to pay three months' salary as severance if an employee is terminated, even if there are plans to hire the employee back in the near future.[10] You were not sure what, if any, implications the difference in labor laws and company policy would have on CVP relationships for SEWMEX (specifically, the mix between variable and short-term fixed costs), but you had a gnawing feeling that it could.

In discussing the effect of this law with you, the president noted that it would be in SEWMEX's best interests to adopt a policy of not terminating employees in times of low demand. This would save the severance pay as well as create greater worker loyalty toward SEWMEX, which is essentially a start-up company. During periods of low demand at SEWMEX, the company would not replace employees who resigned. In reality, however, he felt this would be a limited number of employees. The president indicated that due to varying market demands, there might be periods when an adjustment to production levels is required in one or more of the product lines. The president also explained that SEWMEX would cross-train all operators so that workers could move within and between production lines, a situation that would afford more flexibility in meeting variable market demands.

---

[10] If an employee resigns voluntarily, however, the severance payment is not required.

**Table 3**

Monthly Budgeted Costs. in Pesos. at SEWMEX—Planned Production Levels (per Table 2) (assumed exchange rate. Pesos : USD = 13 : 1)

| Cost Description by Department | Amount (in Pesos) |
|---|---|
| **Cutting and Bundling:** | |
| Indirect Labor | 255 000 |
| Supplies | 50 000 |
| **Production:** | |
| Direct Labor | 1 200 000 |
| Indirect Labor | 300 000 |
| Supplies | 500 000 |
| **Quality:** | |
| Labor | 125 000 |
| Supplies | 5 000 |
| **Maintenance:** | |
| Labor | 200 000 |
| Parts | 160 000 |
| **Shipping:** | |
| Labor | 60 000 |
| Other* | 50 000 |
| *Additional Customs Fees*^ | 40 000 |
| **Human Resources:** | |
| Labor | 40 000 |
| Other* | 10 000 |
| **Administration:** | |
| General* | 750 000 |
| Utilities | 250 000 |
| Other | 100 000 |
| **Miscellaneous:** | |
| Labor | 40 000 |
| Other* | 5 000 |
| **TOTAL** | **4 140 000** |

\* Assume these costs are fixed over the relevant range of planned production. There may be other costs that could be considered fixed depending upon assumptions made.

^ The typical additional cost to send or receive a container. customs brokerage and longshoremen fees. is 5 000 pesos. The current level of planned production at 2 500 000 SAMs requires shipments to consist of one sent container and one received container per week (8 total shipments in a given month). This implies that product valued at 625 000 SAMs is the capacity of an export container. Assume no partial containers will be sent and that, for practical purposes (given the relatively immaterial amount to send or receive a container), this cost will remain as fixed over the entire relevant range.

The president continued, saying that he and the former controller had agreed that in making all calculations for profit-planning purposes they would assume that all product lines in SEWMEX had the same efficiency. That is, because of the cross-training received, all operators are assumed to be equal in terms of their (planned) productivity so that the movement of operators between lines will not affect the productivity of any particular product line. Also, the costs labeled as "production" in Table 3 are to be assigned to product lines (if cost assignment is necessary) based on SAMs associated with each respective line. In essence, these costs represent costs that are traceable to each product (garment) line.

### FOREIGN EXCHANGE RATES

During the meeting, the president noted that in the last few months the peso had begun to fluctuate rather drastically. He mused that such movements were possibly a complicating factor in the profit-planning process since SEWMEX receives revenues in dollars and pays expenses in pesos. The exchange rate (pesos per USD) over the last year has fluctuated between 12 : 1 and 15 : 1. You and he agreed that for initial profit-planning purposes, as reflected in Table 3, an exchange rate of 13 pesos to the USD could be assumed.

## CASE QUESTIONS

(Note: Please check with your instructor to determine whether you are to address optional questions 7 and 8)

1. Discuss what is meant by cost-volume-profit (CVP) analysis and the ways in which CVP can be used as a managerial tool. Include any qualitative factors that may affect the CVP assumptions, particularly with respect to SEWMEX.

2. Cost-Behavior Issues: Define the terms "variable cost" and "fixed cost." Given the facts in the case, identify all fixed and variable costs listed in Table 3. Assume for cost-classification purposes that the relevant activity variable (cost driver) is SAMs (or, equivalently, units produced). Assume further that each line-item cost listed in Table 3 can be classified either as "fixed" or as "variable" with respect to changes in SAMs (units produced). If you feel that the cost under consideration exhibits a "mixed" behavior (i.e., has elements of both fixed and variable cost), make your classification decision on the basis of what you believe to be the primary cost behavior, variable or fixed. Show amounts both in pesos and in USD.

3. Profit-Planning Model
   a. Develop an equation that appropriately reflects the CVP relationships and

depicts the short-term profitability of the SEWMEX plant before taxes. (Hint: your equation should depict pre-tax profit per month, $\pi_B$, as a function of the level of fixed cost per month (FC), total volume, X (in units per month), contribution margin per unit (sp-vc), and a production/sales mix represented by the data reflected in Table 2. Given the unit selling price data in Table1 and the variable costs identified in Question 2 above, you should be able to calculate and use for profit-planning purposes a weighted-average contribution margin ratio and/or weighted-average contribution margin per unit based on the production/sales mix implied by the data in Table 2.)

b. Once the equation for short-term pre-tax profit ($\pi_B$) is developed, use Excel to prepare a profit-volume (PV) graph for the SEWMEX plant. That is, generate a graph of monthly pre-tax profit ($\pi_B$) as a function of monthly sales volume (X). Clearly label the X and Y axes, the X-intercept, the Y-intercept, and the slope of the pre-tax profit function. To generate your graph, you will need to use the weighted-average contribution margin per unit at the current production/sales mix (reflected in Table 2). Your graph should include pre-tax profit ($\pi_B$) for the following values of X (monthly volume): 0 to 70 000, in increments of 5 000 units.

### 4. Breakeven Calculations

a. Based on the *weighted-average contribution margin per unit* that reflects the current production/sales plan (which you used above in Question 3), what is the breakeven point, expressed both in terms of total SAMs (standard allowed minutes) and in terms of total output (units produced), for the SEWMEX factory as a whole? Show your calculations. (Hint: to derive the breakeven point, use the equation for pre-tax profit, $\pi_B$, that you developed in response to Question 3a above. Since revenues are expressed in U.S. dollars and because the dollar is the more stable currency, base all breakeven-point calculations in dollars.) Any assumptions made in your calculations should be noted.

b. Based on a *weighted-average contribution margin ratio*, which reflects the current production/sales plan (Table 2), what is the breakeven point in dollars for the SEWMEX factory as a whole? Show calculations.

c. Use the **Solver** routine in Excel to solve for the overall breakeven point (in total units of product per month, X), given the current production/sales plan (Table 2).

d. Based on the production/sales mix reflected in case Table 2, derive product-line breakeven points (in units per month and in dollars per month).

### 5. Efficiency-Related Issues

a. Based on the data provided in the case (e.g., Table 2), what is the approximate level of planned *plant efficiency* (i.e., total SAM output planned per month, relative to total minutes of all assembly labor in the SEWMEX plant)?

b. Based on the current production/sales mix, what overall (or average) efficiency level at SEWMEX is required to break even on a monthly basis?

c. Prepare a table indicating the monthly pre-tax income, $\pi_B$, that would result from changes in plant efficiency (as defined above in (a)) over the range 50% efficiency to 100% efficiency, in increments of 10%. Assume for purposes of this question that demand changes are the cause of monthly production changes and that SEW will continue to purchase all of SEWMEX's output. Assume, too, that the total number of assembly workers at the SEWMEX plant is unchanged.

d. Assuming labor costs per hour and in total are held constant, what would cause plant efficiency at SEWMEX to change? That is, from the table you prepared in response to part (c) above, what inferences can you draw concerning efficiency changes for SEWMEX?

6. **Summary Report**: Based on the foregoing results and analyses, summarize in a written report meant for the president of SEW the key points, issues, recommendations, and risks that are associated with the profit-planning exercise you just completed. Your report should in some sense be viewed as a consultant's report and as such should be clear, to the point, and polished.

7. (Optional): **Foreign Exchange Rates and Foreign Exchange Risk**

a. What is meant by the term "foreign exchange rate"? In general, what causes foreign exchange rates to vary over time?

b. Do changes in foreign exchange rates benefit or hurt U.S. companies that are doing business in foreign countries?

c. Given the inherent uncertainty associated with currency exchange rates, is there a possibility of reducing the uncertainty? That is, what options are available for controlling or at least addressing this risk? What would you advise the president of SEW to do with respect to foreign exchange risk?

d. Given that SEWMEX receives payment in U.S. dollars and pays expenses in Mexican pesos, what is SEWMEX's greatest risk with regard to the foreign exchange rate?

8. (Optional): **Foreign Exchange Rates—Sensitivity Analysis**: If the exchange rate changes to 15 : 1, what will be the monthly breakeven point (in USD), holding sales mix, productivity (i.e., total output), and selling prices constant? What will be the monthly breakeven point (in USD) if the exchange rate were 11 : 1? What will be the pre-tax income (loss) (in USD) at each of these two exchange rates, assuming plant output and sales mix are as illustrated in Table 2 and at selling prices depicted in Table 1? Prepare a table that compares these results to those obtained under the base-case assumption (i.e., an exchange rate of 13 : 1). What general point can be made on the basis of this sensitivity analysis that you performed?

# 田纳西河流域管理局：电力成本

*Bob G. Wood*
*Salisbury University*

*Steven B. Isbell*
*Tennessee Tech University*

*Cass Larson*
*Tennessee Valley Authority*

## 简介

星期五下午，在驾车回诺克斯维乐（Knoxville）的途中，摩根（Morgan）终于有时间思考一下了。这个星期，她花了大部分时间与多位田纳西河流域管理局（Tennessee Valley Authority，简称 TVA）最大的工业客户见面。摩根是新任的能源供应管理的副总裁，负责编制预期的能源需求计划。该计划必须解决 TVA 在长期战略上如何满足多方利益相关者及其使命的问题，同时保持灵活性以应对近期的财务和经营方面的问题。

## I. 田纳西河流域管理局

TVA 是全国最大的公用电力供应者，由美国政府全资所有。虽然由联邦政府所有，TVA 的资金却并非来自税收；这个公用事业单位的资金来自向用户销售电力的收入。额外的资金需求则通过在金融市场中发行债券借得。TVA 有三重任务：（1）提供可靠的、有价格竞争力的电力；（2）管理田纳西河系及相关的土地，以满足多方面的需求；（3）与当地政府和州政府合作发展经济。TVA 独特的任务已成为它商业活动的基础，为 TVA 达成其商业目标和各项内部的经营活动提供环境条件。

虽然 TVA 的核心任务保持不变，但该行业的形势发生了巨大的变化，前景非常不确定。近年的经济动荡对发电原料的价格和建造新厂的材料成本带来了前所未有的波动。并且，在今后几年可能会立法要求发展更多可再生的清洁能源，这也为该行业带来了高度的不确定性。各项法律的问题，包括

---

\* 本篇译者为杨继良，校订者为赵澄、胡金凤。

最近在北卡罗来纳州提出的一项诉讼，使 TVA 不得不寻求成本高昂的其他发电方式。最大的挑战是，衰退的经济使许多客户不断呼吁，要求 TVA 保持现有的电价不变。

今天会议的核心是讨论 TVA 满足所有能源需求的责任，同时尽可能保持低廉的电价。TVA 去年提供的电力中，大多数来自化石燃料发电厂/火力发电厂（55%）、核电厂（28%）、水力发电厂（4%）、天然气发电厂（1%）和可再生能源发电厂（1%）。此外，由于 TVA 的发电能力不足以满足田纳西河流域的需求，TVA 还从其他供电者那里购入所需电力的 11%。去年，与发电有关的成本中，92% 的成本归结于两个来源：化石燃料和外购电力。核电是 TVA 最有效的发电方式（去年提供 28% 的电力需求，但所耗费的成本却只占总成本的 7%）。水力发电和可再生资源的发电成本最低（投入成本等于零），但却存在效率最差和不可靠的问题。

在过去 20 年中，田纳西河流域的能源需求每年以超过 2.5% 的速度增长。尽管近期的经济衰退让增长速度在短期内有所减缓，但预期未来 20 年内每年仍将增长 1%。虽然经济低迷，但 TVA 现有的发电厂仍不足以满足现有需求。众所周知，TVA 一直以来都向客户提供可靠的电力资源，并且管理局希望维持这一名声。

为提供不断增长的电力需求，TVA 有两种选择：建造新的发电能力，或是外购。管理当局希望只在遇到紧急情况（即在需求超过其发电能力时）才外购。这除了考虑其成本之外，市场价格波动剧烈，也是需要考虑的因素。尽管经济发展放缓，TVA 仍然需要以每四年建造一个新的火力发电厂或核电站的发展速度，才能满足预期的需求量。另外，还要建造一些小型的电厂，应对个别客户的需要。

# II. 绿色革命

摩根在驾车经过埃尔·高尔①的故乡迦太基（Carthage）时，微笑着想到，在对待田纳西河流域的"绿色"问题的态度上，发生了如此巨大的变化。在各级政府对这一问题的关注下，形成了新的环保政策；摩根知道，在提供更清洁、可再生性更强的能源方面，TVA 需要居于领导地位。不过，摩根也知道，绿色资源独特的运行特性和可靠性问题，使他们的选择具有挑战性。

除了考虑更清洁和成本效率更佳的能源外，摩根还不得不考虑到另外一项 TVA 关注的热门话题。除了可再生能源供应方面的选择，TVA 近来还承诺，在增加能源效率以获得更多的节约和应对客户的电量需求方案上，不断加大力度。这些承诺旨在，TVA 系统电力需求最高的时段中，实现最大收益。TVA 的总目标为，到 2014 年年底时，在电力需求最高的时段（通常称为"高峰"时段），减少约 5% 的能源需求量。

---

① Al Gore，美国前副总统，以积极提倡环境保护闻名。——译者

TVA希望通过帮助其客户更有效地使用能源，让整个流域都能节省开支。事实上，TVA的目标是在2017年前从能源效率上实现销售额3.5%的节能，此数相当于这个期间年度发电量增长的0.1%。摩根知道，从表面来看，这一概念简单易懂，但在当前资源有限的情况下，要引入这些项目所需要的新技术和资本费用，还有许多工作要做。

　　另一方面，有些人对提高能源效率的倡议极为怀疑。许多人认为，在当前的经济形势下，近期不应该把钱花费在提高能源效率的方案上。在这方面，摩根有很多尚待完成的工作，必须有所取舍。她想过："投资各项提高能源效率的方案，是不是TVA的最佳选择呢？如果是最佳的选择，那么她的团队怎样才能分析出哪些能源效率提高方案对TAV最有利呢？"

## III. 各种发电方式

　　摩根的思路又回到了更为关键性的问题上，她回忆了TVA最近对一份报告的讨论情况，这份报告归纳了各种发电方式的成本和收益。她知道，她所提出的任何计划都必须考虑到这些因素。报告书的重点包括：

- 煤：粉煤
  - 2011年时，美国发电厂的煤耗占成本的40%以上。
  - 就污染物而言，煤电厂被归入为"高排放"类。
  - 由于对碳排放有严格要求，以及控制碳排放的成本高昂，有关碳排放的法规规定可能让未来的火力发电厂增加50%～100%的成本，还可能必须关闭一些现有的煤电单位。
  - 尽管煤炭价格低廉、在国内可买到，但随着全球日益增长的煤炭使用（尤其在中国，中国平均每星期新启用一座煤电厂），导致煤价格的波动性增加。
  - 煤价不能通过应用衍生工具来进行管理；煤价依靠长期的双边协定来管理，其供应方的财务稳定性一般都比较差。

- 天然气：联合循环
  - 联合循环发电厂围绕一座或多座燃气轮机建成，采用的是与喷气发动机基本相同的技术。
  - 现代的联合循环发电厂的建设成本相对较低、对环境的影响较小，可用来满足基本负荷、中级负荷和高峰时段的需求，因为这种发电厂在需要电力时容易启动、也容易停止。
  - 这些发电厂能很快地建成、效率很高。
  - 近年，天然气已作为联合循环的燃料，与煤炭相比，天然气价格波动显然更大；有关碳排放的法律规定，可能使成本再增加25%。尽管如此，通过财务协定可以在需要该燃料之前更好地锁定天然气的价格。表1是1990～2010年煤与天然气价格的比较。

表 1

1990～2010 年发电厂选择的化石燃料的成本*

| 年份 | 煤（$/MMBTU） | 天然气（$/MMBTU） |
| --- | --- | --- |
| 1990 | 1.46 | 2.32 |
| 1991 | 1.45 | 2.15 |
| 1992 | 1.41 | 2.33 |
| 1993 | 1.39 | 2.56 |
| 1994 | 1.36 | 2.23 |
| 1995 | 1.32 | 1.98 |
| 1996 | 1.29 | 2.64 |
| 1997 | 1.27 | 2.76 |
| 1998 | 1.25 | 2.38 |
| 1999 | 1.22 | 2.57 |
| 2000 | 1.20 | 4.30 |
| 2001 | 1.23 | 4.49 |
| 2002 | 1.25 | 3.53 |
| 2003 | 1.28 | 5.39 |
| 2004 | 1.36 | 5.96 |
| 2005 | 1.54 | 8.21 |
| 2006 | 1.69 | 6.94 |
| 2007 | 1.77 | 7.11 |
| 2008 | 2.07 | 9.01 |
| 2009 | 2.21 | 4.74 |
| 2010 | 2.27 | 5.09 |

\* 《美国能源信息管理局－月刊，能源评论，201》

- **核能**
  - 核电厂使用核裂变所产生的热量，形成蒸气以推动涡轮机来发电。
  - 核电厂的特点是投资成本高、但变动营业成本（包括燃料费用）低。由于变动成本低和设计方面的特点，核电厂在美国都只作为基本负荷发电厂[2]（运行并提供恒定的能源需求）。
  - 2011 年时，全国由核电厂供应的电力约占 20%。
  - 核电厂的建设需要取得核管理委员会的批准，在过去的 16 年里，该委员会未曾批准任何一座新的核电厂。但在 2012 年 2 月，委员会批准了美国南方电力公司建造一座具有两个反应堆的设施。发电行业把此举看作是美

---

[2] 基本负荷发电厂承担电力系统日负荷曲线基本部位负荷的发电厂。基本负荷一般指日负荷曲线最低负荷以下的部分，基本负荷大部分由基本负荷发电厂供应，其余一小部分由夜间低谷负荷时不停机的中间负荷发电厂供应。基本负荷发电厂是系统中运行最经济的，除检修或事故停机外、均连续运行，所带负荷变动较小。——译者

国对扩展核能的许诺。
- 核电厂发电具有"零排放"的特点，但存在废物（消耗的核燃料棒）的处置问题。
- 核电厂的一项优点是，它提供数量庞大的基本负荷电力，却不排放二氧化碳。它可以把稳定可靠的电力，提供给期望扩展或迁移到该流域的各行各业。

- 风力
  - 风力发电厂（有时被称为"风力农场"）用风力推动的涡轮机发电。
  - 风力是一种具有变数的可再生资源，因为是否能得到这种资源，取决于反复无常的气候。美国的东南部风力很小，因而如果风力发电需求量大，就得从美国中部传送电力过来。
  - 2011年时，风力发电提供了美国总电力需求量的3%。如果现有的法律和规定不变，据美国能源信息局估测，到2030年，风力发电将达到20%。
  - 如果使用风力来大规模发电，由于投资成本高昂和发电量难以预测，会使电力成本昂贵。

- 太阳能
  - 太阳能光伏（solar photovoltaic，简称 solar PV）发电使用太阳能电池把阳光直接转变为电力。迄今为止，美国的太阳能光伏设施都很小（大约在1兆瓦[3]或1兆瓦以下）。太阳能电池的发电时间，只有三分之一。
  - 大量生产这一能源需要大面积的土地：发电1兆瓦大约需要2英亩土地。如果要具有相当于一座核电厂的发电能力，太阳能发电厂大约需要面积为4 000英亩的太阳能电池板。
  - 较小的太阳能光伏设施，可以"分散配置"在许多客户的所在地，以避免电力的传送成本。目前这些发电设施，是由少量具有环保意识的客户自建的。TVA有一个项目便是向自行生产太阳能的客户支付奖励金。
  - 主要问题在于成本。成本虽然高，但随着技术进步，成本在不断降低。这与其他多数发电方式的成本正在不断增加的情况，正好相反。

## IV. 电力的特性

重写战略计划最重要的部分，是制定一个增加发电量以应对未来能源需求的资本投资战略，同时尽量降低电价。摩根把从能源信息局取得的成本估计表，保存在她的手提电脑中（见表2）。

---

[3] 兆瓦（英文：megawatt，通常缩略为兆瓦），是一种表示功率的单位，常用来指发电机组在额定情况下每小时能发出来的电量。——译者

表2

估算各种新发电资源的平准成本④（美国）*

| | 利用率（%） | 平准化的资本成本（$/MW-年） | 预计可使用年限 | 平准化的发电成本（$/MWh） |
|---|---|---|---|---|
| 普通煤 | 85% | $515 263 | 30 | $31.20 |
| 粉煤 | 85% | $604 615 | 30 | $29.30 |
| 具有CCS⑤技术的粉煤 | 85% | $689 500 | 30 | $36.70 |
| 普通联合循环 | 87% | $174 525 | 20 | $60.20 |
| 高级联合循环 | 87% | $170 715 | 20 | $56.90 |
| 普通燃料燃烧涡轮 | 30% | $108 011 | 20 | $98.40 |
| 高级燃料燃烧涡轮 | 30% | $101 178 | 20 | $85.00 |
| 先进核电 | 90% | $748 192 | 40 | $24.10 |
| 风力 | 34% | $388 681 | 20 | $18.80 |
| 风力—离岸 | 39% | $546 282 | 20 | $31.20 |
| 太阳能光伏 | 22% | $726 169 | 20 | $19.30 |
| 日光热能 | 31% | $609 381 | 20 | $32.20 |
| 地热能 | 90% | $693 792 | 45 | $27.70 |
| 生物燃料 | 83% | $532 950 | 20 | $37.70 |
| 水力 | 51% | $463 290 | 50 | $16.20 |

*资料来源：能源信息协会。

  投产建成一座发电厂所引起的成本，即资本成本，将在该发电厂的有效使用寿命内摊销。发电的成本在该发电厂运行时发生。必须牢牢记住：正如大部分政府管理的垄断部门一样，TVA必须根据长期的平均成本，确定它的电费费率。

  摩根想起一些团队没有讨论的事。电力不可能储存在电网上。相反，电力必须在生产的同时消耗掉。问题在于电力消耗不但在年度的各季不同，而且每天的各个时段也并不相同。每逢工作日下午的晚些时候和傍晚，需求量会上升。在气候比较暖和的几个月中，这种现象更为明显。在电力行业中，把需求量高的时段称为"高峰负荷"。在其余时段，尤其在凌晨，需求量相当低。当然，电力需求量绝对不会降低到零，因而TVA必须持续地发电，以满足电网上最小的需求量。这一最低的需求量水平，被称为基本负荷。

  电力企业采用多种发电的技术来应对基本负荷和高峰负荷的需求。核电

---

  ④ 平准化电力成本常作为一种可衡量发电厂寿命周期内的最终成本的分析工具。根据生产平准化的定义，平准就是要求生产平稳地、均衡地进行。平准化不仅要达到产量上的均衡，而且还要保证品种、工时和生产负荷的均衡。所以，它实际上是均衡生产的高级阶段。译者姑且理解，平准化成本即这种状况下的成本。以上为译者从资料中所获的认识，供读者参考。——译者

  ⑤ Carbon capture and storage，碳收集与储存。——译者

厂或煤电厂要达到它们的运行功率，需要经过几个小时甚至几天的时间。如果作为高峰负荷发电厂的话，这一特性使它们显得非常低效。因此，采用核电厂和煤电厂应对基本负荷的需求。在一天中电力需求量增加时，可以随时升降其运转的技术（天然气发电厂），以用来供应高峰期需要的额外能源。基本负荷发电厂的固定成本很高，但边际成本很低；高峰负荷发电厂的固定成本比较低，但运行的边际成本要高得多。任何战略计划都必须考虑到总的发电量需要增加多少，而且还要满足不同负荷的需求。这就需要对高峰和基本负荷的需求都作出预测。

不过，还有一项战略需要加以考虑。可以实施"用电需求管理"计划，以降低为满足高峰负荷而增加发电能力的成本。如果有办法能够把高峰时段的电力消耗降下来，把此数移到基本负荷时段（这种做法称为"负荷转移"），则增建发电能力的时间可以推后几年。TVA不能规定每一天何时用电，但有可能通过改变其定价模式，影响电力的耗用量。TVA可不按长期的平均成本确定电费的费率，而采用按"用电时段"确定费率的模式，并根据发电的边际成本额来确定其价格。在基本负荷时段，每千瓦的电价比较低；在高峰负荷时段，随着供应电力的成本提高，费率也相应提高。这一策略能够降低高峰负荷时段的电耗，而增加基本负荷时段的电耗。事实上，总的电耗并无变化，只是把高峰负荷时段的电耗转移到基本负荷时段罢了。这样，TVA可以使用成本较低的基本负荷发电厂提供更多的电力。这也能节省为满足未来高峰负荷的需要而建设新发电能力的成本。

负荷转移并不是一个新概念，然而，由于难以确定客户需要用电的时段，所以不能把这一概念付诸实施。但近来开发的那种"智能电表"⑥ 不但使TVA能够即时监控电力耗用情况，而且也使客户能够跟踪其能源消耗、作出调整，以降低其公用事业费账单。家电制造商甚至还开发了一种"智能"家电，与电网相联结，按定价的实时信息决定开动该家电的时间，使用户能够采用"一旦设定，就可以放手不管"的方法，来管理其能源需求。

虽然这听起来是个理想的解决方法，但客户却一直不愿意接受这种技术。他们认为这一方法无法让各相关方（客户、公用事业和环境）都获益。摩根回忆太平洋天然气和电力公司把智能电表介绍给旧金山湾区时发生的问题，不禁窃笑。县监事会在一次投票中，一致同意中止"智能电表"的安装，他们提出了健康（有人指称这一装置会引起脑瘤）和隐私（收集私人的生活习惯的信息）的问题。如果这一装置都不能售与具有环境意识的加利福尼亚人，那么TAV还有可能把它卖给田纳西河流域的居民吗？

摩根慢慢地收敛了笑容，她想到了与可能使用的这一较新技术有关的其他一些问题。收入和受教育程度比较高的家庭，最有可能购买"智能电表"，利用智能型的家电。阿巴拉契亚在TVA的服务区域内，这一区域的居民身无分文、一贫如洗，许多家庭处于赤贫的边缘。如果TVA执行这一定价模式，并且把安装新电表的成本转嫁给所有的客户，那么这些家庭也将

---

⑥ 向电力用户提供实时的电耗数的电表，帮助用户控制其能源消耗，达到节省开支的目的。——译者

负担这部分的成本,并且他们必定不会购买智能型家电。此外,这些客户中多数人在制造业就业,按日程变换班次,使他们没有管理其能源消耗时间的灵活性。其结果是,按用电时段定价的方法,会使本就难以承担电费的客户雪上加霜。

更为糟糕的是,TVA 可能因补贴高收入家庭而受到指责。目前,收入不平等日益加剧,全国都在议论这一话题,这会让 TVA 陷入不利的情况。但摩根想,这并不是对待事物的正确方法。问题就在于,正确的做法又该如何呢?

## V. 筹资注意事项

TVA 现行费率表是按足够支付经营费用、利息和到期债券兑现、电厂生产耗用燃料和各项杂费的原则设计的。TVA 委员会可以按成本和燃料成本的调节额,每个季度对费率调高一次以抵销燃料价格的变动。

当 TVA 的销售收入不足以弥付其各项费用时,管理局就削减各个职能部门的成本,包括推迟改良性资本支出、限制雇佣新职工、冻结工资。不然,TVA 就借款筹资。从成本观点来讲,这可能是个最佳解决办法,作为一个信用评级为 AAA 的管理局,TVA 可以用显著低于市场的利率借到钱。美国参议院对 TVA 设定的远期债务的上限为 300 亿美元,然而,这个限额已经有四十年未提高过了。近年来,尽管对减少债券已经作了几年的努力,远期债券(这种筹资方法历来留给基建项目使用)的平均额仍保持在 90 亿美元左右。TVA 尚未偿还的长期债券组合的平均利率为 5.5%。虽然过去 TVA 所发行债券的到期日达 50 年之久,但当前经济形势将使新发行的债券到期年限定为 15~30 年之间。考虑到多数发电方法所使用的固定资产的使用年限较长,摩根认为应该发行 30 年期的债券来筹集新的基本建设资金。由于,TVA 目前尚未兑现的债券的到期日比较短,摩根认为她必须采用美国政府公债作为基准。她回忆最近一次与 TVA 各个资深财务人员的会面;他们认为,债券利率需要比当前政府规定的利息上调 80 到 100 个基点(BPS[7])。由于当前经济和政治上的不确定因素非常多,摩根认为似乎应该上调 100 个基点。表 3 列示了目前尚未偿付的 TVA 债券和美国政府债券的利率情况。

另一种增加筹资额的方法是,提高公用事业费率。当然,提高客户的成本从来都不是一个受欢迎的做法,何况 TVA 的任务是尽量降低电费费率。费率低廉对 TVA 非常重要,因为 TVA 的使命是发展田纳西河流域的经济,而能源成本低廉才能使这一地区的工业不断发展。此外,将费率提高以获得所需要的基建资金,必然引起美国整个东南部和首都华盛顿的强烈抗议。

---

[7] basic points 直译就是基点,是金融业内部的一个术语,表示利率或汇率的最小变动单位,如利率的最小变动单位是 0.01%,因此调增 27 个基点,就等于调增 0.27%。——译者

表 3

**TVA 债券** *

| 票息% | 到期日（月-年） | 报价 | 询价 | 到期收益率（%） |
|---|---|---|---|---|
| 6.00 | 3-13 | 103.26 | 103.27 | 0.01 |
| 4.75 | 8-13 | 104.21 | 104.23 | 0.13 |
| 6.25 | 12-17 | 128.12 | 128.30 | 0.76 |
| 6.75 | 11-25 | 148.12 | 148.25 | 0.65 |
| 7.13 | 5-30 | 158.00 | 158.17 | 2.89 |

**美国政府债券**

| 票息% | 到期日（月-年） | 报价 | 询价 | 到期收益率（%） |
|---|---|---|---|---|
| 2.50 | 3-13 | 101.59 | 101.60 | 0.17 |
| 4.25 | 8-13 | 104.30 | 104.33 | 0.17 |
| 2.75 | 12-17 | 111.02 | 111.06 | 0.68 |
| 6.875 | 8-25 | 159.41 | 159.45 | 1.76 |
| 6.25 | 5-30 | 161.91 | 161.99 | 1.22 |
| 5.00 | 5-37 | 149.59 | 149.66 | 1.59 |
| 3.00 | 5-42 | 109.45 | 109.51 | 2.54 |

\* 资料来源：《华尔街日报》2012 年 7 月 23 日。

## VI. 其他注意事项

虽然 TVA 的资本成本非常低，但建设新的发电厂，完全有可能使贷款达到限额。摩根抿紧嘴唇想着，"由于债务上限的缘故，我不知道资本支出宜如何分配。从当前的经济和政治情况来看，有没有可能提高我们的债务上限呢？或者我还是想都不要去想它为好呢？"

当摩根到达诺克斯维乐时，她在左边看到了金斯敦（Kingston）—TVA 的煤电厂，并联想到那场灾难性的事故。煤电厂会产生需要处置的残余物煤灰。在金斯敦电厂，煤灰存储在电厂旁边的一个收集池中。在那一年快过圣诞节的时候，收集池的墙壁裂开了，煤灰污泥淹没了 300 英亩土地，包括一些居民的住宅。TVA 的管理当局反应迅速，尽一切办法扭转形势；但清理成本很高，花费了大约 10 亿美元。现在还不断有要求增强煤炭燃烧的残渣管理的呼声。

除了金斯敦的问题外，TVA 还面对着其他财务困境。由于经济疲软，造成需求减少、没有提高费率的余地。北卡罗来纳州起诉 TVA，要求其遵守空气质量标准，这使 TVA 面临另外 10 亿美元的费用。虽然 TVA 已经制订了一项计划，并且开始对电厂建筑进行升级以改善空气质量，但这一诉讼迫使TVA加速施工的进程，并且在有些情况下开支超过了最初的预算数。最后，TVA还经历着长期干旱，减少了从水坝得到的水力发电，迫使管理局外购高价的电力来补充失去的电力，因为其他的发电设施已满负荷或接近满负荷发电了。摩根想，这些未能预计到的事件，加到一起，相当于一年销售收入的20%。

## VII. 做决策的时候

摩根最终到达诺克斯维尔市区的TVA公司大楼，叹了口气。她应该如何把这些复杂的碎片拼凑成TVA的战略，以满足诸多利益相关方的需要呢？推进TVA战略的关键何在？在应对这两个问题之前，摩根必须着眼于她已经知道的情况。

从最近的10-K报表[8]上，摩根了解到，TVA目前的负载能力为37 188兆瓦；大约40%发电量来自煤电，其余部分主要来自核能、水力和天然气发电厂。来自于可再生资源的发电量不足1%。去年夏天又热又长，使TVA的负载量超过此数，必须从其他发电单位购入电力。

为了确保在未来可对它的服务区域提供可靠、低价的电力，TVA生产电力的方法有多种。各项方法在发电量、现金流量和使用年限方面，各有特性。

摩根想知道，是否应选用使用年限比较长的发电厂更好，如先进的核能或粉煤发电厂，这些电厂从其开始建设日起算的预期使用年限为30年；还是选用使用年限比较短的设施，诸如先进的天然气联合循环电厂、水力发电厂或者太阳能发电厂，其预期使用年限为20年，这些年限较短的设施可便于利用预期的技术和生产效率的进步。

建设项目的成本和使用年限，也相差很大。一座核电厂的成本达55亿美元，远远高于其他发电方式，其建设时间也最长（4年）。煤电厂建设成本比较低（只及核电厂的三分之一，即18亿美元），但建设时间也长达3年。天然气发电厂的建设成本更低（6.5亿美元），也仍然需要2.5年来建设。两种耗用再生能源的电厂的建设时间都较短（1年），但成本相差很大。太阳能发电厂成本为3亿美元，相当于风力发电厂（1 500万美元）的20倍。

资源不同，其发电能力也不同。煤电厂和核能发电厂的发电能力很大（每年分别为2 300兆瓦和2 000兆瓦）。其他几种生产方式的发电能力比较低。天然气发电厂的发电能力为每年720兆瓦，风力发电厂的发电能力为每年150兆瓦，而太阳能发电厂的发电能力为每年100兆瓦。

投入材料的成本，也对各种发电方式预期的年度现金流量有重大影响。现金流量从建设完成的下一年开始，并在该资产的使用寿命内保持不变。由

---

[8] 美国证交会规定的一种年报的格式。——译者

于铀具有使用年限长的性质,因而预期核电厂每年的现金流量为6.8亿美元,比其他发电方法的现金流量显然高出很多。煤电和天然气发电厂的材料投入成本相对较高,因而会减少这两种电厂的年度现金流量,预期其年度现金流量分别为9 700万美元和8 500万美元。风力发电厂预计的年度现金流量为200万美元;太阳能发电厂每年的现金流量为300万美元。

摩根想,"每一种发电方式都有许多独特的因素——发电能力、可靠性、投入成本等。没有一种发电方式有绝对的优势。我应该用哪些因素来比较各种发电方式呢?是否有些因素比其他因素更为重要呢?"

TVA最近公布了要在2018年前关闭几个煤炭发电站的计划,以实现它成为清洁能源领军者的目标。在这些煤炭发电站关闭之前,TVA需要补充5 670兆瓦的发电能力。其中一半的发电能力,将通过把旧的煤电厂转变为燃烧锅炉来实现。其余的发电能力中,至少有70%将以新一代的基本负荷发电来补充;不足之数将从高峰时间段或间歇性传送中得到补足。

至少有一个办法能有所帮助。由于TVA历来以债券的方式筹措新发电设施的建设资金,其享有的低利率能减少贷款的成本。此外,因为TVA在编制其资本预算时没有考虑股权资本成本,应该不难向那少数几位对"财务所知甚少"的董事解释在折现现金流量分析中所使用资本的成本。

TVA的董事会期望她能够按照TVA的资源方针,制订出满足客户需求的计划。摩根在想,每种发电方式的成本和产出特点不同,她应该如何评价这些发电方式呢?此外,其他因素又将如何影响TVA的战略方向呢?会议安排在星期一的早上。摩根认识到,总而言之,她将没有时间去看足球比赛了。

# The Tennessee Valley Authority: The Cost of Power

*Bob G. Wood*
*Salisbury University*

*Steven B. Isbell*
*Tennessee Tech University*

*Cass Larson*
*Tennessee Valley Authority*

## INTRODUCTION

Driving back to Knoxville on Friday afternoon, Morgan finally had some time to think. She'd spent most of the week in Nashville meeting with many of the Tennessee Valley Authority's (TVA) largest industrial customers. As the new VP of energy supply management, Morgan was responsible for formulating a plan to meet expected energy needs. The plan must address how TVA can satisfy its multiple stakeholders and mission in a long-term strategy, while at the same time maintaining the flexibility to address near-term financial and operational challenges.

## I. THE TENNESSEE VALLEY AUTHORITY

TVA is the nation's largest public power provider and is wholly owned by the U.S. government. Although owned by the federal government, TVA is not financed with tax dollars; rather, the utility's funding comes from the sale of power to its customers. Additional funding comes from borrowings using debt issues in the financial market. TVA has a three-fold mission: (1) provide reliable, competitively-priced power, (2) manage the Tennessee River system and associated lands to meet multiple uses, and (3) partner with local and state governments for economic development. TVA's unique mission has served as the foundation of its business endeavors, providing the context for TVA to establish its business objectives and internal processes.

While TVA's core mission has remained constant, the landscape of the industry has changed considerably, and the future remains very uncertain. The recent economic turmoil has caused unprecedented volatility in the prices for commodities that are used as fuel to produce electricity and the cost of materials to build plants. There is also a high level of uncertainty in the industry with respect to potential legislation requiring significantly more renewable and clean energy generation sources in the coming years. Legal issues, including a recent lawsuit in North Carolina, challenged TVA to seek costly alternatives for power generation. On top of these challenges, the lethargic economy has created an uninterrupted stream of calls from customers asking TVA to keep electricity rates where they are.

The major focus of today's meeting was TVA's obligation of meeting all energy needs while at the same time keeping rates as low as possible. Last year, TVA generated the majority of needed electricity using fossil fuel plants (55%), nuclear plants (28%), hydropower plants (4%), natural gas plants (1%), and renewable sources (1%). In addition, TVA purchased 11% of the needed power from other providers, since TVA generation assets were unable to meet the needs of the valley. Of the costs associated with generating electricity last year, 92% came from two sources: fossil fuel costs and purchased power. Nuclear power production is TVA's most efficient production process (providing 28% of the electricity generated last year, but only accounting for 7% of total costs). Electricity generated using hydropower and renewable sources is the least expensive (having zero input cost), but it is also the least efficient and has reliability issues.

The energy needs in the Tennessee Valley have grown at more than 2.5% per year for the last 20 years. Demand is expected to continue to grow at about 1% per year over the next 20 years, even with the recent economic downturn slowing things considerably in the short term. Even with the downturn, TVA's current generation plants are unable to meet current needs. TVA is well known for providing a very reliable source of power to its customers, and the agency wants to maintain that reputation.

Two options exist to supply the increasing power needs: TVA can build new generating capacity or it can buy energy from others. Management wants to limit electricity purchases to emergency situations—periods where demand exceeds generation capacity. In addition to their cost, prices in this market are extremely volatile. Even with the slower economy, TVA needs to build new generating units at the rate of one large coal or nuclear unit every four years to be able to meet forecasted demand. Smaller units will also be constructed to meet individual customers' needs.

## II. THE GREEN REVOLUTION

Driving by Carthage, Al Gore's hometown, Morgan smiled as she thought about how drastically attitudes have changed towards being "green" in the Tennessee Valley. As interest at all levels of government leads to new environmental policies, Morgan knows that TVA will need to provide leadership in the area of providing cleaner, more renewable energy. The unusual operating characteristics and reliability issues of green resources makes their adoption a challenge, however.

In addition to thinking about cleaner and more cost-effective energy sources, Morgan could not help but think of another hot topic of interest for TVA. In addition to renewable supply side alternatives, TVA has recently committed to increasing efforts to gain more savings from energy efficiency and demand response programs. These initiatives are targeted to achieve maximum benefits during the highest periods of power demand on the TVA system. TVA's overall goal is to reduce energy use during times when the demand for power is highest—often referred to as the "peak"—by about 5% by the end of 2014.

By helping consumers use energy more efficiently, TVA is hoping to save money for the entire valley. In fact, TVA is targeting total energy efficiency savings to be about 3.5% of sales by 2017, which would roughly translate to 0.1% annual load growth to that period. Although the concept seems simple on the surface, Morgan knows that there's a lot of work to be done with limited resources, introduction of new technologies, and capital expenses for some of these programs.

On the other hand, some individuals are extremely skeptical of energy efficiency initiatives. Many of these people believe that, given the current shape of the economy, money should not be spent on energy-efficiency programs in the near term. Morgan definitely has her work cut out for her in this area. She wonders: "Is it in TVA's best interest to invest in these energy-efficiency programs? If so, how can her team analyze which energy-efficiency programs are best for TVA?"

## III. POWER GENERATION ALTERNATIVES

Returning to the more critical issue, Morgan remembered a recent discussion at TVA about a report that summarized the benefits and costs of each type of power generation. She knows that any plan she develops must consider these factors. Highlights of the report include:
- Coal: Pulverized
    - Coal accounted for over 40% of power generation in the U.S. in 2011.
    - Coal plants are classified as "high-emitting" with respect to pollutants.
    - Carbon-related legislation could add 50 – 100% to the cost of future coal power generation due to stricter requirements for carbon and expensive carbon controls, possibly even making it necessary to close some existing units.
    - While coal has been a cheap and domestically available fuel source, the

world's increased use of coal generation, particularly in China (China builds a coal plant every week), is causing increased volatility in coal prices.

- Coal prices cannot be managed using derivatives and they rely on longer-term bilateral contracts with suppliers who, in general, have poor financial stability.
- Natural Gas: Combined Cycle
  - Using essentially the same technology used in jet engines, combined cycle plants are built around one or more combustion turbines.
  - Modern combined cycle plants, which have a relatively low construction cost and modest environmental impacts, can be used to meet base-load, intermediate, and peaking demand, since they are easy to start and stop as power is needed.
  - These plants can be built fairly quickly and are very efficient.
  - Natural gas, which fuels combined cycles, has had significantly greater price volatility when compared to coal in recent years, and carbon legislation could add about 25% to the cost. Still, natural gas volatility can be managed using financial contracts to lock in prices well in advance of needing the fuel. Table 1 compares coal and natural gas prices from 1990 to 2010.

Table 1

Cost of Selected Fossil-Fuel at Electric Generating Plants 1990 – 2010 *

| Year | COAL ($/MMBTU) | NATURAL GAS ($/MMBTU) |
|------|----------------|------------------------|
| 1990 | 1.46 | 2.32 |
| 1991 | 1.45 | 2.15 |
| 1992 | 1.41 | 2.33 |
| 1993 | 1.39 | 2.56 |
| 1994 | 1.36 | 2.23 |
| 1995 | 1.32 | 1.98 |
| 1996 | 1.29 | 2.64 |
| 1997 | 1.27 | 2.76 |
| 1998 | 1.25 | 2.38 |
| 1999 | 1.22 | 2.57 |
| 2000 | 1.20 | 4.30 |
| 2001 | 1.23 | 4.49 |
| 2002 | 1.25 | 3.53 |
| 2003 | 1.28 | 5.39 |
| 2004 | 1.36 | 5.96 |
| 2005 | 1.54 | 8.21 |
| 2006 | 1.69 | 6.94 |
| 2007 | 1.77 | 7.11 |
| 2008 | 2.07 | 9.01 |
| 2009 | 2.21 | 4.74 |
| 2010 | 2.27 | 5.09 |

* U.S. Energy Information Administration Monthly, Energy Review, 201

- Nuclear
    - Nuclear power plants use the heat produced by nuclear fission to produce steam that drives a turbine to generate electricity.
    - Nuclear plants are characterized by high investment costs but low variable operating costs, including low fuel expense. Because of the low variable costs and design factors, nuclear plants in the United States operate exclusively as base-load plants (operating and providing energy continuously).
    - Nuclear power supplied almost 20% of the nation's electricity in 2011.
    - Construction of a nuclear plant requires approval from the Nuclear Regulatory Commission, which until this year had not approved the construction of a new plant for 16 years. But in February of 2012, approval was given to the Southern Company for the construction of a two-reactor facility. The industry views this as a commitment to expanding nuclear energy in the United States.
    - Nuclear generation is "zero-emitting" while producing, but has waste disposal (spent nuclear fuel rod) issues.
    - One advantage of nuclear power is that it provides large amounts of base-load electricity without releasing carbon dioxide. This furnishes a steady supply of reliable electricity for industries looking to expand or relocate operations to the valley.
- Wind
    - Wind power plants (sometimes referred to as wind farms) use wind-driven turbines to generate electricity.
    - Wind is a variable renewable resource because its availability depends on the whims of the weather. The Southeast U.S. is fairly wind-poor, and transmission from the middle of the country may be required if wind energy is used in large amounts.
    - Wind supplied 3% of total U.S. power in 2011. Assuming no changes to current law and regulation, the Energy Information Administration estimates an increase to 20% by 2030.
    - The high capital costs and unpredictable generation make wind power costly when used for large generation purposes.
- Solar
    - Solar photovoltaic (solar PV) power uses solar cells to directly convert sunlight to electricity. To date, most of the solar PV installations in the United States have been small (about 1 MW or less). Solar cells produce energy only about one-third of the time.
    - It would take a great deal of land area to produce large quantities of energy—about 2 acres to provide 1 MW of generation. To match the energy of a nuclear unit, it would take around 4 000 acres of solar panels.
    - Smaller photovoltaic solar units could be "distributed" generation in

many customers' locations, which could avoid transmission costs. These units are currently being built by a small number of environmentally sensitive customers. TVA has a program to pay customers a premium for the solar energy they produce.

* The main issue is the cost. Though high, the costs continue to fall because of technological improvements. This is in contrast to the increasing cost of most other generation alternatives.

## IV. THE UNIQUE NATURE OF ELECTRICITY

The biggest part of the rewrite of the strategic plan is developing a strategy for capital investments to increase capacity for future energy needs while at the same time minimizing electricity rates. Morgan keeps the following table of cost estimates from the Energy Information Administration on her laptop (shown in Table 2).

Table 2
Estimated Levelized Cost of New Generation Resources (USA) *

|  | Capacity Factor (%) | Levelized CapitalCost $/MW-year | Estimated Service Life (yrs) | Levelized Cost of Generation $/MWh |
|---|---|---|---|---|
| Conventional Coal | 85% | $515 263 | 30 | $31.20 |
| Pulverized Coal | 85% | $604 615 | 30 | $29.30 |
| Pulverized Coal with CCS | 85% | $689 500 | 30 | $36.70 |
| Conventional Combined Cycle | 87% | $174 525 | 20 | $60.20 |
| Advanced Combined Cycle | 87% | $170 715 | 20 | $56.90 |
| Conventional Combustion Turbine | 30% | $108 011 | 20 | $98.40 |
| Advanced Combustion Turbine | 30% | $101 178 | 20 | $85.00 |
| Advanced Nuclear | 90% | $748 192 | 40 | $24.10 |
| Wind | 34% | $388 681 | 20 | $18.80 |
| Wind-Offshore | 39% | $546 282 | 20 | $31.20 |
| Solar PV | 22% | $726 169 | 20 | $19.30 |
| Solar Thermal | 31% | $609 381 | 20 | $32.20 |
| Geothermal | 90% | $693 792 | 45 | $27.70 |
| Biomass | 83% | $532 950 | 20 | $37.70 |
| Hydro | 51% | $463 290 | 50 | $16.20 |

* Source: Energy Information Administration

Capital costs, the costs that are incurred bringing a generating plant on-line, are amortized over the operating life of the plant. Costs of generation are realized as the generating plant operates. It is important to keep in mind that, like most government-regulated monopolies, TVA must set rates equal to long-run average cost.

Morgan remembered something else that the group failed to talk about. Electricity cannot be stored in the grid. Instead, it is consumed as it is produced. The problem with this is that electricity consumption varies not only by season of the year, but also by the time of day. On late afternoons and early evening on weekdays, demand rises. This increase is more pronounced during warm weather months. These high demand periods are known in the industry as "peak loads." At other times, especially in the very early morning hours, demand is quite low. Of course, electricity demand never falls to zero, so TVA must always be generating power to meet the minimum level of power demanded of the grid. This minimum level is called the "base load."

Electric utilities use different power generation technologies to serve base and peak loads. It can take many hours or even days to get nuclear or coal generation plants up to their functioning power levels. This trait makes them very inefficient as peak load power producers. Instead, they run continuously to serve base load demands. As power demand increases during the day, technologies that can be cycled up and down (natural gas plants) are used to produce the additional energy for the peak load. Base load plants have high fixed costs but very low marginal costs; peak load generators have lower fixed costs but much higher marginal costs of operation. Any strategic plan must take into consideration not only how much to increase total generation capacity, but also how the different loads will be met. This will require that forecasts be made of both peak and base load demands.

There is another strategy that should be considered, however. "Demand side management" programs could be implemented to reduce the costs of adding additional capacity to meet peak load demands. If there were some way to reduce power usage during the peak load times and move that power to the base load periods (a strategy known as "load shifting"), then building additional power generation capacity might be postponed for several years. TVA cannot dictate when power is used during the day, but it might be able to influence power usage by changing its pricing model. Instead of pricing power at long-run average costs, TVA could employ a "time-of-use" pricing model and price electricity close to the marginal cost of producing it. During base load periods, price per kilowatt would be lower; during peak load periods, price per kilowatt would increase with the increased costs of supplying the power. This strategy should reduce energy consumption during peak load periods and increase it during base load periods. In effect, total power usage doesn't change; it just moves from peak load to base load periods. This allows TVA to provide more power from less expensive base load generation plants. It could also save the cost of building additional generation capacity to meet future peak load needs.

Load shifting is not a new idea, but power utilities across the nation have not been able to implement it because of the difficulties of determining exactly what time of day a consumer actually uses a unit of electricity. But recent development of "smart meters" not only allows TVA to monitor power usage instantaneously, but also allows consumers to track their energy use and make adjustments that can reduce their utility bills. Appliance manufacturers are even developing "smart" appliances that communicate with the power grid to use real-time information on pricing and determine the optimum time to run, allowing the consumer to use a "set-it-and-forget-it" approach to managing energy needs.

Though this sounds like the ideal solution, consumers have been reluctant to embrace the technology. They also have trouble believing that the strategy benefits all parties involved—the consumer, the utility, and the environment. Morgan chuckled as she remembered the problems Pacific Gas & Electric had introducing smart meters to the San Francisco Bay area. In a unanimous vote, the County Board of Supervisors imposed a moratorium on "smart meter" installation, citing health (the devices allegedly caused brain tumors) and privacy (the collection of information on private household habits) concerns. If the devices can't be sold to environmentally-conscious Californians, what chance does TVA have with Tennessee Valley residents?

Morgan's smile slowly dissolved as she realized something else about the potential use of the newer technologies. Higher-income and highly-educated households are most likely to purchase the smart meters and to take advantage of the smart appliances. A part of TVA's service area is Appalachia—a region with pockets of extreme poverty where families live on the edge of destitution. If TVA follows this pricing model and passes on the costs of installing the new meters to all of its customers, these families would share those costs and almost certainly not be purchasing the smart appliances. In addition, many of these consumers are employed in manufacturing, doing shift work with schedules that would not allow them the flexibility of managing the timing of their energy use. The result of time-sensitive pricing would actually be increased energy bills for households that could least afford it.

Even worse, TVA could be accused of subsidizing higher-income households. Given the national conversation about increasing income inequality, this would not look good for TVA. But that's not the way to look at things, thought Morgan. The question is, What is the right thing to do?

## V. FUNDING CONSIDERATIONS

TVA's current rate schedule is designed to cover operating expenses, interest and debt issue retirement, production plant fuels, and all other miscellaneous costs. The TVA board is allowed to raise rates as needed to cover costs, and a fuel-cost adjustment can be made on a quarterly basis to offset volatile fuel prices.

During periods in which TVA revenues fail to cover expenses, the agency reduces costs across functional areas, including slowing capital improvements, limiting new hires, and freezing wages. Alternatively, TVA can borrow funds. This solution may be optimal from a cost standpoint in that, as an AAA-rated agency, TVA can borrow money significantly below market rates. TVA's long-term debt ceiling, set by the U. S. Congress, is $30 billion, however. The ceiling has not been raised in the last four decades. Currently, long-term debt (traditionally reserved for capital projects) remains almost $9 billion, despite several years of debt-reduction efforts. TVA's outstanding long-term debt portfolio averages 5.5%. Although TVA has issued debt with maturities of up to 50 years in the past, the current economic climate will limit new issues to maturities of 15 to 30 years. Given the longer-termed asset life of most of the generation alternatives, Morgan believes that a new 30-year debt issue would be used to fund capital construction. Since TVA's current outstanding bond issues are of shorter maturity, Morgan knows that she must use U. S. Government bonds as a benchmark. She remembers a recent meeting with senior treasury officials at TVA; a premium of 80 to 100 basis points over current government rates is expected. Since there is so much uncertainty in today's economic and political environment, Morgan believes that 100 BPS is most likely. Table 3 shows current interest rates for outstanding TVA and U.S Government debt instruments.

Still another alternative to increase funding is to raise utility rates. Increasing the cost to customers is never a popular option, and it is TVA's mandate to keep rates as low as possible. Low rates are especially important given TVA's mission of economic development in the Tennessee Valley, and inexpensive energy costs keeps industry growing in the region. Besides, the outcry following a rate increase large enough to fund capital construction would be heard across the Southeast and in Washington.

### Table 3

**Tennessee Valley Authority Bonds** *

| Coupon % | Maturity (Month-Year) | Bid | Ask | Yield to Maturity % |
|---|---|---|---|---|
| 6.00 | 3 –13 | 103.26 | 103.27 | 0.01 |
| 4.75 | 8 –13 | 104.21 | 104.23 | 0.13 |
| 6.25 | 12 –17 | 128.12 | 128.30 | 0.76 |
| 6.75 | 11 –25 | 148.12 | 148.25 | 0.65 |
| 7.13 | 5 –30 | 158.00 | 158.17 | 2.89 |

**U. S. Government Bonds**

| Coupon % | Maturity (Month-Year) | Bid | Ask | Yield to Maturity % |
|---|---|---|---|---|
| 2.50 | 3 –13 | 101.59 | 101.60 | 0.17 |
| 4.25 | 8 –13 | 104.30 | 104.33 | 0.17 |
| 2.75 | 12 –17 | 111.02 | 111.06 | 0.68 |
| 6.875 | 8 –25 | 159.41 | 159.45 | 1.76 |
| 6.25 | 5 –30 | 161.91 | 161.99 | 1.22 |
| 5.00 | 5 –37 | 149.59 | 149.66 | 1.59 |
| 3.00 | 5 –42 | 109.45 | 109.51 | 2.54 |

\* Source: *Wall Street Journal*, July 23, 2012

## VI. OTHER CONSIDERATIONS

While TVA has an extraordinarily low cost of capital, new generation means that bumping up against the debt ceiling is a real possibility. Morgan pursed her lips, thinking, "Because of the debt ceiling, I don't know the best way to think about rationing capital spending. Given the current economic and political environment, would it be possible to get our debt ceiling raised? Or am I better off to not even think about that?"

As Morgan approached Knoxville, she looked to her left and saw the Kingston-TVA coal facilities and considered that disastrous event. Coal units produce leftover fly ash that requires disposal. At the Kingston plant, the ash was stored in a collection pond near the facilities. Just before Christmas of that year, the walls of the pond ruptured, and the ash sludge flooded about 300 acres of land, including some people's homes. TVA management reacted quickly and did everything they could to right the situation, but at a cost of about $1 billion, the clean-up cost was enormous. There continue to be calls for increased regulation of coal combustion by-products.

TVA faces other financial difficulties on top of the costs associated with the Kingston situation. There's the decreased demand and lack of pricing-increase flexibility due to the weak economy. It is also faced with another $1 billion expense from complying with the air quality standards imposed by a lawsuit with North Carolina. Even though TVA had already developed a plan and had started construction on plant upgrades required for improving air quality, the lawsuit forced TVA to expedite its schedule, and in some cases required more money than originally budgeted. Finally, TVA has experienced a long period of drought, which has reduced hydro generation from dams, forcing the agency to replace that lost energy with expensive purchased power, since other generation assets are producing at or near capacity. Morgan thought how all of these unexpected events, taken together, equal almost 20% of one year's revenue.

## VII. DECISION TIME

Finally, Morgan arrived at the TVA corporate tower in downtown Knoxville and sighed. How should she fit the complicated pieces together to form a strategy for TVA to satisfy its many stakeholders? What are the keys to TVA's strategy going forward? Before tackling these two questions, Morgan must look at what she knows.

From the most recent 10-K, Morgan knows that TVA currently has a 37 188 MW capacity; about 40% of capacity is generated from coal and the remainder is generated primarily by nuclear, hydro, and natural gas plants. Less than 1 percent of current capacity is from renewable resources. Last year's long hot summer caused TVA to exceed this capacity, which required purchasing power from other producers.

TVA has multiple options for producing power in order to ensure its commitment to reliable and affordable electricity to the service area in the future. Each of the options has unique capacities, cash flows, and useful lives.

Morgan wonders whether it would be better to go with longer-lived assets such as advanced nuclear or pulverized coal plants with expected lives of 30 years from the day construction is started, or shorter-lived assets such as advanced natural gas combined cycle, wind generation, or solar photovoltaic plants to take advantage of expected improvements in technology and production efficiency. Each of these alternatives has an expected life of 20 years.

Construction project costs and lengths also vary greatly. The $5.5 billion cost of a nuclear plant dwarfs the other alternatives and also has the longest construction time (4 years). A coal plant is less expensive to build (costing roughly one-third as much— $1.8 billion), but takes almost as long to build (3 years). Although much less expensive to construct ($650 million), a natural gas plant still requires 2.5 years for construction. Both of the renewable energy alternatives have short construction times (1 year); the costs differ significantly. The solar plant cost of $300 million is 20 times the cost of a wind plant ($15 million).

The alternative sources also have different production capacities. Coal and nuclear plants have significant production capacities (2 300 and 2 000 MW per year, respectively). The other alternatives have lower capacities. The gas plant's capacity is 720 MW per year, the wind plant's capacity is 150 MW per year, and the solar plant's capacity is 100 MW per year.

The cost of input materials also significantly affects the expected yearly cash flows from each production source. The cash inflows will begin in the year following the end of construction and will remain constant for the life of the asset. Given the long-lived nature of uranium, the nuclear plant's expected cash flow of $680 million per year is significantly higher than the other alternatives. The relatively high cost of production inputs used in the coal and natural gas plants reduces the expected cash flows from each of these plants to $97 million and $85 million, respectively. The expected yearly cash flow from the wind plant is $2 million; the yearly cash flow from the solar plant is $3 million.

Morgan thought, "There are so many factors that are unique to each of the production alternatives—capacity, reliability, input costs, etc. No one alternative dominates. What factors should I use to compare the alternatives? Are some factors more important than others?"

TVA recently revealed plans to retire multiple coal units by 2018 to comply with its goal to be a leader of clean energy. TVA will need to replace 5 670 MW of generation before these coal units are retired. Half of this generation will be met by converting the old coal plants with combustion turbines. At least 70% of the remaining needed capacity will be met with new base load generation; the remainder can be from peaking or intermittent transmission.

At least one thing should help. Since TVA has traditionally funded new power generation construction with debt, the low interest rates will reduce borrowing costs. In addition, the cost of capital used in discounted cash flow analysis should be easier to explain to those few "financially-challenged" board members, since TVA uses no equity costs in its capital budgeting process.

The TVA board will be looking to her for a plan to meet the customer needs within TVA's resource guidelines. Morgan wonders how she should evaluate the production alternatives, given their different cost and output characteristics. In addition, how do the other factors affect TVA's strategic direction? The meeting is scheduled for early Monday morning. Morgan realized that she wouldn't need those football game tickets after all.

# 业绩考核与报酬
Performance Measurement & Compensation

# 联合利华：一家全球性公司的信息技术服务外包的财务启示

Barbara E. Tarasovich,
Sacred Heart University

## 简介

联合利华的产品几乎在全球的各大商场、药店和超市的货架上都有销售。尽管不是每个人都熟知公司的名称，但联合利华的各个品牌却是家喻户晓，包括凡士林、多芬、好乐门、本杰瑞艾科、家乐和立顿等。公司的使命是"为您的生活增添活力"。然而，为了让公司业务更具有活力，联合利华不仅需要注重提高市场占有率，还需要减少运营成本。信息技术（IT）[①]部门以计算出准确无误的利润为重点，在支持公司使命中扮演了重要的角色，同时它还促使员工更有效的工作。

在竞争激烈的消费品行业中，公司专注于核心竞争力，以提供一个可持续的竞争优势。尽管信息技术的基础构建服务对连接终端用户很关键，但这并不是竞争优势的来源。公司面临的挑战，包括：过时的客户端技术，非标准服务约束了灵活性、可扩展性，和与日俱增的费用。联合利华希望彻底更新它的信息技术基础设施，同时降低部署和维护成本。首席财务官和首席信息官选择了一个商业伙伴，他不仅提供硬件，还提供运行服务、持续的台式机服务和服务中心的支持。本案例将重点关注联合利华在2006年制订的实际业务流程外包的决策。表1列示了联合利华IT部门的组织示意图。

IT服务的外包是一个商业趋势，它在过去10年间大幅增长，并且这一趋势将会继续发展（Plugge and Jannsen，2009）。科技不断变化，IT服务外包可提供最新技术，而公司不需要购进新设备，或为掌握管理IT服务需要的技能（人力资本、知识基础等）而投入大量的资本。管理会计人员需要与IT部门合作，谨慎地制订一个企划案，确定成本削减方案以及外包协议对销售和行政管理费用的影响，同时还要考虑服务的有效性和安全性。对不同的外包协议，如何在财务报告中记录成本也是非常关键的。项目的某些成本需要资本化；而其他成本则确认为当期费用并会影响公司的利润表，减少当期净利润。

---

\* 本篇译者为胡金凤，校订者为余辉、赵澄。
① 信息技术相关术语的解释，请参阅本案例结尾处的"图表3，IT术语表"。——译者

这份企划案必须能够降低所有权总成本[2]，同时确保公司可获得一周七天、一天 24 小时的核心服务。它必须能够帮助联合利华实现显著的成本节约，并带来现金流入。外包的主要目的是获得高质量的 IT 服务，同时让核心的 IT 人员与公司其他人员互动、创新，从而增加公司的现金流和收益。

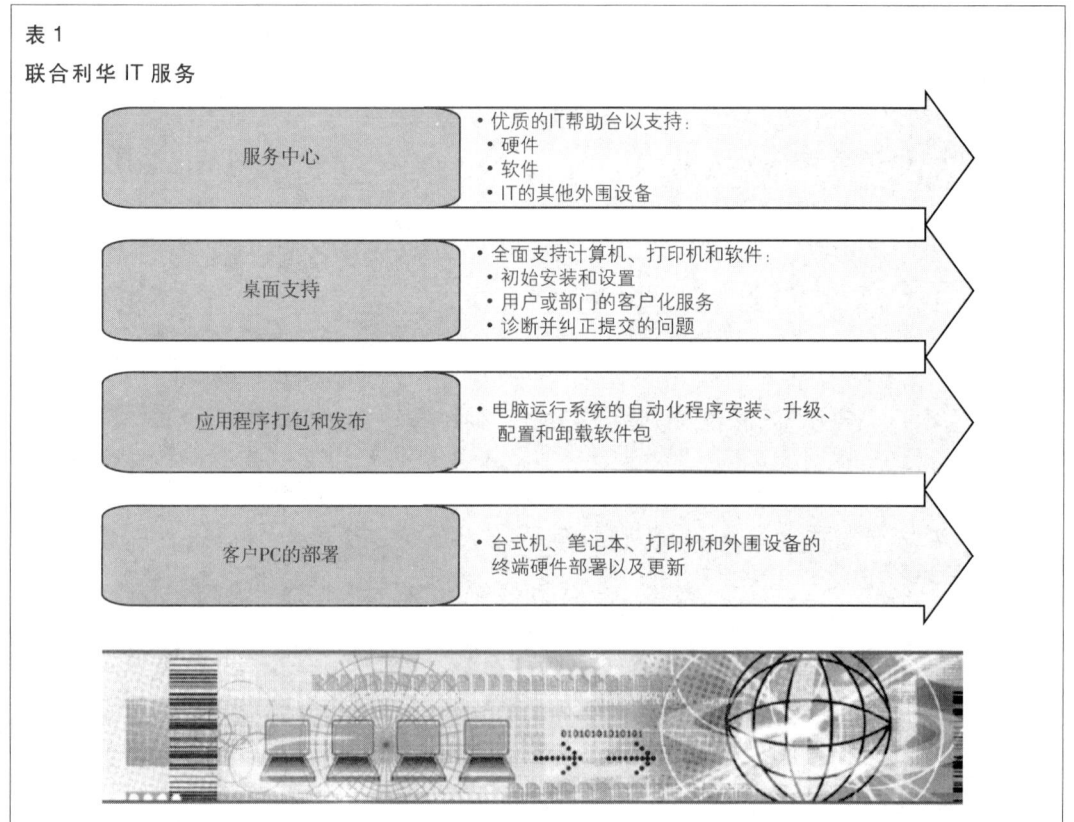

表 1
联合利华 IT 服务

## 公司概述/背景

联合利华是一家制造消费品的跨国公司。图表 1 为公司简介。联合利华的目标为"满足世界各地人们的日常需求——预测我们的消费者和顾客的愿望，并提供具有创造性和竞争力的品牌产品和服务，以提高人们的生活质量"。公司深深扎根于当地文化和全球市场，这使得它（联合利华）充分掌握了当地消费者的相关知识和跨国经验。联合利华有两家母公司：联合利华 PLC，总部位于英国；联合利华 N.V.，总部位于荷兰。[3] 这两家公司基本

---

② 所有权总成本（Total Cost of Ownership），为采购工作中的一项重要方法，其倾向于从全局以及长期的观点，分析企业与供应商发生商品和服务交易的真实成本。它要求企业考虑那些他们认为与采购、占用、使用和处置商品和服务有关的成本或重要的成本。——译者

③ N.V. 为 naamloze vennootschap，即"股份有限公司"的缩写，为荷兰等国家所使用。PLC 为 public limited company 的缩写，为英国所使用。——译者

上各自作为单独的法人经营，但他们由同一个董事会管理，且两者之间由祖铎协议联系着。这些协议使得联合利华在管理、经营、股东权利、目的和使命上实现了统一。这些协议的目的是为了让两个公司的股东处于同等地位，就像他们持有同一家公司的股票一样。

---

**图表1**
**联合利华公司的简介**

**联合利华的结构：**
联合利华由荷兰的联合利华 N.V. 和英国的联合利华 PLC. 两个公司联合经营。

**核心高管：**
董事长：迈克·泰斯库；CEO 兼董事：保罗·波尔曼

**背景：**
联合利华是全球包装消费品的顶级制造商，它的产品畅销于180多个国家，覆盖了非洲、亚洲、拉丁美洲、中东、北美以及西欧。公司的产品涵盖了11个种类，包括护肤品、除臭剂。畅销品牌包括好乐门(蛋黄酱)、家乐(汤类)、立顿(茶)、多芬和力士(香皂) 以及夏士莲(护发品)。

**主要竞争者：**
- 宝洁公司
- 雀巢
- 利洁时集团

**节选的财务数据**（单位为百万美元，根据欧元转换而来）
收入：587亿美元
净利润：56亿美元
净利率：9.59%
员工人数：165 000

---

联合利华最具价值的12个品牌创造了10亿美元的销售额，这20个品牌的销售额占到总销售额的70%。2006年潜在的销量增长为3.8%。联合利华经营的产品有11类（如，护肤品、除臭剂、冰淇淋、茶、调味酱、开胃食品、调料、护发用品、洗涤剂、口腔护理、家用清洁品等），并在其中七个领域居于全球领先的地位。如多芬、力士、旁氏、舒耐等品牌让联合利华成为全球除臭剂和护肤品市场的领导者。立顿、布鲁克邦德、本杰瑞、和路雪这一些品牌让联合利华成为全球冰淇淋和饮料市场的领导者。公司的员工超过了167 000人，并且公司50%以上的业务是在新兴市场中。这些新兴市场是许多公司的未来，特别是像联合利华这样销售漂白剂、阳光肥皂等日常家居用品的公司。新兴市场是指社会或商业活动处于快速成长和产业化过程中的国家。如中国、印度等国家被认为是最大的新兴市场。

# 公司/IT 部门的战略目标

IT 改革的目的是为了构建尖端技术服务，使其在公司总体的"成长之路"战略中发挥关键作用。该战略包括了五年期的具体的销售、利润、收入增长的目标。本案例阐明了，一个与公司总体战略计划相整合的外包项目，何以成为一个竞争优势。为有助于"成长之路"战略，IT 领导团队决定将信息和技术作为关键的驱动力来管理。IT 部门由人员、硬件、软件和流程构成，它们被认为是建立可持续商务活动的一个主要驱动者。"业务与IT融合"这一通俗术语对提供有效的解决方案非常重要，并且对提供降低成本的可选方案也非常重要，因为各消费品公司正都面临着产品利润下降和竞争加剧的困境。简而言之，下列是IT部门需要解决的战略目标：
- 完善的业务和IT运作
- 准确理解用户需求
- 整合管理流程
- 识别引起用户社区共鸣的关键成功因素和指标

IT部门的使命表述为"成为高效的、以客户为中心的IT服务部——提供可靠的优质服务来充分满足业务的需求"。

## 全球信息技术的改革

2006年，联合利华的全球IT部门开始将其管理重点由操作转向服务。IT部门专注于技术流程的简化，以及提供业务敏捷性和灵活性来迅速适应新的商业机会。

一直以来，对IT的定位和价值以及是否应将IT看作像电或天然气这样的商品，公司内存在争论（Harris，2008）。如果将IT作为商品，则应追求成本和缺陷最小化，并避免风险。此外，因为技术的快速进步，IT带来的任何竞争优势都是短暂的。只有当某一项功能达到一定水平的成熟度时，这种形式的讨论才有可能（Glavan，2012）。首席信息官议程中的相关主题已由"下一项技术是什么？"变为"各种服务交付模式的成本为多少？"。对联合利华而言，如IT基础架构库（ITIL）、CobIT（由国际信息系统审计协会为IT管理创立的一个框架（Shuja，2010））和IT治理（Shuja，2010）以及其他标准，可提供可行的路线图和参考模型，来促进建立优质IT服务设施所需要的功能和流程的联合，通过改革让IT的核心与业务相结合，为公司成长做出一些贡献。IT部门所面临的挑战包括：当前的硬件配置、操作系统和办公套件的版本都缺乏更新且过时的。威胁因素包括：

- 由于业务需求和要求在不断变化，所以，容量和扩展性问题变得尤为关键。不论是增加或减少提供的服务，IT部门必须能够迅速的适应以尽量减少管理费用。
- 缺乏必需的管理工具来满足日益增长的提供世界级的客户服务的需求。
- 难以遵守的新IT服务管理流程和规定，如ITIL，而这是提供世界级IT服务的关键要素。它被定义为最佳实践的系列教科书，对优化这些服务的传递和管理的方法提供建议。
- 难以遵守的萨班斯-奥克斯利法案（SOX）的第404号条款。IT通过对公司系统和IT网络中的财务数据进行保密和保护，为公司遵守SOX的推动力提供支持。一个公司没有IT的支持，便不能遵守SOX（第404条）所要求的内部控制结构的测试与生效。如果公司的内部控制结构不恰当，公司会因为违反SOX的条例受到证券交易委员会的惩罚

（Bonnie, Kevin, and Marcia, 2012）。

联合利华的战略为：管理技术部署来帮助业务目标的实现。IT 部门为企业提供建议、帮助和领导能力，尽量提高来自产品和服务的收益。对公司其他部门来说，财务团队与 IT 部门相互合作，成为一个整体。（图表 2 为全球 IT 部门的结构图。）财务部门与 IT 一起工作，建立开发商合作资源、管理外部供应商。此外，财务团队的另一重要作用就是洽谈合同，进而不断改进从风险管理到网络基础设施的所有方面。财务团体也设计信息管理结构、制定采购政策、并分析提供服务的第三方供应商的财务状况。

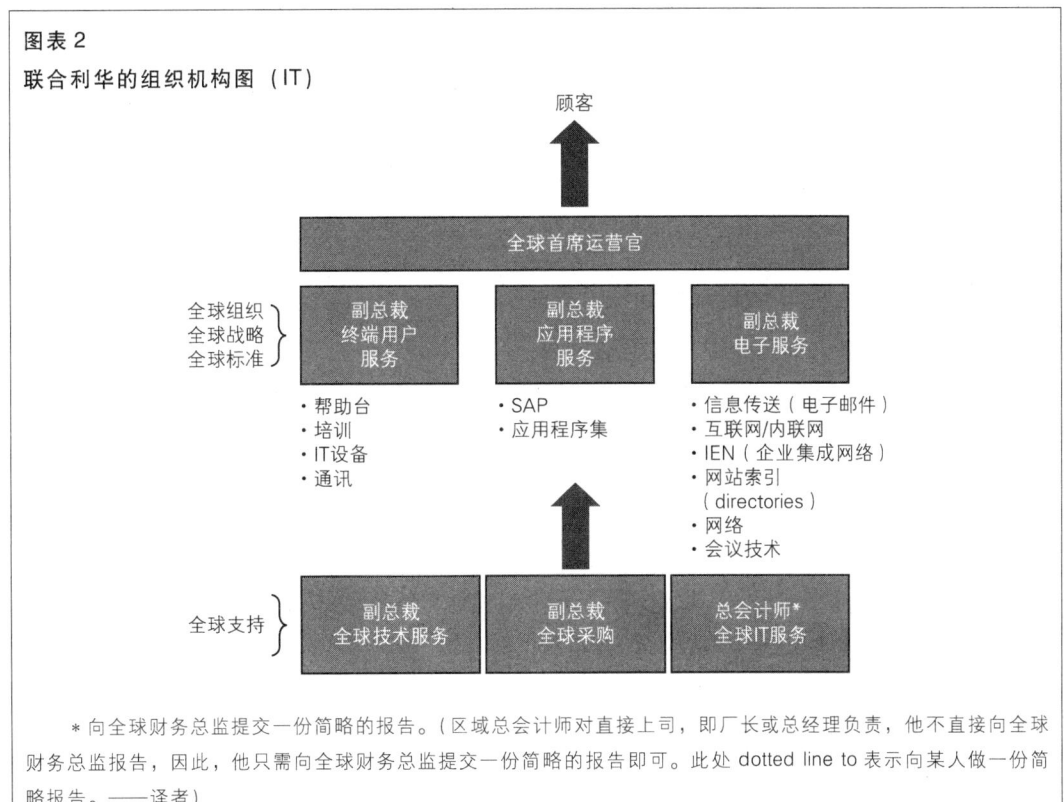

图表 2
联合利华的组织机构图（IT）

* 向全球财务总监提交一份简略的报告。（区域总会计师对直接上司，即厂长或总经理负责，他不直接向全球财务总监报告，因此，他只需向全球财务总监提交一份简略的报告即可。此处 dotted line to 表示向某人做一份简略报告。——译者）

# 外包决策

为确保公司可得到需要的所有电脑和 IT 服务，同时让 IT 部门可以放手去关注业务的增长而不是基础设施的管理，联合利华支持 IT 服务外包的企划案。他们制订的企划案让 IT 部门能够摆脱管理和部署个人电脑（PCs）的行政事务，提高生产力并促使团队为用户提供更好的服务。此外，通过 IT 服务的外包，联合利华可扩展 IT 服务，以适应不断变化的市场环境。

联合利华的财务团队在开发企划案中扮演了重要角色，它为联合利华 2006 年执行 IT 客户服务的外包进行投资和相关成本的处理。考虑到这一方面业务的复杂性质，财务领导团队的任务就是要寻找一种处理和解决的方法，以及为 IT 客户服务建立一个长期计划，包括：
- 复杂、详细、多层次的技术、流程和服务
- 扩展联合利华业务的覆盖地区
- 终端用户帮助台，也被称为客户服务（见图表2）
- 客户基础设施管理和所有权总成本
- 跟上新兴技术的要求
- 工作站和服务器管理——资产的控制和管理
- 安装、移动、增添、更改资产和所有个人计算机设备（如，个人电脑、软件、或打印机）
- 保持良好的职业规划，以吸引、培养并保留高技能的财务和 IT 专业人才

识别项目的成功因素至关重要，来保证团队对可交付实现的关注。在整个改革中，所有的关键成功因素都受到监控。

## 外包的目的

联合利华将 IT 客户服务外包的主要目的：
- 为公司和终端用户提供点对点的台式机生命周期支持
- 解决所有权总成本中关于可预期的长期成本结构的问题
- 改善终端用户的生产率、服务质量和关键技术的访问
- 让终端用户的生产能力与业务需求更相匹配
- 完整的生命周期管理——对于从计划和采购到维护和处置的整个生命周期实施管理
- 基础设施的全球管理，让公司能快速地在全球范围实施并有效地运营，并为持续改进提供基础
- 多个开发商的支持——无缝地支持多样化的、多个开发商的台式和移动（办公）环境
- 采取过渡和转换的工作方法——在服务不中断的条件下，平稳地过渡到新的技术和应用
- 单点接触[④]和问责制

## 风险

对于如此规模庞大的服务转换，有许多风险需要考虑。其中大部分风险会在这些领域的转换中出现，包括服务中心、桌面支持、应用程序打包和发布。一份具备完善且详尽计划的风险评估是必要的，它应包括适当的转折点

---

④ 单点接触是日本住友银行最早创新并实行的。当时住友银行有很多大客户，为了有针对性地为客户提供服务，住友银行设立了许多服务小组，每组有数十人，小组有从事各种业务的专业人才，不仅能对客户提供包括存贷款、外汇结算等业务，还能为客户提供其他服务。这种让客户与银行只接触一个环节就可以把所有的业务、所有的程序都能完成的做法，就是单点接触服务策略。——译者

和继续/暂停决策点。在配置个人电脑设备时，主要风险是终端用户的生产效率受到影响。此外，确保转换过程中数据不会丢失是非常关键的。及时地将正确的设备递送至一个安全环境中，对降低丢失关键信息的风险也是必要的。在服务过渡中，服务中断和受阻还可能影响持续的业务操作。从财务的角度，主要风险不是实现已确定的节省成本。为解决这些风险，联合利华与第三方服务提供者合作，以确保协议中明确了合适的工具和资源，以确保他们按照约定的计划执行部署并管理服务。

# 北美公司的外包功能的概要

2006年，联合利华北美（NA）公司在100个不同地区有17 000终端用户。公司邀请了六个潜在供应商参与这次投标申请书（RFP）的提交，公司不仅仅是要更新现有的所有工作地点的台式机和笔记本，并且还需要管理持续的支持服务。NA的团队总结了，有三家供应商达到了提交申请书的要求，随后，有两家供应商合作提交了一份申请书。

在选择客户服务的供应商时，RFP的目标为：

- 领导"联合利华统一PC项目"的个人电脑部署阶段，提供标准的硬件、程序、工具和一个标准的桌面配置
- 完成新的个人电脑部署后，提供支持服务
- 提供技术改进和服务的灵活性，使得IT创造更多的商业机会
- 做到成本逐年下降
- ITIL定义了计算机处理的最佳实践，根据ITIL的规定更新联合利华的PC环境。

客户服务方案中包括的服务为（见表1）：

- 服务中心——放置计算机设备的场所
- 桌面支持——向用户提供技术支持的机构
- 应用程序打包和发布
- 新PC设备的部署

这些服务是向北美公司所有的业务团队提供的，并最终提供给联合利华的全球IT部门。当前自给自足的当地支持服务模式已转变为了集中支持模式。所有的计算机热线将接入一个集中式的服务中心，并且桌面支持资源将安排在大城市（如，格林威治、多伦多、恩格尔伍德恩克利夫斯和芝加哥）。这些资源也向NA的所有其他网站提供远程支持。中心团队无法提供的支持则由一个派遣服务组解决。

服务提供商必须根据正式的服务水平协议测量所有的服务。所以，为改变现有的"通用服务水平"的终端用户服务（EUS）支持模式，供应商的解决方案将提供服务基线假设。开发商的这一解决方案，在联合利华内以"选择服务、选择成本"为大家所知。财务团队与第三方服务提供商制订了不同的成本模式，为联合利华的业务团队提供了一份服务选项单。例如，业务团队可以选择最高水平的服务（如，铂金级服务—每周七天、每天24小时的服务中心和桌面支持

服务),不过供应商提供的高级支持水平会使成本提高一些。

## 所有权成本和项目节省的预测

表2概括了关于外包IT服务运营的总投资成本,以及转换新设备并由第三方供应商提供服务的一次性项目成本。联合利华必须承担现有的所有程序的软件许可成本。表中还包括了,在全北美工作场所实施新个人电脑的所有一次性资本和项目费用。表2中,EUS的成本反映了在向第三方转换过程中的双重运行成本。这主要包括现有部门中支持EUS的相关人员的成本。合同终止费用反映的是之前在联合利华提供部分职能的第三方供应商终止现有合同的终止费用。

**表2**

**外包投资**

案例中,所有的财务信息均来自真实的项目申请批准(Request for Project approval, RFP)文件——于2005年10月提交给联合利华北美的董事会新设备的一次性资本成本(1 140万美元)和一次性项目费用(1 530万美元)的详细情况如下:

|  | 奥德赛——新个人电脑设备成本 |  |  |  | EUS 的转换<br>(与向第三方转移<br>服务相关) | 合计 |
|---|---|---|---|---|---|---|
|  | 2004 | 2005 | 2006 | 2007/2008 | 2005~2008 |  |
| 资本 | $2.2 | $8.6 | $0.6 | — |  | $11.4 |
| 软件/许可证 |  | 5.1 | 0.6 |  |  |  |
| 服务器(windows 2000/信息传送) |  | 1.3 | 1.3 |  |  |  |
| LAN/WAN 升级 |  | 2.2 |  |  |  |  |
| 客户端(PC)备份 |  | 0.9 |  |  |  |  |
| 一次性项目支出 | $0.5 | $5.5 | $3.7 | $.8 | $4.8 | $15.3 |
| 双重运营/雇员返聘成本 |  | 1.0 | 1.0 |  | 2.5 |  |
| 员工遣散费 |  | 1.1 | 1.1 |  |  |  |
| 终止现有的供应商合同 |  |  |  |  | 2.1 |  |
| 供应商过渡费用 |  | 0.2 | 0.3 | 0.8 |  |  |
| 项目管理成本、差旅费、培训费 |  | 0.9 | 0.3 |  |  |  |
| 应用程序打包 |  | 1.0 |  |  |  |  |
| 通讯工具 |  | 0.3 | 0.3 |  |  |  |
| 软件许可证费用 | 0.5 |  |  |  |  |  |
| 其他,如维护费用 |  | 1.0 | 0.7 |  | 0.2 |  |

表3概括了外包协议所带来的预期节省。这种节约模式将第三方供应商对"每个席位"或"每台个人电脑"的定价与联合利华现有终端用户服务

（EUS）的服务模式成本进行对比。与联合利华当前的营运成本对比，预计每年将节约1 260万美元。

---

**表3**

**项目的节约**

**节约**

通过客户服务的外包协议，2006年的终端用户服务（EUS）的总成本将降低300万美元。三年期的合同预期将节省1 260万美元，主要是因为供应商的每台计算机的运营成本较低，服务内容包括现有的全部，但雇佣的全职人员相当于裁减了50%的全职EUS人员。

下表列示出了项目节省的关键要素：

| 百万美元 | | 2006 | 2007 | 2008 | 2009 | 合计 |
|---|---|---|---|---|---|---|
| 当前的服务模式： | 与雇员相关的成本 | 6.0 | 6.2 | 6.3 | 6.5 | 25.0 |
| | 无线电通讯及相关成本 | 4.0 | 4.1 | 4.2 | 4.3 | 16.6 |
| | 实验室运行脚本程序的成本 | | | | | |
| 联合利华的环境 | 1.0 | 1.0 | 1.1 | 1.1 | 4.2 |
| | 总成本 | 11.0 | 11.3 | 11.6 | 11.9 | 45.8 |
| 每台电脑的服务提供商成本：* | | 8.0 | 8.2 | 8.4 | 8.6 | 33.2 |
| 节省： | | 3.0 | 3.1 | 3.2 | 3.3 | 12.6 |

*定价是在约定的每季度的席位（注：一台计算机设备则为一个席位）价格基础上作出。这项协议在不改变定价结构的条件下，在席位数量上给予一定的灵活性。坐席数量每季度审核。

---

# 评价外包协议的成功

服务外包协议的实施，在极大程度上使联合利华总体的IT战略远景得以实现。它引入简化的技术与流程，并为迅速适应新的商业机会、重组和重建等提供了灵活性。部署的成功被认为是一个关键的里程碑。总会计师与IT服务的副总裁一起合作，确保项目严格按照计划进行管理，并实现节省目标。此外，终端用户和IT人员会对服务水平协议进行检测和评估，以确保提供的服务水平与计划相一致。

# 案例要求

1. 为实现这项倡议的使命，必须正确处理的关键成功因素有哪些？
2. 对如此规模庞大的服务转换，有许多风险因素需要考虑。其中大部分风险会在这些领域的转换中出现，包括服务中心、桌面支持以及应用程序打包和发布。你认为服务外包中的主要风险是什么？应该如何缓解这些风险？
3. 财务团队是否考虑了外包给第三方的过程中的所有成本，或者你能否指出任何遗漏的成本？
4. 联合利华如何确保外包早期取得的成本节约在未来可以继续获得？

5. 联合利华在审视将其全球组织的某一区域的服务转换到第三方供应商时,是否可能考虑过其他外包方法,你能否指出这些方法?

---

**图表 3**
**IT 术语表**

**应用程序** IT 应用程序为软件的术语,在业务中可利用这类软件帮助公司解决问题。当"企业"与"应用程序"两个词结合起来,通常是指用于大型、复杂的组织的软件平台。

**桌面支持** 为用户提供技术帮助的部门。

**终端客户服务(EUS)** 在 IT 部门中,"终端用户"是指实际使用计算机设备的员工。

**企业集成网络(IEN)** 集成网络是在同一个框架中进行通讯和分布式计算机的管理。

**基础设施服务** IT 基础设施由整个组织中常见的设备、系统、软件和服务构成。

**信息技术基础构架(ITIL)** ITIL 是广泛采用的 IT 服务管理方法。它为公司提供了实用的框架来识别、规划、传送和支持 IT 服务。

**信息传送** 是指通讯网络内的文本、图像、语音、电报、传真、邮件、传呼和电子数据交换(EDI)的存储、交换和管理。

**网络** 是建立起一组计算机之间的相互沟通。你的网络可以是一个小型系统,通过电缆可以进行物理连接(一个局域网—LAN);你也可以建立一个较大型的网络,同时连接不同的网络(称为广域网—WANs)

**SAP** SAP 是一个国际公司,它提供管理业务流程的软件、解决方案和服务。

---

# 参考文献

Beasley, M., Bradford, M., Pagach, D. (2004) Outsourcing? At Your Own Risk, *Strategic Finance*, 86, 1, 22–29.

Bonnie, K. K., Kevin, W. K., & Marcia, W. W. (2012) Determinants of the persistence of internal control weaknesses. *Accounting Horizons*, 26(2), 307–333.

Glavan, L. (2012) Performance Measurement System for Process-Oriented Companies, *Journal of American Academy of Business*, 19, 2.

Harris, M. (2008) *The Business Value of IT: Managing Risks, Optimizing Performance and Measuring Results*, Auerbach Publications, New York, 21.

Krell, E. (2006) What's Wrong with IT Outsourcing and How to Fix It, *Business Strategy Magazine*, 8, 18–24.

Osheroff, M. (2005) Outsourcing Successfully, *Strategic Finance*, 87, 6, 23.

Plugge, A. & Janssen, M. (2009) Managing Change in IT Outsourcing Agreements, *Strategic Outsourcing*, 257–274.

Shuja, A. (2010) ITIL Service Management: Implementation and Operation. Retrieved from https://www.isaca.org.

# Unilever: The Financial Implications of Outsourcing Information Technology Services in a Global Organization

*Barbara E. Tarasovich,*
*Sacred Heart University*

## INTRODUCTION

Unilever products are found on the shelves of almost every large grocery store, drug store, and super store around the world. Although the company's name isn't familiar to everyone, Unilever's brands are household names that include *Vaseline Intensive Care*, *Dove*, *Hellmann's*, *Ben & Jerry's*, *Axe*, *Knorr*, and *Lipton*. The company's mission is to add vitality to life. To add vitality to its own business, however, Unilever not only needed to focus on increasing market share, but also on reducing operating costs levels. The Information Technology (IT) department played a key role in supporting this mission by developing an unerring focus on the bottom line while also enabling employees to do their jobs more effectively.

In the highly-competitive consumer products industry, the company focused their attention on core competencies to provide a sustainable competitive advantage. While IT infrastructure services are critical for connecting end users, they aren't a source of competitive advantage. The company faced the challenge of outdated client technology, non-standard services inhibiting flexibility, scalability, and an ever-increasing amount of overhead. Unilever wanted to completely refresh its IT infrastructure while reducing deployment and maintenance costs. The CFO and CIO chose a business partner that wouldn't only provide the hardware, but also the implementation services, ongoing desk-side services, and Service Center support. This case will focus on the actual business process outsourcing decision made by Unilever in 2006. A diagram of Unilever's IT department is presented in Table 1.

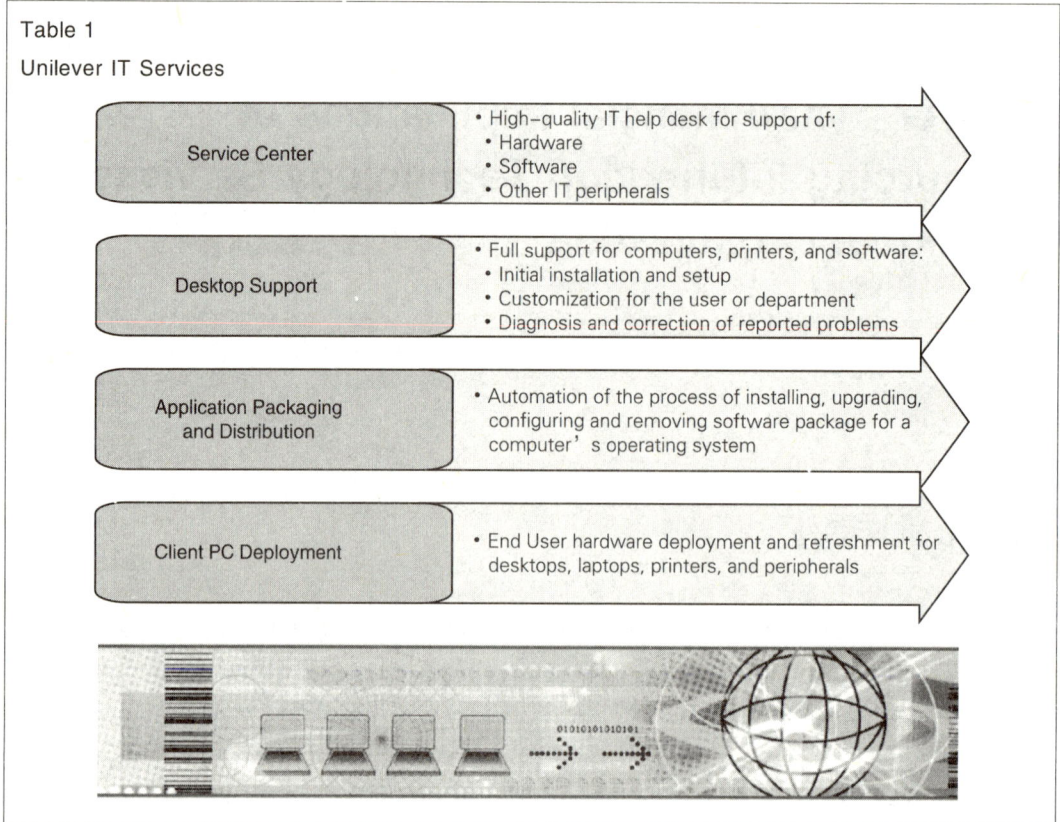

Table 1
Unilever IT Services

Outsourcing of IT services is a business trend that has dramatically increased in the past 10 years and is expected to continue (Plugge and Jannsen, 2009). Technology is constantly changing and the outsourcing of IT services can provide the latest technology without the organization making large capital investments in new equipment or acquiring the skills (human capital, knowledge base, and so on) needed to manage IT services. Management accounting professionals need to partner with the IT department to carefully develop a business case that identifies cost-cutting options and the impact of an outsourcing agreement on selling, and general and administrative expenses, while also considering availability and security of services. It's also critical to have a good idea as to how costs are recorded in the financial records for different outsourcing arrangements. Some of the project costs require capitalization, while others are recorded as immediate expense and impact the income statement of the company, reducing its net profit. The business case must achieve lower total cost of ownership, while delivering critical services 24 hours a day, seven days a week. It must also help Unilever achieve significant cost savings while generating cash. A primary objective of outsourcing is to achieve high-quality IT service delivery while enabling core IT personnel to interact and innovate with the rest of the company, thereby increasing the company's cash flow and earnings.

## COMPANY DESCRIPTION/BACKGROUND

Unilever is a global manufacturer of consumer products. A company profile is included as Exhibit 1. Unilever's purpose is to "meet the everyday needs of people everywhere—to anticipate the aspirations of our consumers and customers and to respond creatively and competitively with branded products and services which raise the quality of life." The company has deep roots in local cultures and markets around the world giving it a wealth of knowledge and international expertise about local consumers. Unilever has two parent companies: Unilever PLC, based in the United Kingdom, and Unilever N.V., based in the Netherlands. The two companies, which operate virtually as a single corporation, are run by a single Board of Directors and are linked by a number of agreements. These agreements enable Unilever to achieve unity of management, operations, shareholders' rights, purpose, and mission. The objective of these agreements is to allow the shareholders of both companies the same position as if they held stock in a single company.

---

Exhibit 1
Unilever Company Profile

**UNILEVER STRUCTURE:**
Unilever is the operating arm of Netherlands-based Unilever N.V. and UK-based Unilever PLC.

**KEY EXCECUTIVES:**
Chairman: Michael Treschow; CEO and Director: Paul Polman

**BACKGROUND:**
A top maker of packaged consumer goods worldwide, Unilever products are sold in more than 180 countries throughout Africa, Asia, Latin America, the Middle East, North America, and Western Europe. The company's offerings span 11 categories, including skin care and deodorant. Best-selling brands include *Hellmann's* (mayonnaise), *Knorr* (soups), *Lipton* (tea), *Dove* and *Lux* (soaps), and *Sunsilk* (hair care).

**TOP COMPETITORS:**
- The Procter & Gamble Company
- Nestlé
- Reckitt Benckiser Group

**Selected Financial Data (USD $ in millions, translated from EUR €)**
Revenues: $58.7 billion
Net Profit: $5.6 billion
Net Profit Margin: 9.59%
Number of Employees: 165 000

---

Unilever's top 12 brands generate sales of $1 billion and the top 20 brands account for 70% of sales. Underlying volume growth in 2006 was 3.8%. Unilever operates in 11 product areas (i.e., skin care, deodorant, ice cream, tea, spreads, savoury, dressings, hair care, laundry, oral care, and household cleaning) and is a global leader in seven of them. Brands like *Dove*, *Lux*, *Pond's* and *Rexona* have made Unilever a global leader in the deodorant and skin care markets. *Lipton*, *Brooke Bond*, *Ben & Jerry's* and *Heartbrand* are among the brands that have made Unilever a global leader in the ice cream and beverage markets. The company employs more than 167,000 people and more than 50% of their business is in emerging markets. These emerging markets are the future for many companies, particularly for Unilever, which sells everyday household products such as bleach and *Sunlight* soap. Emerging markets are defined as countries where social or business activity is in the process of rapid growth and industrialization. Countries such as China and India are considered to be the largest.

## COMPANY/IT STRATEGIC GOALS

The goal of the transformation of IT is to build leading-edge technology services capable of playing a pivotal role in the company's overall "Path to Growth" strategy. This strategy includes very specific targets for sales, margins, and earnings growth over a five-year period. The case illustrates how an outsourcing program, integrated with an organization's overall strategic plan, can be a competitive advantage. To contribute to the "Path to Growth" strategy, the IT leadership team determined that information and technologies would need to be managed as a critical enabler. The people, hardware, software, and processes that make up the IT organization were considered a primary driver for developing sustainable business practices. The commonly used term "business and IT alignment" is extremely important to the provision of efficient solutions, but also to the provision of lower cost alternatives—as consumer goods organizations are faced with lower product margins and increased competition. In short, the following are the strategic goals that need to be addressed by the IT organization:

- Flawless business and IT operations
- True understanding of user needs
- Integrated management processes
- Identify key success factors and metrics that resonate with the user community

The mission statement for the IT organization is "to be a high-performance, customer-focused IT service organization – providing dependable, quality services that fully meet the needs of the business."

## TRANSFORMATION OF GLOBAL INFORMATION TECHNOLOGY

In 2006, Unilever's global IT organization began to shift its management focus from operations to services. The IT organization was focused on the simplification of technology processes along with providing the business agility and flexibility to quickly adjust to new business opportunities.

Companies have been debating the role and value of IT (Harris, 2008) and whether IT should be treated as a commodity like electricity or gas. By keeping IT as a commodity, costs and vulnerabilities are minimized and risk-taking is avoided. In addition, any competitive advantage gained through IT is short-lived because of the speed of technological advances. This form of debate is only possible when a function has reached a certain level of maturity (Glavan, 2012). Relevant topics in the CIO agenda have shifted from, "which technology is next?" to "which service delivery model at what cost?" For Unilever, standards like IT Infrastructure Library (ITIL), CobIT (a framework created by ISACA for IT management (Shuja, 2010)), and IT Governance (Shuja, 2010), among others, provide actionable roadmaps and a reference model that facilitate the functional and process alignment required to establish a high-quality IT Services Utility, releasing the core of IT to engage with the business through innovation and to make other contributions for growth. Challenges facing the IT organization include current hardware configurations, operating systems, and Office Suite software versions that lack updates or are obsolete. Threats included:

- Capacity and Scalability issues are critical because business needs and requirements are constantly changing. The IT organization must be able to adapt quickly, either with an increase or decrease in services provided, to minimize overhead costs.
- A paucity of the management tools necessary for meeting the increasing demand to deliver world class Client Services.
- Difficulty complying with new IT service management processes and regulations such as ITIL, which is a critical component of providing world class IT services. It's defined as a series of best practice books that provide recommendations on ways to optimize their delivery or management of those services.
- Difficulty complying with Sarbanes-Oxley (SOX) regulations, Section 404. IT supports the corporation's drive to comply with SOX by securing and protecting financial data in the company's systems and IT network. Without IT support, a corporation simply can't comply with the testing and validation of the internal control structure required by SOX (Section 404). If the internal control structure of the company is inadequate, the company will be subject to retribution from the Securities & Exchange Commission, for noncompliance with SOX regulations (Bonnie, Kevin, and Marcia, 2012.)

Unilever's strategy is to manage technology deployment to support business goals. The IT organization provides advice, assistance, and leadership to the business to maximize benefits from the products and services available. The finance team works together with the IT organization and acts as one face to the rest of the company. (Exhibit 2 includes an organizational chart of the global IT organization.) The finance organization works with IT to establish vendor partnering sources and manage external suppliers. In addition, an important role of the finance team is to negotiate contracts to continuously improve everything from risk management to network infrastructures. The finance team also designs information management structures, sets policies for sourcing, and performs financial analyses of the services provided by third-party suppliers.

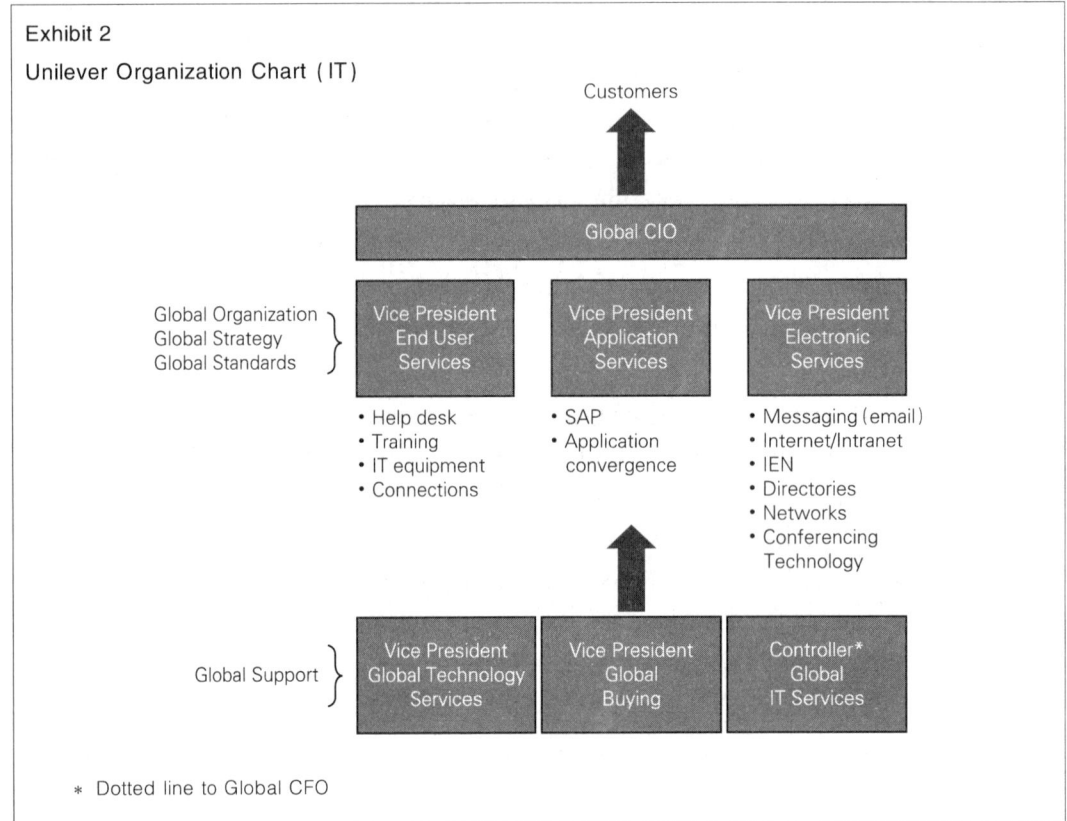

## OUTSOURCING DECISION

Unilever supported the business case for outsourcing IT services by ensuring that they would get all computers and IT services needed, while freeing the department to focus on growing the business instead of managing infrastructure services. They made the case that relieving the IT department of the administrative burden of managing and deploying personal computers (PCs) would enhance productivity and enable the team to provide better services to users. In addition, by outsourcing IT services, Unilever was able to scale IT support to adapt the changing market conditions.

Unilever's finance team played a key role in developing the business case for proceeding with the investments and associated costs required to carry out the outsourcing of Unilever's IT Client Services in 2006. The Finance Leadership Team was tasked with finding a way to address and solve, as well as establish a long-term plan for IT Client Services, given the complex nature of the area, including:

- Complex, detailed, and multi-layered technologies, processes, and services
- Regional spreading of Unilever business
- End user help desk, also known as Client Services (See Exhibit two)
- Total cost of ownership and management of client infrastructure
- The need to keep up with emerging technology
- Workstation and server management—asset control and administration
- Install, move, add, and change assets and all personal computing equipment (e.g., PCs, software, or printers.)
- Keep up a career plan to attract, develop, and retain highly skilled finance and IT professionals

It was critical to identify the project success factors to keep the team focused on the implementation deliverables. All of the critical success factors were monitored throughout the transformation.

# GOALS OF OUTSOURCING

Unilever's main goals of outsourcing IT client services were to:

- Provide end-to-end desktop lifecycle support for the organization and the end user
- Address total-cost-of-ownership concerns with a predictable long-term cost structure
- Improve end-user productivity, quality of service, and critical skill access
- Better align end-user capabilities with business requirements
- Complete lifecycle management—manages a lifecycle of service from planning and procurement through support and disposal
- Global managed infrastructure enabling rapid, global implementation and efficient operations; provides the foundation for continuous improvements
- Multi-vendor support—seamlessly supports a heterogeneous, multi-vendor desktop and mobile environment
- Transition and transformation methodology—enable a smooth transition to new technologies and applications without service disruption
- Single point of contact and accountability

## RISKS

With transformation of services of this magnitude, there are a number of risks to consider. The majority of these risks arise during the transformation in the Service Center, Desktop Support, and Application Packaging and Distribution areas. A risk assessment is necessary with a developed, detailed plan, which includes appropriate milestones and go/no-go decision points. One of the major risks in deployment of PC equipment is disruption of end-user productivity. In addition, ensuring that no data is lost in the transformation is critical. Delivering the correct equipment in a timely manner in a secure environment is also necessary to mitigate the risk of losing critical information. Service interruption and obstacles during the services transition may also impact on-going business operations. From a financial perspective, a major risk is not delivering the identified savings. To address these risks, Unilever worked with the third-party service provider to ensure the agreement identified the appropriate tools and resources to be used to ensure that they performed the deployment and management of services according to the agreed plan.

## SUMMARY OF OUTSOURCED FUNCTIONS IN NORTH AMERICA

In 2006, Unilever North America (NA) had 17 000 end users in 100 distinct locations. The company invited six potential suppliers to participate in a Request for Proposal (RFP) to not only upgrade the existing desktops and notebook computers at all these locations, but also manage the on-going support services. The NA team concluded that three suppliers met the requirements to submit proposals and, subsequently, two suppliers partnered to submit one proposal.

The objectives of the RFP in selecting this Client Services supplier were:
- Lead the PC deployment phase of the One Unilever PC Programme, offering standard hardware, processes, tools, and a standard desktop configuration
- Provide support services upon the completion of the new PC deployment
- Deliver technological improvements and service flexibility that will allow IT to contribute further to business opportunities
- Offer year-over-year declining costs
- Refresh Unilever's PC environment as dictated by ITIL, which defines computing best practices

The services included in the Client Services Proposal are (See Table 1):
- Service Center—The facility where the computing equipment resides
- Desktop Support—The organization that provides assistance to users

of technology
- Application Packaging and Distribution
- New PC Equipment Deployment

These services were to be offered to all business groups in NA and eventually to Unilever's global IT organization. The existing hands-on, local support services model was changed into a centralized support model. All computing calls would go into a centralized Service Center, and Desktop Support resources will be placed in large locations (i.e. Greenwich, Toronto, Englewood Cliffs, and Chicago). These resources would also provide remote support for all other sites in NA. Any support that can't be provided by the central team will be handled by a dispatch service.

The service provider is required to measure all services against formal service level agreements. So, in changing from the existing End User Services (EUS) support model of "one service level fits all," the vendor solution will offer Service Baseline Assumptions. This vendor solution is known within Unilever as "Choice of Service, Choice of Cost." The finance team developed different cost models with the third-party service providers to offer a menu of services to the Unilever business groups. For example, the business group could select the highest level of service (i.e. Platinum—seven by 24 Service Center and Desktop Support), but the cost would be higher, reflecting the premium support level provided by the supplier.

# COST OF OWNERSHIP AND PROGRAM SAVINGS FORECAST

Table 2 outlines the total investments cost related to outsourcing the IT services operation and one-time project costs to transition to new equipment and services provided by the third-party vendor. Unilever was required to incur the software licensing costs for all existing programs. The table also includes all one-time capital and project expense to implement new PCs in all NA locations. The EUS costs in Table 2 reflect the dual running costs while the transition to the third party is in process. This includes, primarily, employee related costs of the existing departments supporting EUS. The contract termination fees reflect the termination fee of an existing contract with a third-party provider, previously supporting part of the internal function within Unilever.

Table 2

Outsourcing Investment

( All financial information in the case was provided by Unilever from the actual Request for Project approval ( RFP ) document-Submitted to the Unilever NA Board of Directors during October 2005. )

One-time capital costs ( $11.4 million) for new equipment and one-time project expense ( $15.3 million) are detailed below:

|  | Odyssey-New PC Equipment Costs |  |  |  | EUS Transformation (related to transfer of services to 3rd party provider) | Total |
|---|---|---|---|---|---|---|
|  | 2004 | 2005 | 2006 | 2007/2008 | 2005 – 2008 |  |
| Capital | $2.2 | $8.6 | $0.6 | — |  | $11.4 |
| Software/Licenses |  | 5.1 | 0.6 |  |  |  |
| Servers (W2K/Messaging) | 1.3 | 1.3 |  |  |  |  |
| LAN/WAN Upgrade |  | 2.2 |  |  |  |  |
| Client (PC) Back Up | 0.9 |  |  |  |  |  |
| One Time Project Expense | $0.5 | $5.5 | $3.7 | $.8 | $4.8 | $15.3 |
| Dual Running/Employee Backfill Costs |  | 1.0 | 1.0 |  | 2.5 |  |
| Employee Severance |  | 1.1 | 1.1 |  |  |  |
| Existing Supplier Contract Termination |  |  |  |  | 2.1 |  |
| Supplier Transition Fee |  | 0.2 | 0.3 | 0.8 |  |  |
| Project Management Costs, Travel, Training |  | 0.9 | 0.3 |  |  |  |
| Application Packaging |  | 1.0 |  |  |  |  |
| Messaging Implementation |  | 0.3 | 0.3 |  |  |  |
| Software License Fees | 0.5 |  |  |  |  |  |
| Other, e.g. Maintenance |  | 1.0 | 0.7 |  | 0.2 |  |

Table 3 outlines the project savings as a result of the outsourcing agreement. The savings model compares the "per seat" or "per PC" pricing of the third-party supplier to the existing service model cost of Unilever's EUS. The annual savings was projected to be $12.6 million as compared to Unilever's current operating costs.

## Table 3
### Project Savings

**Savings**

As a result of the Client Services outsourcing agreement, total End User Services (EUS) costs will be reduced by $3 million in 2006. Expected savings over the three-year life of the contract is $12.6 million and is primarily a result of the supplier's lower operational cost per seat, including a complete replacement of the existing services solution and a 50% EUS full time equivalent head count reduction.

Following is a table outlining the key components of the program savings:

| $ Millions | | 2006 | 2007 | 2008 | 2009 | Total |
|---|---|---|---|---|---|---|
| Current Service Model: | Employee related costs | 6.0 | 6.2 | 6.3 | 6.5 | 25.0 |
| | Telecommunications and related costs | 4.0 | 4.1 | 4.2 | 4.3 | 16.6 |
| | Lab to script applications to run in | | | | | |
| Unilever's environment | 1.0 | 1.0 | 1.1 | 1.1 | 4.2 | |
| | Total Costs | 11.0 | 11.3 | 11.6 | 11.9 | 45.8 |
| Service Provider Costs Per Seat: * | | 8.0 | 8.2 | 8.4 | 8.6 | 33.2 |
| Savings: | | 3.0 | 3.1 | 3.2 | 3.3 | 12.6 |

\* The pricing is based on an agreed upon seat price per quarter. The agreement allows for some flexibility in number of seats with no change in pricing structure. The seat count will be reviewed on a quarterly basis.

# MEASURING SUCCESS OF THE OUTSOURCING AGREEMENT

The implementation of the outsourced services agreement critically enabled Unilever's overall IT strategic vision. It introduced simplified technology and processes, and provided flexibility to quickly adjust to new business opportunities, reorganizations, and restructurings. Success of the deployment was measured by key milestones. The controller worked with the VP of IT services to ensure the project was managed according to plan and delivered targeted savings. In addition, service-level agreements were monitored and reviewed by end users and IT staff to ensure the level of service provided was in accordance with the plan.

# CASE REQUIREMENTS

1. What were the critical success factors, those things that must go right, for this initiative to achieve its mission?

2. With transformation of services of this magnitude, there are a number of risks to consider. The majority of these risks will arise during the transformation in the areas of Service Center, Desktop Support, and Application Packaging and Distribution. What do you think are the main risks in outsourcing this service?

How can these risks be mitigated?

3. Did the finance team consider all costs when outsourcing to a third party or can you identify any costs that may have been missed?

4. What can Unilever do to ensure the savings realized in the early years of outsourcing will continue in the future?

5. Can you identify any other approaches to outsourcing that Unilever may have considered when examining the transfer of services in one region of a global organization to a third-party supplier?

---

**Exhibit 3**
**Glossary of IT Terms**

**Applications** An IT application is the term used for software that a business would use to assist the organization in solving problems. When the word "enterprise" is combined with "application," it usually refers to a software platform that is used for large, complex organizations.

**Desktop Support** The organization that provides assistance to users of technology.

**End User Services (EUS)** In an IT organization, "end users" are those employees actually using computer equipment.

**Integrated Enterprise Network (IEN)** An integrated network is the management of telecommunications and distributed computing systems within the same framework.

**Infrastructure Services** IT infrastructure consists of the equipment, systems, software, and services used in common across an organization.

**ITIL** ITIL is a widely adopted approach for IT service management. It provides a practical framework for identifying, planning, delivering, and supporting IT services to the business.

**Messaging** is the storage, exchange, and management of text, images, voice, telex, fax, e-mail, paging, and Electronic Data Interchange (EDI) over a communications network.

**Network** a group of computers set up to communicate with one another. Your network can be a small system that's physically connected by cables (a LAN), or you can connect separate networks together to form larger networks (called WANs).

**SAP** SAP is a global company that provides software, solutions, and services to manage business processes.

---

# REFERENCES

Beasley, M., Bradford, M., Pagach, D. (2004) Outsourcing? At Your Own Risk, *Strategic Finance*, 86, 1, 22–29.

Bonnie, K. K., Kevin, W. K., & Marcia, W. W. (2012) Determinants of the persistence of internal control weaknesses. *Accounting Horizons*, 26 (2), 307–333.

Glavan, L. (2012) Performance Measurement System for Process-Oriented

Companies, *Journal of American Academy of Business*, 19, 2.

Harris, M. (2008) *The Business Value of IT: Managing Risks, Optimizing Performance and Measuring Results*, Auerbach Publications, New York, 21.

Krell, E. (2006) What's Wrong with IT Outsourcing and How to Fix It, *Business Strategy Magazine*, 8, 18 – 24.

Osheroff, M. (2005) Outsourcing Successfully, *Strategic Finance*, 87, 6, 23.

Plugge, A. & Janssen, M. (2009) Managing Change in IT Outsourcing Agreements, *Strategic Outsourcing*, 257 – 274.

Shuja, A. (2010) ITIL Service Management: Implementation and Operation. Retrieved from https://www.isaca.org.

# 公司治理与职业道德
## Corporate Governance & Ethics

# 詹森制药：一出公司治理的角色扮演[①]

J. Kay Keels
Coastal Carolina University

Norman T. Sheehan
University of Saskatchewan

## 简介

2012年1月，詹森（Jensen）制药董事会召开了一次特别会议。为了增强做决策时的响应性和凝聚力，詹森制药设置的董事会规模相对较小，这意味着每一位董事会成员必须在数个委员会中任职。作为报酬，詹森制药的董事们可以获得公司的股票期权，不过只能在特定的期间行权和售出。根据各董事任职的委员会的个数和这些委员会会面的次数，各董事每年有望获得20 000到100 000股的股票期权。

詹森制药是一家比较小的非上市公司。迄今为止，詹森制药成功实现了它的使命——通过使用有效的药物治疗，帮助病人延长寿命、免除痛苦。Dekanor保持着3亿美元的销量，是詹森制药销量最大的药。它是詹森制药的一种"重磅产品"，占到了詹森制药年收入的1/3。Dekanor是一种抑制α神经的镇痛剂（如，止痛药）。Dekanor在三年多前投入临床使用，很快就成为医生们喜爱的药方，用于治疗患有严重慢性偏头疼的病人。詹森制药目前的研究部门经理，H. 菲利普斯（H. Phillips）带领他的团队将Dekanor推向市场，Dekanor被看做是菲利普斯和其他团队成员（如公司信息总监）的"事业成就"。詹森制药的信息总监曾帮助此药在空前短的时间内通过了食品及药物管理局（FDA）的临床试验。

有谣言称FDA正在考虑禁止Dekanor，董事会召开此次特别会议正是要讨论这一谣言。董事会会议文件在会议召开前一天已发送给董事会成员，其中包括很多的财务、法律和医药专业术语，有一些董事会成员可能对此不熟悉。文件总结如下：

- Dekanor的开发，总共经历了六年的时间，比大多数其他药物少两到

---

\* 本篇译者为陈秀云，校订者为胡金凤、赵澄。

[①] 这一则案例是虚构的，公司的名称和药品都不存在，所以都维持原文，没有翻译。这种角色扮演的方法，常被大的服务公司（如"联合包裹服务公司，UPS"）采用来培训员工，使员工熟悉有关方面会对某种情况如何反应，以提高自己的服务水平。——译者

三年，这得益于詹森应对 FDA 审批流程的技巧。Dekanor 的疗效在 1 100 位病人身上进行了检验，这是 FDA 可接受的最低人数，检验成本共计 6.75 亿美元。该药通过了 FDA 的临床试验，没有任何问题，所以目前销售的 Dekanor 的药物说明书和其他镇痛剂相同（即，药物说明书上概述了服用 Dekanor 的可能副作用，但未提到存在死亡风险）。

- 很多病人报告对 Dekanor 有很高的满意度，因为在对抗慢性偏头痛方面，它比竞争对手的药物更有效。
- 然而，自从被推行，Dekanor 就和大量不良心血管事件（特别是心脏病）相关，一些事件甚至致人死亡。
- 一项独立研究发现的证据表明，这些死亡案例中有一些可能是 Dekanor 导致的；但由于所研究的病人数量不够大，无法得出结论。一位来自常春藤名牌大学的杰出科学家领导的这项研究，他呼吁增加对 Dekanor 的研究，来证明 Dekanor "很可能是一枚定时炸弹"。
- 自从发布了这项独立研究，一些医生公开拒绝给他们的病人开 Dekanor。因为詹森制药没有相关的替代药品，这些医生开始给病人开竞争者的药物，尽管这种药有效性较低。
- 关于 Dekanor 的这些争议，一些网站上出现了回应，表示支持 Dekanor。许多这样的网站聚集了 Dekanor 的使用者，他们请求詹森和大型医学团体把 Dekanor 留在市场上。分发给董事会成员的文件中引用了一些网站上的信息，如 "Dekanor 让我重获我的生活。我现在能和我的孩子们玩耍并在社区做志愿者。感谢 Dekanor！！！" 以及 "请让我一直使用 Dekanor。我需要它来对抗我的头痛。" 另外，也有这样的评论："Dekanor 从我身边夺走了我的妈妈。Dekanor 是一个杀手！！！"
- 据估计，要证明 Dekanor 是安全的药物，至少得花费三年、耗资 1 200 万美元开展一项大规模的独立性临床试验。
- 其他制药公司被发现故意销售危害病人健康的药物后，均遭到了诉讼和罚款，罚款金额依据死亡人数和公司的过失（即该公司对于死亡应付多大程度的责任）从 5 000 万美元到 50 亿美元不等。
- Dekanor 的盈利目前约占詹森年度利润 2.5 亿美元的一半，如果 Dekanor 被禁，在詹森制药正在开发的产品中还没有其他药物有可能取代 Dekanor 的盈利能力。
- 据估计，如果在说明书中明确说明心脏病发作的风险，可能导致销售下降 50%。另一方面，余下的 50% 的现有患者对 Dekanor 非常满意，不太可能转而使用竞争对手的药物。
- 一家竞争对手制药公司刚刚宣布计划下月推行一种药，也用于治疗偏头痛症状，未证明有致命的副作用。
- 因为詹森目前是一家非上市公司，它的股票在场外交易市场[②]公开交

---

[②] 场外交易市场，又称柜台交易或店头交易市场，指在交易所外由证券买卖双方当面议价成交的市场。它没有固定的场所，其交易主要利用电话进行，交易的证券以不在交易所上市的证券为主。——译者

易。当那份独立研究的结果公布时，詹森的股票价格下降了 22%。詹森目前在场外交易市场的股票价格是每股 17 美元，这是从一年前处于高位的 30 美元降下来的。詹森制药外发的股票有 5 300 万股。

- 詹森的董事会意识到如果要成功开发新药并使其进入市场，詹森需要投入更多在研究上。为此，董事会已经就是否应该让詹森在纽约证券交易所（NYSE）上市展开讨论，这样通过 IPO 获得的收益可形成急需的研发资金。

为了给董事会提供更多的信息来决定 Dekanor 的命运，詹森的高管团队也被邀参加会议。董事会主席（同时也是公司 CEO）计划召开会议为 Dekanor 提出三项备选方案。董事会在会议结束前必须在三项备选方案中选出一项：

1. 立即停止销售 Dekanor，召回所有存货，直到有一项独立的临床试验可以成功地证明 Dekanor 没有致使病人提早死亡。

2. 增加一条警告标签，明确提示服用 Dekanor 可能导致不良心血管事件，从而可能会致人死亡，停止所有直接面向消费者的 Dekanor 广告和面向医生的 Dekanor 促销，但仍向需要该药的医生进行销售。

3. 继续积极努力的营销 Dekanor，采取任何必要的法律、政治和其他行动来避免 FDA 禁止 Dekanor。

---

**詹森的董事会成员和高管成员参加有关 Dekanor 特别董事会议**

1. C. 詹森（C. Jensen），医学博士，CEO 和董事会主席（所有董事委员会的当然成员）：C. 詹森担心降低 Dekanor 的销量将对詹森制药未来的股价产生影响（C. 詹森拥有单个最大宗的詹森股票，以目前的场外交易市场股价计算的价值为 9 000 万美元）以及詹森制药通过首次公开募股（IPO）筹集资金的能力。然而，作为公司创始人唯一的孩子，C. 詹森也非常关心他的形象和詹森制药的形象。

2. M. 詹森（M. Jensen），C. 詹森的后代，董事会成员（审计、风险和胜任能力委员会*成员，任命委员会成员）：M. 詹森经营一家咨询事务所，MJ 联合事务所，事务所开展的多数业务都与詹森制药公司有关。M. 詹森还有将近 4% 的詹森股票，是其父亲 C. 詹森所给。M. 詹森一直在推动董事会迅速进行 IPO 来为新药开发筹集资金。M. 詹森认为，目前公司的管理团队对股东的意见响应不力，对此他感到担心。他的言论最近被华尔街日报引用，他说，"需要提醒詹森制药的管理团队，是詹森制药的股票拥有者雇佣了他们，而非利益相关者。"

3. L. Vayan，董事会成员（管理委员会主席，薪酬委员会成员）：在制药行业有着 28 年的经验，Vayan 知道所有的药物都带有一定的风险。Vayan 是一家药物供应公司——RAV 制药的 CEO，这家公司是詹森制药最大的供应商之一。Vayan 拥有 30 万股股票期权。

4. D. 查尔斯（D. Charles），已退休，董事会成员（ARCo 委员会主席，任命委员会主席，管理委员会成员）：作为一名退休的保险经理，查尔斯非常关心 Dekanor 问题的隐含责任。在上一次的董事会会议中，查尔斯要求詹森制药增加董事和高管（D&O）的责任保险，将投保额增加到每位经理 1 000 万美元，但是这一要求尚未批准。查尔斯拥有相当多的詹森股票和股票期权。

5. B. 加里森（B. Garrison），医学博士，董事会成员（薪酬委员会主席，任命委员会成员，ARCo 委员会成员）：作为一名执业医生，加里森几年来一直给病人处方开 Dekanor，没有发生过任何问题。事实上，加里森和那些开 Dekanor 超过三年的医生交流后发现，Dekanor 是有价值的。加里森拥有 50 000 股詹森股票和 300 000 股股票期权。

6. Y. 波伊克（Y. Boiki），董事会成员（ARCo*委员会、薪酬委员会以及管理委员会的成员）：这是波伊克在詹森医药参加的首次董事会会议。詹森制药的 CEO 和董事会主席 C. 詹森以及子女现在所住的房子是波伊克的公司在去年建造的。波伊克在与市政机构打交道时所展现的生意头脑和能力令 C. 詹森印象深刻，于是他最近把波伊克聘请进詹森制药董事会。

7. H. 菲利普斯，医学博士，研究部门经理：菲利普斯帮助 Dekanor 在空前短的时间内推向市场，并节省了预算。就为了这个原因，菲利普斯在三年前就被任命为研究部门经理。菲利普斯意识到那些死亡事例与 Dekanor 有关，但还是常说，"与酒精、烟草相比，Dekanor 是一种非常安全的药；服用 Dekanor 甚至比驾驶时发短信安全！"菲利普斯有相当多的股票期权。

8. J. 万斯（J. Vance），法学博士，公司法律顾问：万斯是一位知名的诉讼、代理律师，精通于游说 FDA 以及与之争辩。万斯有相当多的股票和股票期权用作他/她的退休基金。

9. E. 罗林斯（E. Rollins），医学博士，哲学博士，研究部门助理经理：罗林斯是拥有如此高职位的最年轻的研究科学家。罗林斯既是制药行业最聪明的新星之一，又是 FDA 前任主席约翰·李（John Lee）的一名助理，这让她获得杰出的声望。李博士最强烈的信念中有一项就是，医药学专业和制药行业应该永远不做危害人们生命的事情。由于罗林斯新近加入詹森制药，尚未持有任何股票或股票期权。

10. D. 斯通（D. Stone），公共关系经理：斯通负责塑造公司的公共形象，邀请他来参加会议是为了确定詹森公司能够为董事会所做的任何选择"编造"积极的理由。斯通持有 200 000 股股票期权。

11. R. 约翰逊（R. Johnson），注册管理会计师，副总裁，财务总监（CFO）：约翰逊主要关心公司的财务业绩。约翰逊时常提醒董事会，Dekanor 销售量的任何显著下滑将会明显危害詹森制药的未来盈利能力。约翰逊也将会提醒董事会，詹森制药的其他两种最畅销药品的专利权两年后即将终止。约翰逊持有相当多的股票和股票期权。

12. L. 古德森（L. Goodson），人力资源副总裁：古德森被广泛认为是一位人道主义者，这意味着，他与人来往时，古德森的同情、正直、公正的价值标准起到核心作用。大家都知道古德森对公司的一个争论感到不安，即詹森制药必须将股东的需求置于利益相关者的关心之上。

13. N. 格林（N. Greene），市场营销副总裁：自 Dekanor 三年前引进市场以来，格林领导了一场非常成功的市场营销活动。格林很有信心只要公司继续强势营销 Dekanor，詹森制药的营销团队能继续产生稳健的收入额。

14. T. 加西亚（T. Garcia），信息总监（CIO）：加西亚是一位杰出的信息总监，非常谨慎地保存着有关詹森制药的药物测试试验的每一个文件，其中一些文件是没有发送给 FDA 或者向公众公开的。加西亚持有许多股票和股票期权。

\* ARCo（Audit, Risk, and Compliance）Committee，即审计、风险和合规委员会，缩写为 ARCo 委员会。——译者

# 学习指南：

1. 在上课之前阅读案例背景信息和指定读物。

2. 当讨论到角色扮演时，教师将在上课之前或在课上为案例中的 14 个角色找好表演的学生和替补扮演者。

3. 作为一名指定角色的扮演者，你应该和你的替补扮演者谈谈，理解你的指定角色，思考该角色在董事会对 Dekanor 讨论中应该关注什么，并做好笔记。在董事会会议前不要和其他角色扮演者分享和你角色相关的任何私人信息。

4. 根据你对指定角色的想法去进行表演，并准备在董事会会议中陈述你倾向选择的备选方案，解释你为什么支持这种备选方案。在董事会讨论时，你可以咨询你的替补扮演者（他/她应该坐在你旁边），但请注意在和替补扮演者交流时不要打断或干扰其他的董事会成员。

5. 董事会会议将定好时间，在休会之前董事会必须达成决议。

# 14 位角色扮演者各自的角色

教师请注意：学生们应该只获得他们各自角色的资料。每位角色扮演者都不应该获得其他角色的任何信息或说明。

### 角色：C. 詹森，医学博士
詹森制药的 CEO 和董事会主席

作为詹森制药的董事会主席兼 CEO，你将负责引导讨论并确保每位成员都可表达其想法。你必须带领董事会在既定的时间内达成决议，因为一些董事会成员已经预订好航班，在休会后就得离开。

你对各种会议的总体观点是：尽量对一个问题的不同方面加以讨论，然后达成决议。从法律上讲，达成决议需要大多数投票通过。你倾向于达成共识的决策，但是在任何情况下，在一场会议结束时必须进行正式投票。作为董事会主席，你不参加投票，除非结果为平票时，你的投票将打破平局。董事会的决策，无论是达成共识还是大多数投票通过，都必须形成正式的会议记录，以供股票持有者今后查阅。

从个人角度，你有两个想法：（1）你担心降低 Dekanor 的销量将对詹森制药未来的股价产生影响（你拥有单个最大宗的詹森股票，以目前的场外交易市场股价计算的价值为 9 000 万美元），以及詹森制药通过首次公开募股（IPO）筹资的能力。（2）另一方面，你还有义务使这家公司——这家你引领着走过最快速发展阶段的公司——保持自己诚实、正直的形象。为履行这一承诺，詹森应通过行动使公众信服，它致力于病人的福利而不仅仅是为其股东的财富。最后，你知道这将决定后人如何评价你和你的家族（这家公司的创始者）。

作为詹森制药的董事会主席，你将：

1. 当老师提示时，宣布召开董事会特别会议；
2. 评述 Dekanor 的每项方案；
3. 请与会人员发言，包括自我介绍、解释自己认为董事会应该做出的选择（即，选项 1、2 或 3）以及支持该选择的原因；
4. 确保每人都有机会发言；
5. 到规定时间时或当老师提示时，请董事会成员投票。（注意：只有五位董事会成员有权利投票。除非投票结果为平票，否则董事会主席不参加投票。）

### 角色：M. 詹森
董事会主席 C. 詹森的子女，詹森制药董事会成员，MJ 联合事务所主任、咨询师

你经营着一家咨询事务所，MJ 联合事务所，这家事务所的多数业务来自詹森制药。你拥有将近 4% 的詹森股票，这是你的父亲 C. 詹森给你的。你重复地提醒其他董事会成员，你拥有的股票数量排名第二，按照目前的股

票价格，价值3 600万美元。你还拥有300 000股的股票期权，这是你在任职董事的期间获得的，股票期权价值几百万美元。去年，你的股票和股票期权的价值下降幅度超过3 000万美元，因此你非常关心FDA的Dekanor禁令将对詹森制药的未来股票价格和公司进行IPO的能力产生怎样的影响。你从一出生就和制药行业紧密相连，你敏锐地意识到詹森制药要想长期存续下去的话，需要投资开发新药，所以你一直催促董事会让詹森制药尽快在纽约证券交易所上市，然后进行IPO。

管理层对利益相关者需求的积极响应，让你最近变得越来越烦恼。在华尔街日报的一篇广泛引起注意的声明中，你陈述道，"需要提醒詹森制药的管理团队，是詹森制药的股票拥有者而非利益相关者雇佣了他们。"

华盛顿的一位公司说客最近给你发来一条建议。他建议通过跟健康与人力资源部（FDA隶属于该部门）现任部长合作，或许可向FDA施加政治压力。该部长可能愿意推迟FDA的禁令，直到有独立的试验能够证明Dekanor是安全的，而这一结果预计三、四年后才能得到。最好的一种结果是说服这位部长否决FDA提议的任何禁令，因为颁发禁令这一举措代表着FDA开出了先例，这会增加FDA的权力，而以药物公司和自由企业制度为代价。让部长处理这项计划可能需要公司为总统改选活动做一些重要的财务贡献。不管哪种手段都会为詹森医药赢得必要的时间来完成IPO，通过IPO筹得的资金使公司可以开发一些新型"重磅"药来取代Dekanor。

**角色：L. VAYAN**
詹森制药董事会成员，RAV制药CEO

你在制药行业有28年的经验，在一些大型国际制药公司做了12年高级经理，最近的8年你在一家医药供应公司（RAV制药）担任CEO。詹森制药是你的一个较大的客户，在RAV的销售额中占到将近10%。因为现金流问题，詹森制药已经有6个月的购货发票未支付，现在欠RAV800万美元。你已服务于詹森董事会有四年的时间，拥有300 000股的股票期权，但到目前为止，你未持有该公司股票。

你从一些行业知情人士那里获知，在北美地区，处方药比非法药品害死的人还要多。考虑到所有的药品都带有一定的风险，你赞成让病人和他们的医生来决定是否使用该药。你不确定董事会将面临怎样的法律风险，但你觉得对詹森制药来说最好的方法是保持对FDA的压力，继续积极营销Dekanor，公司应尽其所能避免该药被禁止。否则，你害怕你的詹森股票期权将不值钱了，还有詹森欠RAV的800万美元也将无法追还。

**角色：D. 查尔斯**
詹森制药董事会成员，一家保险公司已退休的CEO

12年前你第一次被选入詹森制药的董事会，当时你是一家知名保险公司的CEO。作为詹森制药ARCo（审计、风险和合规）委员会的主席，这次会议的召开使你感到恼怒，原因有二：首先，虽然你听到传言说Dekanor

是不安全的，但管理层仍然一遍又一遍地告诉你它是安全的；其次，按惯例你今天本要去参加高尔夫四人常规赛，为了参加这次会议你不得不在最后时刻取消原本的活动。

作为一名已退休的保险经理，你充分意识到 Dekanor 问题的隐含责任。在上次的董事会会议上，你请求詹森制药改变对其董事和高管的责任保险（D&O 保险）政策，将投保额增加到每位董事 1 000 万美元，但是这项请求尚未获准。另外，即便董事会投票同意为 Dekanor 产品在标签上增加一项警告，你怀疑等詹森制药的董事日后被发现有疏忽之处时，每位董事 1 000 万美元的保费是否足够偿还个人债务。

综上所述，你的专业经验告诉你应该考虑保守的做法。你想把这些问题拿到会议上讨论，董事会还从没讨论过自身的风险承受水平。董事会可以承受多大的风险，而难以承受多大的风险？你想确保詹森医药董事会做出正确的决定，因为你拥有该公司大量的股票和股票期权，你指望着从这些股票、期权的持有中获得收入来支持你退休后的生活。

### 角色：B. 加里森，医学博士
詹森制药董事会成员，执业医生

你意识到不利的宣传正围绕着 Dekanor。作为一名执业医生，你三年来一直给病人开 Dekanor，并没有发现任何问题。在上一届的美国医学协会会议上，和你交流的其他医生也报告了相似的经历。你认为应该向所有医生发出呼吁，向 FDA 将禁止 Dekanor 的威胁表示抗议，因为医生有权开出最有效的药，而禁令侵犯了医生的这一权力。事实上，和你的交流医生中，一些医生已经使用 Dekanor 三年多了，这说明 Dekanor 是有价值的。

你做了八年的董事会成员，拥有 50 000 股詹森制药的股票，并因服务于詹森董事会而获得 300 000 股股票期权的奖励。当你今早查看詹森制药的场外交易市场股票价格时，你发现这些股票期权中 120 000 股的行权价格低于目前 17 美元的股票价格，所以你急于避免在这次会议中对 Dekanor 做出任何轻率的决定。

### 角色：Y. 波伊克
詹森制药董事会成员，一家房地产开发公司的 CEO

这是詹森制药召集你来参加的首个董事会会议。你是当地一家成功的房地产公司的 CEO。詹森制药的 CEO 兼董事会主席 C. 詹森以及他孩子现在所住的房子是你的公司在去年建造的。你在和市政机构打交道时所展现的生意头脑和能力让 C. 詹森印象深刻，于是他最近把你聘请进詹森制药董事会做一名独立董事。后来他们通知你将加入詹森制药的 ARCo（审计，风险与合规）委员会、薪酬委员会以及管理委员会。

因为这是你在詹森制药董事会和高管团队面前的首次亮相，你想给大家留下一个好印象。如果被催着做选择，不得不承认你会非常紧张，因为你还没准备好对这项重大问题做出投票。你的专长是土木工程和建设，你觉得自己毫无准备，就像一个大学生没有复习就走进期末考试考场一样。你后悔自己对制药行业和这个行业的法律问题的知识不足、接触不多，就加入了董事会。

在参加这次特殊会议之前，你对 Dekanor 的印象非常好，因为你的岳母在服用 Dekanor，她对这个药的评价非常高。当然，作为一名董事，你对个人责任问题感到忧虑，并且不想和对人类有害的任何产品搭上边。到了最后，你只是想适应董事的工作，所以你将随大流来搞好关系。

### 角色：H. 菲利普斯，医学博士，哲学博士
#### 詹森制药研究部门经理

你帮助公司在空前短的时间内把 Dekanor 推向市场，并节省了预算。仅因为此，你在三年前被任命为研究部门经理，你目前仍担任该职位。作为詹森制药研究部门的经理，你意识到那些死亡事例与 Dekanor 有关，但你还是常说，"与酒精、烟草相比，Dekanor 是一种非常安全的药；服用 Dekanor 甚至比驾驶时发短信安全！"

尽管它是詹森制药生产的唯一一种帮助缓解偏头痛症状的药，但你知道它有副作用。你觉得只是因为詹森制药高超的营销、直接面向消费者的广告和积极向医生推广的销售力，才使得 Dekanor 在面对竞争对手的竞争时，经营得这么好。你想再次提醒董事会，现在像詹森制药这样研究预算很少的公司要开发和引进新药进入市场越来越难，因为 FDA 要求的试验是漫长而详尽无遗的。现在开发并向市场推广一种新药需将近 10 亿美元。制药公司通常测试 5 000 到 10 000 种化合物，检验它们治疗疾病的能力，其中只有 4 到 5 种可以进入下一阶段，即在人类受试者身上做临床试验。通常，在人身上测验的化合物中只有一种将得到 FDA 的认可，然后推向市场。你将告诉董事会，如果没有从 Dekanor 获得的利润，除非詹森制药迅速进行 IPO 募集到研究所需的资金，否则詹森制药没有其他资源为研究新药筹集资金。

自从被任命为研究部门经理，你获得了相当多的詹森制药股票期权的奖励，有机会的话，你想行使股票期权，为你的孩子积攒教育基金。

### 角色：J. 万斯，法学博士
#### 詹森制药的公司法律咨询

你想向董事会提出两种法律方案。第一种方案是与 FDA 协商给 Dekanor 一项黑框警告，取代禁止 Dekanor 的决定。黑框警告是 FDA 发布的最强警告，它置于药物的标签上来警告患者服用该药可能带来生命危险。要求增加黑框警告标签是 FDA 在市场上禁止一种药之前的最后一步。你觉得向 FDA 施加一些压力可以说服它接受这一方案。

第二种方案是一种更积极的方案，这是詹森制药的另一位律师向你建议的。她在去年就看到了 Dekanor 显露的问题，她觉得使用法律手段来拖延 FDA 的任何行动是可行的。她觉得亚特兰大的法官肯特（Kent）（你私下认

识的某人）可能愿意对 FDA 的任何行动下禁令。这一禁令可以避免 FDA 禁止 Dekanor，直到正式召开听证会。听证会的结果，如果不利，还可以上诉。实际上，这案子会在法院拖上个 3~5 年，使詹森制药有机会进行 IPO，筹集资金，研发新药。你持有大量的股票和股票期权，你希望积累一笔资金，过几年安逸的退休日子。

### 角色：E. 罗林斯，医学博士，哲学博士
**詹森制药研究部门助理经理**

你是管理团队的最新成员，也是提升到公司如此高位的最年轻的研究科学家。在你早期作为约翰·李博士的助理时，你便享有国际声誉，是制药行业最聪明年轻的新星。约翰·李是备受尊重的一位科学家，也是 FDA 的前任主席。李博士坚信：最重要的是，医学专业，甚至是延伸到制药行业，应该永远不做危害人们生命的事情。他还是 FDA 的一位热心支持者，在维护国家健康和福利方面起到重要作用。作为你的导师，李博士潜移默化地向你灌输同样的价值观。

你来到詹森制药时间不长，所以没有持有任何股票期权。然而，你所获得的好声誉，实际上确保你将有一份非常长远且高收益的工作。所以，你不想做会触怒你的导师或破坏你在科学界声誉的任何事。你参与了一项研究，这项研究由一位常春藤盟校的研究人员主导，研究结果表明服用 Dekanor 可能会增加心脏病发作的风险。你知道她是一位杰出的研究人员，有着无可挑剔的原则，如果她找到 Dekanor 有危险的证据，这一定是基于可靠的、科学的研究。

在你看来，你觉得董事会没有完全了解继续销售 Dekanor 所牵涉的风险。你想以一种不惹恼上司 H. 菲利普斯（他强烈支持继续销售该药，而你完全有理由质疑他）的方式，提醒董事会：詹森制药的最终目的是让人们生活得更好，而不是挣钱。

### 角色：D. 斯通
**詹森制药的公共关系经理**

作为公司与公众之间，特别是与大多数的新闻媒体之间的主要沟通桥梁，你有责任塑造公司的形象。因为在特别会议上要讨论的问题非常敏感，所达成的决议将对詹森制药产生非常大的影响，你被邀请参加会议以确保无论公司做出怎样的选择，你都能为董事会的选择"编造"正面的理由。

你有两点想法可以让每种选择都处于有利的局面。如果董事会选择方案 1，从市场上移除 Dekanor，你将使用强生公司（J & J）对于泰勒诺（Tylenol，药名）的经验作为指导。强生公司一发现有人干预泰勒诺，并且有个人受到伤害，它便立即从市场上撤掉所有的泰勒诺。这一决策短期来说使强生公司付出昂贵的代价，但是这一行动为强生公司树立起了重视病人健康高于公司利润的声誉；这种声誉多年来有效地影响着强生公司。你觉得现在移除 Dekanor 是一个强有力的例子，显示詹森制药关心它的患者多于利

润，詹森便可以利用这种声誉有效地营销它的其他药品。

如果董事会决定采取方案 2 或 3，那么你将提议双管齐下。首先，你将着手设计一项活动诋毁那位常春藤名牌大学出身的独立研究人员。其次，你打算抨击这项研究的前提，表明这项研究没有充分地控制住预先存在的心脏状况，这可以解释为什么 Dekanor 更多地被发现与心脏病发作相关。如果你能使公众确信该研究人员不具备胜任能力、她的研究有瑕疵，这将大大削弱它对 FDA 禁止 Dekanor 的影响。

### 角色：R. 约翰逊，注册管理会计师
詹森制药的副总裁，财务总监（CFO）

作为公司的 CFO，你主要关心的是公司的财务绩效（尽管你也拥有大量的詹森股票期权，你依赖它作为你的退休金）。你不是董事会的成员；然而，你参加了所有的董事会会议，以便解答董事会的任何决策对公司最终盈亏产生的影响。你将提醒董事会，Dekanor 销售的任何显著下降可能会转变利润上强劲增长的趋势，而这种趋势为现任 CEO 领导下的詹森制药业绩的特点。另外，任何这样的不利趋势将进一步促使詹森制药的股价下降，明显损害它进行 IPO 的能力。你还希望董事会明白，为研发筹集资金的能力是詹森制药长期成功的关键，因为如果 Dekanor 的销量下降，目前生产线上没有一种药可以弥补其损失的收入。另外，詹森制药的另外两种畅销药品的专利权两到三年后即将到期，也就是说这些药带来的收入将大幅度下降。

如果你感到生气，你可能还会提到你不喜欢的研究部门经理 H. 菲利普斯。自从三年前引进 Dekanor 后，他没有将任何新药成功引向市场，这意味着研究部门经理过去取得的成绩只是"昙花一现"而已。你还可以利用这个机会向董事会说明，如果詹森制药想要生存，就需要雇佣新的研究部门经理，因为詹森制药的未来在于向市场推出新药。因为你的红利，你的股票期权价值，以及你的工作依赖于这家公司财务的健康状况，你将很大的个人赌注压在拒绝或延迟任何将 Dekanor 从市场撤掉的行动。

### 角色：L. 古德森
詹森制药的人力资源副总裁

作为人力资源部门的经理，你主要关心的是公司的员工。你被公认为一位人道主义者；无论是对于你个人，还是作为一个人力资源专业人员，同情、正直和公正的价值标准都非常重要。对于詹森制药必须将股东对利润的关心置于利益相关者对患者健康的关心之上的争论，你感到极为不安。即便你拥有 40 000 股股票期权，你个人对股东和利益相关者之争仍有明确的答案。如果这个问题丢给你，你会实践詹森制药的使命，将患者的健康顾虑置于股东利润的需求之上。

你不是董事会成员，但是你参加所有的董事会会议，就董事会决策可能如何影响詹森制药员工的福利提供建议。你知道将 Dekanor 立即从市场撤掉的决策会带来人力资源的噩梦，因为这一决策意味着将关掉詹森制药的一项

或多项生产设备和其中一间研发实验室。其结果将造成几百人失去工作，公司会交给你来决定谁将离开。虽然你会告诉董事会停止销售Dekanor会给很多的詹森员工带来消极影响，你还是愿意看到Dekanor立即从市场上撤掉，你觉得只有当它已被证明是安全时，它才应该重新进入市场。

### 角色：N. 格林
詹森制药的营销副总裁

作为营销副总裁，自Dekanor三年前引进市场以来，你领导了一场非常成功的市场营销活动。你很有信心只要公司继续强势营销Dekanor，你的营销团队能继续产生强劲的绩效。考虑到目前正围绕着Dekanor的负面宣传，你赞成直接面向消费者和医生开展一项新广告活动。

你不是董事会成员，但你参加所有的董事会会议，当讨论到营销问题时，为大家提供信息。在今天的会议中，你将首先提醒董事会，对手公司突然发布了一种治疗偏头痛的新药，你担心如果詹森制药在这个时候召回Dekanor进行独立试验，或者如果詹森制药甚至停止对Dekanor的积极促销，竞争对手的新药将会窃取Dekanor的大部分（即便不是全部）市场份额。考虑到这一情况，你希望制订一项特别有效的方案，支持将Dekanor保留在市场上并开展新一轮的营销活动。你知道你在另一行业一家知名公司的CEO候选人的名单上，如果你愿成为这一职位的最终竞争者，你现在需要给人留下深刻的印象。

### 角色：T. 加西亚
詹森制药的信息总监

作为一位信息总监，你为维护詹森制药的信息系统而勤勉工作。制药行业的竞争要求公司的信息安全做到最好。新的和尚未申请专利的各项药物总是成为那些想要窃取公司秘密的人最惯常的目标，因为下一项"重磅"药物可能价值数十亿。

你非常谨慎地保存着从Dekanor最初研发以来的每一项相关文件。你非常有信心，Dekanor所有的电子文件都很安全，不会遭到任何方式的非法黑客攻击。然而，如果FDA开始正式的调查，你细心保存下来的Dekanor记录可能最终会危害公司。因为在Dekanor早期的试验中有一些关于副作用的令人不安的发现，这些资料从未发送给FDA或向公众公开。你认为静悄悄地组织一个小团队是个好主意，可以为采取迅速果断的行动来销毁任何可能带来危害的文件做准备。你意识到最后你可能会成为最终的替罪羊，不管选择实施哪种方案。

# Jensen Pharma: A Governance Role-Play

*J. Kay Keels*
*Coastal Carolina University*

*Norman T. Sheehan*
*University of Saskatchewan*

## INTRODUCTION

It is January 2012, and a special meeting of the Jensen Pharma board has been called. Jensen has a relatively small board in order to enhance its decision-making responsiveness and cohesiveness, which means that each board member must serve on several committees. Jensen's directors are compensated with Jensen stock options, which can only be exercised and sold at certain periods. A director can be expected to be awarded anywhere from 20 000 to 100 000 stock options each year depending on the number of committees he/she serves on and how many times these committees meet during the year.

Jensen is a relatively small, unlisted corporation. To date, Jensen has successfully delivered on its mission to help its patients live longer, pain-free lives through the use of effective pharmaceutical treatments. With sales of $ 300 million, Dekanor is Jensen's largest seller. It is a "blockbuster drug" that accounts for one-third of Jensen's annual revenues. Dekanor is an analgesic (i. e., painkiller) that is in the alpha-suppressing neural class of drugs. Dekanor was introduced over three years ago and quickly rose to be doctors' favorite prescription for patients suffering from acute chronic migraine pain. Jensen's current director of research, H. Phillips, led the team that brought Dekanor to the market, and Dekanor is seen to be a "career-maker" for Phillips and the other team members, such as the CIO, who were instrumental in getting the drug through the U. S. Food and Drug Administration (FDA) clinical trials in record time.

This special board meeting has been called to discuss a rumor that the FDA is considering banning Dekanor. The board meeting documents, which were sent out the day prior to meeting, include many financial, legal, and medical terms with which some board members may not be familiar. These documents are summarized here:

- Dekanor went through a total of six years of development, which is two to three years less than most other drugs, due to Jensen's skill in managing the FDA approval process. Dekanor's efficacy was tested on 1 100 patients, which is the minimum number the FDA will accept, at a cost of $675 million. The drug passed through the FDA clinical trials without any issues, so Dekanor is currently sold with the same drug product label information as other analgesic drugs (i. e., the drug label information outlines potential side effects of taking Dekanor, but does not mention the risk of death).

- Many patients report very high satisfaction with Dekanor, as it is more effective in combating chronic migraine pain than rival medications.

- Since being introduced, however, Dekanor has been associated with a large number of adverse cardiovascular events (typically heart attacks), some of which have resulted in death.

- An independent study found evidence to suggest that Dekanor may have contributed to some of these deaths; however, the number of patients studied was not large enough to be conclusive. The researcher who led the study, a prominent scientist from an Ivy League school, called for more studies of Dekanor, arguing that Dekanor "could very well be a ticking time bomb."

- Since the independent study was published, some doctors have publicly refused to prescribe Dekanor to their patients. Since Jensen has no alternative drug, these doctors began prescribing a rival's pain reliever for their patients, even though it is less effective.

- In response to the controversy surrounding Dekanor, some websites have emerged in support of Dekanor. Many of these websites are filled with Dekanor users pleading with Jensen and the larger medical community to keep Dekanor on the market. The document distributed to board members provides quotes from several websites carrying messages such as, "Dekanor has allowed me to live my life again. I can now play with my children and volunteer in the community. Thanks Dekanor!!!" and "Please keep Dekanor for me. I need it to survive my headaches." Still, there are also comments such as, "Dekanor stole my mother from me. Dekanor is a KILLER!!!"

- It is estimated that it will take a minimum of three years and $12 million for a large-scale, independent clinical trial to prove that Dekanor is a safe drug.

- Other pharmaceutical firms that have been found to knowingly sell drugs that harmed patients have faced lawsuits and been assessed fines between $50 million and $5 billion, depending on the number of deaths and culpability (i. e., how much blame could be assigned to the company for the deaths).

- Dekanor currently produces about half of Jensen's yearly profits of $250 million, and Jensen Pharma has no other drugs in its product development pipeline that have the potential to replace Dekanor's profits if it is banned.

• It is estimated that adding a drug warning label that clearly specifies the heart attack risk could result in a 50% drop in sales. On the other hand, the remaining 50% of existing patients are very satisfied with Dekanor and are not likely to switch to a rival's drug.

• A rival pharmaceutical firm has just announced that it plans to introduce a drug next month that also treats migraine symptoms with no proven fatal side effects.

• As Jensen is currently an unlisted corporation, its shares are publicly traded on the over-the-counter market. When the results of the independent study became public, Jensen's stock price decreased by 22%. Jensen's current over-the-counter stock price is $17 per share, which is down from a high of $30 a year ago. There are 53 million shares of Jensen Pharma outstanding.

• Jensen's board recognizes that it needs to spend even more on research if it is to successfully develop and bring new drugs to the market. To that end, the board has been in discussions about whether Jensen should be listed on the New York Stock Exchange (NYSE), so that the proceeds from an initial public offering (IPO) could be used to generate the much needed research funds.

In order to provide additional information to the board, Jensen's senior management team has been asked to attend the meeting to decide Dekanor's fate. The board chair (also the CEO) plans to open the meeting by proposing three alternatives for Dekanor. The board must select one of these alternatives by the end of the meeting:

1. Stop sales of Dekanor immediately and recall all inventory until an independent clinical trial has satisfactorily proven that Dekanor is not causing patients to die prematurely.

2. Add a warning label that clearly states that taking Dekanor may lead to adverse cardiovascular events that may result in death, and stop all direct advertising to consumers and promotion of Dekanor to doctors, but continue to sell it to those doctors who request it.

3. Continue efforts to market Dekanor aggressively and take any necessary legal, political, and other actions to prevent the FDA from banning Dekanor.

## Jensen's Board Members and Senior Management Team Members Attending the Special Dekanor Board Meeting

1. **C. Jensen, M. D., CEO and chairperson of the board (ex-officio member of all board committees):** C. Jensen is concerned about the effect that a reduction in Dekanor's sales will have on Jensen's future share price (C. Jensen owns the single largest block of Jensen shares, worth $90 million at the current over-the-counter market share price), and its ability to raise funds through an initial public offering. Still, as the only child of the founder, C. Jensen is also very concerned about preserving his image and the image of Jensen Pharma.

2. **M. Jensen, offspring of C. Jensen, member of the board (member of ARCo and Nominating Committees):** M. Jensen operates a consulting firm, MJ Associates, which does most of its business with Jensen Pharma. M. Jensen owns almost 4% of Jensen stock, which was given by the parent, C. Jensen. M. Jensen has been pushing the board to execute an initial public offering (IPO) quickly in order to fund the development of new drugs. Concerned about the current management team's lack of responsiveness to Jensen's shareholders, M. Jensen was recently quoted in The Wall Street Journal saying, "Jensen's management team needs to be reminded that they were hired by Jensen's shareholders, NOT its stakeholders."

3. **L. Vayan, member of the board (chair of Governance Committee, member of Compensation Committee):** With 28 years of experience in the pharmaceutical industry, Vayan knows that all drugs carry some risk. Vayan is the CEO of RAV Pharmaceuticals, a pharmaceutical supply company that is one of Jensen's largest suppliers. Vayan has 300 000 stock options.

4. **D. Charles, retired, member of the board (chair of ARCo and Nominating Committees and member of Governance Committee):** As a retired insurance executive, Charles is very concerned about the liability implications of the Dekanor issue. At the last board meeting, Charles requested that Jensen increase its liability coverage on its directors and officers (D&O) insurance policy to $10 million per director, but this request has not been honored yet. Charles owns a considerable amount of Jensen stock and stock options.

5. **B. Garrison, M. D., member of the board (chair of Compensation Committee, member of Nomination and ARCo Committees):** As a practicing physician, Garrison has been prescribing Dekanor to patients for years without any issues. The fact that the doctors that Garrison talks to have been using Dekanor for over three years indicates that it has value. Garrison owns 50 000 shares of Jensen stock as well as 300 000 stock options.

6. **Y. Boiki, member of the board (member of ARCo, Compensation, and Governance Committees):** This is Boiki's first board meeting with Jensen Pharma. Last year, Boiki's firm built the mansions that C. Jensen, CEO and chair of Jensen, and his offspring now occupy. C. Jensen was so impressed with Boiki's business acumen and ability to handle the municipal authorities that he recently recruited Boiki to Jensen's board.

7. **H. Phillips, M. D., Ph. D., director of research:** Phillips was instrumental in getting Dekanor on the market in record time and under budget. For that reason alone, Phillips was named director of research three years ago. Phillips is aware of the deaths linked to Dekanor but often says, "It is a very safe drug when compared to alcohol and tobacco; it is even safer to take Dekanor than texting while driving!" Phillips has a significant number of stock options.

8. **J. Vance, J. D., corporate legal counsel:** Vance is a high profile litigator and attorney who is well-versed in lobbying and fighting the FDA. Vance has a significant number of shares and share options that will be used to fund his/her retirement.

9. **E. Rollins, M. D., Ph. D., assistant director of research:** Rollins is the youngest research scientist ever to hold to such a high corporate position. Rollins earned a stellar reputation as one of the pharmaceutical industry's brightest young stars while working as an assistant to Dr. John Lee, a former head of the FDA. One of Dr. Lee's strongest beliefs was that the medical profession and pharmaceutical industry should never do anything that would endanger people's lives. Given that Rollins recently joined Jensen, Rollins does not own any shares or share options.

10. **D. Stone, director of public relations:** Stone is responsible for shaping the company's public image and has been invited to the meeting to be certain that Jensen can "spin" whatever option the board chooses in a positive way. Stone has 200 000 share options.

**11. R. Johnson, CMA, vice president and CFO:** Johnson's principal concern is for the company's financial performance. Johnson constantly reminds the board that any significant drop in the sales of Dekanor would significantly hurt Jensen's future profitability. Johnson will also remind the board that the patents on Jensen's other two best-selling drugs will expire in the next two years. Johnson has a significant number of shares and options.

**12. L. Goodson, vice president of human resources:** Goodson is widely recognized as a humanist, meaning the values of compassion, integrity, and justice play a central role in Goodson's dealings with others. Goodson is known to be uncomfortable with the argument that Jensen must place shareholders' demands above stakeholders' concerns.

**13. N. Greene, vice president of marketing:** Greene has led a very successful marketing campaign for Dekanor since it was introduced to the market three years ago. Greene is very confident that Jensen's marketing group can continue to generate strong revenue numbers as long as the company continues to market Dekanor aggressively.

**14. T. Garcia, chief information officer:** Garcia is an excellent CIO, meticulously keeping every file relating to Jensen's drug testing trials, some of which have never been released to the FDA or the public. Garcia has a number of shares and share options.

## INSTRUCTIONS TO STUDENTS:

1. Read the case background information and the assigned readings prior to the class.

2. Roles for the 14 role-players and understudies will be assigned by the instructor in advance of class or in the class when the role-play is to be discussed.

3. As a designated role-player, you should meet with your understudy, read your assigned role, and prepare notes on points your character should emphasize during the board's discussion of Dekanor. Do not share any of the private information contained in your role with other role-players prior to the board meeting.

4. Acting as you think your assigned character would, be prepared to state your preferred alternative during the board meeting and explain why you support that alternative. During the board discussion, you may consult with your understudy (who should sit near you), but be discreet so as not to interrupt or distract other board members.

5. The board meeting will be timed, and the board must reach a decision before adjournment.

## ROLES FOR EACH OF THE 14 ROLE-PLAYERS

Note to instructors: Students should receive copies of their assigned roles only. No role-player should be given any information or description about any of the other role-players' roles.

## ROLE OF C. JENSEN, M. D.

### CEO and chairperson of the board, Jensen Pharma

As Jensen's board chair and CEO, you will be responsible for directing the discussion and ensuring that everyone is heard. You must lead the board to a decision by the end of the time available, since some board members have to leave immediately after adjournment to make a scheduled flight.

Your general philosophy about meetings is to try to allow for various sides of the issue to be discussed before a decision is reached. Legally speaking, a majority vote is required to reach a decision. You prefer a consensus decision, but in any case, a formal vote must be taken at the end of the meeting. As board chair, you do not vote unless there is a tie, at which time your vote will break the tie. The board's decision, whether by consensus or by majority vote, must be formally recorded in the meeting's minutes to be available to stockholders at a later date.

Personally, you are of two minds: (1) You are concerned about the effect that a reduction in Dekanor's sales will have on Jensen's future share price (you own the single largest block of Jensen shares, which are worth $90 million at the current over-the-counter market share price) and the firm's ability to raise funds through an initial public offering. (2) On the other hand, you are also committed to having this company—which you have led through its period of greatest growth—maintain its image of honesty and integrity. To honor this commitment, Jensen must act in ways that convince the public that it is devoted to its patients' well-being, not just the wealth of its shareholders. Ultimately, you know that is how you and your family (which founded the company) will be judged in history.

As chair of the Jensen Pharma board, you will:

1. Call the special board meeting to order when indicated by the instructor;
2. Review each option for Dekanor;
3. Ask each individual at the meeting to introduce him/herself and explain what option he/she thinks the board should choose (i.e., option 1, 2, or 3) and why he/she supports this option;
4. Ensure that everyone has a chance to speak; and
5. Call for a vote of the board when time expires or when directed to do so by the instructor. (NB: Only the five board members are allowed to vote. The chair does not vote unless there is a tie.)

## ROLE OF M. JENSEN

### Offspring of C. Jensen (board chair), member of Jensen's board of directors and president of MJ Associates, consultants

You operate a consulting firm, MJ Associates, which does most of its business with Jensen Pharma. You own almost 4% of Jensen stock, which was given to you by your parent, C. Jensen. As you repeatedly remind the other board members, you own the second largest block of stock, worth $36 million at the current share price. You also own 300 000 stock options that you earned during your tenure as a board member, which are worth several more millions. The value of your shares and options have dropped over $30 million in the last year, so you are very concerned about the potential effects that the FDA's ban of Dekanor could have on Jensen's future share price and the firm's ability to execute an initial public offering. Having been closely involved in the drug industry since birth, you are acutely aware of Jensen's need to invest funds into the development of new drugs if it is to survive in the longer term, and thus you have been pushing the board to list Jensen on the NYSE quickly, and then do an initial public offering (IPO).

You have recently become increasingly disturbed about management's apparent responsiveness to stakeholders' demands. In a well-publicized statement that appeared in The Wall Street Journal, you stated, "Jensen's management team needs to be reminded that they were hired by Jensen's shareholders, NOT its stakeholders."

A suggestion was recently sent to you by a corporate lobbyist in Washington. He suggests that it might be possible to bring political pressure to bear on the FDA by securing the cooperation of the current secretary of the Department of Health and Human Services (of which the FDA is an agency). The secretary might be willing to postpone the FDA ban until independent testing can show Dekanor is safe, a result that is anticipated within three to four years. In the best case, the secretary might even be persuaded to overrule any ban proposed by the FDA, since the ban would represent a major precedent that increases the power of the FDA at the expense of drug companies and their rights to free enterprise. Getting the secretary to go along with this plan might require some major financial contributions to the president's re-election campaign. Either way, these tactics would buy Jensen the time it needs to complete an IPO, the proceeds from which would allow the firm to develop some new blockbuster drugs to replace Dekanor.

### ROLE OF L. VAYAN
Member of Jensen's board of directors and CEO of RAV Pharmaceuticals

You have 28 years of experience in the pharmaceutical industry, having served 12 years as a senior manager in several large international pharmaceutical companies, and the last 8 years as a CEO of a pharmaceutical supply company, RAV Pharmaceuticals. Jensen is one of your larger customers, making up almost 10% of RAV's sales. Due to cash flow problems, Jensen has not paid its invoices for six months and now owes RAV $8 million. You have served on the board for four years and have 300 000 stock options, but, to date, you own no stock.

You have heard from several industry insiders that prescription drugs kill more people in North America than illegal drugs. Given that all drugs carry some risk, you favor permitting patients and their doctors to decide what is best for them. Although you are unsure of the board's legal exposure, you feel that the best path for Jensen is to maintain pressure on the FDA, to continue to aggressively market Dekanor, and to do whatever the firm can to avoid having the drug banned. Otherwise, you fear that your Jensen stock options will be worthless, and the $8 million owed to RAV will never be paid.

### ROLE OF D. CHARLES
#### Member of Jensen's board and retired CEO of an insurance company

You were first elected to Jensen's board 12 years ago when you were the CEO of a well known insurance company. As chair of Jensen's ARCo (Audit, Risk, and Compliance) Committee, you were annoyed when this meeting was called, for two reasons: First, while you have heard allegations that Dekanor is not safe, you have nonetheless been told repeatedly by management that it is safe. And second, you were supposed to play golf with your usual foursome today and had to cancel at the last minute in order to attend this meeting.

As a retired insurance executive, you are well aware of the liability implications of the Dekanor issue. At the last board meeting, you requested that Jensen increase its liability coverage on its directors and officers (D&O) insurance policy to $10 million per director, but this request has not been honored yet. Still, even if the board votes to add a warning to Dekanor's product label, you doubt that $10 million in D&O insurance will be enough to cover the personal liability if Jensen's directors are later found negligent.

Given this, your professional experience indicates a conservative approach should be considered. You want to bring up these issues in the meeting, as well as the fact the board has never discussed its risk tolerance level. How much risk is the board comfortable with, and how much risk is too much? You want to ensure that Jensen's board makes the right decision, as you own a considerable amount of its stock and stock options, and you are counting on the proceeds from these holdings to fund the rest of your retirement.

### ROLE OF B. GARRISON, M.D.
#### Member of Jensen's board of directors and practicing physician

You are aware of the bad publicity surrounding Dekanor. As a practicing physician, you have been prescribing Dekanor to your patients for three years, and you have seen nothing wrong with it. At the last American Medical Association meeting, other doctors with whom you have spoken reported similar experiences. Your thought is that an appeal should be sent to all doctors to protest the FDA's threat to ban Dekanor on the grounds that a ban would be violating a physician's right to prescribe the most effective drugs. The fact that some of the doctors you talked to have been using Dekanor for over three years indicates that it has value.

You have been a member of the board of directors for eight years and own 50 000 shares of Jensen stock as well as 300 000 stock options that you have been awarded for serving on Jensen's board. When you checked Jensen's over-the-counter share price this morning, you saw that 120 000 of these stock options are still exercisable at prices lower than the current stock price of $17, so you are eager to avoid any imprudent decisions regarding Dekanor at this meeting.

### ROLE OF Y. BOIKI
### Member of Jensen's board of directors and CEO
### of a property development firm

You have just been summoned to your first board meeting with Jensen Pharma. You are the CEO of a successful local property development firm. Last year, your firm developed the land and built the mansions that C. Jensen, CEO and chair of Jensen Pharma, and his offspring now occupy. C. Jensen was so impressed with your business acumen and ability to handle the authorities that he recently recruited you to fill the position as an independent director on Jensen's board. You have been since informed you that you will be appointed to Jensen's ARCo (Audit, Risk, and Compliance), Compensation, and Governance Committees.

As this is your first introduction to Jensen Pharma's board and its senior management team, you want to make a good impression. If pushed, you would admit to feeling very nervous, as you are ill prepared to vote on such an important issue. Given that your background is in civil engineering and construction, you feel as unprepared as a university student walking into a final exam without ever having opened the text. You regret that you have not had more education and exposure to the pharmaceutical industry and its legal issues before joining the board.

You have come to the special meeting with very positive impressions of Dekanor, as your mother-in-law uses it and speaks very highly of it. You are, of course, worried about the personal liability issues as a director and do not want to be associated with any product that causes harm to humans. At the end of the day, however, you just want to fit in, so you will "go along, to get along."

## ROLE OF H. PHILLIPS, M. D. , PH. D.
### Director of research, Jensen Pharma

You were instrumental in getting Dekanor on the market in record time and under budget. For that reason alone, you were named director of research three years ago, the position you currently hold. As head of Jensen's research division, you are aware of the deaths linked to Dekanor. As you often tell anyone who will listen, however, "It is a very safe drug when compared to alcohol and tobacco; it is even safer to take Dekanor than texting while driving!"

Although it is the only product of its kind that Jensen produces to help lessen migraine symptoms, you know there are negative side effects. You feel that it is only because of Jensen's superior marketing, its direct advertising to consumers, and its aggressive sales force pushing it on physicians that Dekanor has fared so well against rival migraine drugs. You want to remind the board again that it has become increasingly difficult for companies with smaller research budgets, like Jensen, to develop and bring new products to the market because of the lengthy and exhaustive testing requirements of the FDA. It now requires almost $1 billion to develop and bring a new drug to market. Drug companies typically test 5 000 to 10 000 compounds for their ability to treat a disease, and of these only 4 to 5 make it to the next phase, which is clinical testing on human subjects. Typically, only one of the compounds tested on humans will be approved by the FDA and then brought to market. You will tell the board that without the profits from Dekanor, Jensen will not have the resources to finance new drug research unless Jensen quickly does an initial public offering to raise the needed research funds.

You have been awarded a significant amount of Jensen stock options since being named director of research and would like to have a chance to exercise these so you can fund your children's educations.

## ROLE OF J. VANCE, J. D.
### Corporate legal counsel, Jensen Pharma

You want to present two legal options to the board. The first is to negotiate with the FDA to place a black box warning on Dekanor in lieu of banning Dekanor. Black box warnings, the strongest issued by the FDA, are placed on a drug's label to alert patients to life-threatening risks associated with the drug. Requiring a black box warning label is the last step that the FDA will take before banning that drug from the market. You feel the FDA can be persuaded to accept this option with some arm twisting.

A second, much more aggressive option was suggested to you by another Jensen attorney. She has seen the Dekanor issue develop over the past year, and she thinks that it would be possible to delay any action by the FDA using legal means. She suggests that Judge Kent of Atlanta (someone you know personally) would be willing to serve an injunction on any FDA action. This injunction would prohibit the FDA from banning Dekanor until a formal hearing could be held. The results of the hearing, if unfavorable, could be appealed. In effect, the case could be tied up in the courts for three to five years, allowing Jensen time to execute an initial public offering to fund the development of new drugs. You have been given a significant number of shares and options that you hope will fund a prosperous retirement in a few years.

### ROLE OF E. ROLLINS, M. D., PH. D.
#### Assistant director of research, Jensen Pharma

You are the newest member of the management team and the youngest research scientist ever to be promoted to such a high corporate position. You earned an international reputation as one of the brightest young stars in the pharmaceutical industry very early in your career when you worked as the assistant to Dr. John Lee, a highly respected member of the scientific community and former head of the FDA. One of Dr. Lee's strongest beliefs was that, above all, the medical profession—and, by extension, the pharmaceutical industry—should never do anything that would endanger people's lives. He was also a fervent advocate of the FDA and the important role that it plays in maintaining the nation's health and welfare. As your mentor, Dr. Lee instilled those same values in you.

You have not been with Jensen very long, so you do not own any stock options. Your highly regarded reputation, however, practically ensures that you will have a very long and highly lucrative career. Therefore, you do not want to do anything that would displease your mentor or damage your standing in the scientific community. You studied with the researcher at the Ivy League university who led the study that indicated that taking Dekanor may increase the risk of heart attacks. You know this individual is an outstanding researcher with impeccable standards, and if she found evidence that Dekanor is dangerous, it is based on solid, scientific research.

In your opinion, you do not feel the board fully understands the risks involved with keeping Dekanor available for sale. You want to remind the board, in a way that will not alienate your boss, H. Phillips (whom you have every reason to suspect will strongly support continuing the sale of the drug), that the ultimate purpose of Jensen Pharma is to make people's lives better, not to make money.

### ROLE OF D. STONE
#### Director of public relations, Jensen Pharma

As the company's primary interface with the public and most especially with the press, you are responsible for shaping the company's image. Since the issues to be discussed at the special meeting are so sensitive and the decision will have such a huge impact on Jensen, you have been invited to the meeting to be certain that you can "spin" whatever option the board chooses in a positive way.

You have two ideas to help place a favorable spin on each option. If the board goes with Option 1, to remove Dekanor from the market, you will use Johnson & Johnson's (J&J) experience with Tylenol as a guide. Once J&J found that an individual was tampering with Tylenol and individuals were being harmed, it immediately removed all Tylenol from the market. This decision was very costly for J&J in the short term, but this action built J&J's reputation as being a company that puts its patients' well being ahead of profitability; a reputation that J&J effectively leveraged for years. You feel that by removing Dekanor at this point, Jensen could make a strong case that the company cares for its patients more than profits, and Jensen could then leverage this reputation to market its other drugs effectively.

If the board decides to proceed with Option 2 or 3, then you will propose a two-pronged attack. First, you will begin a campaign designed to smear the reputation of the independent researcher at the Ivy League school. Second, you plan to attack the premise of the research study, perhaps by arguing that the study did not adequately control for pre-existing heart conditions, which may explain why Dekanor was found to be associated with a higher incidence of heart attacks. If you can convince the public to believe that the researcher is incompetent and her study is flawed, this will significantly lessen the pressure on the FDA to ban Dekanor.

### ROLE OF R. JOHNSON, CMA
#### Vice president and CFO, Jensen Pharma

As CFO of the corporation, your principal concern is for the company's financial performance (although you also own a significant number of Jensen stock options, which you are relying on to fund your retirement). You are not a member of the board; nonetheless, you attend all board meetings in order to speak to the effect any board decisions may have on the company's bottom line. You will remind the board that any significant drop in the sales of Dekanor would reverse the trend of strong growth in profits that has been characteristic of Jensen's performance under the leadership of its current CEO. In addition, any such adverse trend would further drive down Jensen's share price and significantly hurt its ability to execute an initial public offering (IPO). You also want to make the board understands that the ability to fund R&D is the key to Jensen's long-term success, as there are no drugs in the pipeline to replace the lost revenue if Dekanor's sales slump. In addition, the patents on the other two of Jensen's best-selling drugs will expire in the next two to three years, which means the income from these drugs will fall significantly.

If you are feeling grumpy, you may also add that the research director, H. Phillips, whom you dislike, has not successfully introduced any new drugs to the market since Dekanor three years ago, meaning the research director is a "one-hit wonder." You can also use this opportunity to point out to the board that if Jensen is to survive, it needs to hire a new research director, as its future lies in bringing new drugs to market. Since your bonus, the value of your stock options, and also your job depend upon the well-being of the company's financial condition, you have a substantial personal stake in rejecting or delaying any action that would remove Dekanor from the market.

### ROLE OF L. GOODSON
#### Vice president of human resources, Jensen Pharma

As head of human resources, your primary concern is for the company's employees. You are widely known as a humanist; the values of compassion, integrity, and justice are very important to you as a person and as an HR professional. You are extremely uncomfortable with the argument that Jensen must place shareholders' concerns for profits above stakeholders' concerns for patients' well-being. Even though you have 40 000 stock options, you personally can see a clear answer to the debate of shareholder versus stakeholder. If it were left to you, you would live Jensen's mission and place patients' health concerns over the shareholders' desire for profits.

You are not a member of the board, but you attend all board meetings in order to provide advice as to how board decisions may impact the well-being of Jensen's employees. You know that a decision to remove Dekanor from the market immediately would create a human resources nightmare, as the decision would mean closing one or more of Jensen's production facilities as well as one of its R&D labs. As a result, several hundred people would lose their jobs, and it would fall to you to decide who has to go. While you will inform the board of the negative impact a decision to stop selling Dekanor would have on many of Jensen's employees, you would like to see Dekanor removed from the market immediately, and you feel that it should only be re-introduced when it has been proven safe.

### ROLE OF N. GREENE
#### Vice president of marketing, Jensen Pharma

As vice president of marketing, you have led a very successful marketing campaign for Dekanor since it was introduced to the market three years ago. You have every confidence that your marketing group can continue to turn in a strong performance as long as the company continues to market Dekanor aggressively. Given the negative publicity currently surrounding Dekanor, you favor instituting a new advertising campaign aimed directly at consumers and physicians.

You are not a member of the board, but you attend all board meetings to provide input on marketing issues when called upon. At today's meeting, you will begin by reminding the board that a new migraine drug is due to be released by a rival firm shortly, and you fear that if Jensen recalls Dekanor at this time to conduct independent testing, or if Jensen even stops aggressively promoting it, the rival's new drug will steal most, if not all, of Dekanor's market share. Given this, you want to make an especially strong case to keep Dekanor on the market and to launch a new marketing campaign. You know that you are on the short list of CEO candidates at a well-known firm in another industry, and if you are to be considered as a finalist for this position, you need to make a strong impression right now.

### ROLE OF T. GARCIA
#### Chief information officer, Jensen Pharma

As chief information officer, you have worked diligently to protect Jensen Pharma's information systems. Competing in the pharmaceutical industry requires the very best in corporate information security. New and unpatented drugs are the frequent targets of those who seek to steal company secrets because the next big blockbuster drug can be worth billions.

You have meticulously kept every file relevant to Dekanor since the early days of its initial development, and you feel very confident that all of the Dekanor computer files are safe from any sort of illegal hacking. If the FDA begins formal investigations, however, your careful preservation of the Dekanor records could end up harming the company, since there were some troubling findings of side effects in the early testing of Dekanor that were never released to the FDA or made public. You are thinking that it might be a good idea to very quietly put together a small team that would be prepared to take immediate and decisive action to destroy any potentially damaging files. You realize that you could end up being the ultimate scapegoat, regardless of which way things go.

# Alchemy——一则内部审计案例

*Herbert Snyder*
*North Dakota State University*

*James Clifton*
*North Dakota State University*

*William Bowlin*
*North Dakota State University*

## 公司简介

  Auditing Alchemy 公司（以下一律简称 AA 公司）成立于 1998 年，是一家私有制的制造企业。AA 公司生产各种工业用的球体。AA 公司是行业内最好的球体生产商，并向美国政府和其他一些航空合约商销售他们的球体。这种球以两种形式进行出售：绿色的和金色的球体。第三种形式的红色球体，是生产过程中的副产品。

  尽管没有公开上市交易，AA 公司早在十多年前就已经成立了内部审计部门。这个部门内设有审计执行主管（chief audit executive，CAE），负责向董事会报告，以及向执行总裁做行政报告。除了主管以外，该部门还有另外三名内部审计人员。在 AA 公司内，该部门职责广泛，但这些职责主要是防止和调查舞弊行为，以保证财产的安全。

## 问题界定：一项可能存在的舞弊

  西尔维娅·托伦斯（Sylvia Torrance）是 AA 公司的 CEO。从 2006 年度开始，她就对 AA 公司的制造产出深感不安。尽管销售活跃，并且利润也保持在一个可接受的水平上，然而，销售利润却越来越少，制造费用也越来越高。因此，她安排了一次与 AA 公司审计执行主管（CAE）——布雷特·安德森（Bret Anderson）的会面，讨论这一情况。

  西尔维娅·托伦斯（CEO，以 ST 表示）与布雷特·安德森（CAE，以 BA 表示）之间的谈话：

---

\* 本篇译者为赵澄，校订者为胡金凤、余辉。

ST：感谢你今天顺道来访。我不确定我们公司是否存在问题，但是，财务情况看似不妙。利润水平尚可接受，但我们本应该做得更好。公司的毛利率已经从2005年的27%下降到2006年25%。公司两年之间的销售价格和营运费用基本保持不变。

BA：确切地说，你认为公司什么地方有问题呢？

ST：这恰恰就是问题所在。我无法具体指出哪里有问题，但是，在我看来，公司的财务情况确实有问题。净利润仍是可接受的，但我就是对一些事情感到不安。财务人员做了一些初步分析，它可能与遗漏登记的存货有关。让我来为你讲讲我们到目前为止的发现。

首先，对公司的仓库进行了一个全面的清查。存货的实物保护，是我见过的最安全的保护。我们也对内部控制进行了全面的检查；它们（内部控制）设计得很好，更重要的是，内部控制制度正按照设计预期的那样运行。我相信，如果存货存在遗漏登记的问题，那么，问题一定是出在存货入库前的生产过程中。

我们生产金色球体和绿色球体的单位原材料成本在过去的几年里上涨很多。我们使用的是标准成本体系，并为所生产的每种类型的球制定了标准材料成本。标准材料成本如下：一个金色球体的标准成本是348美元，绿色球体的标准成本是90美元。去年，与标准相比，我们的标准成本目标基本实现，即：金色球体349美元，绿色球体89美元，但今年却没有实现。今年的金色球体的材料成本上涨了2%，达到356美元。

我们进一步将材料成本差异分解为价格差异和用量差异。如我所预期的，价格差异接近零，因为采购部告诉我，公司原材料的采购价格并没有提高。事实上，整个成本差异主要来自耗用量的变化。与之前年度相比，今年我们在生产中使用了更多的原材料。

同时，在过去的六个季度里，我们的完工产品成本/原材料存货比率却保持不变，这表明我们在生产过程中使用的原材料数量与上一年一样。在过去几年里，我们采用的是永续盘存制，而不是手工盘点制，因为手工盘点制存在人工成本。

最后，我们还发现，我们采购的原材料比去年增加了。

我知道这是一个信息的大杂烩，但是，它向我们指出，与我们制定的标准量相比，我们用了更多的原材料。我与生产经理谈过，问她是否能找出我们使用这么多原材料的原因，如因购入新设备而员工未进行充分培训、原材料质量较差，或是对机器未作预防维护。但是她说这些因素都不是问题。我不知道我还能做什么，所以，我想看看你能否帮得上忙，你可以调查一下这个问题吗？

BA：当然可以，你是怀疑存在舞弊吗？

ST：我不知道。我不清楚具体存在什么问题，但我们的钱和利润与我们应该拥有的不一致，并且现在是市场繁荣期。还有可能是什么原因呢？

BA：我也不清楚，但是，在我们提出像"舞弊"这样的原因之前，我需要进行更加详细的调查。一项彻底的舞弊检查将会造成连锁反应，使得人人自危，即便他们是诚实可靠的。我要说的是，我会进行一些快速地检测，看看是否会暴露一些事情，然后我们再决定，事情是否如你想的那么糟糕。

# 作业

这则案例有三项独立的作业，每一项作业都有特定的预期结果，如下：

**作业 1：**

假设你是布雷特·安德森，并已经获得了如图表 1 所示的员工劳动生产率信息。

你能提供哪些证据，证明是否需要进行进一步调查？为支撑你的决定，请提供具体的计算，并根据计算结果进行描述性分析。请记住，任何的进一步调查都将在员工之间造成混乱，因此，提出要执行的任何建议都需要强有力的证据。如果你决定执行调查，你所提供的证据是否表明存在舞弊行为？请解释存在或不存在舞弊的原因。

---

**图表 1**

**员工年初至今的生产**

参考 Excel 文件：表 T1 – AA 公司生产数据.xls①

**作业 2：**

这项作业需要使用 AA 公司的视频，你可以从下面的地址下载并查看：http://134.129.81.111/~alchemy/ 该文件约 1.4GB，高速连接的话，需要花费 4～6 分钟下载。该视频是 AVI 格式，因而可以在大部分的视频播放器上播放。视频时长约 7 分钟。

你可以多次观看视频，但关于工作地点的信息，除了作业 1 中所使用的，我们无法提供更多的额外信息。

视频会带你了解并解释 AA 公司球体生产过程。

以你从视频中观察到的 AA 公司工作场地为基础，回答如下问题：

1. 内部控制系统中，能够防范谎报球体存货的优点有哪些？
2. 是否存在盗窃昂贵的球体而不被发现的可能性？如果有，盗窃行为是如何实现的？
3. 如果存在盗窃球体的可能，是否有足够证据证明盗窃行为已经发生？并解释原因。

**作业 3：**

1. 根据你对作业 1 和作业 2 的分析，你可能需要额外的信息来帮助你确定：如果 AA 公司存在舞弊行为，那么是谁以及如何在 AA 公司进行舞弊行为。请以书面（复印件或电子邮件，由教师指定）形式将你的要求写给你的导师。你所要求的任何信息都必须是能够合法获得的。有些信息可能需要以法院传票形式来获得，但只有当你提供的解释足以让法官相信时，法院才会提供帮助。

2. 根据你从作业 1 和作业 2 所收集和分析的全部信息，撰写该舞弊案的最终报告书。你的报告中至少应该列示证明舞弊行为确实发生的证据，舞弊行为的途径，可能的嫌疑人或多个嫌疑人，并提供支撑你认定嫌疑人的证据。

在你的分析中，优势和劣势分别是什么？如果可以，你还能做哪些事情让你的分析更加可信？你还会建议哪些行动方案？

关于 AA 公司产品和制作流程的摘要信息如下：

---

① Excel 文件可到经济科学出版社网站（www.esp.com.cn）的"在线资源"中下载。

## AA 公司生产流程概述

正如案例前面所述的，AA 公司生产和销售两类球体：绿色球体和金色球体。绿色和金色球体都有相当高的价值。一个金色球体所需的原材料是绿色球体所需原材料的四倍，并以约 10 倍于成本的价格进行销售。绿色和金色球体都很轻便。

用来生产球体的原材料本身价值不菲，生产投入也被严格监测。所有投入生产流程的原材料最终都转变为了球体的产成品，但并不是所有的球体都有商业价值。除了绿色和金色球体，生产过程中还会产出红色球体。为了生产绿色和金色球体，必将生产出一些红色球体，然而，他们本身没有商业价值。因此，球体的数量——红色球体、绿色球体和金色球体——与投入生产的单位产品原材料相匹配。绿色和金色球体完工之后被送到 AA 公司的仓库。红色球体，由于无商业价值，在核实后被丢弃掉。

# Alchemy-An Internal Auditing Case

*Herbert Snyder*
*North Dakota State University*

*James Clifton*
*North Dakota State University*

*William Bowlin*
*North Dakota State University*

## INTRODUCTION TO AUDITING ALCHEMY

Auditing Alchemy (AA) is a privately-held manufacturing company established in 1998. AA manufactures spheres that are used in a variety of industrial applications. AA is the top sphere producer in the industry and also sells spheres to the U. S. government and other aerospace contracts. The spheres are sold in two forms: green and gold. A third form of sphere, red, is also a by-product of the manufacturing process.

Although it is not publicly traded, AA has had an internal audit department for more than a decade. The department has a chief audit executive (CAE) who reports to the board of directors and who reports administratively to the CEO. The department has three other internal auditors, in addition to the director. The department has broad responsibilities within AA, but among its duties are deterring and investigating fraud and safeguarding assets.

## PROBLEM DEFINITION: A POSSIBLE FRAUD

Sylvia Torrance is Auditing Alchemy's CEO. She had been feeling uneasy about AA's manufacturing output since the beginning of calendar year 2006. Although sales were brisk and profits remained at an acceptable level, there seemed to be less profit from sales and higher expenses for manufacturing. As a result, she scheduled a meeting with AA's CAE Bret Anderson to discuss the situation.

Conversation between Sylvia Torrance (CEO) and Bret Anderson:

ST: Thanks for stopping by today. I'm not sure if we have a problem here, but something doesn't seem right about our finances. Profit level is acceptable, but we should be doing better. Our gross margin percentage has dropped from 27% in 2005 to 25% so far in 2006. Our selling price and operating expenses are pretty consistent between the two years.

BA: What is it exactly that doesn't seem right to you?

ST: That's just the problem. I can't quite put my finger on it, but the financials for the company just don't look right to me. The bottom line is still healthy, but I'm just not comfortable with things. The CFO's staff has done some preliminary analyses, and it appears there might be a problem with missing inventory. Let me lay out for you what we have found so far.

First, there was an extensive examination of our warehouse. The physical protection for inventory is the most secure I've ever seen. We also did a complete review of the internal controls; they're well-designed and, more importantly, they actually work the way their intended. I am confident that if there is a problem with missing inventory, it has to occur in manufacturing, before it reaches the warehouse.

Our raw material cost per unit to produce a gold sphere and a green sphere is up significantly over the last couple of years. We use a standard cost system and consequently develop a standard material cost for each type of sphere produced. Our standard material cost is $348 for a gold sphere and $90 for the green sphere. Last year our costs were just about on target ($349 for gold spheres and $89 for green spheres) compared to the standard, but not this year. This year the material cost for the gold spheres has increased 2% to $356.

We further broke the materials cost variance into a price variance and a usage variance. The price variance was near zero as I had expected, since Purchasing had told me there was no increase in the price we were paying for raw materials. In fact, the whole cost variance was made up of the usage variance. We used more raw material in producing this year's usable spheres than we had in previous years.

At the same time, however, our cost of goods manufactured/raw material inventory ratio is pretty consistent over the most recent six quarters, indicating that we are using about the same amount of raw material in our production process as we have previously. We use a perpetual inventory system and have not done a manual inventory count in a couple of years because of the cost of doing this.

Finally, we have also noticed that our raw material purchases are up over last year.

I know that this is a hodge-podge of information, but it all points to us using more materials than we should. I've talked with the production manager about whether she can identify any reason why we would be using more materials, such as labor not being sufficiently trained on the new machinery we bought, raw materials being a poorer quality, or machinery not having the preventive maintenance being done. But she said none of those factors are a problem. I'm at a loss as to what more I can do, so I'm seeing if you might be able to help. Will you look into it?

BA: Of course. Do you suspect fraud?

ST: I don't know. I'm not sure what the problem is, but we don't seem to have the money and profits we ought to and the market is booming. What else could it be?

BA: I'm not sure, but before we start shaking things up with a word like "fraud," I should look into things in more detail. A full-blown fraud examination costs a bundle and it puts everybody on edge, even if they're honest. Tell you what. I'll run some quick diagnostics and see if anything falls out, and then we can decide whether things are as bad as you think they are.

## ASSIGNMENT

There are three separate tasks for this case, each of which has a specific set of deliverables, as follows:

TASK 1:

Imagine you are Bret Anderson and have been provided the following employee productivity information.

What evidence can you provide that further investigation is or is not needed? Provide specific calculations to support your decision, as well as a narrative analysis of what the calculations demonstrated to you. Keep in mind that any further investigation will be disruptive, so any recommendation to proceed will require strong evidence. If you decide to proceed, is the evidence you produce indicative that fraud has occurred? Explain why or why not.

EXHIBIT 1:

Year-to-date production by employeeRefer to Excel file: T1_AA_Prod_Data.xls

TASK 2:

This task uses the Auditing Alchemy video, which may be viewed by downloading the file from: http://134.129.81.111/~alchemy/

The file is approximately 1.4GB and requires about 4-6 minutes to download on a high-speed connection. The video is an AVI format, which should run on most computer media players. The video runs approximately 7 minutes.

You may view the video more than one time, but no additional information about the workplace is available other than what was used for Task 1.

The video will lead you though a tour and explanation of the Auditing Alchemy sphere production process.

Based on your observations of the Auditing Alchemy workplace in the video, answer the following questions:

1. What are the strengths of the internal control system that protects the sphere inventory from misstatement?
2. Is it possible to steal the valuable spheres without detection, and if so, how is this accomplished?
3. If it is possible to steal spheres, is there enough evidence to support that a crime has been committed? Why or why not?

TASK 3:

1. Based on your analysis from Tasks 1 and 2, you may request additional information to help you decide if and who may have perpetrated fraud at Auditing Alchemy. Any request should be made in writing (hard copy or email, as your instructor specifies) to your instructor. Whatever information you ask for must be legally obtainable. It may be possible to obtain information that requires a court order, but this will be supplied only if you provide an explanation that would be sufficient to convince a judge.

2. Write your final fraud report based on any information you have collected and the analysis from Tasks 1 and 2. At a minimum, your report should list predication for believing a fraud has occurred, a mechanism by which the fraud could be perpetrated, a likely suspect or suspects, and evidence that supports your choice of a suspect.

What are the strengths and weaknesses in your case? What else could you do (if anything) to make the case stronger? What other courses of action would you advise?

Summary information concerning AA's products and manufacturing process follow.

# SUMMARY OF AUDITING ALCHEMY'S MANUFACTURING PROCESS

As noted earlier in the case, AA produces and sells two varieties of spheres: green and gold. Both green and gold spheres have considerable value. A gold sphere requires nearly four times as much raw material as a green sphere and sells for approximately ten times the cost. Both green and gold spheres are portable.

The raw materials that are used to produce spheres have value in and of themselves, and the manufacturing inputs are closely monitored. All of the raw materials that go into the process result in the production of spheres, but not all of the spheres have commercial value. In addition to the green and gold spheres, the manufacturing process also results in the production of red spheres. Some red spheres must be produced in order to manufacture either green or gold spheres; however, they have no commercial value in and of themselves. As a result, the number of spheres—red, green, and gold—is reconciled with the raw material inputs for each production. The green and gold spheres are subsequently sent off to AA's warehouse. The red spheres, having no commercial value, are discarded after the run's reconciliation.

# 可持续发展
# Sustainability

# 索莱亚的可持续战略部署

*Jan Bell*
*Babson College*

*S. Sinan Erzurumlu*
*Babson College*

*Holly Fowler*
*Babson College M'10*

## 简介

这是发生在2010年的事,索莱亚公司正对可持续战略绩效衡量方法展开试点(见图表1),公司开发出一个基于网络的绩效仪表盘[1]供驻场经理(site manager)[2]和客户[3]代表使用。当时,索莱亚管理层认为这一新的仪表盘将成为公司实施可持续战略的一个关键手段。

玛丽亚·玻卡友(Maria Porcayo)索莱亚的湖畔医院会计部经理,她接待了两位检查该企业可持续发展情况的审计人员,希瑟(Heather)和瑞西(Rishi)。"很高兴见到你们,"玛丽亚先说道。"两位来此审计我们的可持续性,让我有点紧张。但若能获得你们的建议,告诉我们在提高客户绩效方面如何改进的话,紧张也是值得的。我的区域经理(district manager,简称DM)和我均支持索莱亚的可持续发展计划,并且对你们选择来我这儿探访感到激动。我们将在上午10点会见汤姆·苏利文(Tom Sullivan)。他是医院的副总裁,负责设施管理,是我的主要客户联络人。他会和我们待上一整天,并希望你们起草好报告后给他一份。"

---

\* 本篇译者为陈秀云,校订者为余辉、赵澄。

[1] 提到仪表盘,一般最先想到的是汽车仪表盘,即司机方向盘正前方位置安装了许多仪表的"盘",能够反映各方面情况(例如速度、用油情况、空调情况)。如果把运营企业比喻成开车,那么便可把综合反映企业绩效管理情况的程序或软件形象地称作绩效仪表盘(performance dashboard)。陈为民(2007)将绩效仪表盘定义为"一种建立在企业信息和数据整合架构上的多层次应用程序,它能使企业更加有效地进行绩效度量、监测、管理"。——译者

[2] 驻场服务是一种专业服务方式,常用于外包公司,这类公司派驻专业人员或团队长期在客户现场,向客户提供各种专业支持服务。本案例中索莱亚的驻场服务是指在客户单位建立运营点提供专业的餐饮或设备管理服务,驻场经理为该运营点的经理人员。——译者

[3] 请注意,文中的"客户"和"顾客"指代的是不同群体。"客户"一词在案例原文使用client表示,指索莱亚产品或服务的购买者。案例中索莱亚公司的服务对象有公司、教育机构和政府部门,也就是说索莱亚是为各类组织提供服务的,而这些组织又有自己的服务对象,文中称为"顾客",案例原文中以customer表示。——译者

**图表 1**
**可持续性仪表盘的开发**

2011年年底，索莱亚为驻场经理们推出了一项基于网络的仪表盘。仪表盘收集了运营点的市场、地理、规模和服务范围的相关信息。它包括的五类主要问题与"照亮未来"计划的各项承诺密切相关。

- 碳
- 水
- 废弃物
- 卫生与健康
- 社区

每一大类中都列出详细的问题和为达到目标而建议的行为。这一工具包括的问题超过450项，涵盖了所有主要类别。根据运营点收集的客户统计数据，对这些问题进行了加权处理；每个运营点对五项类别中的每一项会分别得到一个分数（满分为100）。

包括在碳这一大类中的一些问题，举例如下：

| 团队参与和行动 |
| --- |
| 你们为所有员工组织过关于能源保护的培训和月度例会吗？ |
| 你们是否就你们对能源保护的努力进行了交流并邀请顾客/客户参与呢？ |
| 你们设定能源节约目标了吗？ |
| 如果是的，你们是否宣传你们的目标、记录进展并公布结果呢？ |
| **照明** |
| 在所有的照明灯中，是否至少有95%是中央控制的，并且/或配有定时器或运动传感器？ |
| 你们是否用能源之星®的节能灯、LED灯（发光二极管）或极光灯（使用调光灯与调光开关）来替换白炽灯和卤素灯？ |
| 你们的运营点是否用T8或T5灯与电子镇流器替换了T12日光灯和电感镇流器呢（并尽量拆掉不需要的灯泡）？ |
| **空调通风系统（HVAC）** |
| 你们的运营点在排气罩上安装侧面板了吗？ |
| 你们的运营点是否对空调通风系统进行中央控制？ |
| 你们是否贴隔热膜来阻挡太阳的热能——使用高质量的薄膜和专业的安装工？*（注意：能源的投资回收需要的时间较久，但顾客的满意度是即时的。） |

资料来源：公司报告。

"玛丽亚，谢谢你到机场接我们并安排我们的到访。在电邮交流后，能最终见到你本人，实在是太好了。"希瑟应道。

玛丽亚继续说道，"我们希望在你们的报告中，我们的表现相当不错，也希望你们向汤姆提出宝贵的建议。他想知道医院现在有哪些可持续产品和服务。卫生和健康问题对他很重要，但也得考虑环境。最近，医院的一些员工成立了一个委员会，为减少湖畔医院的碳排放量出谋划策。"

瑞西插嘴道，"我希望你自愿加入了那个员工委员会。"

"是的，"玛丽亚回应道，"我是其中一员，但是我需要向委员会提出一些出色的新观点，所以我正指望着二位帮忙呢。我们的供应商给了我们一台机器用来回收泡沫,所以,至少我已经有了一些投入。"

"什么,回收泡沫?我不确定我相信那种可能性,"希瑟说,"所以我得去看看那台机器!但你们考虑到泡沫问题,这思路是对的。""谢谢你能加入到我们的试点中来,"她继续说,"但我可不想燃起你们的希望,期冀我们今天就能为你的客户提供新产品。我们是来取得你们营运点有关可持续性的基本指标数据。我们的方法是看看你们是否正在使用有利于环境的清洁用品,就如何改进我们的厨房和其他场所的绩效提供建议,并使你们意识到最佳实践的做法。我们关注营养与健康、回收、设备选择和水电使用等问题。我们要了解你们的可持续性指标的情况;并为接下来的步骤给出建议,对一段时间后的改进进行测评。"

瑞西补充辩护道,"我知道每个人都想销售产品和服务,但是现在我们正在努力开发和实施衡量可持续性的指标,并在公司内部培训可持续问题的专家。"

玛丽亚回应道,"你们知道我们参与了"好公民"行动的试点活动吗?你们今天会在湖畔医院看到人们用印有"好公民"字样的马克杯来喝饮料。令我失望的是,我们没有把"好公民"活动继续下去,因为从那时起我没有任何东西可以提供给汤姆,而他一直希望我们提供一些东西。现在医院的顾客都希望选用来自本地的产品;这似乎真的很流行。"④

希瑟反对说,"玛丽亚,你知道"本地"一词对你的顾客意味着什么吗?它意味着伊利诺伊州吗?还是提供食品的50或100英里范围之内呢?我这么问是因为对"本地"的含义并没有一个公认的标准。我们正与供应链管理及风险管理人员一起,来定义"本地"一词,并保证如果我们给某物贴上"本地"标签,我们能保证它确实来自本地。这意味着我们的经销商得建立起标准,来保证本地种植者所提供食物的来源、安全性和质量。"

"那会对食物价格产生怎样的影响?我们主要的供应商会参与吗?"玛丽亚问道。"如果我通过大型供应商进行采购,我的区域经理将获得一些折扣,这会增加他的毛利,所以他确实很关注我购货的事情,也和我谈了这个事。那些折扣影响他的盈亏,但对我没有影响。我的业绩以销售额的增加和从医院合同中获得的利润来评估。我要尽我所能让客户开心。但是,我不希望我的区域经理失去从主要供应商那里购买商品而获得的回报,因为我的绩效也是由他来评估的。"⑤

"我知道了,玛丽亚,我们能意识到各位驻场经理面临的挑战。你带我

---

④ 索莱亚驻湖畔医院的运营点希望为该医院这一客户提供持续服务,所以为医院员工准备了一种纪念品性质的礼物(马克杯),杯上印有"好公民(Good Citizen)"字样。该运营点把向自己购买商品的单位称为"好公民",因为索莱亚支持有利于环保的可持续行为。这样做是一项试点行动,公司希望因此而增加业务量。——译者

⑤ 如果区域经理从大公司采购,采购量大,就可以得到比较高的折扣,使他的区域绩效高,也因而提高了索莱亚的利润。与此同时,区域经理也可以得到较高的奖金或薪金。问题在于玛丽亚为之提供餐饮服务的湖畔医院需要新鲜的、本地产的食品,因而向规模大的供应商采购的数量就会减少,得不到从大量采购获得的折扣也会降低,索莱亚的利润会降低,区域经理的绩效评价可能会受到影响。因此,他会对玛丽亚不满,有可能在对玛丽亚进行绩效评估时给出较低的评价,玛丽亚对此感到不安。——译者

去看看你所说的回收泡沫塑料的机器,我们和汤姆会合,然后开始今天的工作,你说怎么样?我们保证会尽全力帮助你和你的客户,"瑞西回复道。

## 公司背景——索莱亚有限公司

  索莱亚有限公司,始自20世纪60年代后期西班牙的一家小型驻场餐饮服务公司。1975年,创立者卡尔·索乌坦(Carl Soltan)和内德·阿瑞尔(Ned Arrea)扩展了公司的业务范围,将设施管理服务纳入了经营范围,并同时展开一场富有闯劲的国际市场营销活动。在20年里,索莱亚在全球60个国家经营,拥有公司、教育机构和政府部门等30 000多个客户。

  自公司总部落户马德里,高级管理团队便重点关注战略、公众与投资者关系,以及对整个公司的经营进行总体监督。各个分部总裁(divisional President)、副总裁和区域经理(area/district manager)立足于他们各自的指定市场区域,对本区域的经营负责。公司将各分部进一步分为区域和运营点。⑥ 在各分部中,每一个市场(商业的、教育的和政府的)有一个副总裁负责资产收益率。区域经理和驻场经理分别对利润和预算的贡献毛益负责。各区域的职能经理服务于区域层次,为各个市场的经理提供支持,他们既向分部总裁汇报工作,又向马德里总部负责该职能的副总裁汇报工作。这种组织方式构成了一种矩阵结构(见图表2)。决策制定的权力是分散化的,仅受战略计划的宽泛引导。

### 供应管理团队

  索莱亚有3 500多个供应商为其分散在不同区域的客户提供所需产品,所以供应管理团队(Supply Management Group,简称SMG)是公司成功的一项关键要素。SMG管理顾客的采购订单,并使用经销商网络为顾客安排送货。索莱亚的货物大多购自主要经销商,但也会向区域供应商购买。SMG还负责开发和维持与供应商稳定的长期关系,以保证所购产品的质量和数量。

  SMG以两种主要的方式为索莱亚的盈利做出贡献。首先,该团队通过汇聚世界各地客户的订单向供应商申请折扣。这些供应商的折扣直接增加索莱亚的毛利,在一些区域每年增加的毛利润高达20%。这一部分毛利再根据各区域经理从公司的主要供应商那里购买货物的数量,分配到各个区域,增加区域经理的毛利润。第二,SMG通过向客户展示,特定产品能降低成本和/或能给客户带来驻场销售收入(比如塑料杯、瓶装水),以此鼓励客户购买这些产品。这两点对提高客户的满意度和维系客户都产生了积极的影响。结果,SMG在索莱亚经营的方法上起了重要作用。

---

  ⑥ 按前所述,可推测索莱亚公司的业务结构大致是这样的:公司设在马德里的总公司(headquarter)→设在某一国家或地区的分部(division,如案例中的北美分部)→分部内的运营区域(area/district,如案例中的伊利诺斯州)→该区域所包括的驻场运营点(site,案例中玛丽亚就是一位驻场经理)。——译者

**图表 2**
**索莱亚的组织结构图**

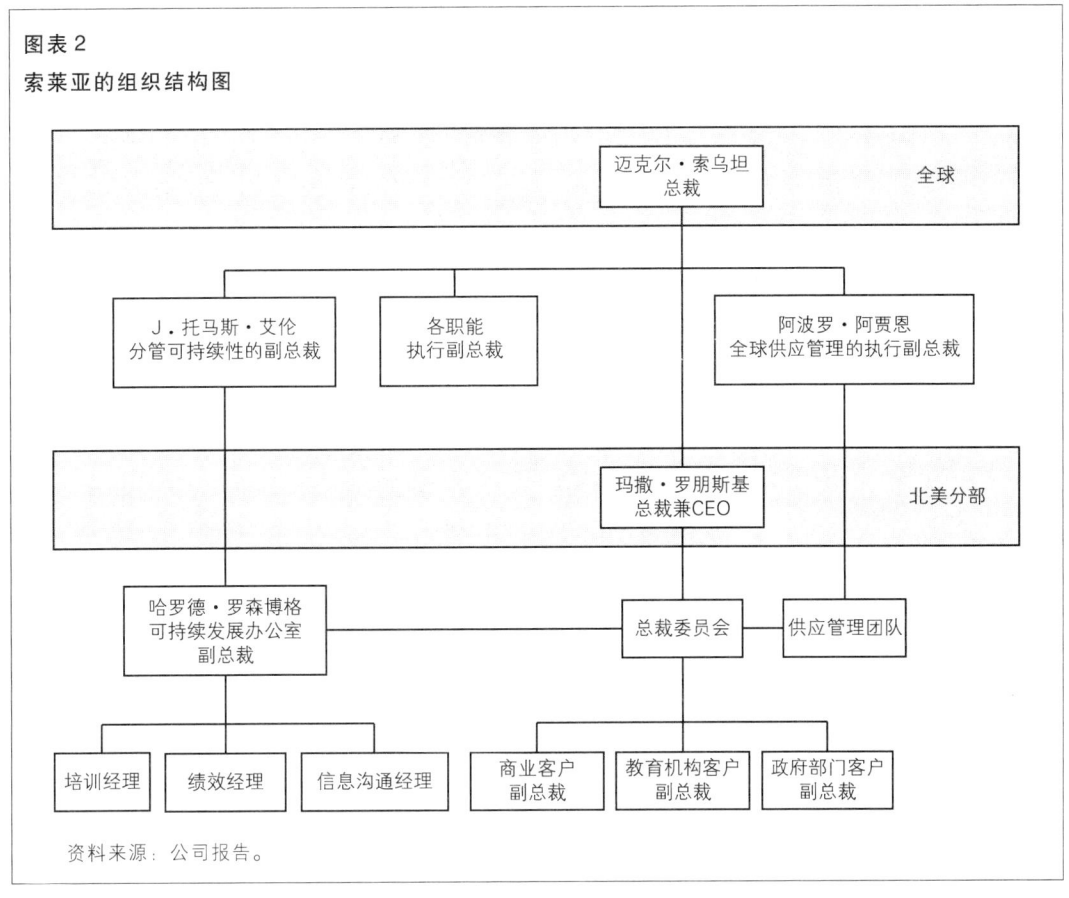

资料来源：公司报告。

一个供应管理的经理团队担当了 SMG 和驻场经理的联络人。通过常规的商业电话，这些经理让驻场经理了解认可的供应商和受青睐的产品，以便从采购中获得更多的供应商折扣，让其客户享受较低的价格。这些管理人员被视为"供应链管理"商业模式的推进者。

在北美分部，SMG 根据索莱亚的五步战略性供应链流程开发了一个采购流程。

第 1 步——形成分类大纲

第 2 步——建立分类采购战略

第 3 步——建立价值主张[7]

第 4 步——完成合同

第 5 步——实施和执行

SMG 从它的区域合同供应商那里直接得到采购历史记录，而其主要经销商会向它提供总的索莱亚采购量［以库存量单位（SKU）[8] 表示］的报

---

[7] 价值主张（value proposition），即公司通过其产品和服务所能向消费者提供的价值。——译者根据《有道词典》

[8] 库存量单位（stock keeping unit，简称 SKU），即库存进出计量的单位，可以是以件、盒、托盘等为单位。SKU 是对于大型配送中心物流管理的一个必要的方法。现在已经被我们引申为产品统一编号的简称，每种产品均对应有唯一的 SKU 号。（引自百度百科）——译者

告。通过了解客户的汇总采购量，负责北美供应的管理层能够就竞争性的定价、严格的食品安全项目、赔偿和保险项目以及支持和数据管理，与供应商进行谈判。

SMG经常在市场上寻找那些价格优惠的供应商。通过资格预审的潜在供应商，SMG会依据众多的因素对其进行评估，这些因素包括革新、服务范围、商品的供应、满足需求的能力、价格、服务水平以及满足索莱亚质量保证要求的能力。所有选定的供应商需要签订一个供应商行为规范（见图表3）。索莱亚的程序要求，食品供应商定期接受一家专业的第三方公司的检查。这些检查确保：

- 制造设备能够生产安全、优质的产品。
- 产品的生产遵循常规的要求和规格。
- 应用了有效的控制措施来确保稳定的性能。
- 管理层致力于食品安全和高品质。

---

**图表3**
**索莱亚的供应商行为规范**

**卫生与安全指南**
供应商必须一同履行索莱亚的承诺，提供一个安全、卫生的工作场所，公平对待员工并遵守本地法律。

**环境指南**
索莱亚将主动寻觅与我们同样承诺保护环境的供应商。供应商应遵守联邦、州和地方所有的环境法律。

**劳动力**
索莱亚将不容许其供应商使用契约劳工*、奴隶、债役劳工或其他强迫的非自愿劳工。索莱亚的供应商不得雇佣所在国家或区域的法定雇佣年龄以下的工人。索莱亚将优先选择其劳动力反映出客户和顾客多样性的供应商。

**工资和工时**
供应商支付的工资不得低于法律规定的最低工资，也不得低于普遍的市场价。供应商应按照本地准则或所在国家和区域适用的法律维持合理的员工工时。

**社区参与**
索莱亚追求与供应商一起成为地政府和社区的伙伴，来改进其所在社区与服务社区的教育、文化和社会福利。

**道德标准**
索莱亚力求识别那些开展业务时使用的道德标准与我们自身一致的供应商。索莱亚的道德标准详细公布在我们的网站上。

**传达**
供应商应采取合适的步骤来确保将这一准则传达给其员工，并将其贯穿在他们自己的供应链中。

资料来源：公司报告

---

\* 契约劳工（indentured labor），是一种近似奴隶的工人。在美国初立国时，美国人到英国去为因欠债而受拘留的犯人赎身，成为契约工。这些契约工需在美国劳苦工作多年，只供膳宿，不给工资。这是违反美国宪法的，因而从1787年起成为非法。——译者

## 对于可持续战略

进入21世纪初期,公司对环境和社会可持续发展的活动的兴趣增加,索莱亚收到大量对可持续性实践信息的要求。作为回应,索莱亚将可持续问题委派给执行副总裁 J. 托马斯·艾伦(J. Thomas Allen)。在他的带领下,公司于2004年发布了首个公司的社会责任报告。在这份报告中,索莱亚就可持续的、盈利的绩效做出公开承诺,管理层将该承诺定义为"对我们经营涉及的环境、客户的健康、客户的顾客以及全球社会,我们要采取保护和修复环境的方式来运营。"在此报告的最后,索莱亚宣布其目标为,在提高盈利性的同时将新的可持续进程融入日常经营决策中。

北美分部成为索莱亚可持续承诺的试点。在公司2004年的社会责任报告发布之后,艾伦立即组织了一个特别小组来开发称作"好公民"的产品线,以此来回应顾客对可持续性产品迅速增长的需要。索莱亚的区域和驻场经理们对"好市民"感到兴奋,但是分部总裁很快意识到那些产品设计不佳,在向客户高度吹捧一番之后,很快地取消了那条产品线。以此为鉴,艾伦在索莱亚的北美分部建立起可持续发展办公室(Office of Sustainability,简称OS)。他雇佣可持续发展专家哈罗德·罗森博格(Harold Rothenberg)担任这一新办公室的领导。罗森博格第一年要和艾伦以及索莱亚北美总裁委员会的下属委员会一起工作,为北美分部设计战略。

罗森博格通过一年的计划设计出一个雄心勃勃的战略:索莱亚北美分部不能仅向那些感兴趣并愿意额外支付高价的客户提供具有可持续性的产品,更应通过提供有关可持续问题的专家建议,和整个市场共享各项创新,使可持续变为正常服务的组成部分;衡量客户的绩效改进;积极地与各个区域的利益相关者团体、非政府组织(NGO)和贸易联盟合作,优先考虑他们的各项持续性问题。罗森博格告诉利益相关者群体,"我们希望通过提供以可持续性为导向的各项实践和服务,增强与客户的关系,因为他们可看到选用可持续性的做法能带来积极的成长。他们的成功就是我们的成功。"

通过向客户提出新的做法、服务和更多的食品选择,索莱亚北美分部期望使它的客户更加成功——尤其希望他们能够更好地预测和回应其顾客的需求。通过这些行动和利益相关者、非政府组织以及贸易联盟的参与,公司最终将被公认为行业中关于可持续发展知识和实践的领军者。这将让索莱亚的品牌效应增强,管理层更加理性,顾客维系能力提高,新业务的竞价效益更高,差异化的产品和服务在市场中产生的毛利更高。

## 将可持续发展融入日常经营

将可持续发展融入索莱亚的日常经营需要实质性的改变。公司将开发出一个有关可持续发展的仪表盘来反映各项期望的实现情况、指导经营决策并提供可持续绩效的考核。为了对成功实施可持续战略提供必要的结构,罗森博格设立了三个经理级的职位来负责培训、绩效和沟通。这三个部门高度融合，与经理定期会面讨论进展，并寻求合作的新方式。

**培训经理**：关注于开发最佳实践；培训各项问题的专家；创作教育材料；主办一些活动和项目，让员工学习和分享索莱亚各个市场的最佳实践。

**绩效经理**：与公司总部和北美分部总裁委员会一起工作，北美分部为经营建立了时间目标和绩效指标。该部门还负责开发和实施驻场经理使用的绩效仪表盘。

**信息沟通经理**：与利益相关者建立内、外部合作关系；寻求利益相关者对可持续承诺、目标和优先权的认可；沟通所倡议的行动与行动的结果。

### 考核进展

2004年，罗森博格及其团队在公司创建了一种基于网络的互联网可持续管理数据库（InternetSustainability Managementdatabase，简称ISM）。索莱亚各区域的关键人员可获得这一在线工具的访问权。到2010年年底时，该数据库共记录了将近1 000例"最佳实践"。仅北美分部就有超过100项行动在列，它们是由35人分别提出的。

然而，也不全都是好消息。多数行动所包括的细节不充分，无法证明该项实践的实效，或无法供其他人仿效该实践；同时，公司对输入系统的内容进行过滤和验证的能力不足。然而，在2010年公司社会责任报告书中，这些计划的回应被列作索莱亚取得进展的证据。这令北美可持续发展办公室的一些经理们感到不满，他们支持对ISM进行修正，要求输入的数据得到更严格的控制。"我们不符合透明报告的标准——我想我们还没有抓住足够的细节，"一位可持续发展办公室的经理如是说。

罗森博格承认ISM的局限性，因而加速了对可持续仪表盘的开发。新仪表盘的开发考虑到了三项目标：有助于向区域和驻场经理报告本地行动和关键的绩效指标；分享最佳实践和鼓励内部的评价标准；加强与内、外部利益相关者的沟通。

2011年中期，新仪表盘向100个运营点发布，仪表盘的界面让驻场经理和客户能有效追踪该运营点在可持续承诺方面所取得的进展。新的仪表盘包括五个受关注的方面：碳、水、废弃物、卫生与健康，以及社区。通过运营点的客户统计信息和驻场经理的反馈来分析运营点的产品与实践，该仪表盘可以显示出每一个受关注的领域应如何改进来达到"最佳实践"。

罗森博格与其可持续发展办公室团队还开发了一项仪表盘功能，使仪表盘能对输入的信息进行筛选，找出领先的运营点。一旦一个运营点被识别为领先的运营点，可持续发展办公室的代表将核实并验证该运营点的实践，将其作为范例供其他运营点学习效仿。同时，内部分析人员将检查可持续实践如何影响运营点的毛利，如果必要，会提出建议对其进行改进。

### "照亮未来计划"

2009年，艾伦公开宣布了索莱亚的"照亮未来计划"，这样一组计划由索莱亚必须遵守的10项可持续承诺构成（见图表4）。每一项承诺包括完成的时间目标、相关的指标，以及支持这些目标的公司政策和程序。

---

**图表4**
**索莱亚的可持续承诺（"照亮未来计划"）**

1. 我们将采购本地、应季或可持续种植与培养的产品。
2. 我们将增加可回收和可重复利用物品的采购量。
3. 我们将增加公平贸易认证产品的采购量。
4. 我们将提供可循环再生的鱼类及其他海产品。
5. 我们将采购并倡导利用高能效的设备。
6. 我们将减少产生的废物量并将油炸油*100%处理掉。
7. 我们将在全部的运营点和客户场地减少碳排放和水资源的流失。
8. 我们将增加能够促进员工、客户和顾客健康的产品和项目。
9. 我们将支持本地社区的项目，雇佣和培训本地的劳动力。
10. 我们将保证遵守"供应商行为准则"。

资料来源：公司报告

\* 油炸油（fryer oil），即已用来炸过食物的油，美国有专门向餐馆收集这些油，并加工成工业用的石油制品的企业。——译者

---

"照亮未来计划"应该使供应管理与可持续战略相一致。由于市场的需求和主动出击的管理者们的努力，在不同区域已有部分产品种类达到了部分可持续承诺。比如，西欧分部的鱼与海产品类的经理和供应者们致力于可持续的工作已经多年，他们刚好在发布"照亮未来计划"的数月前，从国际海洋理事会（Marine Stewardship Council，简称MSC）那里取得来之不易的可持续认证。

在某些领域，供应管理人员能迅速地接纳"照亮未来计划"。尤其是在休闲场所、美术馆、动物园和水族市场，这些地方的潜在客户通常要求竞标的供应者们提供可持续的产品和服务，管理者们把该承诺作为一种对策，使客户们相信索莱亚对待可持续问题的态度是认真的。"当我们能够向客户展示我们为完成'照亮未来计划'而采取的行动时，"一位休闲市场的供应经理说，"我们正向他们展示我们所走的可持续道路。我们认为客户想要某种具体的证据。"

## 持续的挑战

可持续战略遇到了来自一些领域的内部阻力，包括在"照亮未来计划"和"2016进取计划"之间察觉到的利益冲突，后者是一项独立的公司行动，旨在大幅地增加利润。同时，一些经理们感到了来自"照亮未来计划"的威胁，因为公司的绩效评估和激励系统（见图表5）主要以利润为基础，从而与完成公司的其他行动相悖。

> **图表 5**
> **绩效管理与激励系统**
>
> 索莱亚有一个复杂的绩效管理系统供在客户那里的驻场经理人员和所有员工使用。该系统需要员工和他/她的管理者共同来复审适用于评估员工绩效的目标与行为的标准。在复审了这些标准之后，员工按照索莱亚的标准对自己的绩效进行自我评估，同时经理对其员工进行评估，员工签字接受经理的意见，然后由员工提出改进工作的计划。
>
> 在索莱亚的管理绩效系统中的项目，每个项目的绩效评估结果用为 1~5 分来表示，评估结果来自绩效的财务目标与价值行为两方面得分的平均数，其权重分别为 60% 和 40%。
>
> 为了说明该系统，以下是驻场经理对于商业客户有关财务目标和价值行为的评估标准。
>
> **财务目标（权重 60%）**
> 1. 实现预算毛利
> 2. 销售收入增加
> 3. 建立一个团队
> 4. 配套销售服务/产品
> 5. 检查食品安全/人身安全
> 6. 实施部门计划（支持员工认可的项目和对顾客满意度的调查）
>
> **价值行为（权重 40%）**
> 1. 服务于客户与顾客（主动了解客户需求，建立融洽的关系，展现专业的行为）
> 2. 驱动力与可靠性（热心、热情、激情和正直）
> 3. 建立多样化的团队（增加多样性和包容性）
> 4. 人际关系（与客户、监督者、员工、经理以及供应商一起，建立并维持专业、信任、积极的工作关系。）
> 5. 管理和激发员工的绩效（通过提供有用的反馈、认可和奖励成就，激发员工达到超乎预期的绩效。）
> 6. 管理单位财务（理解财务数据，识别影响财务绩效的关键因素，使预算、绩效与战略相符合。）
> 7. 确保质量管理（实施，监督，管理质量经营程序。）
>
> 根据绩效评估的结果，经理人员的奖金可高达全年工资的 20%。但整个北美分部必须完成预算利润的 95%，该分部的人员才能获得奖金。
>
> 资料来源：公司文件节选。
>
> ＊交叉销售（Cross Selling），就是发现现有客户的多种需求，并通过满足其需求而实现销售多种相关的服务或产品的营销方式。（参考自百度百科。）——译者

## "2016 进取计划"

2008 年，公司与一组外部咨询人员签订协约，以寻求改善北美分部财务绩效的机会。结果，"2016 进取计划"提出到 2016 年时销售收入要翻番，营业利润要达到原来的三倍。该计划由一个任务小组来负责，其成员大多来自供应管理团队。

"2016 进取计划"的一项主要战略是关注供应链的效率，这项战略得到了可持续发展办公室和供应管理团队的共同关注，因为它对供应链三个方面有直接影响，即运送频率、库存合理化和供应商选择。

对供应管理人员来说，运送频率的效率有可能通过运送量和订单频率的最优化而提高。这么做减少了物流成本和途中的运送卡车的数量。这与可持续发展办公室建议的可持续运输行动相一致，该办公室建议供应管理团队检查自己的订单模式，引进最小订单量的概念以防止"量小而频繁的"运送模式。降低运送频率即推进了可持续发展，又降低了成本，同时还能满足"照亮未来计划"和"2016 进取计划"的要求。

其他影响供应链、库存（SKU）合理化和供应商选择的因素似乎都能获得供应管理团队的认可，但却给可持续发展办公室造成了问题。库存合理化有利于提高绩效，比如通过改进稳定性而提高质量，通过增加批量买进的机会而降低成本。供应商选择有利于通过主要的分销渠道来（汇总）采购（量），从而最大限度地获得数量折扣。然而，尽管这些因素可以减少多达20%的采购成本，但它们却与索莱亚"照亮未来计划"的承诺相冲突。

目前，湖畔医院使用的泡沫塑料似乎在库存合理化和可持续绩效之间呈现出一种矛盾。供应经理用泡沫塑料盘子替换了可回收的纸盘和杯子，因为公司的主要供应商能以非常优惠的价格提供泡沫塑料盘子，这直接影响运营点的盈利性。当运营点的可持续发展委员会提出反对时，供应经理便要求供应商安装泡沫塑料压实设备。这一设备贴有"泡沫塑料回收"的标签，并放置于餐饮设施的明显位置供顾客使用。然而，这些被压实的泡沫数量并没有被回收，而是和常规垃圾一起被拉走；因为库存合理化带来的短期收益，超过了"照亮未来计划"正试图创造的长期盈利。

"照亮未来计划"提倡像采购本地产品这样的活动，而这会减少供应商的折扣。虽然这些活动降低了短期利润，但它通过提高顾客的忠诚度和吸引新业务的能力，会对索莱亚的品牌带来长期的提升。正如罗森博格曾害怕的，各种类别的供应管理人员对这些建议抱有敌对的态度，并为这些活动贴上了给索莱亚的盈利性带来"经济上不负责任和危险的"威胁的标签。

罗森博格还认为供应商折扣将对供应管理团队的评估和区域经理的绩效产生影响。具体来说，所产生的供应商折扣也是评估供应管理团队的部分标准，因为区域经理可根据采购比例获得供应商折扣，并直接增加到他们的毛利中。因为对区域经理的评估是以利润为基础，则获得的供应商折扣更多，评估结果更好。高层管理者认为，供应管理团队中的大多数人和区域经理们，将会继续反对"照亮未来计划"，除非评估系统有显著的改变。

### 客户关系

复杂的客户关系使得将可持续融入索莱亚的经营实践成为一件难事。即使有可选的可持续性方案，也无法确定客户是否参与和遵守。这对索莱亚食品经营的影响尤甚，而食品是索莱亚传统的收入来源项目。[9] 客户们希望、甚至会要求索莱亚提供可持续方案，但通常不愿意支付额外的预付费用，即便这会令他们获得更多的长期利润，他们依然期望由索莱亚来承担可持续的成本。另外，索莱亚自身通常也不愿意投资于可持续性实践。

索莱亚经理们面临的另一固有的难题是确保客户能贯彻实施。比如，最

---

⑨ 本句话的英文原文为"This particularly affected Solea's food operations, which was also a traditional revenue source for Solea's clients."根据上下文，译者猜测是原作者表述有误，食品应是索莱亚的传统收入来源。因为索莱亚的客户包括企业、教育机构和政府部门，这些组织的传统收入来源项目不会是餐饮；而索莱亚最初是经营餐饮服务的，后又增加了设施管理服务。——译者

近一个客户和索莱亚签订合同,要求使用可降解的盘子和餐具,这满足了该客户的顾客对可持续产品的要求。然而,这样的盘子在使用后,却被简单地扔进了垃圾箱,因为客户不想做额外的工作,也不愿意付出堆制肥料的成本。

在索莱亚继续努力去适应自己提出的要求时,很多客户的行动却只求对自己有利,并要求索莱亚自己承担费用去满足那些标准。如果成千上万的客户期望索莱亚遵循他们特定的可持续性指导方针,索莱亚将面临令人不快的选择:要么满足客户的指导方针并承担额外费用,要么因拒绝遵守指导方针而令客户不满。客户的个体行动也限制了索莱亚就可持续性问题向客户提供有关专家建议的能力,而这是战略计划的一部分。

**其他挑战**

成本管理显然是向可持续的管理提出了一项挑战,因为可持续项目的采购价格可能比非可持续项目更高。值得注意的是,可持续发展办公室手头并没有索莱亚特定采购项目的生命周期(即从购买到废弃整个周期,译者)的成本数据,因此要分析可持续性的经济意义就更难了。"我们确实发现一种方法,能够更好地获得成本数据,"一位区域经理补充道,"这不仅对我们自己的可持续性观点很重要,而且对我们向客户和供应商交流这一信息的能力也很重要。"

索莱亚的顾客关系管理系统没有把可持续性作为投标输赢的一个理由。然而一些征询方案要求公司在投标时展示最低水平的可持续性绩效,可持续发展办公室曾被告知,过去就发生过因为索莱亚没有可持续产品而失去客户的事情。

风险消减[10]是管理层要面对的另一潜在的问题,特别是涉及本地食品采购时。索莱亚的很多客户希望得到产自本地的货物,因为他们自己的顾客有这样的需求。但是,索莱亚并没有规定允许运营点直接从供应商处采购。相反,公司的战略是依赖于区域经销商在既定区域采购可持续的产品。因缺乏相应的规定,供应管理团队把采购产自本地货物的活动视为高风险的领域。

挑战也存在于政府部门,这是索莱亚的主要市场之一。根据联邦法律,索莱亚需要与政府客户分享供应商折扣,因为政府客户也对折扣作出了贡献。可以料想,其他市场的客户也对折扣问题变得更加老练,在努力争取和索莱亚共享供应商折扣。面对严峻的竞争和不景气的经济,索莱亚开始迁就这些客户,因为与客户续签合同的时间已近。负责可持续的经理相信,提供给政府和其他客户的折扣可能最终扩展到整个市场,从而会破坏索莱亚的定价策略并威胁到其商业模式。

萎靡不振的经济进一步加剧了"照亮未来计划"原本就已面临的挑战。"照亮未来计划"原本是在强劲的、而非衰退的经济基础上提出来的。索莱

---

[10] 风险消减(Risk mitigation),是风险管理过程的第二个阶段,牵涉到确定风险消减策略、风险和安全控制措施的优先级选定、制定安全计划并实施控制措施等活动。(引自《下一代网络安全》)——译者

亚的一些经理建议，在经济复苏之前修改甚至放弃承诺。有一份电子往来邮件径直发送给了艾伦和他供应管理团队搭档，邮件中批评了可持续办公室在当前的经济环境下推进那些对财务不负责任的可持续发展"最佳实践"是危险的。对于罗森博格和可持续发展办公室经理来说，建立并鼓励最佳实践的尝试通常遭到供应管理人员的抵制。供应管理团队反对可持续办公室的观点导致很多供应管理人员反对可持续行动，从而阻碍了组织的变革。罗森博格向艾伦抱怨说，他发现长期盈利性被放置于短期盈利之后，这会损害到公司的发展。罗森博格在写给艾伦的一封电邮中建议说，"在当前问题下，重新思考战略或许是最好的。我们将与可持续发展办公室的经理们会晤，来讨论其他备选方案。"

## 权衡可持续性与公司利益

艾伦和罗森博格认为，为了保证可持续性成为索莱亚的一贯做法，需要对可持续的行动做出进一步的改变。在他们看来，通过财务分析支持最佳实践是必要的。另外，需要将可持续绩效与正式的绩效评估和激励系统联系起来，不是只在仪表盘上进行追踪。

财务部门一些感兴趣的员工自愿贡献时间来收集和分析可持续实践的有关数据，诸如一次性餐具与可重复使用的瓷器餐具的对比。但是这一工作预计进展缓慢，因为对比需要差异分析，单单对从信息系统获得的常规成本数据进行分析是不够的。可持续发展办公室的近期战略是直接与各个市场（例如，公司、健康护理、教育）一起工作，以取消目前系统中的那些不太恰当的激励，并与公司一起，将可持续性正式纳入绩效系统。

公司希望得出一些结果，因此来自公司的压力明显越来越大。在2011年7月的电邮中，艾伦告诉罗森博格"高层领导希望给媒体一些材料，证明我们正在兑现我们的承诺。我们已经发布有关供应类别和仪表盘的新闻稿，表示在供应类别方面已实施了"照亮未来计划"。现在的确是公布新的进展报告的时候了，我们应该宣布一些显著的胜利。"

艾伦意识到，如果没有证据表明可持续实践可提高盈利性，大多数供应管理人员将继续拒绝执行"照亮未来计划"。该团队还将抵制与可持续实践纳入绩效评估系统有关的任何行动，除非有相同的证据说服他们来实施"照亮未来计划"。"除非我们得到财务分析数据来支持我们的声明，证明可持续能够促进盈利性，"艾伦告诉罗森博格和各位可持续发展办公室的经理，"不然，我们无法在我们的工作中取得进展，将可持续性融入日常的经营。"

# Deploying Sustainability at Solea

*Jan Bell*
*Babson College*

*S. Sinan Erzurumlu*
*Babson College*

*Holly Fowler*
*Babson College M'10*

## INTRODUCTION

The following transpired in 2010 during a pilot of Solea's sustainability performance measurement tool (see Exhibit 1), which was being developed into a web-based performance dashboard for site managers and client representatives. At the time, Solea management believed the new dashboard would be a critical component to the implementation of the company's sustainability strategy.

Maria Porcayo, manager of Solea's Lakeshore Hospital account, greeted the two visiting sustainability auditors, Heather and Rishi. "It's good to meet you," Maria began. "I'm a little nervous that you guys are here to audit our sustainability, but it'll be worth it if we get some suggestions about how we can contribute to our client's performance. My district manager (DM) and I support Solea's sustainability initiative and are excited that you've picked my site to visit. We'll be meeting with Tom Sullivan at 10 a.m. He is the hospital's vice president for facilities management and my main client liaison. He'll spend the day with us and wants a copy of your report when you draft it."

"Thanks, Maria, for picking us up at the airport and arranging our visit. It's great to finally meet you in person after our email conversations," Heather replied.

Maria continued, "We hope we'll look pretty good in your report, and that you'll make suggestions that Tom will find valuable. He wants to know what sustainability products and services exist for hospitals. Health and wellness issues are important to him, but the environment is also a concern. Some of the hospital staff recently set up a committee to develop ways to reduce Lakeshore's

> **Exhibit 1**
>
> **Development of the Sustainability Dashboard**
>
> Solea launched a web-based dashboard for site managers in late 2011. The dashboard collected information about the market, location, size, and scope of services at the site. It included questions on five major categories tied to commitments in the Bright Future plan.
>
> - Carbon
> - Water
> - Waste
> - Health and wellness
> - Community
>
> Each major category contained detailed questions that communicated suggested behaviors. The tool contained over 450 questions spread across the major categories. These questions were weighted based on the demographic data collected on the site; each site got a score out of 100 on each of the five categories.
>
> As an example, the following were some of the questions included in the carbon category:
>
> | |
> |---|
> | TEAM ENGAGEMENT AND BEHAVIORS |
> | Do you have organized training and monthly meetings for all of your workers about energy conservation? |
> | Do you communicate your energy conservation efforts and ask for participation from your customers/clients? |
> | Have you established energy savings goals? |
> | If yes, do you advertise your goals, chart progress, and post results? |
> | LIGHTING |
> | Are at least 95% of all the lights centrally controlled and/or equipped with timers or motion sensors? |
> | Have you replaced incandescent and halogen lamps with ENERGY STAR® compact fluorescent lamps, LEDs, or induction lighting (use dimmable lamps with dimming switches)? |
> | Has your site replaced T12 fluorescent lamps and magnetic ballasts with T8 or T5 lamps and electronic ballasts (de-lamp where possible)? |
> | HVAC |
> | Has your site installed side panels on exhaust hoods? |
> | Does your site have centralized controllers for the HVAC system? |
> | Have you installed window film to block sun-generated heat—use high quality film and professional installer?* (Note: Energy payback is longer, however customer satisfaction is immediate.) |
>
> Source: Company reports.

carbon footprint."

Rishi interjected, "I hope you volunteered to be on that staff committee."

"Yes," Maria replied, "I'm on it, but I need some cool new ideas to offer, so I'm counting on you guys. Our supplier gave us a machine that recycles foam, so at least I've had that input."

"Recycling foam, huh? Not sure I believe that's possible," Heather said, "so I have to see that machine! But you're on the right track to be concerned with foam." Thanks for agreeing to participate in our pilot test," she continued, "but I don't want to get your hopes up about new products that we can offer your client today. We're here to get baseline metrics on your site's sustainability. Our approach is to see if you are using environmentally friendly cleaning products, to make suggestions about how to improve performance in the kitchen and other spaces we operate, and to make you aware of best practices. We focus on things like nutrition and wellness, recycling, equipment selection, and the use of water and utilities. We get a read on where you are on sustainability metrics; make suggestions for next steps, and over time measure improvement."

Rishi added, a little defensively, "I know everyone wants products and services to sell, but right now we're working hard to develop and implement this measurement tool and train internal sustainability experts."

Maria replied, "Did you know that we participated in the pilot of the Good Citizen offer? You're going to see people today refilling their Good Citizen mugs. I'm personally disappointed that we discontinued Good Citizen, because I haven't had anything to offer Tom since then and he's been asking for something. Right now the hospital's customers want the option of locally sourced products; that seems to be really popular."

Heather countered, "Maria, do you know what local means to your customers? Does it mean the state of Illinois or within 50 or 100 miles of where the food is served? I ask because there isn't a shared standard for what local means. We're working with the folks from supply management and risk management to define local and to assure that if we label it local, we know that it is local. That means that our distributors have to develop standards so they can guarantee food source, safety, and quality from local growers."

"What's that going to do to food prices? Are our prime vendors going to participate?" asked Maria. "My district manager gets discounts that increase his gross margin if I purchase through large vendors, so he really watches my purchases and talks to me about it. Those discounts impact his bottom line but not mine. I'm evaluated on increasing sales and on the profit made on the hospital contract. I've got to do what it takes to keep my client happy. But, I don't want my DM to lose out on the rewards from purchasing from prime vendors, because he evaluates me, too."

"I hear you, Maria, and we're aware of the challenges that site managers face. What do you say you show me the machine that allegedly recycles foam and we meet up with Tom and get this day started? We promise to help you with your client the best we can," replied Rishi.

# COMPANY BACKGROUND—SOLEA, INC.

Solea, Inc., originated as a small on-site food services company in Spain in the late 1960s. In 1975, its founders, Carl Soltan and Ned Arrea, expanded the company's scope to include facilities management services and simultaneously initiated an aggressive international marketing campaign. Within two decades, Solea was operating in 60 countries, with over 30 000 corporate, education, and government clients.

From its corporate headquarters based in Madrid, the senior executive team focused primarily on strategy and public and investor relations while providing general oversight of all company operations. Divisional presidents, vice presidents, and area managers responsible for regional operations were based in their assigned market regions, which were further divided into districts and sites. Within divisions, each market (commercial, education, and government) had a vice president responsible for return on assets. District and site managers were responsible for profits and budgeted contribution, respectively. Functional area managers served at the division level. They supported managers across all markets and reported to both the division president and the appropriate functional executive vice president at headquarters in Madrid. This approach constituted a matrix structure (see Exhibit 2). Decision making, loosely guided by strategic plans, was decentralized.

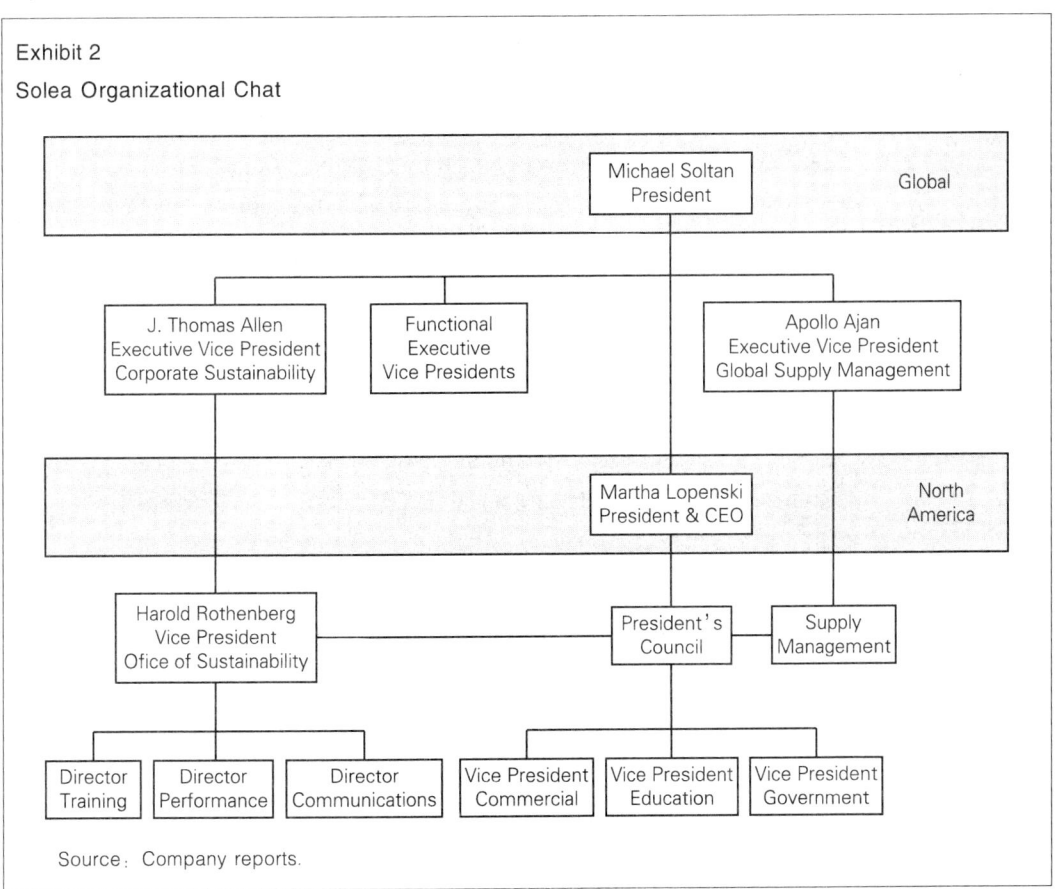

Exhibit 2
Solea Organizational Chat

Source: Company reports.

## SUPPLY MANAGEMENT GROUP

Solea's geographically diverse clients required products from more than 3 500 suppliers, so the Supply Management Group (SMG) was a key factor for success. SMG managed customers' purchase orders and arranged delivery to customer sites using a network of distributors. Solea used major distributors for most of its purchases, but also relied on regional suppliers. The group was also responsible for developing and maintaining reliable long-term relationships with suppliers to guarantee quality and availability of products.

SMG contributed to Solea's profitability in two major ways. First, the group arranged vendor discounts by aggregating orders from worldwide clients. These vendor discounts were added directly to Solea's gross margin, with an increase of as much as 20% annually in some regions. This profit was added to each district manager's gross margin based on how much the respective site managers had purchased from the company's major vendors. Second, SMG encouraged the purchase of specific products (e.g., foam cups, bottled water) by demonstrating to clients that these products reduced costs and/or led to client site sales revenue. Taken together, these actions had a positive influence on both client satisfaction and retention. And as a result, SMG had a significant role in the Solea's approach to doing business.

A team of supply management managers acted as liaisons between the SMG and site managers. Through regular business calls, these managers made site managers aware of approved vendors and favored products so that purchases would yield large vendor allowances and low prices to their clients. These managers were considered "promoters" of Supply Management's business model.

Within North America, SMG developed a procurement process based on Solea's five-step strategic sourcing process:

Step 1 – Outline the category

Step 2 – Develop category sourcing strategy

Step 3 – Create the value proposition

Step 4 – Finalize contract

Step 5 – Implement and execute

SMG received a purchasing history directly from its regionally contracted suppliers, while its major distributors provided reports that aggregated Solea's purchase volume by SKU level. By having knowledge of its aggregate volume across clients, Supply Management North America was able to negotiate competitive pricing, stringent food safety programs, indemnity and insurance programs, and support and data management.

SMG routinely scanned the market for vendors that might be willing to provide favorable pricing. After pre-qualifying potential suppliers, SMG evaluated bids based on numerous factors, including innovation; scope of services; availability of product; ability to meet demand; price; service level; and ability to meet Solea's quality assurance requirements. All selected suppliers were required to sign a Supplier Code of Conduct (see Exhibit 3). Solea's procedures obliged food vendors to be regularly inspected by a professional third-party firm. These inspections ensured that:

- Manufacturing facilities were able to produce safe, high-quality products.
- Product manufacturing followed regulatory requirements and specifications.
- Effective control measures were applied for consistent performance.
- Management was dedicated to food safety and high quality.

---

Exhibit 3

Solea's Supplier Code of Conduct

HEALTH AND SAFETY GUIDELINES
Suppliers must share Solea's commitment to providing a safe and healthy workplace and to treating employees fairly and in compliance with local laws.

ENVIRONMENTAL GUIDELINES
Solea will actively seek suppliers that share our commitment to protecting the environment. Suppliers shall abide by all federal, state, and local environmental laws.

LABOR FORCE
Solea shall not tolerate the use of indentured, slave, bonded, or other forced involuntary labor by its suppliers. Suppliers are prohibited from using workers under the legal age of employment in any country or local jurisdiction where the supplier performs work for Solea. Solea will give preference to suppliers whose workforce mirrors the diversity of its clients and customers.

WAGES AND WORKING HOURS
Suppliers shall not pay less than the minimum wage in accordance with local laws or the prevailing market, whichever is higher. Suppliers shall maintain reasonable employee work hours in compliance with local standards and applicable national laws of the countries and regions in which the supplier does business.

COMMUNITY INVOLVEMENT
Solea seeks to work with suppliers that partner with local governments and communities to improve the educational, cultural, economic, and social well-being of the communities in which they live and serve.

ETHICAL STANDARDS
Solea seeks to idenify suppliers that conduct business with ethical standards consistent with our own. Solea's ethical standards are detailed on our website.

COMMUNICATION
Suppliers should take appropriate steps to ensure tha this code is communicated to their employees and throughout their own supply chains.

Source: Company reports.

# TOWARD SUSTAINABILITY

In the early 2000s, corporate interest in environmentally and socially sustainable activities grew as Solea was inundated with requests for information on the company's sustainability practices. In response, Solea assigned sustainability to Executive Vice President J. Thomas Allen, under whose leadership the first corporate social responsibility report was published in 2004. In this report, Solea made a public commitment to sustainable, profitable performance, which management defined as "doing business in a way that protects and restores the environment and the health and well-being of our clients, their customers, and the global community in which we operate." To this end, Solea declared its intention to incorporate new sustainable processes into its daily operational decisions while improving profitability.

The North American region became the testing ground for Solea's commitment to sustainability. Immediately following the release of the 2004 corporate social responsibility report, Allen organized a task force to develop a product line called "Good Citizen" in response to the growing client demand for sustainable products. "Good Citizen" was met with excitement by Solea's district and site managers, but the division president quickly became aware that the products were poorly designed and eliminated the product line shortly after its highly-touted introduction to clients. As a result of this experience, Allen set up the Office of Sustainability (OS) within Solea's North America Division. He hired Harold Rothenberg, a sustainability expert, to head the new office. Rothenberg spent his first year working with Allen and a subcommittee of Solea's North American President's Council to develop a strategy for North America.

The outcome of Rothenberg's year of planning was an ambitious strategy: Rather than providing sustainable products only to interested clients willing to pay a premium, Solea North America would make sustainability a part of normal service offerings by providing expert advice on sustainability issues and sharing innovations across its markets; measuring its clients' performance improvements; and engaging actively with stakeholder groups, NGOs, and trade associations to prioritize sustainability issues by region. "Our hope is that by providing sustainability-oriented practices and services, we'll strengthen our relationship with our clients as they see the positive growth that comes from making sustainable choices," Rothenberg told a gathering of stakeholders. "Their success is our success."

By presenting clients with new practices, services, and expanded food options, Solea North America expected to make its clients more successful-particularly as they would be better able to anticipate and respond to the needs of their own customers. Through these actions and engagement with stakeholders, NGOs, and trade associations, the company would ultimately be recognized as a leader in sustainability knowledge and practice within its industry. This would enhance Solea's brand, management reasoned, and result in improved customer retention, higher bid yields for new business, and higher gross margins for differentiated products and services in the market.

# INTEGRATING SUSTAINABILITY INTO DAILY OPERATIONS

Integrating sustainability into Solea's daily operations required substantial changes. A sustainability dashboard would be developed to communicate expectations, guide operational decisions, and provide measures of sustainability performance. To provide the necessary structure for the sustainability strategy to succeed, Rothenberg created three director-level positions to head training, performance, and communications. These three departments were highly integrated, with the directors meeting regularly to discuss progress and to find new ways to collaborate.

**Director of Training:** Focused on developing best practices; training subject matter experts; creating educational materials; and sponsoring activities and events for employees to learn and share best practices across Solea's markets.

**Director of Performance:** Working with corporate headquarters and the North American President's Council, this area established timed goals and performance metrics for operations. This department was also responsible for developing and implementing the performance dashboard to be used by site managers.

**Director of Communications:** Established internal and external partnerships with stakeholders; sought stakeholder validation of sustainability commitments, goals, and priorities; and communicated initiatives and outcomes.

## MEASURING PROGRESS

In 2004, Rothenberg and his team at corporate had created a web-based ISM (Internet Sustainability Management database). Key Solea personnel across regions were granted access to the online tool. Through 2010, the tool registered almost 1 000 "best practices." For North America alone, there were over 100 initiatives listed, posted by 35 different people.

The news wasn't all good, however. Most initiatives contained insufficient detail for validation of the practice's impact or to allow others to copy the practice, and at the same time the input into the system surpassed corporate's resources to filter and verify content. Nevertheless, the responses were used to provide evidence of Solea's progress in the 2010 corporate social responsibility report. This frustrated some North American OS directors, who advocated for a revision of ISM that allowed for more rigorous control over data entered. "We're not living up to standards of transparent reporting-I just don't think we're capturing enough detail yet," said one OS director.

Acknowledging ISM's limitations, Rothenberg sped up the development of the sustainability dashboard. The new tool was developed with three objectives in mind: To facilitate the reporting of local initiatives and key performance indicators among district and site managers; to share best practices and encourage internal benchmarks; and to strengthen internal and external communication with stakeholders.

In mid-2011, the dashboard was released to 100 sites with an interface that allowed site managers and clients to effectively track a site's progress toward sustainability commitments. The new dashboard contained five focus areas: carbon, water, waste, health and wellness, and community. Using demographic information about the site as well as responses from site managers to questions about a site's products and practices, the tool suggested "best practice" improvements for each focus area.

Rothenberg and his OS team also developed a dashboard function that would allow the tool to sort through input to identify "best in class" sites. Once a site was identified as such, OS representatives would verify and document the site's practices to create a model for other sites to follow. At the same time, internal analysts would examine how the sustainability practices were impacting the site's profit contribution and, if necessary, make recommendations to improve that impact.

## BRIGHT FUTURE PLAN

In 2009, Allen publicly announced Solea's Bright Future Plan, a set of 10 sustainability commitments by which Solea would abide (see Exhibit 4). Each commitment included timed goals for achievement, relevant metrics, as well as corporate policies and procedures to support these goals.

The Bright Future Plan should align supply management with the sustainability strategy. A few product categories in various regions had already achieved several of the sustainability commitments due to market demand and proactive managers. For example, the manager and suppliers of the Western Europe region's fish and seafood category had been working toward sustainability for several years, achieving the Marine Stewardship Council's hard-earned sustainability certification just months prior to the release of the Bright Future Plan.

On some fronts, the Bright Future Plan was immediately embraced by supply management. Particularly in the leisure, museum, zoo, and aquarium markets, where potential clients often required bidders to offer sustainable products and services, managers viewed the commitments as a resource for convincing clients

> **Exhibit 4**
>
> **Solea's 10 Sustainability Commitments (The Bright Future Plan)**
>
> 1. We will source local, seasonal, or sustainably-grown and raised products.
> 2. We will increase the purchase of items that can be recycled and reused.
> 3. We will increase the purchase of items sourced from fairly and responsibly certified sources.
> 4. We will supply sustainable fish and seafood.
> 5. We will purchase and promote energy-efficient equipment.
> 6. We will reduce waste generated and divert 100% of fryer oil.
> 7. We will reduce our carbon and water intensity across all our operations and clients' sites.
> 8. We will increase products and programs that promote health and wellness for our employees, clients, and customers.
> 9. We will support local community projects and employ and train a local workforce.
> 10. We will ensure compliance with the Supplier Code of Conduct.
>
> Source: Company reports.

that Solea was serious about sustainability. "When we can show clients the steps we've taken to meet the Bright Future Plan," one leisure market supply manager said, "we're showing them that we walk our sustainability talk. We think clients want some kind of concrete evidence."

# ONGOING CHALLENGES

The sustainability strategy met its share of internal resistance from several fronts, including a perceived conflict of interests between the Bright Future Plan and a separate company initiative, Initiative 2016, which aimed to substantially increase profits. At the same time, some managers felt threatened by the Bright Future Plan because the company's performance evaluation and incentive system (see Exhibit 5) was based largely on profits, with no allowance for achievement of other company initiatives.

## INITIATIVE 2016

In 2008, corporate contracted a group of external consultants to identify opportunities to improve the North American region's financial performance. The result, Initiative 2016, called for doubling sales and tripling operating profit by 2016. The responsibility for Initiative 2016 was charged to a task force mostly staffed by supply managers.

One of the primary strategies of Initiative 2016 focused on supply chain efficiency. This interested both OS and SMG since it had direct implications for three aspects of the supply chain, namely delivery frequency, SKU rationalization, and vendor choice.

For supply management personnel, delivery frequency held the potential to increase efficiency by optimizing both drop size and order frequency. Doing so decreased logistics costs and reduced the number of delivery trucks on the road. This

**Exhibit 5**

**Performance Management and Incentive System**

Solea had an elaborate performance management system for all employee levels down to a manager located at a client site. The system required both the employee and his/her manager to review Solea's standards for goals and behaviors appropriate to the employee being evaluated. The review of Solea's standards was followed by the employee performing a self-evaluation, the manager evaluating the employee, the employee signing off on the manager's review, and the employee creating a development plan for improvement.

The items included in Solea's performance management system were each evaluated on a 1–5 scale with the average in each of two sections— financial and value behaviors—weighed 60% and 40% respectively.

To illustrate that system, the following were the evaluation criteria for the financial objectives and value behaviors for site managers for commercial accounts.

Financial Objectives (60% weight)
1. Attainment of budgeted profit contribution
2. Revenue sales growth
3. Developing a team
4. Cross selling services/products
5. Food safety/physical safety audit
6. Implementation of division initiatives (approved employee recognition programs and customer satisfaction survey)

Value Behaviors (40% weight)
1. Serving clients and customers (proactively understanding client needs, establishing rapport, displaying professional behavior.)
2. Drive and dependability (eagerness, enthusiasm, passion, and integrity)
3. Building a diverse team (increasing diversity and inclusion)
4. Interpersonal relations (develop and maintain professional, trusting, positive working relationship with clients, supervisors, staff, managers, customers, andvendors.)
5. Managing employee performance and development (inspire employees beyond expectations, motivate by providing meaningful feedback, recognize and reward accomplshments.)
6. Managing unit finances (understand financial data, identify key factors affecting financial performance, align budgets and performance with strategy.)
7. Ensuring quality operations (implement, monitor, and manage quality operating prcedures.)

The results of the performance review could result in a bonus to the manager up to 20% of salary for the year. No one within North America received any bonus until North America made 95% of its budgeted profit, however.

Source: Extracted from company documents.

---

aligned with sustainable delivery initiatives suggested by OS, which had recommended that supply management review its ordering patterns and introduce minimum orders to discourage "little and often" delivery patterns. Reducing delivery frequency satisfied both the Bright Future Plan and Initiative 2016 by reducing cost while boosting sustainability.

The other factors affecting the supply chain, SKU rationalization and vendor choice, appeared to meet the approval of the SMG, but posed a problem for OS. SKU rationalization offered performance benefits such as increased quality through greater consistency and cost reduction through better bulk buying opportunities. Vendor choice favored purchasing through prime distribution channels, which maximized volume discounts. These factors, however, while reducing purchase costs by up to 20%, simultaneously conflicted with Solea's Bright Future Plan commitments.

Current foam use at Lakeshore Hospital appeared to present a conflict between SKU rationalization and sustainability performance. The supply manager had replaced recyclable paper plates and cups with foam dishes because a prime distributor could provide the latter at very favorable prices, directly impacting site profitability. When pushback came from the site's sustainability committee, the manager had the distributor install foam-compacting equipment. This equipment was labeled "Foam Recycling" and prominently placed in the dining facilities for customers' use. Rather than being recycled, however, the compacted foam was hauled away with the regular trash, as the short-term benefits of SKU rationalization trumped the long-term profitability that the Bright Future Plan was trying to create.

The Bright Future Plan called for activities like purchasing local products, which would reduce vendor discounts. While these actions would lead to long-term improvements to Solea's brand by increasing its customer retention and ability to win new business, they hurt short-run profits. As Rothenberg had feared, supply management personnel in many categories reacted to these recommendations with hostility, labeling them as "economically irresponsible and risky" threats to Solea's profitability.

Rothenberg also considered the effect vendor discounts could have on evaluations of SMG and district manager performance. Specifically, SMG was evaluated partially on the vendor discounts generated, with district managers having their pro rata share of vendor discounts added directly to their gross margin. Because district managers were evaluated on profits, a greater number of vendor discounts produced better evaluations. Unless the evaluation system was dramatically altered, senior management believed that the majority of the SMG and district managers would continue to resist the Bright Future Plan.

## CLIENT RELATIONSHIPS

Complex client relationships also contributed to the difficulty of integrating sustainability into Solea's business practices. Even when a sustainable option was made available, client participation and compliance was not a given. This particularly affected Solea's food operations, which was also a traditional revenue source for Solea's clients. Clients wanted and even demanded sustainable options from Solea, but were often unwilling to pay the additional upfront cost even when it would lead to greater long-term profits, expecting Solea to shoulder the cost. Additionally, Solea itself was often reluctant to invest in sustainable practices.

Assuring client follow-through was another inherent difficulty Solea's managers faced. For instance, one recent client contracted for compostable plates and flatware, which satisfied its customers' desire for sustainable offerings. Once the dishes had been used, however, they were simply thrown into the garbage because the client did not want the additional work effort and cost of composting the items.

And while Solea was continuing to struggle to accommodate its own directives, many clients were developing initiatives customized to their circumstances and asking Solea to meet those standards at its own expense. If thousands of clients expected compliance to their specific sustainability guidelines, Solea would face the unpalatable option of either meeting the guidelines and paying the additional expense, or displeasing clients by refusing to conform. Individual client initiatives also limited Solea's ability to offer its clients expert advice on sustainability issues, a part of the strategic plan.

## OTHER CHALLENGES

Cost management presented an obvious challenge to managing sustainability, as the purchase price for sustainable items could be higher than for nonsustainable items. Of note, OS did not have life-cycle costing data on hand for specific Solea purchases, thus making analysis of the economics of sustainability more difficult. "We've really got to find a way to do better capturing cost data," one district manager stated, adding, "This is important not only for our own view of sustainability, but also for our ability to communicate this information to clients and suppliers."

Solea's customer relationship management system did not code sustainability as a reason for winning or losing bids and clients. Yet some requests for proposals required minimum levels of sustainability performance to bid, and OS had been told that clients had been lost in the past because Solea didn't have sustainability offerings.

Risk mitigation was another potential problem facing management, specifically as it related to local food purchases. Many of Solea's clients wanted locally-sourced items, in accordance with their own customers' demands. However, Solea did not have processes that allowed sites to purchase directly from suppliers. Instead, the company's strategy was to rely on regional distributors to procure sustainable items within a given region. Without the necessary processes in place, SMG viewed the purchase of locally-sourced items as an area of high risk.

Challenges existed in the government sector as well, one of Solea's major markets. Under federal law, Solea was required to share vendor discounts with the government accounts that contributed to them. Unsurprisingly, clients in other markets became more sophisticated about discounts and were pushing Solea to share vendor discounts with them, too. Faced with tough competition and a bad economy, Solea began accommodating these clients as their contracts came up for renewal. Sustainability directors believed that the discounting offered to government and other clients might eventually spread across all markets, thus disrupting Solea's pricing strategy and threatening its business model.

The faltering economy served to further exacerbate the challenges already facing the Bright Future Plan. The Bright Future Plan had been designed with a robust economy in mind, rather than an economic recession. Some Solea executives were now suggesting that the commitments be adapted, even discarded, until the economy recovered. In an exchange of emails that went all the way up to Allen and his supply management counterparts, OS was accused by SMG of dangerously promoting sustainability "best practices" that were financially irresponsible in light of the current economy. To Rothenberg and the OS directors, attempts to establish and encourage best practices seemed to be often met with resistance from supply management personnel. SMG's arguments against OS turned many supply management personnel against the sustainability initiative, thereby stalling organizational change. Rothenberg complained to Allen that he perceived short-run profits as being privileged over long-term profitability, to the detriment of the company. In an email exchange between Allen and Rothenberg, Rothenberg suggested, "Perhaps it would be best to rethink strategy in light of current issues. We will meet with OS directors to discuss alternatives."

## BALANCING SUSTAINABILITY AND COMPANY INTERESTS

Allen and Rothenberg believed that in order to assure that sustainability became a way of life for Solea, further changes to the sustainability initiatives would be required. In their view, it was imperative for best practices to be supported by financial analysis. Additionally, sustainability performance needed to be linked to the formal performance evaluation and incentive system, not just tracked on the dashboard.

Several interested employees of the financial department volunteered their time to collect and analyze data on sustainable practices such as the use of disposable versus reusable china, but such work was expected to progress slowly since comparisons required differential analysis, not routine cost data captured by the information system. The near-term strategy of the OS was to work directly with the markets (e.g., corporate, health care, education) to eliminate some of the more perverse incentives that the current system rewarded and to work with corporate to get sustainability into the formal performance system.

Pressure from corporate to produce results was readily apparent and growing. In a July 2011 email, Allen told Rothenberg that "senior leadership wants something to give the media that shows we're making good on our commitments. We've already issued press releases on the supply categories that have implemented Bright Future Plan and on the dashboard. But it is definitely time for fresh progress to report, some clear wins."

Allen was aware that without evidence that sustainable practices would increase profitability, most members of SMG would continue to refuse to follow the Bright Future Plan. The group would also resist any move to include sustainable practices in the performance evaluation system unless they had the same evidence needed to convince them to implement the Bright Future Plan. "Until we get financial analysis supporting our claim that sustainability fosters profitability," Allen told Rothenberg and the OS directors, "we cannot progress in our efforts to integrate sustainability into daily operations."